Methods of Rhetorical Criticism

Under the Advisory Editorship of
J. Jeffery Auer

Methods of Rhetorical Criticism
A Twentieth-Century Perspective

Robert L. Scott
Bernard L. Brock

Harper & Row, Publishers
New York, Evanston, San Francisco, London

METHODS OF RHETORICAL CRITICISM
A Twentieth-Century Perspective

Copyright © 1972 by Robert L. Scott and Bernard L. Brock
Printed in the United States of America. All rights reserved. No part of this book
may be used or reproduced in any manner whatsoever without written permission except in the case of brief quotations embodied in critical articles and
reviews. For information address Harper & Row, Publishers, Incorporated,
49 East 33rd Street, New York, N.Y. 10016.

Standard Book Number: 06-045842-9
LIBRARY OF CONGRESS CATALOG CARD NUMBER: 72-174522

Contents

Preface

The criticism of rhetorical discourse is steadily assuming a more vital role in American life. So pervasive and varied are the efforts of some to influence the beliefs and actions of others that our very environment is taking on a rather distinctly rhetorical character. Coming to some understanding of these efforts in various media of communication has energized critics in such academic departments as English, political science, sociology, journalism, and history to describe and evaluate the flow of public address. Popular journalism is becoming increasingly filled with what we would call rhetorical criticism.

The increased use and diversity of criticism has resulted in such a proliferation of terms and methods that the field of rhetorical criticism appears chaotic to the novice. One is apt to be driven either to oversimplify critical form so as to include all methods or to make criticism so individual as virtually to exclude any method. We would hope that this book responds to the current confusion in criticism by hitting between these two extremes. No one should believe that his favorite nomenclature or method for dealing with those phenomena is apt to be universally adopted. We certainly have no such illusion that ours will be so adopted—not even in that fraction of consciousness of humanity and its ways that we know as academic departments of speech-communication. We do believe, however, that there has been a rather strong and useful tradition of rhetorical criticism in such departments. Moreover, we believe that that tradition has been affected by some important evolutionary forces.

In order to describe those forces and to make possible a way of looking at them that may prove useful for many interested in rhetorical criticism, we have undertaken to assemble this book. A key assumption is that Thomas S. Kuhn is right in arguing that modes of thought dominate the structures scientists find in the reality they describe and manipulate. He calls these modes "paradigms." We believe that Kuhn's concept is useful in considering the regularities in what rhetorical criticism has been in departments like ours and, more importantly, in understanding the situation that critics are in regarding their tradition and present inclinations. We have argued that rhetorical criticism has taken certain shapes in the past and that the present indicates certain potentials for the future. Those arguments will have to stand as readers use and scrutinize this book. We hope that even if many are inclined to reject the way we have typified the reality presented to us by critical activity that these readers will find their rejections meaningful acts in reformulating the reality.

In addition to our describing the abstract forms, we have gathered together two sorts of illustrative materials: essays stating what criticism is or should be and essays actually undertaking the criticism of rhetorical discourse. These essays have been selected from among scores of others that we might have included. If we have chosen well, then the substance of our arguments depends most heavily on these two sorts of illustrations. Clearly we owe a great debt to those scholars who have allowed us to use their writing for our purposes. They should not be held responsible for the purposes that we have brought to them. But we do thank them again for their kind permissions.

Arguments with our colleagues have been instrumental in forming our thought, but these have been too numerous to mention with justice. We hope that some of our friends will see reflected here some influences that they might approve. If they do not see some that make them uneasy, we shall feel that we have not done our job well.

We are most in debt to the tradition that we have mentioned, even though both of us believe that substantially we reject that tradition. We know, however, that no one can say sensibly that he has rejected a tradition unless he has been strongly influenced by it. Only then can a rejection be meaningful. As labels go, Mr. Scott sees himself operating from an "experiential" perspective and Mr. Brock from one of the "new rhetorics."

R. L. S.
B. L. B.
Minneapolis
October 1971

Methods of Rhetorical Criticism

An Introduction to Rhetorical Criticism

T HE Nixon Zigzag," "The Lockheed Scandal," "Vine-yard Victory," and "Black Arts for Black Youth" are titles that virtually leap out at us as we leaf through newspapers or magazines. In response we may feel a mixture of curiosity, disdain, or any number of emotions. But if we focus even momentarily on what is written, we are apt to respond in some way.

Not all our responses are critical. Nor are all the articles we glance at critical. But many are. Every day our experiences make us aware of circum-stances that seem to cry out for explanations. What we feel moving within us at these moments of special questioning may be called "the critical impulse." But what is this impulse? It is difficult to pinpoint. Perhaps it is a queasy feeling or the urge to run or to strike out. Often it manifests itself by verbalizing agreement or disagreement. At other times the critical impulse is formed into a guarded intellectual state-ment.

The Province of Criticism

Although what we call the critical impulse is a vague feeling that cannot be defined with precision, man sets some boundaries for him-self as critic. Of the phenomena that surround him, he does not under-take to criticize those that might be called natural. If he were to say, "I am a critic of the rocks and hills, of bees and flowers," the statement would strike us as whimsy. He might well find himself puzzled when confronting the objects of nature and raise questions to pursue in hope of finding answers, but we do not think of such work as criticism. Rather, it is to the work of man himself that we turn when moved by the critical impulse.

The vibrations of the air may be considered to be an aspect of the physics of sound. The phenomena of pitch and overtone may be taken to be constituents of harmony and counterpoint. But it is to musical composition and performance that the critic turns.

One can quite readily compose a list of works that are relevant to criticism: theater and literature, sculpture and music, cinema and dance. These we tend to call "art." And although we are not so likely to list them initially, we commonly find references to the art of war (or, less often, the art of peace), to the art of government, or even to the art of marriage. These human relationships in which we find ourselves involved, although unique as particular occurrences, partake of tradi-tions, of institutions, of plans; they are, in short, human productions.

The distinction we tend to make between "fine art" and "practical art" is beguiling. Notice that although we may criticize the practice of the art of government or the performance of a musical composition, in the former case we are less likely to think of ourselves as critics or our product as criticism. Our feeling is that, like natural phenomena, which are not subject to criticism, the practical arts are instruments to aid man's living, whereas the fine arts express man's humanity. Right here, however, the line between the fine and the practical begins to fade as one asks, "What is *living?* Is it simply staying alive?" The line becomes even more obscure if one inserts the term good, as in "What is a good life?"

Clearly, we cannot settle such questions here, but we may point out that the critical impulse has again manifested itself in our responses, and, we trust, in those of our readers. Man does not simply live in an environment; he creates instruments and institutions for living, which he uses, discards, and re-creates. And he sees and assesses what he does. In fact, he seems scarcely able to keep himself from "sizing it up."

But how does one size up in a critical sense? If we simply see a piece of copper, we do not criticize it. As metallurgists, we may question its properties and determine, for example, that it is copper of a certain purity. We begin to size up critically when we see in something a purpose for human use. We may perceive that a particular piece of copper in a peculiar shape is useful for plumbing. Given our interests and abilities, we may say, "He certainly sweats a nice joint."

To speak of "sweating a joint" may be quite foreign to some readers. "I wouldn't think of criticizing one; in fact, I wouldn't know one if I saw one," might be a possible response, and one that helps us make a point. The more we know about some human enterprise, and the more salient it is to our interests, the more likely we are to feel the critical impulse. In fact, consciously or unconsciously we often repress the critical impulse, saying, in effect, "Let me know more about it first."

This observation raises the question, Can't one just know about something without criticizing it? Our position is that (1) knowing about something and (2) recognizing that the object of interest has in some respect become entwined with human purposes in the creation of a human product will lead to criticism. But this position does not preclude answering the question positively. In fact, the impulse to know things in-and-of-themselves may be referred to as the scientific impulse.

We may make several assertions about the scientific impulse with a fair degree of confidence. First, the impulse predates what nearly everyone today calls "science." Ways of knowing things-in-and-of-themselves and the knowledge that scientific procedures presuppose were both so rudimentary and sketchy until the last few centuries that science in a contemporary sense was scarcely possible. Another way

of saying all of this is that science itself has a history and precondi-
tions. A second assertion we can make is that designating something
as a science, or even as an object for scientific scrutiny, entails an
arbitrary narrowing of focus. Thomas H. Huxley recognized this problem when he was explaining the Darwinian theory of natural selection
in accounting for the evolution of species. The idea of "nature" (another way of saying things-in-and-of-themselves) must be restricted to
those parts of the phenomenal world in which man does not play "the
part of immediate cause."[1]

The scientific impulse has become science, then, both historically
and operationally, through a series of limitations. The power of science
lies in large part in these limitations. If we remember this fact, we shall
not go wrong in asking, "Can't we just know about something without
criticizing it?" Nor shall we go wrong in believing that finding out
about things-as-they-are may be a useful predisposition to criticism.

Too often, however, we believe that we can dispose of all important
questions by "scientific" procedures. "The scientist is one of the cultural heroes of our age." With this sentence Edwin Black begins his
important book on rhetorical criticism.[2] However, with the crises of
war, race, and environment, the accomplishments of science seem a
little less heroic. Of course, scientists as scientists have not sought the
role of heroes, although some of them as politicians may have done so.

Even now some scientists are in revolt and are arguing that the bulk
of their research is not relevant to the most serious problems facing
humanity.[3] Such revolts do not indicate a new science as much as a
fresh political conscience for the men of science. These revolts may
also indicate the critical impulse.

We have no formulary solution to the problem that C. P. Snow popu-
larized as "the two cultures,"[4] but we do believe that the ground for
rapprochement is being prepared by a contemporary awareness of the
inevitability of man's participation in whatever it is he takes to be the
facts of the matter.[5]

[1] *Thomas H. Huxley, "The Struggle for Existence in Human Society,"* Evolution and Ethics, *New York, Appleton-Century-Crofts, 1899, p. 202.*

[2] *Edwin Black,* Rhetorical Criticism: A Study in Method, *New York, Macmillan,
1965, p. 1.*

[3] *See, for example, "Scientists' 'Relevant' Study Asked,"* Minneapolis Star
(July 22, 1970), p. 5A.

[4] *C. P. Snow,* The Two Cultures and a Second Look, *Cambridge, Cambridge
University Press, 1964.*

[5] *For a discussion from another point of view of some of the problems of the
interaction of science and criticism, see Robert L. Scott, "A Rhetoric of Facts:
Arthur Larson's Stance as a Persuader,"* Speech Monographs, *XXXV, 2 (June
1968), 109–121. Edwin Black, in the source cited previously, begins his book
on criticism with a comparison of science and criticism.*

If we are correct in saying that a new humanism is evident in man's capacity to look critically at his own creations, including what he has created as scientist, then the critical impulse seems central to humaneness. But our perception of the welter of activity around us may be wrong and, surely, is biased. The bias is a commitment to criticism, but such commitment should not blind us to the contributions of science, nor to the humaneness of the scientific impulse. If recent history has witnessed a blindness to the limits of science, surely there must be a contrary possibility of a blindness to the limits of criticism. If our analysis suggests that there must be a balance between these impulses, then that balance will result from continuing interactions that will constantly threaten imbalance.

Rather than define "criticism," we have discussed the vague notion of a critical impulse, arguing that such an impulse manifests itself naturally as a man becomes knowledgeable about any human activity and as he sees that this activity is salient to his purposes as a fully functioning man. We would argue that man cannot completely repress the critical impulse because it is a part of learning how to act toward something or someone. Knowing about something necessarily includes knowing how to behave toward it. We recognize, moreover, that although we claim the impulse is natural, it is difficult to imagine a common set of circumstances in which a man depends on that impulse alone. Traditions of criticism surround him and direct his attention and help him formulate methods of dealing critically with the objects of his interest.

Rhetoric as an Object of Criticism

Rhetoric may be defined as the human effort to induce cooperation through the use of symbols. Most definitions tend to give rise to troublesome questions of inclusion and exclusion; this definition is no exception.

First, the limits of rhetoric are imprecise. The simple request, "Please pass the salt," is an example of the use of symbols to induce cooperation. On the other hand, such requests, if repeatedly ignored, may be reinforced with angry shouts and kicks. Although normally we would exclude simple, conventional requests and physical coercion from the concept of rhetoric, no one can draw the boundaries easily. If the notion of voluntary cooperation, that is, that which involves choice on the part of those responding to symbolic inducements, is necessary to define rhetoric, then certainly the everyday conventions that groups respond to are germane; moreover, threats of coercion are much more common than coercion itself, and often succeed. The question, Has one *really* cooperated if he accedes to conventional requests or to threats? calls attention to the difficulty of making distinctions and also to the need for criticism.[6]

Second, an ambiguity of this sort appears in the question, Does rhetoric refer to the process of inducing cooperation or to the product of that process? The obvious answer is that it refers to both, but the answer does not reduce the ambiguity. Historically and currently, the word has been and is used in both senses.

Traditionally, one thinks of criticism in terms of the products of human creation. One is used to thinking of criticism in regard to paintings, novels, and speeches. "Rhetorical criticism" and "speech criticism" are often taken as synonymous. When the living voice was the only practical public means to induce cooperation, speeches nearly exhausted the possibilities of rhetoric. The printing press ended that circumstance. Although the marvels of electronic media have again brought the living voice and visage back to prominence, the forms of presentation stagger the capacity of speeches to contain them. The spot commercial and the Presidential press conference both seem designed to induce cooperation through the use of symbols.

The products of rhetoric, then, are multitudinous. Part of the task of rhetorical criticism is to find a focus, to pick products that will be fruitful to criticize.

But the very idea of product, as traditional as it is for the critic, may be detrimental to the deepest fulfillment of the critical impulse if it is taken as a limit. This conclusion is especially apparent if one follows carefully the implications of the existence of any product, say an ordinary public speech. Where does the speech start? Where does it end? Does it start in the mind of the speaker as he interacts with his social and physical environment? Immediately we are likely to see relationships between his thought, its formation and expression, and similar thoughts, formations, and expressions. We are apt to become aware that the context in which the speech occurs is a rhetorical context. The critic may find himself less interested in commenting on specific speeches as speeches than in typifying the verbal, and perhaps the nonverbal, forms that permeate many speeches and seem to constitute some discernible phenomena.[7] Our effort here is not to typify a par-

[6] *An exceedingly interesting piece of criticism focuses on a specific case illustrative of the interaction of persuasion and coercion. See James R. Andrews, "The Rhetoric of Coercion and Persuasion: The Reform Bill of 1832,"* The Quarterly Journal of Speech, *LVI, 2 (April 1970), 187–195.*

[7] *See, for example Franklyn Haiman, "The Rhetoric of the Streets: Some Legal and Ethical Considerations,"* The Quarterly Journal of Speech, *LIII, 2 (April 1967), 99–114; Robert L. Scott and Donald K. Smith, "The Rhetoric of Confrontation,"* The Quarterly Journal of Speech, *LV, 1 (February 1969), 1–8; and Parke G. Burgess, "The Rhetoric of Black Power: A Moral Demand?"* The Quarterly Journal of Speech, *LV, 2 (April 1969), 122–133.*

ticular kind of criticism but rather to point out that ones focus may easily shift from a distinct product toward the process that apparently brings the product into being.

The rhetorical critic may be concerned with such traditional objects as speeches and editorials,[8] or he may be interested in scrutinizing less traditional objects, such as novels and plays,[9] from a rhetorical point of view. He may sense that some event or campaign or movement formed of congeries of rhetorical products will yield to his efforts.[10] Whatever his endeavor, however, it is aroused by his sense of the importance of man's effort to induce cooperation through the use of symbols. Since the critic will wish to bring his audience closer to his own point of view regarding some phenomena, his communication will probably display a deeply rhetorical characteristic. To say that critical comment on rhetoric will likely be rhetorical itself, however, leads to the question: What are the purposes of rhetorical criticism?

Purposes of Rhetorical Criticism

The rhetorical impulse reveals its own purposes. In one sense, the plural *purposes* must be used; in another, when the critic works well, the purposes of rhetorical criticism tend to merge into a unique whole, all present, and yet all subordinate to the purpose of that instance.

The critic's attention is drawn to a certain phenomenon. He sees, but he perceives that his experience is not universally shared. In part, his function is to indicate, to point out, to draw the attention of others to the phenomenon. Since he is not working with something that is simply there, he must show the phenomenal aspects of whatever object he focuses on. In this first respect, his purpose is descriptive.

With more or less awareness of the implications of his activity, the critic endows with meaning the phenomenon to which he attends. We say that he endows it because the meaning shaped in his descriptions is one among several possibilities. In the very act of singling out from among the welter of his experiences those aspects he will set forth as constituting a phenomenon—the impact of a single speech, the career of a speaker, the outlines of a campaign, the sort of argument that typifies a repeated phenomenon in like circumstances, and so on—he

---

[8] *For an interesting rhetorical case study of newspaper reporting, see Meredith W. Berg and David M. Berg, "The Rhetoric of War Preparation: The New York Press in 1898," Journalism Quarterly, XLV, 4 (Winter 1968), 653–660.*
[9] *See, for example, Ray Lynn Anderson, "The Rhetoric of Science Fiction," unpublished Ph.D. dissertation, Minneapolis, University of Minnesota, 1968.*
[10] *See, for example, James R. Andrews, "Confrontation at Columbia: A Case Study in Coercive Rhetoric," The Quarterly Journal of Speech, LV, 1 (February 1969), 9–16; Leland Griffith, "The Anti-Masonic Persuasion," unpublished Ph.D. dissertation, Ithaca, N.Y., Cornell University, 1950.*

begins to shape the meaning of the phenomenon for anyone who attends to his critique. In taking responsibility for his shapings, the critic's purpose becomes interpretive.

Finally, the critic judges. In some way or another, implicitly or explicitly, he says that the rhetoric, product or process, is well done or ill. On what basis does he judge? We shall turn to that question shortly.

Many rhetorical critics would like to ignore the evaluative purpose of criticism. Some pointedly exclude evaluation by labeling their efforts "descriptive," as if to say that this is their sole purpose. Although we can understand some of the motivations for such limitations, we believe that evaluation cannot be excluded entirely. The descriptive act, in and of itself, implies that the phenomenon as described is worth attending to.

The primary purposes of rhetorical criticism are to describe, to interpret, and to evaluate. These purposes tend to merge into one another. One purpose prepares for the next; the one that follows reflects back on the one that has been explicated.

The process of calling attention to a phenomenon, interpreting it, and judging it, will inevitably result in a product that is designed, more or less consciously, to be persuasive. The critic says implicitly, "See as I see, know as I know, value as I value." If we are correct in our interpretation of the critical act, then when that act is directed toward rhetorical objects, which are themselves potentially persuasive, the critic enters into the arena of argument inhabited by the object he criticizes.

Just as the critic may choose to deemphasize the evaluative function of criticism, he may wish to minimize the persuasive potential of his work. Nevertheless, he should be prepared to recognize the possible social consequences, for if rhetoric seeks to induce the cooperation of others, then the seeking and the cooperation achieved will have consequences.

Criticism is a potent social force. Although academic critics seem quite chary of it, popular critics are much less cautious. For example, those who criticize Presidential speaking, formally or informally, whether or not they call themselves rhetorical critics, usually embrace vigorously the possibility of a persuasive impact of their acts.

In addition to the primary purposes of description, interpretation, evaluation, and, we would add, persuasion, rhetorical criticism may have a number of secondary purposes. Primary purposes include those that seem to adhere to the act of criticism itself; secondary purposes are any others that the act may be made to serve.

Clearly in the critical impulse lies the motivation to learn about things. The pedagogical function of rhetorical criticism stretches back to antiquity. Choosing model speeches for the students to imitate was an early critical act. The question was, What speeches are worth saving and studying? In addition to the basic evaluation necessary, interpretation was needed, that is, the schoolboy had to understand the speech in his own way, if imitation of it was not simply to be slavish.[11]

Closely allied to the pedagogical function is the theoretical. Criticism may serve theoretical motivations in two ways: First, it may give rise to insights that can then be phrased as principles for further use or hypotheses for further testing. Second, criticism may serve as a test. If conventional principles are sound, then they should be confirmed in the practice of good speakers. Again, descriptive, interpretative, and evaluative functions are necessary to serve adequately these secondary purposes.[12]

In addition to learning about rhetoric, one may undertake the study of rhetorical criticism to learn about other matters, such as those involved in speaking, writing, or other symbolic actions. One's motivation may be historical, biographical, or cultural. Indeed, rhetorical materials are artifacts, and, therefore, are the evidence for reconstructing the lives and ways of the people who produced these materials.

Criteria for Rhetorical Criticism

If evaluation continually manifests itself in criticism, then the question, On what grounds shall I evaluate? is inevitable. The question is difficult to deal with.

The difficulty first arises out of the multiplicity of purposes that criticism can serve. If, at its best, a piece of criticism subordinates the ordinary purposes to a unique whole, then the criteria appropriate to the critical act may be unique. But if we leave the matter at this point, we have simply refused to answer an honest question: Is there no standard common to all acts of rhetorical criticism?

The most common standard asserted is that of effect. Since rhetorical acts are normally viewed as instrumental, as indeed the phrase "inducing cooperation" may be taken, then is not success in using the instrument the final measure? If, for example, the purpose of a Presidential campaign is to elect the candidate, then the candidate elected has mounted a good campaign.

As tempting as this pragmatic evaluation may be, the critic who invokes it so simply is likely to find himself in some embarrassing positions. May not the success in a campaign, for example, be attributed

---

[11] *For an excellent discussion of the classical notion of* imitatio, *see Donald Leman Clark,* Rhetoric in Greco-Roman Education, *New York, Columbia University Press, 1957, chap. 6.*

[12] *For a vigorous criticism of the contention that rhetorical criticism can serve these purposes well, see Phillip K. Tompkins, "Rhetorical Criticism: Wrong Medium?" Central States Speech Journal, XIII, 1 (Winter 1962), 90–95.*

more to the ineptness of the opposition than to the adequacy of the winner? Long before the New Left was arguing that neither American political party gives the citizens an adequate choice, some people on the political right were saying almost the same thing. Hence, one of the slogans of the 1964 campaign: "A choice, not an echo." Are not some of the most successful persuaders, on the face of what they say, disreputable, and some of the best unsuccessful? Would the criterion of effect lead us to conclude that Adolph Hitler was one of the finest speakers of history and Demosthenes among the poorest? Was Martin Luther King, Jr., successful?

The answers to these questions are not simple, but two conclusions are indicated. First, we tend to shift our perspective. For example, we can say that Hitler was good in one respect and bad in another, or that Martin Luther King, Jr., was overwhelmingly successful, given the circumstances within which his rhetoric worked. Second, in spite of the difficulties that the criterion of effect entails, it is impossible to do without this criterion altogether. Although the question, Is one success as good as another? indicates the ultimate shortcoming of that criterion, the very question assumes some weight when applied to the notion of effect.

We have scarcely discussed all of the difficulties. Some of these arise from traditional uncertainties, such as linking causes with effects in any circumstance. Again the difficulties are compounded by the necessity to focus on a few effects among many, since it is an impossible task to be aware of all the possible effects of any complex, human action. The shifting of perspective mentioned in the last paragraph may be one of turning from immediate effects to long-run effects.

Motivated in part by the difficulties of assessing effect and in part by their concept of rhetoric, some critics examine the process of persuasion and then appeal to artistic criteria to evaluate. Such an appeal may be thought of as the doctrine of effectiveness in contrast to the doctrine of effect. Authority for this doctrine is drawn from Aristotle, who defines rhetoric as "the faculty of observing in any given case the available means of persuasion." Focusing on the means, not the ends, the point of rhetoric is "not simply to succeed in persuading, but rather to discover the means of coming as near such success as the circumstances of each particular case allow."[13]

Appealing to artistic criteria assumes that there are well-recognized principles that can be embodied concretely in particular works. Today many critics might question such an assumption. Indeed, because of such an inclination to question the notion that there are clearly recog-

---

[13] *Aristotle,* Rhetoric (*W. Rhys Roberts trans.*) *1355^b26; 1355^b10.*

nized, artistic principles to which the critic may appeal, we have undertaken to compile this book.

If a critic is to appeal to the doctrine of effectiveness, what will be the source of his critical criteria? The very assumption of principles that are used in such a way that they can be appealed to as criteria suggests that authority or tradition will be their source. But why should a critic follow a particular tradition or authority? Two reasons are given as possible explanations, although they are not always clearly distinct from one another. The first is that the authority or tradition seems consistent with practice, which may be a way of appealing obliquely to the doctrine of effect. The second is that the authority or tradition seems internally consistent and the principles are coherent with one another and with the sense of good practice with which the critic and his immediate culture feel comfortable.

In considering traditional criteria, whatever the theoretical vocabulary may be, one senses the potential interactions of product and process in the doctrines of effect and effectiveness. We do not mean to suggest the comfortable compromise of a platitudinous "at best all work together," which is obviously true but not helpful. What we see is a circularity in which the appeal to good practice helps to establish principle and the appeal to principle helps to determine good practice. Often the observation of circularity is offered as a refutation of the efficacy of whatever exhibits that characteristic. We do not offer our observation in a refutative sense, however. We believe that such circularity is inevitably a part of building a tradition. If the critic rejects a tradition, he will probably do so either because it fails to do what it promises or because he appeals to standards that are outside the tradition.

Often rhetorical critics appeal to standards that are outside rhetoric. The tendency to make ethical judgments about the goodness of rhetoric is often such an appeal; perhaps it is inevitably such an appeal. In any case, critics often do submit rhetoric to ethical or moral judgments.

The doctrine of effect leads to the judgment of rhetoric as good pragmatically; that is, whatever the given ends, the rhetorical means seem causally important in reaching them. The doctrine of effectiveness leads to the judgment of rhetoric as a qualified good, that is, given a sense of good means, the rhetoric in question is an embodiment of such means. To make a moral judgment of rhetoric may be to extend the doctrine of effect—to argue that some ultimate goals are or are not enhanced by the rhetoric in question. On the other hand, such a judgment may be focused on means, on the assumption that some means are per se valuable whereas others are destructive to human value.

Recently some critics have argued that although most ethical evaluations of rhetoric have indeed been an appeal beyond the rhetorical itself to nonrhetorical standards, the critic may find an intrinsically rhetorical ethic. We cannot argue the questions raised by such a potentiality in this introduction, but the notion, as it is now being worked out, is one of the most exciting problems in contemporary rhetorical theory.[14]

The State of the Art of Rhetorical Criticism

We have raised many more questions than we have answered. Nevertheless, we have made a number of assertions that might be argued at some length. In short, looking at rhetorical criticism as it is revealed in practice, the nature of the art seems uncertain and unclear. Issues to be settled are basic ones, not ones of application of accepted procedures to commonly perceived problems.

Probably the most important recent book to be published on rhetorical criticism is Edwin Black's *Rhetorical Criticism: A Study in Method.*[15] In it he identified and objected to a tradition that appeared to have been well accepted for more than thirty years. This tradition he called neo-Aristotelian criticism.

We believe that Professor Black was astoundingly accurate in his assessment. Although we may disagree in some details, in our opinion his descriptions of and arguments about the insufficiency of neo-Aristotelianism are penetrating.[16] But Professor Black's voice was not so lonely as it seemed when he first raised it. Although he drew together, better than any other single person, feelings that the old assumptions were not adequate for the tasks at hand, he was scarcely alone in his convictions.

We are in the midst of a disintegrating tradition. Perhaps rhetorical criticism now is transitional; from it will grow a fresh tradition. Of the latter point, we cannot be certain; of the former we are convinced.

Thomas S. Kuhn's picture of *The Structure of Scientific Revolutions*[17] may be instructive in understanding the state of rhetorical criticism at this moment. Kuhn's own thought is revolutionary. He rejects the well-established notion that scientific knowledge grows by a gradual accu-

[14] *For an excellent idea of the potentialities now envisioned, see Parke G. Burgess, "The Rhetoric of Moral Conflict,"* The Quarterly Journal of Speech, *LVI, 2 (April 1970), 120–130.*

[15] *Edwin Black,* Rhetorical Criticism: A Study in Method, *New York, Macmillan, 1965.*

[16] *Our fundamental disagreement with Professor Black stems from his argument that in a time of crisis in values the lack of shared values makes* logos *(in the sense of enthymemes based on culturally assumed premises) impossible. For a critique of the book see Robert L. Scott,* The Quarterly Journal of Speech, *LI, 3 (October 1965), 333–338.*

[17] *Thomas S. Kuhn,* The Structure of Scientific Revolutions, *Chicago, University of Chicago Press, 1962. (The book is also available in a paperback Phoenix edition from the University of Chicago Press.)*

mulation of knowledge; in such a process errors are sifted out and replaced by fresh hypotheses, which are verified and developed into an orderly, unified pattern. If the unified pattern does not exist, this view contends, the hypothesis is assumed to be the goal of a progression proceeding from the engrained ignorance and misinformation of prescientific culture to the full explanation of nature in-and-of-itself.

Kuhn argues that science grows by fits and starts. That fundamental to change, which may not be progress at all, is the construction of a fresh "paradigm." By paradigm he means an imaginative picture of what reality is like. Rather than being noncultural, scientists form a community, or community of interests. When a number are convinced of the efficacy of a particular paradigm, usually resulting from the insight of an unusually creative thinker, the work of "ordinary science" begins. Ordinary science is the clarifying and testing of innumerable hypotheses implied by the paradigm. As this work progesses, the inadequacies, the lacunae, and the contradictions of the paradigm become more apparent and more bothersome. At first these are simply ignored—for they can be ignored until scientists have worked out other problems from among the myriad hypotheses that can be stated in the various branches of science. Finally, however, the old paradigm breaks down from the weight of its inadequacies, which are really the dissatisfactions (one might almost say "the lack of faith") of scientists in it. Other paradigms compete for the loyalties of scientific workers—for working to the pattern of a paradigm is an excellent definition of such loyalty.

Whether or not the sort of rhetorical criticism that grew up in the speech departments of American colleges and universities during the past fifty years would qualify as *paradigmatic* is probably arguable. But a strong tradition, the roots of which are best revealed by Herbert Wichelns's 1925 essay, "The Literary Criticism of Oratory," did grow (see Chapter 2). The inadequacies of the tradition were undoubtedly always apparent, but they began to impress themselves on more and more rhetorical critics in the 1960s. Searching for alternative frames of reference, critics have turned in a number of directions. By gathering together both theoretical essays about criticism and examples of criticism, we shall try to indicate some of the most promising of these directions, letting the critics who take them speak for themselves.

The Pattern of This Book

Whether or not any of the critical probings now apparent will build into a fresh paradigm is not clear. We rather believe that the efforts we shall try to describe are pre-paradigmatic, so we have divided the book into two general sections—a traditional perspective and breaks from the tradition.

Within the traditional perspective we have identified two approaches: neo-Aristotelian and historical. The dominant tradition emphasizes that the speaker role determines the choices that make speeches. Historical effects seem best explained in terms of the choices of a dominant individual (or individuals) who sizes up the circumstances in which he and his fellows struggle and interprets and expresses them in such a way as to demonstrate leadership. The man who speaks out in a time of crisis arouses the interest of the traditional critic.

In the break from the traditional perspective we have observed two general tendencies. First, the tendency to move the orientation of the criticism from the speaker to the critic. Second, the tendency to replace the Aristotelian rhetorical theory with some other theory as the starting point for criticism.

Criticism that has a critic's orientation we call the "experiential perspective." The critic's experience—the rhetorical standards he has established throughout years of extensive reading and varied contacts —is drawn on creatively as a starting point for his rhetorical criticism. Experiential criticism is probably more diverse than any other, but two approaches, which stand out within this perspective, are what we call the "eclectic" and the "sociocultural-psychological."

Criticism that attempts to replace Aristotelian theory will be referred to as the "perspective of the 'New Rhetorics.' " The critics of the New Rhetorics believe that there is an underlying theory capable of informing criticism generally, although they by no means agree on what that theory should be. We shall refer to two tendencies within this perspective: one that we shall call the "grammatical-semantical approach" and one that we shall call the "dramatistic approach."

In each section of this anthology we shall endeavor, first, to explain the critical perspective; second, to represent it with theoretical essays; and, third, to illustrate it with criticism embodying the relevant theory.

We believe that agreement was complete enough and practice consistent enough to justify our referring to the traditional perspective of rhetorical criticism as a paradigm. But, in organizing the breaks from tradition into two categories, we do not mean to imply that these are clearly unified countertraditions. We do think that the nature of these tendencies, the assumptions underlying them, and their theoretical implications are well enough formed to warrant the categories and subcategories that we shall make. But we also believe that the circumstance of criticism is quite fluid and that the tendencies involved may form themselves in ways that we can scarcely predict.

Again, although we shall first take up one "new perspective" and then the other, we do so for the convenience of discussion and not to imply any sort of temporal or final priority.

Some Recent Books on Rhetorical Criticism

Black, Edwin, *Rhetorical Criticism: A Study in Method,* New York, Mac-millan, 1965.

Cathcart, Robert, *Post Communication: Critical Analysis and Evaluation,* Indianapolis, Bobbs-Merrill, 1966.

Hillbruner, Anthony, *Critical Dimensions: The Art of Public Address Criticism,* New York, Random House, 1966.

Linsley, William A. (ed.), *Speech Criticism: Methods and Materials,* Dubuque, Iowa, William C. Brown, 1968.

Nichols, Marie Hochmuth, *Rhetoric and Criticism,* Baton Rouge, Louisiana State University Press, 1963.

Nilsen, Thomas R. (ed.), *Essays on Rhetorical Criticism,* New York, Random House, 1968.

Thonssen, Lester, and Baird, A. Craig, *Speech Criticism: The Development of Standards for Rhetorical Appraisal,* New York, Ronald Press, 1948. (Second edition, with Waldo Braden, 1970.)

The Traditional Perspective

WE have discussed a "critical impulse," suggesting that it inheres in the process of making some phenomena a part of human experience; in fact, the critical impulse is central to the human experience. The impulse can be studied because man continually formalizes and institutionalizes it to serve his needs.

In the academic work of speech departments, a traditional perspective for rhetorical criticism took shape during the first half of the twentieth century. Herbert Wichelns laid the cornerstone with his essay, "The Literary Criticism of Oratory."[1] The basic outlines Wichelns laid down were given the fullest detail by Lester Thonssen and A. Craig Baird in *Speech Criticism*.[2] Representative of the sort of criticism that drew on the paradigm are the essays in the three volume series, *History and Criticism of American Public Address,* sponsored by the Speech Association of America; Volumes I and II were edited by W. N. Brigance[3] and Volume III by Marie Hochmuth Nichols.[4]

The paradigm took shape during the ferment of departmentalization of American higher education. At the beginning of the twentieth century some of the traditional, broad disciplines began to splinter, and new fields such as psychology, sociology, and political science sought to establish unique identities. Speech, or what some people called oratory and drama, was in a similar position. In 1898 Brander Matthews wrote that "an oration or a drama shall be judged not as literature only, but also in accordance with the principles of its own art."[5] Matthews accepted a basic link between speech and literature and attempted to establish, in addition, some unique characteristics for oratory and drama. The drive for differentiation was intensified as the discipline of speech became increasingly separate from English departments. The separation was symbolized by the formation of the National Association of Academic Teachers of Public Address in 1915 (renamed the Speech Association of America in 1946, and the Speech Communication Association in 1970).

[1] *Herbert Wichelns, "The Literary Criticism of Oratory," in A. M. Drummond (ed.), Rhetoric and Public Speaking in honor of James A. Winans, New York, Century, 1925.*

[2] *Lester Thonssen and A. Craig Baird,* Speech Criticism, *New York, Ronald Press, 1948. Second edition, Waldo Braden, 1970.*

[3] *W. Norwood Brigance (ed.), A History of American Public Address, vols. I and II, New York, McGraw-Hill, 1943.*

[4] *Marie Hochmuth Nichols (ed.),* History and Criticism of American Public Address, vol. III, London, Longmans, Green, 1955.

[5] *Brander Matthews, "The Relation of Drama to Literature," Forum (January 1898), 630–640 in Thomas R. Nilsen (ed.), Essays on Rhetorical Criticism, New York, Random House, 1968, p. 4.*

In his formative essay, after exhaustively reviewing available work, Herbert Wichelns concluded that "we have not much serious criticism of oratory." He sought to establish a framework for such criticism. For two reasons we believe that it is fair to cite Wichelns's essay as the beginning of the paradigm that has since dominated. First, he sets forth a difference between literature and rhetoric that is still generally accepted—rhetoric is concerned with effect and literature with permanence. Second, his fundamental outline for criticism was accepted by most critics for at least thirty years.

In *Speech Criticism,* the first book in the field devoted solely to the theory and method of criticizing speeches, Lester Thonssen and A. Craig Baird extended the traditional perspective as defined by Wichelns. Although the authors surveyed much of the history of rhetoric and drew examples from twentieth-century criticism, essentially they took the Aristotelian rhetorical theory and historical method suggested by Wichelns and developed them into a more complex series of patterns.

Finally, in 1955 Marie Hochmuth Nichols published the third volume of *History and Criticism of American Public Address,* supplementing William Norwood Brigance's two volumes released in 1943. These works include the critical efforts of forty scholars in the field of speech and demonstrate the application of the basic patterns to traditional criticism. However, the application was uneven and at times deviated significantly from the ideal. Wichelns, and later Thonssen and Baird, stressed making judgments about the effects of rhetoric, but these critical essays tended to stress description, stopping shy of evaluation. The thrust of traditional criticism apparently brought many critics to look upon their art as that of identifying conventional rhetorical strategies and presenting an account of the speaker and the times.

Within the traditional perspective two strains or approaches stand out: the neo-Aristotelian and the historical. Some critics weave the two approaches into a unified work, but often they stand quite separately. The roots of these approaches can be found in Wichelns's discussion of three types of criticism. The first, he writes, is "predominantly personal or biographical" and "goes behind the work to the man." The second "attempts to hold the scales even between the biographical and the literary [rhetorical] interest. . . . The third is occupied with the work and tends to ignore the man."

The nomenclature common to traditional criticism is derived from Aristotle's *Rhetoric.* To stress that the pattern is derived from the ancient source, Edwin Black labels it "neo-Aristotelian," a move which seems to us wise and which we have adopted.[6]

[6] *Edwin Black,* Rhetorical Criticism: A Study in Method, *New York, Macmillan, 1965,* passim, *esp. p. 31.*

In his 1925 essay, Herbert Wichelns listed the necessary elements for neo-Aristotelian criticism: "the speaker's personality as a conditioning factor . . . the public character of the man . . . a description of the speaker's audience . . . the leading ideas with which he plied his hearers—his topics, the motives to which he appealed, the nature of the proofs he offered . . . the surviving texts to what was actually uttered . . . the speaker's mode of arrangement and his mode of expression . . . his habit of preparation and his manner of delivery . . . diction and sentence movement . . . the effect of the discourse on its immediate hearers." This impressive list of Aristotelian topics became the rhetorical ideal for the neo-Aristotelian critic, who, after 1948, drew from the heavily detailed Aristotelianism of Thonssen and Baird's *Speech Criticism.*

The ideal prescribed by Wichelns was quite ambitious because its method, essentially, required the critic to describe and analyze in depth all aspects of the historical and rhetorical elements that surround a rhetorical act. In practice few critics were able to achieve the ideal, even though the neo-Aristotelian approach dominated the literature of rhetorical criticism for thirty years. In studying the three volumes of *History and Criticism of American Public Address,* Black concluded that fifteen of the forty essays employ this pattern and that the neo-Aristotelian influence significantly affected many of the remaining twenty-five essays.[7]

Following our pattern for including essays in this anthology, one setting forth and another applying theory, we have chosen two essays to illustrate neo-Aristotelian criticism: Herbert Wichelns's "The Literary Criticism of Oratory" and Marie Hochmuth Nichols's "Abraham Lincoln's First Inaugural Address." We have already commented on the significance of Wichelns's work. Professor Nichols's essay represents the neo-Aristotelian tradition at its best. She does an excellent job of discussing all of the elements initially set forth by Wichelns, weaving history and rhetorical analysis together quite effectively. In the process, the essay typifies the common neo-Aristotelian bent, stressing description and interpretation rather than evaluation.

Wichelns's three types of criticism, which we have noted above, describe a continuum of emphasis, one end of which is "predominantly personal or biographical." We have chosen to label emphasis on this end of the scale as "historical." The neo-Aristotelian perspective tends to shortcut the demanding traditional criticism by focusing on the *work* from an Aristotelian point of view; the historical perspective tends to reduce the complete traditional pattern by concentrating on the *his-*

[7] Ibid., *p. 28.*

torical elements of the person and the times. The historical perspective assumes a causal relation between events in history and public address. Viewing public address as both formed by and formative of the events of history, the historical critic analyzes as essential to his study the interrelationship of rhetoric and its times. Ernest Wrage, an historical critic, believed that American public address should be approached as a study in the history of ideas. From his perspective the critical act is viewed as "tracing out an American intellectual pattern." We offer his essay "Public Address: A Study in Social and Intellectual History" as representative of the *theory* of the historical approach and, as an *application* of that approach, "The Little World of Barry Goldwater."

Characteristics of the Traditional Perspective

In spite of their different emphases, the neo-Aristotelian and the historical approaches share a common heritage, perspective, and several assumptions. Their common heritage starts with the classical rhetoricians, especially Aristotle, so that subsequent rhetorical history served as an illustration and refinement of what has become known as the "classical canon." The point of departure for traditional criticism is well indicated in Wichelns's words, "one must conceive of the public man as influencing the men of his own times by the power of his discourse." It is in this light that the traditional critic sees Aristotle's famous definition of rhetoric as "the faculty of observing in any given case the available means of persuasion."[8] The traditional critic focuses on the speaker as the center of interest; we refer to his perspective as a *speaker orientation*. He is likely to see the historical context as posing problems for a speaker and to consider the speaker's response to his problems from a number of approaches which can be represented by such questions as: What strategies or rhetorical principles does the speaker employ in his message? How did the speaker adapt to his audience? How did the speaker take advantage of the historical setting and occasion? It is not simply that the traditional perspective examines the interaction among the speaker, message, occasion, and audience, but that the interaction is always viewed through the speaker's eyes. Aristotle's principles are taken as choices that a speaker must make. If the question, Is the rhetoric good for society? evolves, the critic is likely to put it aside as not relevant since he is, in effect, "giving the speaker his purposes." Thus, the traditional perspective tends to be amoral, attempting to raise and answer technical problems.

The traditional approach, with its speaker orientation, seems to as-

---

[8] *1355ᵇ26. Aristotle's* Rhetoric *is readily available in several editions. We are citing the W. Rhys Roberts translation, which may be found in an inexpensive Modern Library edition by Random House.*

sume that society is relatively stable if not static and that people, circumstances, and rhetorical principles remain fundamentally unchanged throughout history. It assumes that rhetoricians have discovered the essential principles of public persuasion and that for this reason the critic's primary concern should be to describe the use of the traditional principles, along with modern variations in the ongoing public address.

The traditional critic is apt to scrutinize historical rather than contemporary public address because greater objectivity can be attained and the details of the events better documented. If he strives for objectivity and believes that rhetorical principles reflect a relatively stable reality, then it will follow that an accurate reconstruction of history will be his goal.

All divisions of human activity must be suspected of being arbitrary to some degree, but we believe that a traditional perspective is observable in much twentieth-century rhetorical criticism. To the extent that this perspective could be labeled "paradigmatic," it was dominant and, for a time, unchallenged. The subordinate approaches, which we call the neo-Aristotelian and the historical, are often distinct and sometimes merged as critics approach the ideal set by Wichelns.

The traditional perspective represents a special formalizing of the critical impulse. As the traditional perspective came to be questioned, other forms of the impulse took shape. To study the breaks from tradition, however, we believe that a strong sense of the dominant mode must be obtained, and we present the selections illustrating the traditional perspective, in theory and application, as a means of gaining that understanding.

The Neo-Aristotelian Approach

THE Literary Criticism of Oratory
by Herbert A. Wichelns

I

Samuel Johnson once projected a history of criticism "as it relates to judging of authors." Had the great eighteenth-century critic ever carried out his intention, he would have included some interesting comments on the orators and their judges. Histories of criticism, in whole or in part, we now have, and histories of orators. But that section of the history of criticism which deals with judging of orators is still unwritten. Yet the problem is an interesting one, and one which involves some important conceptions. Oratory—the waning influence of which is often discussed in current periodicals—has definitely lost the established place in literature that it once had. Demosthenes and Cicero, Bossuet and Burke, all hold their places in literary histories. But Webster inspires more than one modern critic to ponder the question whether oratory is literature; and if we may judge by the emphasis of literary historians generally, both in England and in America, oratory is either an outcast or a poor relation. What are the reasons for this change? It is a question not easily answered. Involved in it is some shift in the conception of oratory or of literature, or of both; nor can these conceptions have changed except in response to the life of which oratory, as well as literature, is part.

This essay, it should be said, is merely an attempt to spy out the land, to see what some critics have said of some orators, to discover what their mode of criticism has been. The discussion is limited in the main to Burke and a few nineteenth-century figures—Webster, Lincoln, Gladstone, Bright, Cobden—and to the verdicts on these found in the surveys of literary history, in critical essays, in histories of oratory, and in biographies.

Of course, we are not here concerned with the disparagement of oratory. With that, John Morley once dealt in a phrase: "Yet, after all, to disparage eloquence is to depreciate mankind."[1] Nor is the praise of eloquence of moment here. What interests us is the method of the critic: his standards, his categories of judgment, what he regards as important. These will show, not so much what he thinks of a great and

From *Studies in Rhetoric and Public Speaking in Honor of James Albert Winans,* by Pupils and Colleagues. Copyright © 1925, by The Century Company. Reprinted by courtesy of Appleton-Century-Crofts, Educational Division, Meredith Corporation. Mr. Wichelns is Professor Emeritus of Speech, Cornell University.

[1] Life of William Ewart Gladstone, *New York, 1903, II, 593.*

ancient literary type, as how he thinks in dealing with that type. The chief aim is to know how critics have spoken of orators.

We have not much serious criticism of oratory. The reasons are patent. Oratory is intimately associated with statecraft; it is bound up with the things of the moment; its occasion, its terms, its background, can often be understood only by the careful student of history. Again, the publication of orations as pamphlets leaves us free to regard any speech merely as an essay, as a literary effort deposited at the shrine of the muses in hope of being blessed with immortality. This view is encouraged by the difficulty of reconstructing the conditions under which the speech was delivered; by the doubt, often, whether the printed text of the speech represents what was actually said, or what the orator elaborated afterwards. Burke's corrections are said to have been the despair of his printers.[2] Some of Chatham's speeches, by a paradox of fate, have been reported to us by Samuel Johnson, whose style is as remote as possible from that of the Great Commoner, and who wrote without even having heard the speeches pronounced.[3] Only in comparatively recent times has parliamentary reporting pretended to give full records of what was actually said; and even now speeches are published for literary or political purposes which justify the corrector's pencil in changes both great and small. Under such conditions the historical study of speech making is far from easy.

Yet the conditions of democracy necessitate both the making of speeches and the study of the art. It is true that other ways of influencing opinion have long been practiced, that oratory is no longer the chief means of communicating ideas to the masses. And the change is emphasized by the fact that the newer methods are now beginning to be investigated, sometimes from the point of view of the political student, sometimes from that of the "publicity expert." But, human nature being what it is, there is no likelihood that face to face persuasion will cease to be a principal mode of exerting influence, whether in courts, in senate-houses, or on the platform. It follows that the critical study of oratorical method is the study, not of a mode outworn, but of a permanent and important human activity.

Upon the great figures of the past who have used the art of public address, countless judgments have been given. These judgments have varied with the bias and preoccupation of the critics, who have been historians, biographers, or literary men, and have written accordingly. The context in which we find criticism of speeches, we must, for the purposes of this essay at least, both note and set aside. For though the aim of the critic conditions his approach to our more limited problem—

[2] Select Works, *ed. E. J. Payne, Oxford, 1892, I, xxxviii.*
[3] *Basil Williams,* Life of William Pitt, *New York, 1913, II, 335–337.*

the method of dealing with oratory—still we find that an historian may view an orator in the same light as does a biographer or an essayist. The literary form in which criticism of oratory is set does not afford a classification of the critics.

"There are," says a critic of literary critics, "three definite points, on one of which, or all of which, criticism must base itself. There is the date, and the author, and the work."[4] The points on which writers base their judgments of orators do afford a classification. The man, his work, his times, are the necessary common topics of criticism; no one of them can be wholly disregarded by any critic. But mere difference in emphasis on one or another of them is important enough to suggest a rough grouping. The writers with whom this essay deals give but a subordinate position to the date; they are interested chiefly in the man or in his works. Accordingly, we have as the first type of criticism that which is predominantly personal or biographical, is occupied with the character and the mind of the orator, goes behind the work to the man. The second type attempts to hold the scales even between the biographical and the literary interest. The third is occupied with the work and tends to ignore the man. These three classes, then, seem to represent the practice of modern writers in dealing with orators. Each merits a more detailed examination.

II

We may begin with that type of critic whose interest is in personality, who seeks the man behind the work. Critics of this type furnish forth the appreciative essays and the occasional addresses on the orators. They are as the sands of the sea. Lord Rosebery's two speeches on Burke, Whitelaw Reid's on Lincoln and on Burke, may stand as examples of the character sketch.[5] The second part of Birrell's essay on Burke will serve for the mental character sketch (the first half of the essay is biographical); other examples are Sir Walter Raleigh's essay on Burke and that by Robert Lynd.[6] All these emphasize the concrete nature of Burke's thought, the realism of his imagination, his peculiar combination of breadth of vision with intensity; they pass to the guiding principles of his thought: his hatred of abstraction, his love of order and of settled ways. But they do not occupy themselves with Burke as a speaker, nor even with him as a writer; their first and their last concern is with the man rather than with his works; and their method is to fuse

---

[4] *D. Nichol Smith,* Functions of Criticism, *Oxford, 1909, p. 15.*
[5] *See Rosebery,* Appreciations and Addresses, *London, 1899, and Whitelaw Reid,* American and English Studies, *New York, 1913, II.*
[6] *See Augustine Birrell,* Obiter Dicta, *New York, 1887, II; Walter Raleigh,* Some Authors, *Oxford, 1923; Robert Lynd,* Books and Authors. *London, 1922.*

into a single impression whatever of knowledge or opinion they may have of the orator's life and works. These critics, in dealing with the public speaker, think of him as something other than a speaker. Since this type of writing makes but an indirect contribution to our judgment of the orator, there is no need of a more extended account of the method, except as we find it combined with a discussion of the orator's works.

III

Embedded in biographies and histories of literature, we find another type of criticism, that which combines the sketch of mind and character with some discussion of style. Of the general interest of such essays there can be no doubt. Nine-tenths of so-called literary criticism deals with the lives and personalities of authors, and for the obvious reason that every one is interested in them, whereas few will follow a technical study, however broadly based. At its best, the type of study that starts with the orator's mind and character is justified by the fact that nothing can better illuminate his work as a persuader of men. But when not at its best, the description of a man's general cast of mind stands utterly unrelated to his art: the critic fails to fuse his comment on the individual with his comment on the artist; and as a result we get some statements about the man, and some statements about the orator, but neither casts light on the other. Almost any of the literary histories will supply examples of the gulf that may yawn between a stylistic study and a study of personality.

The best example of the successful combination of the two strains is Grierson's essay on Burke in the *Cambridge History of English Literature.* In this, Burke's style, though in largest outline only, is seen to emerge from the essential nature of the man. Yet of this essay, too, it must be said that the analysis of the orator is incomplete, being overshadowed by the treatment of Burke as a writer, though, as we shall see, the passages on style have the rare virtue of keeping to the high road of criticism. The majority of critics who use the mixed method, however, do not make their study of personality fruitful for a study of style, do not separate literary style from oratorical style even to the extent that Grierson does, and do conceive of literary style as a matter of details. In fact, most of the critics of this group tend to supply a discussion of style by jotting down what has occurred to them about the author's management of words; and in the main, they notice the lesser strokes of literary art, but not its broader aspects. They have an eye for tactics, but not for strategy. This is the more strange, as these same writers habitually take large views of the orator himself, considered as a personality, and because they often remark the speaker's great themes and his leading ideas. The management of ideas—what the

Romans called invention and disposition—the critics do not observe; their practice is the *salto mortale* from the largest to the smallest considerations. And it needs no mention that a critic who does not observe the management of ideas even from the point of view of structure and arrangement can have nothing to say of the adaptation of ideas to the orator's audience.

It is thus with Professor McLaughlin in his chapter in the *Cambridge History of American Literature* on Clay and Calhoun and some lesser lights. The pages are covered with such expressions as diffuse, florid, diction restrained and strong, neatly phrased, power of attack, invective, gracious persuasiveness. Of the structure of the speeches by which Clay and Calhoun exercised their influence—nothing. The drive of ideas is not represented. The background of habitual feeling which the orators at times appealed to and at times modified, is hinted at in a passage about Clay's awakening the spirit of nationalism, and in another passage contrasting the full-blooded oratory of Benton with the more polished speech of Quincy and Everett; but these are the merest hints. In the main, style for McLaughlin is neither the expression of personality nor the order and movement given to thought, but a thing of shreds and patches. It is thus, too, with Morley's pages on Burke's style in his life of the orator, and with Lodge's treatment of Webster in his life of the great American. A rather better analysis, though on the same plane of detail, may be used as an example. Oliver Elton says of Burke:

He embodies, more powerfully than any one, the mental tendencies and changes that are seen gathering force through the eighteenth century. A volume of positive knowledge, critically sifted and ascertained; a constructive vision of the past and its institutions; the imagination, under this guidance, everywhere at play; all these elements unite in Burke. His main field is political philosophy. . . . His favorite form is oratory, uttered or written. His medium is prose, and the work of his later years, alone, outweighs all contemporary prose in power. . . . His whole body of production has the unity of some large cathedral, whose successive accretions reveal the natural growth of a single mind, without any change or essential break. . . .

Already [in the Thoughts *and in the* Observations*] the characteristics of Burke's thought and style appear, as well as his profound conversance with constitutional history, finance, and affairs. There is a constant reference to general principles, as in the famous defence of Party. The maxims that come into play go far beyond the occasion. There is a perpetual ground-swell of passion, embanked and held in check, but ever breaking out into sombre irony and sometimes into figure; but metaphors and other tropes are not yet very frequent. . . .*

In the art of unfolding and amplifying, Burke is the rival of the ancients. . . .

In the speech on Conciliation the [oft-repeated] key-word is peace. . . . This iteration makes us see the stubborn faces on the opposite benches. There is contempt in it; their ears must be dinned, they must remember the word peace through the long intricate survey that is to follow. . . .

Often he has a turn that would have aroused the fervor of the great appreciator known to us by the name of Longinus. In his speech on Economical Reform (1780) Burke risks an appeal, in the face of the Commons, to the example of the enemy. He has described . . . the reforms of the French revenue. He says: "The French have imitated us; let us, through them, imitate ourselves, ourselves in our better and happier days." A speaker who was willing to offend for the sake of startling, and to defeat his purpose, would simply have said, "The French have imitated us; let us imitate them." Burke comes to the verge of this imprudence, but he sees the outcry on the lips of the adversary, and silences them by the word ourselves; and then, seizing the moment of bewilderment, repeats it and explains it by the noble past; he does not say when those days were; the days of Elizabeth or of Cromwell? Let the House choose! This is true oratory, honest diplomacy.[7]

Here, in some twenty pages, we have but two hints that Burke had to put his ideas in a form adapted to his audience; only the reiterated *peace* in all Burke's writings reminds the critic of Burke's hearers; only one stroke of tact draws his attention. Most of his account is devoted to Burke's style in the limited use of the term: to his power of amplification—his conduct of the paragraph, his use of clauses now long, now short—to his figures, comparisons, and metaphors, to his management of the sentence pattern, and to his rhythms. For Professor Elton, evidently, Burke was a man, and a mind, and an artist in prose; but he was not an orator. Interest in the minutiae of style has kept Elton from bringing his view of Burke the man to bear on his view of Burke's writings. The fusing point evidently is in the strategic purpose of the works, in their function as speeches. By holding steadily to the conception of Burke as a public man, one could make the analysis of mind and the analysis of art more illuminating for each other than Elton does.

It cannot be said that in all respects Stephenson's chapter on Lincoln in the *Cambridge History of American Literature* is more successful than Elton's treatment of Burke; but it is a better interweaving of the biographical and the literary strands of interest. Stephenson's study of the

---

[7] *Oliver Elton,* Survey of English Literature, *1780–1830, I, 234–53, published by The Macmillan Company.*

personality of Lincoln is directly and persistently used in the study of Lincoln's style:

Is it fanciful to find a connection between the way in which his mysticism develops—its atmospheric, non-dogmatic pervasiveness—and the way in which his style develops? Certainly the literary part of him works into all the portions of his utterance with the gradualness of daylight through a shadowy wood. . . . And it is to be noted that the literary quality . . . is of the whole, not of the detail. It does not appear as a gift of phrases. Rather it is the slow unfolding of those two original characteristics, taste and rhythm. What is growing is the degree of both things. The man is becoming deeper, and as he does so he imposes himself, in this atmospheric way, more steadily on his language.[8]

The psychology of mystical experience may appear a poor support for the study of style. It is but one factor of many, and Stephenson may justly be reproached for leaning too heavily upon it. Compared to Grierson's subtler analysis of Burke's mind and art, the essay of Stephenson seems forced and one-sided. Yet he illuminates his subject more than many of the writers so far mentioned, because he begins with a vigorous effort to bring his knowledge of the man to bear upon his interpretation of the work. But though we find in Stephenson's pages a suggestive study of Lincoln as literary man, we find no special regard for Lincoln as orator. The qualities of style that Stephenson mentions are the qualities of prose generally:

At last he has his second manner, a manner quite his own. It is not his final manner, the one that was to give him his assured place in literature. However, in a wonderful blend of simplicity, directness, candor, joined with a clearness beyond praise, and a delightful cadence, it has outstripped every other politician of the hour. And back of its words, subtly affecting its phrases, . . . is that brooding sadness which was to be with him to the end.[9]

The final manner, it appears, is a sublimation of the qualities of the earlier, which was "keen, powerful, full of character, melodious, impressive";[10] and it is a sublimation which has the power to awaken the imagination by its flexibility, directness, pregnancy, wealth.

In this we have nothing new, unless it be the choice of stylistic categories that emphasize the larger pattern of ideas rather than the minute

---

[8] Cambridge History of American Literature, *New York, 1921, III, 374–5.*
[9] Cambridge History of American Literature, *III, 378.*
[10] Ibid., *pp. 381–2.*

pattern of grammatical units, such as we have found in Elton and to some extent shall find in Saintsbury; it must be granted, too, that Stephenson has dispensed with detail and gained his larger view at the cost of no little vagueness. "Two things," says Stephenson of the Lincoln of 1849–1858, "grew upon him. The first was his understanding of men, the generality of men. . . . The other thing that grew upon him was his power to reach and influence them through words."[11] We have here the text for any study of Lincoln as orator; but the study itself this critic does not give us.

Elton's characterization of Burke's style stands out from the usual run of superficial comment by the closeness of its analysis and its regard for the architectonic element. Stephenson's characterization of Lincoln's style is distinguished by a vigorous if forced effort to unite the study of the man and of the work. With both we may contrast a better essay, by a critic of greater insight. Grierson says of Burke:

What Burke has of the deeper spirit of that movement [the romantic revival] is seen not so much in the poetic imagery of his finest prose as in the philosophical imagination which informs his conception of the state, in virtue of which he transcends the rationalism of the century. . . . This temper of Burke's mind is reflected in his prose. . . . To the direct, conversational prose of Dryden and Swift, changed social circumstances and the influence of Johnson had given a more oratorical cast, more dignity and weight, but, also, more of heaviness and conventional elegance. From the latter faults, Burke is saved by his passionate temperament, his ardent imagination, and the fact that he was a speaker conscious always of his audience. . . . [Burke] could delight, astound, and convince an audience. He did not easily conciliate and win them over. He lacked the first essential and index of the conciliatory speaker, lenitas vocis; his voice was harsh and unmusical, his gesture ungainly. . . . And, even in the text of his speeches there is a strain of irony and scorn which is not well fitted to conciliate. . . . We have evidence that he could do both things on which Cicero lays stress—move his audience to tears and delight them by his wit. . . . Yet, neither pathos nor humor is Burke's forte. . . . Burke's unique power as an orator lies in the peculiar interpenetration of thought and passion. Like the poet and the prophet, he thinks most profoundly when he thinks most passionately. When he is not deeply moved, his oratory verges toward the turgid; when he indulges feeling for his own sake, as in parts of Letters on a Regicide Peace, it becomes hysterical. But, in his greatest speeches and pamphlets, the passion of Burke's mind shows itself in the luminous thoughts which it emits, in the imagery which at once

[11] Ibid., p. 377.

moves and *teaches, throwing a flood of light not only on the point in question, but on the whole neighboring sphere of man's moral and political nature.*[12]

The most notable feature of these passages is not their recognition that Burke was a speaker, but their recognition that his being a speaker conditioned his style, and that he is to be judged in part at least as one who attempted to influence men by the spoken word. Grierson, like Elton, attends to the element of structure and has something to say of the nature of Burke's prose; but, unlike Elton, he distinguishes this from the description of Burke's oratory—although without maintaining the distinction: he illustrates Burke's peculiar oratorical power from a pamphlet as readily as from a speech. His categories seem less mechanical than those of Elton, who is more concerned with the development of the paragraph than with the general cast of Burke's style; nor is his judgment warped, as is Stephenson's, by having a theory to market. Each has suffered from the necessity of compression. Yet, all told, Grierson realizes better than the others that Burke's task was not merely to express his thoughts and his feelings in distinguished prose, but to communicate his thoughts and his feelings effectively. It is hardly true, however, that Grierson has in mind the actual audience of Burke; the audience of Grierson's vision seems to be universalized, to consist of the judicious listeners or readers of any age. Those judicious listeners have no practical interest in the situation; they have only a philosophical and æsthetic interest.

Of Taine in his description of Burke it cannot be said that he descends to the minutiæ of style. He deals with his author's character and ideas, as do all the critics of this group, but his comments on style are simply a single impression, vivid and picturesque:

Burke had one of those fertile and precise imaginations which believes that finished knowledge is an inner view, which never quits a subject without having clothed it in its colors and forms. . . . To all these powers of mind, which constitute a man of system, he added all those energies of heart which constitute an enthusiast. . . . He brought to politics a horror of crime, a vivacity and sincerity of conscience, a sensibility, which seem suitable only to a young man.

. . . The vast amount of his works rolls impetuously in a current of eloquence. Sometimes a spoken or written discourse needs a whole volume to unfold the train of his multiplied proofs and courageous

---

[12] *From H. J. C. Grierson in* Cambridge History of English Literature, *XI, 30–35 by Cambridge University Press (1914). Abridgements by permission of the publisher.*

anger. It is either the exposé of a ministry, or the whole history of Brit-
ish India, or the complete theory of revolutions . . . which comes
down like a vast overflowing stream. . . . Doubtless there is foam on
its eddies, mud in its bed; thousands of strange creatures sport wildly
on its surface: he does not select, he lavishes. . . . Nothing strikes
him as in excess. . . . He continues half a barbarian, battening in ex-
aggeration and violence; but his fire is so sustained, his conviction so
strong, his emotion so warm and abundant, that we suffer him to go on,
forget our repugnance, see in his irregularities and his trespasses only
the outpourings of a great heart and a deep mind, too open and too
full.[13]

This is brilliant writing, unencumbered by the subaltern's interest in
tactics, but it is strategy as described by a war-correspondent, not by
a general. We get from it little light on how Burke solved the problem
that confronts every orator: so to present ideas as to bring them into
the consciousness of his hearers.

Where the critic divides his interest between the man and the work,
without allowing either interest to predominate, he is often compelled
to consider the work *in toto,* and we get only observations so generalized as not to include consideration of the form of the work. The speech
is not thought of as essentially a means of influence; it is regarded as
a specimen of prose, or as an example of philosophic thought. The
date, the historical interest, the orator's own intention, are often lost
from view; and criticism suffers in consequence.

IV

We have seen that the critic who is occupied chiefly with the orator
as a man can contribute, although indirectly, to the study of the orator
as such, and that the critic who divides his attention between the man
and the work must effect a fusion of the two interests if he is to help
materially in the understanding of the orator. We come now to critics
more distinctly literary in aim. Within this group several classes may be
discriminated: the first comprises the judicial critics; the second includes the interpretative critics who take the point of view of literary
style generally, regarding the speech as an essay, or as a specimen of
prose; the third and last group is composed of the writers who tend to
regard the speech as a special literary form.

The type of criticism that attempts a judicial evaluation of the literary
merits of the work—of the orator's "literary remains"—tends to center
the inquiry on the question: Is this literature? The futility of the question

[13] *H. A. Taine,* History of English Literature, *tr. H. Van Laun, London, 1878,*
II, 81–3.

appears equally in the affirmative and in the negative replies to it. The fault is less with the query, however, than with the hastiness of the answers generally given. For the most part, the critics who raise this problem are not disposed really to consider it: they formulate no conception either of literature or of oratory; they will not consider their own literary standards critically and comprehensively. In short, the question is employed as a way to dispose briefly of the subject of a lecture or of a short essay in a survey of a national literature.

Thus Phelps, in his treatment of Webster and Lincoln in *Some Makers of American Literature,*[14] tells us that they have a place in literature by virtue of their style, gives us some excerpts from Lincoln and some comments on Webster's politics, but offers no reasoned criticism. St. Peter swings wide the gates of the literary heaven, but does not explain his action. We may suspect that the solemn award of a "place in literature" sometimes conceals the absence of any real principle of judgment.

Professor Trent is less easily satisfied that Webster deserves a "place in literature." He grants Webster's power to stimulate patriotism, his sonorous dignity and massiveness, his clearness and strength of style, his powers of dramatic description. But he finds only occasional splendor of imagination, discovers no soaring quality of intelligence, and is not dazzled by his philosophy or his grasp of history. Mr. Trent would like more vivacity and humor and color in Webster's style.[15] This mode of deciding Webster's place in or out of literature is important to us only as it reveals the critic's method of judging. Trent looks for clearness and strength, imagination, philosophic grasp, vivacity, humor, color in style. This is excellent so far as it goes, but goes no further than to suggest some qualities which are to be sought in any and all works of literary art in dramas, in essays, in lyric poems, as well as in speeches.

Let us take a third judge. Gosse will not allow Burke to be a complete master of English prose: "Notwithstanding all its magnificence, it appears to me that the prose of Burke lacks the variety, the delicacy, the modulated music of the very finest writers."[16] Gosse adds that Burke lacks flexibility, humor, and pathos. As critical method, this is one with that of Trent.

Gosse, with his question about mastery of prose, does not directly ask, "Is this literature?" Henry Cabot Lodge does, and his treatment of Webster (in the *Cambridge History of American Literature*) is curious.

---

[14] *Boston, 1923.*

[15] *W. P. Trent,* History of American Literature, 1607–1865, *New York, 1917,* pp. 576–7.

[16] *Edmund Gosse,* History of Eighteenth Century English Literature, 1660–1780, *London, 1889, pp. 365–6.*

Lodge is concerned to show that Webster belongs to literature, and to explain the quality in his work that gives him a place among the best makers of literature. The test applied is permanence: Is Webster still read? The answer is, yes, for he is part of every schoolboy's education, and is the most quoted author in Congress. The sight of a literary critic resigning the judicial bench to the schoolmaster and the Congressman is an enjoyable one; as enjoyable as Mr. H. L. Mencken's reaction to it would be; but one could wish for grounds more relative than this. Mr. Lodge goes on to account for Webster's permanence: it lies in his power to impart to rhetoric the literary touch. The distinction between rhetoric and literature is not explained, but apparently the matter lies thus: rhetorical verse may be poetry; Byron is an example. Rhetorical prose is not literature until there is added the literary touch. We get a clue as to how the literary touch may be added: put in something imaginative, something that strikes the hearer at once. The example chosen by Lodge is a passage from Webster in which the imaginative or literary touch is given by the single word "mildew."[17] This method of criticism, too, we may reduce to that of Trent, with the exception that only one quality—imagination—is requisite for admission to the literary Valhalla.

Whether the critic's standard be imagination, or this together with other qualities such as intelligence, vivacity, humor, or whether it be merely "style," undefined and unexplained, the point of view is always that of the printed page. The oration is lost from view, and becomes an exercise in prose, musical, colorful, varied, and delicate, but, so far as the critic is concerned, formless and purposeless. Distinctions of literary type or kind are erased; the architectonic element is neglected; and the speech is regarded as a musical meditation might be regarded: as a kind of harmonious musing that drifts pleasantly along, with little of inner form and nothing of objective purpose. This, it should be recognized, is not the result of judicial criticism so much as the result of the attempt to decide too hastily whether a given work is to be admitted into the canon of literature.

V

It is, perhaps, natural for the historian of literature to reduce all literary production to one standard, and thus to discuss only the common elements in all prose. One can understand also that the biographer, when in the course of his task he must turn literary critic, finds himself often inadequately equipped and his judgment of little value, except on the scale of literature generally rather than of oratory or of any given type. More is to be expected, however, of those who set up

[17] Cambridge History of American Literature, *New York, 1918, II, 101.*

as literary critics in the first instance: those who deal directly with Webster's style, or with Lincoln as man of letters. We shall find such critics as Whipple, Hazlitt, and Saintsbury devoting themselves to the description of literary style in the orators whom they discuss. Like the summary judicial critics we have mentioned, their center of interest is the work; but they are less hurried than Gosse and Lodge and Phelps and Trent; and their aim is not judgment so much as understanding. Yet their interpretations, in the main, take the point of view of the printed page, of the prose essay. Only to a slight degree is there a shift to another point of view, that of the orator in relation to the audience on whom he exerts his influence; the immediate public begins to loom a little larger; the essential nature of the oration as a type begins to be suggested.

Saintsbury has a procedure which much resembles that of Elton, though we must note the fact that the former omits consideration of Burke as a personality and centers attention on his work. We saw that Elton, in his passages on Burke's style, attends both to the larger elements of structure and to such relatively minute points as the management of the sentence and the clause. In Saintsbury the range of considerations is the same. At times, indeed, the juxtaposition of large and small ideas is ludicrous, as when one sentence ends by awarding to Burke literary immortality, and the next describes the sentences of an early work as "short and crisp, arranged with succinct antithetic parallels, which seldom exceed a single pair of clauses."[18] The award of immortality is not, it should be said, based entirely on the shortness of Burke's sentences in his earliest works. Indeed much of Saintsbury's comment is of decided interest:

The style of Burke is necessarily to be considered throughout as conditioned by oratory. . . . In other words, he was first of all a rhetorician, and probably the greatest that modern times have ever produced. But his rhetoric always inclined much more to the written than to the spoken form, with results annoying perhaps to him at the time, but even to him satisfactory afterwards, and an inestimable gain to the world. . . .

The most important of these properties of Burke's style, in so far as it is possible to enumerate them here, are as follows. First of all, and most distinctive, so much so as to have escaped no competent critic, is a very curious and, until his example made it imitable, nearly unique faculty of building up an argument or a picture by a succession of complementary strokes, not added at haphazard but growing out of and

[18] *G. E. B. Saintsbury,* Short History of English Literature, *New York, 1915, p. 630.*

onto one another. No one has ever been such a master of the best and grandest kind of the figure called . . . Amplification, and this . . . is the direct implement by which he achieves his greatest effects.

. . . The piece [Present Discontents] may be said to consist of a certain number of specially labored paragraphs in which the arguments or pictures just spoken of are put as forcibly as the author can put them, and as a rule in a succession of shortish sentences, built up and glued together with the strength and flexibility of a newly fashioned fishing-rod. In the intervals the texts thus given are turned about, commented on, justified, or discussed in detail, in a rhetoric for the most part, though not always, rather less serried, less evidently burnished, and in less full dress. And this general arrangement proceeds through the rest of his works.[19]

After a number of comments on Burke's skill in handling various kinds of ornament, such as humor, epigram, simile, Saintsbury returns to the idea that Burke's special and definite weapon was "imaginative argument, and the marshalling of vast masses of complicated detail into properly rhetorical battalions or (to alter the image) mosaic pictures of enduring beauty."[20] Saintsbury's attitude toward the communicative, impulsive nature of the orator's task is indicated in a passage on the well-known description of Windsor Castle. This description the critic terms "at once . . . a perfect harmonic chord, a complete visual picture, and a forcible argument."[21] It is significant that he adds, "The minor rhetoric, the suasive purpose [presumably the argumentative intent] must be kept in view; if it be left out the thing loses"; and holds Burke "far below Browne, who had no needs of purpose."[22] It is less important that a critic think well of the suasive purpose than that he reckon with it, and of Saintsbury at least it must be said that he recognizes it, although grudgingly; but it cannot be said that Saintsbury has a clear conception of rhetoric as the art of communication: sometimes it means the art of prose, sometimes that of suasion.

Hazlitt's method of dealing with Burke resembles Taine's as Saintsbury's resembles that of Elton. In Hazlitt we have a critic who deals with style in the large; details of rhythm, of sentence pattern, of imagery, are ignored. His principal criticism of Burke as orator is contained in the well-known contrast with Chatham, really a contrast of mind and temperament in relation to oratorical style. He follows this with some excellent comment on Burke's prose style; nothing more is said of his

[19] Ibid., *pp. 629–30.*
[20] Ibid., *p. 631.*
[21] Ibid.
[22] Ibid.

oratory; only in a few passages do we get a flash of light on the relation of Burke to his audience, as in the remark about his eagerness to impress his reader, and in the description of his conversational quality. It is notable too that Hazlitt finds those works which never had the form of speeches the most significant and most typical of Burke's style.

> *Burke was so far from being a gaudy or flowery writer, that he was one of the severest writers we have. His words are the most like things; his style is the most strictly limited to the subject. He unites every extreme and every variety of composition; the lowest and the meanest words and descriptions with the highest. . . . He had no other object but to produce the strongest impression on his reader, by giving the truest, the most characteristic, the fullest, and most forcible description of things, trusting to the power of his own mind to mold them into grace and beauty. . . . Burke most frequently produced an effect by the remoteness and novelty of his combinations, by the force of contrast, by the striking manner in which the most opposite and unpromising materials were harmoniously blended together; not by laying his hands on all the fine things he could think of, but by bringing together those things which he knew would blaze out into glorious light by their collision.*[23]

Twelve years after writing the essay from which we have quoted, Hazlitt had occasion to revise his estimate of Burke as a statesman; but his sketch of Burke's style is essentially unaltered.[24] In Hazlitt we find a sense of style as an instrument of communication; that sense is no stronger in dealing with Burke's speeches than in dealing with his pamphlets, but it gives to Hazlitt's criticisms a reality not often found. What is lacking is a clear sense of Burke's communicative impulse, of his persuasive purpose, as operating in a concrete situation. Hazlitt does not suggest the background of Burke's speeches, ignores the events that called them forth. He views his subject, in a sense, as Grierson does: as speaking to the judicious but disinterested hearer of any age other than Burke's own. But the problem of the speaker, as well as of the pamphleteer, is to interest men here and now; the understanding of that problem requires, on the part of the critic, a strong historical sense for the ideas and attitudes of the people (not merely of their leaders), and a full knowledge of the public opinion of the times in which the orator spoke. This we do not find in Hazlitt.

Two recent writers on Lincoln commit the opposite error: they devote

[23] Sketches and Essays, *ed. W. C. Hazlitt, London, 1872, II, 420–1.*
[24] Political Essays with Sketches of Public Characters, *London, 1819, pp. 264–79.*

themselves so completely to description of the situation in which Lincoln wrote as to leave no room for criticism. L. E. Robinson's *Lincoln as Man of Letters*[25] is a biography rewritten around Lincoln's writings. It is nothing more. Instead of giving us a criticism, Professor Robinson has furnished us with some of the materials of the critic; his own judgments are too largely laudatory to cast much light. The book, therefore, is not all that its title implies. A single chapter of accurate summary and evaluation would do much to increase our understanding of Lincoln as man of letters, even though it said nothing of Lincoln as speaker. A chapter or two on Lincoln's work in various kinds—letters, state papers, speeches—would help us to a finer discrimination than Professor Robinson's book offers. Again, the proper estimate of style in any satisfactory sense requires us to do more than to weigh the soundness of an author's thought and to notice the isolated beauties of his expression. Something should be said of structure, something of adaptation to the immediate audience, whose convictions and habits of thought, whose literary usages, and whose general cultural background all condition the work both of writer and speaker. Mr. Robinson has given us the political situation as a problem in controlling political forces, with little regard to the force even of public opinion, and with almost none to the cultural background. Lincoln's works, therefore, emerge as items in a political sequence, but not as resultants of the life of his time.

Some of the deficiencies of Robinson's volume are supplied by Dodge's essay, *Lincoln as Master of Words*.[26] Dodge considers, more definitely than Robinson, the types in which Lincoln worked: he separates messages from campaign speeches, letters from occasional addresses. He has an eye on Lincoln's relation to his audience, but this manifests itself chiefly in an account of the immediate reception of a work. Reports of newspaper comments on the speeches may be a notable addition to Lincolniana; supported by more political information and more insight than Mr. Dodge's short book reveals, they might become an aid to the critical evaluation of the speeches. But in themselves they are neither a criticism nor an interpretation of Lincoln's mastery of words.

Robinson and Dodge, then, stand at opposite poles to Saintsbury and Hazlitt. The date is put in opposition to the work as a center of critical interest. If the two writers on Lincoln lack a full perception of their author's background, they do not lack a sense of its importance. If the critics of Burke do not produce a complete and rounded criticism, neither do they lose themselves in preparatory studies. Each method is incomplete; each should supplement the other.

[25] *New York, 1923.*
[26] *New York, 1924.*

We turn now to a critic who neglects the contribution of history to the study of oratory, but who has two compensating merits: the merit of recognizing the types in which his subject worked, and the merit of remembering that an orator has as his audience, not posterity, but certain classes of his own contemporaries. Whipple's essay on Webster is open to attack from various directions: it is padded, it "dates," it is overlaudatory, it is overpatriotic, it lacks distinction of style. But there is wheat in the chaff. Scattered through the customary discussion of Webster's choice of words, his power of epithet, his compactness of statement, his images, the development of his style, are definite suggestions of a new point of view. It is the point of view of the actual audience. To Whipple, at times at least, Webster was not a writer, but a speaker; the critic tries to imagine the man, and also his hearers; he thinks of the speech as a communication to a certain body of auditors. A phrase often betrays a mental attitude; Whipple alone of the critics we have mentioned would have written of "the eloquence, the moral power, he infused into his reasoning, so as to make the dullest citation of legal authority *tell* on the minds he addressed."[27] Nor would any other writer of this group have attempted to distinguish the types of audience Webster met. That Whipple's effort is a rambling and incoherent one, is not here in point. Nor is it pertinent that the critic goes completely astray in explaining why Webster's speeches have the nature of "organic formations, or at least of skilful engineering or architectural constructions"; though to say that the art of giving objective reality to a speech consists only of "a happy collocation and combination of words"[28] is certainly as far as possible from explaining Webster's sense of structure. What is significant in Whipple's essay is the occasional indication of a point of view that includes the audience. Such an indication is the passage in which the critic explains the source of Webster's influence:

What gave Webster his immense influence over the opinion of the people of New England, was first, his power of so "putting things" that everybody could understand his statements; secondly, his power of so framing his arguments that all the steps, from one point to another, in a logical series, could be clearly apprehended by every intelligent farmer or mechanic who had a thoughtful interest in the affairs of the country; and thirdly, his power of inflaming the sentiment of patriotism in all honest and well-intentioned men by overwhelming appeals to that sen-

27 E. P. Whipple, "Daniel Webster as a Master of English Style," in American Literature, *Boston, 1887, p. 157.*
28 Ibid., *p. 208.*

timent, so that after convincing their understandings, he clinched the matter by sweeping away their wills.

Perhaps to these sources of influence may be added . . . a genuine respect for the intellect, as well as for the manhood, of average men.[29]

In various ways the descriptive critics recognize the orator's function. In some, that recognition takes the form of a regard to the background of the speeches; in others, it takes the form of a regard to the effectiveness of the work, though that effectiveness is often construed as for the reader rather than for the listener. The "minor rhetoric, the suasive purpose" is beginning to be felt, though not always recognized and never fully taken into account.

VI

The distinction involved in the presence of a persuasive purpose is clearly recognized by some of those who have written on oratory, and by some biographers and historians. The writers now to be mentioned are aware, more keenly than any of those we have so far met, of the speech as a literary form—or if not as a literary form, then as a form of power; they tend accordingly to deal with the orator's work as limited by the conditions of the platform and the occasion, and to summon history to the aid of criticism.

The method of approach of the critics of oratory as oratory is well put by Lord Curzon at the beginning of his essay, *Modern Parliamentary Eloquence:*

In dealing with the Parliamentary speakers of our time I shall, accordingly, confine myself to those whom I have myself heard, or for whom I can quote the testimony of others who heard them; and I shall not regard them as prose writers or literary men, still less as purveyors of instruction to their own or to future generations, but as men who produced, by the exercise of certain talents of speech, a definite impression upon contemporary audiences, and whose reputation for eloquence must be judged by that test, and that test alone.[30]

The last phrase, "that test alone," would be scanned; the judgment of orators is not solely to be determined by the impression of contemporary audiences. For the present it will be enough to note the topics touched in Curzon's anecdotes and reminiscences—his lecture is far from a systematic or searching inquiry into the subject, and is of interest rather for its method of approach than for any considered study

[29] Ibid., *p. 144.*
[30] *London, 1914, p. 7.*

of an orator or of a period. We value him for his promises rather than for his performance. Curzon deals with the relative rank of speakers, with the comparative value of various speeches by a single man, with the orator's appearance and demeanor, with his mode of preparation and of delivery, with his mastery of epigram or image. Skill in seizing upon the dominant characteristics of each of his subjects saves the author from the worst triviality of reminiscence. Throughout, the point of view is that of the man experienced in public life discussing the eloquence of other public men, most of whom he had known and actually heard. That this is not the point of view of criticism in any strict sense, is of course true; but the *naïveté* and directness of this observer correct forcibly some of the extravagances we have been examining.

The lecture on Chatham as an orator by H. M. Butler exemplifies a very different method arising from a different subject and purpose. The lecturer is thinking, he tells us, "of Oratory partly as an art, partly as a branch of literature, partly as a power of making history."[31] His method is first to touch lightly upon Chatham's early training and upon his mode of preparing and delivering his speeches; next, to present some of the general judgments upon the Great Commoner, whether of contemporaries or of later historians; then to re-create a few of the most important speeches, partly by picturing the historical setting, partly by quotation, partly by the comments of contemporary writers. The purpose of the essay is "to reawaken, however faintly, some echoes of the kingly voice of a genuine Patriot, of whom his country is still justly proud."[32] The patriotic purpose we may ignore, but the wish to reconstruct the *mise en scène* of Chatham's speeches, to put the modern Oxford audience at the point of view of those who listened to the voice of Pitt, saw the flash of his eye and felt the force of his noble bearing, this is a purpose different from that of the critics whom we have examined. It may be objected that Butler's lecture has the defects of its method: the amenities observed by a Cambridge don delivering a formal lecture at Oxford keeps us from getting on with the subject; the brevity of the discourse prevents anything like a full treatment; the aim, revivification of the past, must be very broadly interpreted if it is to be really critical. Let us admit these things; it still is true that in a few pages the essential features of Pitt's eloquence are brought vividly before us, and that this is accomplished by thinking of the speech as originally delivered to its first audience rather than as read by the modern reader.

The same sense of the speaker in his relation to his audience appears in Lecky's account of Burke. This account, too, is marked by the

---

[31] Lord Chatham as an Orator, *Oxford, 1912, p. 5.*
[32] Ibid., *pp. 39–40.*

use of contemporary witnesses, and of comparisons with Burke's great rivals. But let Lecky's method speak in part for itself:

He spoke too often, too vehemently, and much too long; and his elo-quence, though in the highest degree intellectual, powerful, various, and original, was not well adapted to a popular audience. He had little or nothing of that fire and majesty of declamation with which Chatham thrilled his hearers, and often almost overawed opposition; and as a par-liamentary debater he was far inferior to Charles Fox. . . . Burke was not inferior to Fox in readiness, and in the power of clear and cogent reasoning. His wit, though not of the highest order, was only equalled by that of Townshend, Sheridan, and perhaps North, and it rarely failed in its effect upon the House. He far surpassed every other speaker in the copiousness and correctness of his diction, in the range of knowl-edge he brought to bear on every subject of debate, in the richness and variety of his imagination, in the gorgeous beauty of his descriptive passages, in the depth of the philosophical reflections and the felicity of the personal sketches which he delighted in scattering over his speeches. But these gifts were frequently marred by a strange want of judgment, measure, and self-control. His speeches were full of epi-sodes and digressions, of excessive ornamentation and illustration, of dissertations on general principles of politics, which were invaluable in themselves, but very unpalatable to a tired or excited House waiting eagerly for a division.[33]

These sentences suggest, and the pages from which they are ex-cerpted show, that historical imagination has led Lecky to regard Burke as primarily a speaker, both limited and formed by the conditions of his platform; and they exemplify, too, a happier use of stylistic cate-gories than do the essays of Curzon and Butler. The requirements of the historian's art have fused the character sketch and the literary criti-cism; the fusing agent has been the conception of Burke as a public man, and of his work as public address. Both Lecky's biographical in-terpretation and his literary criticism are less subtle than that of Grier-son; but Lecky is more definitely guided in his treatment of Burke by the conception of oratory as a special form of the literature of power and as a form molded always by the pressure of the time.

The merits of Lecky are contained, in ampler form, in Morley's bi-ography of Gladstone. The long and varied career of the great parlia-mentarian makes a general summary and final judgment difficult and perhaps inadvisable; Morley does not attempt them. But his running

[33] *W. E. H. Lecky,* History of England in the Eighteenth Century, *New York, 1888, III, 203–4.*

account of Gladstone as orator, if assembled from his thousand pages, is an admirable example of what can be done by one who has the point of view of the public man, sympathy with his subject, and understanding of the speaker's art. Morley gives us much contemporary reporting: the descriptions and judgments of journalists at various stages in Gladstone's career, the impression made by the speeches upon delivery, comparison with other speakers of the time. Here history is contemporary: the biographer was himself the witness of much that he describes, and has the experienced parliamentarian's flair for the scene and the situation. Gladstone's temperament and physical equipment for the platform, his training in the art of speaking, the nature of his chief appeals, the factor of character and personality, these are some of the topics repeatedly touched. There is added a sense for the permanent results of Gladstone's speaking: not the votes in the House merely, but the changed state of public opinion brought about by the speeches.

Mr. Gladstone conquered the House, because he was saturated with a subject and its arguments; because he could state and enforce his case; because he plainly believed every word he said, and earnestly wished to press the same belief into the minds of his hearers; finally because he was from the first an eager and a powerful athlete. . . . Yet with this inborn readiness for combat, nobody was less addicted to aggression or provocation. . . .

In finance, the most important of all the many fields of his activity, Mr. Gladstone had the signal distinction of creating the public opinion by which he worked, and warming the climate in which his projects throve. . . . Nobody denies that he was often declamatory and discursive, that he often overargued and overrefined; [but] he nowhere exerted greater influence than in that department of affairs where words out of relation to fact are most surely exposed. If he often carried the proper rhetorical arts of amplification and development to excess, yet the basis of fact was both sound and clear. . . . Just as Macaulay made thousands read history, who before had turned from it as dry and repulsive, so Mr. Gladstone made thousands eager to follow the public balance-sheet, and the whole nation became his audience. . . .

[In the Midlothian campaign] it was the orator of concrete detail, of inductive instances, of energetic and immediate object; the orator confidently and by sure touch startling into watchfulness the whole spirit of civil duty in man; elastic and supple, pressing fact and figure with a fervid insistence that was known from his career and character to be neither forced nor feigned, but to be himself. In a word, it was a man— a man impressing himself upon the kindled throngs by the breadth of

his survey of great affairs of life and nations, by the depth of his vision, by the power of his stroke.[34]

Objections may be made to Morley's method, chiefly on the ground of omissions. Though much is done to re-create the scene, though ample use is made of the date and the man, there is little formal analysis of the work. It is as if one had come from the House of Commons after hearing the speeches, stirred to enthusiasm but a little confused by the wealth of argument; not as if one came from a calm study of the speeches; not even as if one had corrected personal impressions by such a study. Of the structure of the speeches, little is said; but a few perorations are quoted; the details of style, one feels, although noticed at too great length by some critics, might well receive a modicum of attention here.

Although these deficiencies of Morley's treatment are not supplied by Bryce in his short and popular sketch of Gladstone, there is a summary which well supplements the running account offered by Morley. It has the merit of dealing explicitly with the orator as orator, and it offers more analysis and an adequate judgment by a qualified critic.

Twenty years hence Mr. Gladstone's [speeches] will not be read, except of course by historians. They are too long, too diffuse, too minute in their handling of details, too elaborately qualified in their enunciation of general principles. They contain few epigrams and few . . . weighty thoughts put into telling phrases. . . . The style, in short, is not sufficiently rich or finished to give a perpetual interest to matters whose practical importance has vanished. . . .

If, on the other hand, Mr. Gladstone be judged by the impression he made on his own time, his place will be high in the front rank. . . . His oratory had many conspicuous merits. There was a lively imagination, which enabled him to relieve even dull matter by pleasing figures, together with a large command of quotations and illustrations. . . . There was admirable lucidity and accuracy in exposition. There was great skill in the disposition and marshalling of his arguments, and finally . . . there was a wonderful variety and grace of appropriate gesture. But above and beyond everything else which enthralled the listener, there were four qualities, two specially conspicuous in the substance of his eloquence—inventiveness and elevation; two not less remarkable in his manner—force in the delivery, expressive modulation in the voice.[35]

[34] Life of William Ewart Gladstone, *I, 193–4; II, 54–5, 593.*
[35] Gladstone, his Characteristics as Man and Statesman, *New York, 1898, pp. 41–4.*

One is tempted to say that Morley has provided the historical setting, Bryce the critical verdict. The statement would be only partially true, for Morley does much more than set the scene. He enacts the drama; and thus he conveys his judgment—not, it is true, in the form of a critical estimate, but in the course of his narrative. The difference between these two excellent accounts is a difference in emphasis. The one lays stress on the setting; the other takes it for granted. The one tries to suggest his judgment by description; the other employs the formal categories of criticism.

Less full and rounded than either of these descriptions of an orator's style is Trevelyan's estimate of Bright. Yet in a few pages the biographer has indicated clearly the two distinguishing features of Bright's eloquence—the moral weight he carried with his audience, the persuasiveness of his visible earnestness and of his reputation for integrity, and his "sense for the value of words and for the rhythm of words and sentences";[36] has drawn a contrast between Bright and Gladstone; and has added a description of Bright's mode of work, together with some comments on the permanence of the speeches and various examples of details of his style. Only the mass and weight of that style are not represented.

If we leave the biographers and return to those who, like Curzon and Butler, have written directly upon eloquence, we find little of importance. Of the two general histories of oratory that we have in English, Hardwicke's[37] is so ill organized and so ill written as to be negligible; that by Sears[38] may deserve mention. It is uneven and inaccurate. It is rather a popular handbook which strings together the great names than a history: the author does not seriously consider the evolution of oratory. His sketches are of unequal merit; some give way to the interest in mere anecdote; some yield too large a place to biographical detail; others are given over to moralizing. Sears touches most of the topics of rhetorical criticism without making the point of view of public address dominant; his work is too episodic for that. And any given criticism shows marked defects in execution. It would not be fair to compare Sears's show-piece, his chapter on Webster, with Morley or Bryce on Gladstone; but compare it with Trevelyan's few pages on Bright. With far greater economy, Trevelyan tells us more of Bright as a speaker than Sears can of Webster. The *History of Oratory* gives us little more than hints and suggestions of a good method.

With a single exception, the collections of eloquence have no criti-

---

[36] *G. M. Trevelyan,* Life of John Bright, *Boston, 1913, p. 384.*
[37] *Henry Hardwicke,* History of Oratory and Orators, *New York, 1896.*
[38] *Lorenzo Sears,* History of Oratory, *Chicago, 1896.*

cal significance. The exception is *Select British Eloquence,*[39] edited by Chauncey A. Goodrich, who prefaced the works of each of his orators with a sketch partly biographical and partly critical. The criticisms of Goodrich, like those of Sears, are of unequal value; some are slight, yet none descends to mere anecdote, and at his best, as in the characterizations of the eloquence of Chatham, Fox, and Burke, Goodrich reveals a more powerful grasp and a more comprehensive view of his problem than does Sears, as well as a more consistent view of his subject as a speaker. Sears at times takes the point of view of the printed page; Goodrich consistently thinks of the speeches he discusses as intended for oral delivery.

Goodrich's topics of criticism are: the orator's training, mode of work, personal (physical) qualifications, character as known to his audience, range of powers, dominant traits as a speaker. He deals too, of course, with those topics to which certain of the critics we have noticed confine themselves: illustration, ornament, gift of phrase, diction, wit, imagination, arrangement. But these he does not overemphasize, nor view as independent of their effect upon an audience. Thus he can say of Chatham's sentence structure: "The sentences are not rounded or balanced periods, but are made up of short clauses, which flash themselves upon the mind with all the vividness of distinct ideas, and yet are closely connected together as tending to the same point, and uniting to form larger masses of thought."[40] Perhaps the best brief indication of Goodrich's quality is his statement of Fox's "leading peculiarities."[41] According to Goodrich, Fox had a luminous simplicity, which combined unity of impression with irregular arrangement; he took everything in the concrete; he struck instantly at the heart of his subject, going to the issue at once; he did not amplify, he repeated; he rarely employed a preconceived order of argument; reasoning was his *forte,* but it was the reasoning of the debater; he abounded in *hits*—abrupt and startling turns of thought—and in side-blows delivered in passing; he was often dramatic; he had astonishing skill in turning the course of debate to his own advantage. Here is the point of view of public address, expressed as clearly as in Morley or in Curzon, though in a different idiom, and without the biographer's fulness of treatment.

But probably the best single specimen of the kind of criticism now under discussion is Morley's chapter on Cobden as an agitator. This is as admirable a summary sketch as the same writer's account of Gladstone is a detailed historical picture. Bryce's brief essay on Gladstone is inferior to it both in the range of its technical criticisms and in

[39] *New York, 1852.*
[40] *P. 75.*
[41] *P. 461.*

the extent to which the critic realizes the situation in which his subject was an actor. In a few pages Morley has drawn the physical characteristics of his subject, his bent of mind, temperament, idiosyncrasies; has compared and contrasted Cobden with his great associate, Bright; has given us contemporary judgments; has sketched out the dominant quality of his style, its variety and range; has noted Cobden's attitude to his hearers, his view of human nature; and has dealt with the impression given by Cobden's printed speeches and the total impression of his personality on the platform. The method, the angle of approach, the categories of description or of criticism, are the same as those employed in the great life of Gladstone; but we find them here condensed into twenty pages. It will be worth while to present the most interesting parts of Morley's criticism, if only for comparison with some of the passages already given:

I have asked many scores of those who knew him, Conservatives as well as Liberals, what this secret [of his oratorical success] was, and in no single case did my interlocutor fail to begin, and in nearly every case he ended as he had begun, with the word persuasiveness. *Cobden made his way to men's hearts by the union which they saw in him of simplicity, earnestness, and conviction, with a singular facility of exposition. This facility consisted in a remarkable power of apt and homely illustration, and a curious ingenuity in framing the argument that happened to be wanted. Besides his skill in thus hitting on the right argument, Cobden had the oratorical art of presenting it in the way that made its admission to the understanding of a listener easy and undenied. He always seemed to have made exactly the right degree of allowance for the difficulty with which men follow a speech, as compared with the ease of following the same argument on a printed page. . . .*

Though he abounded in matter, Cobden can hardly be described as copious. He is neat and pointed, nor is his argument ever left unclinched; but he permits himself no large excursions. What he was thinking of was the matter immediately in hand, the audience before his eyes, the point that would tell best then and there, and would be most likely to remain in men's recollections. . . . What is remarkable is, that while he kept close to the matter and substance of his case, and resorted comparatively little to sarcasm, humor, invective, pathos, or the other elements that are catalogued in manuals of rhetoric, yet no speaker was ever further removed from prosiness, or came into more real and sympathetic contact with his audience. . . .

After all, it is not tropes and perorations that make the popular speaker; it is the whole impression of his personality. We who only read them can discern certain admirable qualities in Cobden's speeches; aptness in choosing topics, lucidity in presenting them, buoyant con-

*fidence in pressing them home. But those who listened to them felt
much more than all this. They were delighted by mingled vivacity and
ease, by directness, by spontaneousness and reality, by the charm
. . . of personal friendliness and undisguised cordiality.*[42]

These passages are written in the spirit of the critic of public speaking. They have the point of view that is but faintly suggested in Elton
and Grierson, that Saintsbury recognizes but does not use, and Hazlitt
uses but does not recognize, and that Whipple, however irregularly,
both understands and employs. But such critics as Curzon and Butler,
Sears and Goodrich, Trevelyan and Bryce, think differently of their
problem; they take the point of view of public address consistently and
without question. Morley's superiority is not in conception, but in execution. In all the writers of this group, whether historians, biographers,
or professed students of oratory, there is a consciousness that oratory
is partly an art, partly a power of making history, and occasionally a
branch of literature. Style is less considered for its own sake than for
its effect in a given situation. The question of literary immortality is regarded as beside the mark, or else, as in Bryce, as a separate question requiring separate consideration. There are, of course, differences
of emphasis. Some of the biographers may be thought to deal too
lightly with style. Sears perhaps thinks too little of the time, of the
drama of the situation, and too much of style. But we have arrived at a
different attitude towards the orator; his function is recognized for what
it is: the art of influencing men in some concrete situation. Neither the
personal nor the literary evaluation is the primary object. The critic
speaks of the orator as a public man whose function it is to exert his
influence by speech.

VII

Any attempt to sum up the results of this casual survey of what some
writers have said of some public speakers must deal with the differences between literary criticism as represented by Gosse and Trent,
by Elton and Grierson, and rhetorical criticism as represented by Curzon, Morley, Bryce, and Trevelyan. The literary critics seem at first
to have no common point of view and no agreement as to the categories of judgment or description. But by reading between their lines
and searching for the main endeavor of these critics, one can discover
at least a unity of purpose. Different in method as are Gosse, Elton,
Saintsbury, Whipple, Hazlitt, the ends they have in view are not different.

---

[42] Life of Richard Cobden, *Boston, 1881, pp. 130–2.*

Coupled with almost every description of the excellences of prose and with every attempt to describe the man in connection with his work, is the same effort as we find clearly and even arbitrarily expressed by those whom we have termed judicial critics. All the literary critics unite in the attempt to interpret the permanent value that they find in the work under consideration. That permanent value is not precisely indicated by the term beauty, but the two strands of æsthetic excellence and permanence are clearly found, not only in the avowed judicial criticism but in those writers who emphasize description rather than judgment. Thus Grierson says of Burke:

His preoccupation at every juncture with the fundamental issues of wise government, and the splendor of the eloquence in which he set forth these principles, an eloquence in which the wisdom of his thought and the felicity of his language and imagery seem inseparable from one another . . . have made his speeches and pamphlets a source of perennial freshness and interest.[43]

Perhaps a critic of temper different from Grierson's—Saintsbury, for example—would turn from the wisdom of Burke's thought to the felicity of his language and imagery. But always there is implicit in the critic's mind the absolute standard of a timeless world: the wisdom of Burke's thought (found in the principles to which his mind always gravitates rather than in his decisions on points of policy) and the felicity of his language are not considered as of an age, but for all time. Whether the critic considers the technical excellence merely, or both technique and substance, his preoccupation is with that which age cannot wither nor custom stale. (From this point of view, the distinction between the speech and the pamphlet is of no moment, and Elton wisely speaks of Burke's favorite form as "oratory, uttered or written";[44] for a speech cannot be the subject of a permanent evaluation unless it is preserved in print.)

This is the implied attitude of all the literary critics. On this common ground their differences disappear or become merely differences of method or of competence. They are all, in various ways, interpreters of the permanent and universal values they find in the works of which they treat. Nor can there be any quarrel with this attitude—unless all standards be swept away. The impressionist and the historian of the evolution of literature as a self-contained activity may deny the utility or the possibility of a truly judicial criticism. But the human mind insists upon

[43] Cambridge History of English Literature, *New York, 1914, XI, 8.*
[44] *Oliver Elton,* Survey of English Literature, 1780–1830, *London, 1912, I,* 234.

judgment *sub specie æternitatis.* The motive often appears as a merely practical one: the reader wishes to be apprised of the best that has been said and thought in all ages; he is less concerned with the descent of literary species or with the critic's adventures among masterpieces than with the perennial freshness and interest those masterpieces may hold for him. There is, of course, much more than a practical motive to justify the interest in permanent values; but this is not the place to raise a moot question of general critical theory. We wished only to note the common ground of literary criticism in its preoccupation with the thought and the eloquence which is permanent.

If now we turn to rhetorical criticism as we found it exemplified in the preceding section, we find that its point of view is patently single. It is not concerned with permanence, nor yet with beauty. It is concerned with effect. It regards a speech as a communication to a specific audience, and holds its business to be the analysis and appreciation of the orator's method of imparting his ideas to his hearers.

Rhetoric, however, is a word that requires explanation; its use in connection with criticism is neither general nor consistent. The merely deprecatory sense in which it is often applied to bombast or false ornament need not delay us. The limited meaning which confines the term to the devices of a correct and even of an elegant prose style—in the sense of manner of writing and speaking—may also be eliminated, as likewise the broad interpretation which makes rhetoric inclusive of all style whether in prose or in poetry. There remain some definitions which have greater promise. We may mention first that of Aristotle: "the faculty of observing in any given case the available means of persuasion";[45] this readily turns into the art of persuasion, as the editors of the *New English Dictionary* recognize when they define rhetoric as "the art of using language so as to persuade or influence others." The gloss on "persuade" afforded by the additional term "influence" is worthy of note. Jebb achieves the same result by defining rhetoric as "the art of using language in such a way as to produce a desired impression upon the hearer or reader."[46] There is yet a fourth definition, one which serves to illuminate the others as well as to emphasize their essential agreement: "taken broadly [rhetoric is] the science and art of communication in language";[47] the framers of this definition add that to throw the emphasis on communication is to emphasize prose, poetry being regarded as more distinctly expressive than communicative. A German writer has made a similar distinction between poetic as the art

[45] Rhetoric, *ii, 2, tr. W. Rhys Roberts in* The Works of Aristotle, *XI, Oxford, 1924.*
[46] *Article "Rhetoric" in the* Encyclopaedia Britannica, *9th and 11th editions.*
[47] *J. L. Gerig and F. N. Scott, article "Rhetoric" in the* New International Encyclopaedia.

of poetry and rhetoric as the art of prose, but rather on the basis that prose is of the intellect, poetry of the imagination.[48] Wackernagel's basis for the distinction will hardly stand in face of the attitude of modern psychology to the "faculties"; yet the distinction itself is suggestive, and it does not contravene the more significant opposition of expression and communication. That opposition has been well stated, though with some exaggeration, by Professor Hudson:

The writer in pure literature has his eye on his subject; his subject has filled his mind and engaged his interest, and he must tell about it; his task is expression; his form and style are organic with his subject. The writer of rhetorical discourse has his eye upon the audience and occasion; his task is persuasion; his form and style are organic with the occasion.[49]

The element of the author's personality should not be lost from sight in the case of the writer of pure literature; nor may the critic think of the audience and the occasion as alone conditioning the work of the composer of rhetorical discourse, unless indeed he include in the occasion both the personality of the speaker and the subject. The distinction is better put by Professor Baldwin:

Rhetoric meant to the ancient world the art of instructing and moving men in their affairs; poetic the art of sharpening and expanding their vision. . . . The one is composition of ideas; the other, composition of images. In the one field life is discussed; in the other it is presented. The type of the one is a public address, moving us to assent and action; the type of the other is a play, showing us [an] action moving to an end of character. The one argues and urges; the other represents. Though both appeal to imagination, the method of rhetoric is logical; the method of poetic, as well as its detail, is imaginative.[50]

It is noteworthy that in this passage there is nothing to oppose poetry, in its common acceptation of verse, to prose. Indeed, in discussing the four forms of discourse usually treated in textbooks, Baldwin explicitly classes exposition and argument under rhetoric, leaving narrative and description to the other field. But rhetoric has been applied to the art of prose by some who include under the term even non-

[48] *K. H. W. Wackernagel,* Poetik, Rhetorik und Stilistik, *ed. L. Sieber, Halle, 1873, p. 11.*
[49] *H. H. Hudson, "The Field of Rhetoric,"* Quarterly Journal of Speech Education, *IX (1923), 177. See also the same writer's "Rhetoric and Poetry," ibid., X (1924), 143 ff.*
[50] *C. S. Baldwin,* Ancient Rhetoric and Poetic, *New York, 1924, p. 134.*

metrical works of fiction. This is the attitude of Wackernagel, already mentioned, and of Saintsbury, who observes that Aristotle's *Rhetoric* holds, "if not intentionally, yet actually, something of the same position towards Prose as that which the *Poetics* holds towards verse."[51] In Saintsbury's view, the *Rhetoric* achieves this position in virtue of its third book, that on style and arrangement: the first two books contain "a great deal of matter which has either the faintest connection with literary criticism or else no connection with it at all."[52] Saintsbury finds it objectionable in Aristotle that to him, "prose as prose is merely and avowedly a secondary consideration: it is always in the main, and sometimes wholly, a mere necessary instrument of divers practical purposes,"[53] and that "he does not *wish* to consider a piece of prose as a work of art destined, first of all, if not finally, to fulfil its own laws on the one hand, and to give pleasure on the other."[54] The distinction between verse and prose has often troubled the waters of criticism. The explanation is probably that the outer form of a work is more easily understood and more constantly present to the mind than is the real form. Yet it is strange that those who find the distinction between verse and prose important should parallel this with a distinction between imagination and intellect, as if a novel had more affinities with a speech than with an epic. It is strange, too, that Saintsbury's own phrase about the right way to consider a "piece of prose"—as a work of art destined "to fulfil its own laws"—did not suggest to him the fundamental importance of a distinction between what he terms the minor or suasive rhetoric on the one hand, and on the other poetic, whether or not in verse. For poetry always is free to fulfil its own law, but the writer of rhetorical discourse is, in a sense, perpetually in bondage to the occasion and the audience; and in that fact we find the line of cleavage between rhetoric and poetic.

The distinction between rhetoric as theory of public address and poetic as theory of pure literature, says Professor Baldwin, "seems not to have controlled any consecutive movement of modern criticism."[55] That it has not controlled the procedure of critics in dealing with orators is indicated in the foregoing pages; yet we have found, too, many suggestions of a better method, and some few critical performances against which the only charge is overcondensation.

Rhetorical criticism is necessarily analytical. The scheme of a rhetorical study includes the element of the speaker's personality as a conditioning factor; it includes also the public character of the man—not

---

[51] *G. E. B. Saintsbury,* History of Criticism and Literary Taste in Europe, *New York, 1900, I, 39.*

[52] Ibid., *p. 42.*

[53] History of Criticism and Literary Taste in Europe, *p. 48.*

[54] Ibid., *p. 52.*

[55] Op. cit., *p. 4.*

what he was, but what he was thought to be. It requires a description of the speaker's audience, and of the leading ideas with which he plied his hearers—his topics, the motives to which he appealed, the nature of the proofs he offered. These will reveal his own judgment of human nature in his audiences, and also his judgment on the questions which he discussed. Attention must be paid, too, to the relation of the surviving texts to what was actually uttered: in case the nature of the changes is known, there may be occasion to consider adaptation to two audiences—that which heard and that which read. Nor can rhetorical criticism omit the speaker's mode of arrangement and his mode of expression, nor his habit of preparation and his manner of delivery from the platform; though the last two are perhaps less significant. "Style" —in the sense which corresponds to diction and sentence movement— must receive attention, but only as one among various means that secure for the speaker ready access to the minds of his auditors. Finally, the effect of the discourse on its immediate hearers is not to be ignored, neither in the testimony of witnesses, nor in the record of events. And throughout such a study one must conceive of the public man as influencing the men of his own times by the power of his discourse.

VIII

What is the relation of rhetorical criticism, so understood, to literary criticism? The latter is at once broader and more limited than rhetorical criticism. It is broader because of its concern with permanent values; because it takes no account of special purpose nor of immediate effect; because it views a literary work as the voice of a human spirit addressing itself to men of all ages and times; because the critic speaks as the spectator of all time and all existence. But this universalizing of attitude brings its own limits with it: the influence of the period is necessarily relegated to the background; interpretation in the light of the writer's intention and of his situation may be ignored or slighted; and the speaker who directed his words to a definite and limited group of hearers may be made to address a universal audience. The result can only be confusion. In short, the point of view of literary criticism is proper only to its own objects, the permanent works. Upon such as are found to lie without the pale, the verdict of literary criticism is of negative value merely, and its interpretation is false and misleading, because it proceeds upon a wrong assumption. If Henry Clay and Charles Fox are to be dealt with at all, it must not be on the assumption that their works, in respect of wisdom and eloquence, are or ought to be sources of perennial freshness and interest. Morley has put the matter well:

The statesman who makes or dominates a crisis, who has to rouse and mold the mind of senate or nation, has something else to think about than the production of literary masterpieces. The great political

speech, which for that matter is a sort of drama, is not made by pas-
sages for elegant extract or anthologies, but by personality, movement,
climax, spectacle, and the action of the time.[56]

But we cannot always divorce rhetorical criticism from literary. In
the case of Fox or Clay or Cobden, as opposed to Fielding or Addison
or De Quincy, it is proper to do so; the fact that language is a common
medium to the writer of rhetorical discourse and to the writer in pure
literature will give to the critics of each a common vocabulary of
stylistic terms, but not a common standard. In the case of Burke the
relation of the two points of view is more complex. Burke belongs to
literature; but in all his important works he was a practitioner of public
address written or uttered. Since his approach to *belles-lettres* was
through rhetoric, it follows that rhetorical criticism is at least a preliminary to literary criticism, for it will erect the factual basis for the understanding of the works: will not merely explain allusions and establish
dates, but recall the setting, reconstruct the author's own intention, and
analyze his method. But the rhetorical inquiry is more than a mere preliminary; it permeates and governs all subsequent interpretation and
criticism. For the statesman in letters is a statesman still: compare
Burke to Charles Lamb, or even to Montaigne, and it is clear that the
public man is in a sense inseparable from his audience. A statesman's
wisdom and eloquence are not to be read without some share of his
own sense of the body politic, and of the body politic not merely as a
construct of thought, but as a living human society. A speech, like a
satire, like a comedy of manners, grows directly out of a social situation; it is a man's response to a condition in human affairs. However
broadly typical the situation may be when its essential elements are
laid bare, it never appears without its coverings. On no plane of
thought—philosophical, literary, political—is Burke to be understood
without reference to the great events in America, India, France, which
evoked his eloquence; nor is he to be understood without reference to
the state of English society. (It is this last that is lacking in Grierson's
essay: the page of comment on Burke's qualities in actual debate wants
its supplement in some account of the House of Commons and the national life it represented. Perhaps the latter is the more needful to a
full understanding of the abiding excellence in Burke's pages.) Something of the spirit of Morley's chapter on Cobden, and more of the
spirit of the social historian (which Morley has in other parts of the
biography) is necessary to the literary critic in dealing with the statesman who is also a man of letters.

In the case of Burke, then, one of the functions of rhetorical criticism

[56] Life of William Ewart Gladstone, *II, 589–90.*

is as a preliminary, but an essential and governing preliminary, to the literary criticism which occupies itself with the permanent values of wisdom and of eloquence, of thought and of beauty, that are found in the works of the orator.

Rhetorical criticism may also be regarded as an end in itself. Even Burke may be studied from that point of view alone. Fox and Cobden and the majority of public speakers are not to be regarded from any other. No one will offer Cobden's works a place in pure literature. Yet the method of the great agitator has a place in the history of his times. That place is not in the history of *belles-lettres;* nor is it in the literary history which is a "survey of the life of a people as expressed in their writings." The idea of "writings" is a merely mechanical one; it does not really provide a point of view or a method; it is a book-maker's cloak for many and diverse points of view. Such a compilation as the *Cambridge History of American Literature,* for example, in spite of the excellence of single essays, may not unjustly be characterized as an uneven commentary on the literary life of the country and as a still more uneven commentary on its social and political life. It may be questioned whether the scant treatment of public men in such a compilation throws light either on the creators of pure literature, or on the makers of rhetorical discourse, or on the life of the times.

Rhetorical criticism lies at the boundary of politics (in the broadest sense) and literature; its atmosphere is that of the public life,[57] its tools are those of literature, its concern is with the ideas of the people as influenced by their leaders. The effective wielder of public discourse, like the military man, belongs to social and political history because he is one of its makers. Like the soldier, he has an art of his own which is the source of his power; but the soldier's art is distinct from the life which his conquests affect. The rhetorician's art represents a natural and normal process within that life. It includes the work of the speaker, of the pamphleteer, of the writer of editorials, and of the sermon maker. It is to be thought of as the art of popularization. Its practitioners are the Huxleys, not the Darwins, of science; the Jeffersons, not the Lockes and the Rousseaus, of politics.

Of late years the art of popularization has received a degree of attention: propaganda and publicity have been words much used; the influence of the press has been discussed; there have been some studies of public opinion. Professor Robinson's *Humanizing of Knowledge*[58] is a cogent statement of the need for popularization by the instructed element in the state, and of the need for a technique in doing

---

[57] *For a popular but suggestive presentation of the background of rhetorical discourse, see J. A. Spender,* The Public Life, *New York, 1925.*
[58] *New York, 1923.*

so. But the book indicates, too, how little is known of the methods its author so earnestly desires to see put to use. Yet ever since Homer's day men have woven the web of words and counsel in the face of all. And ever since Aristotle's day there has been a mode of analysis of public address. Perhaps the preoccupation of literary criticism with "style" rather than with composition in the large has diverted interest from the more significant problem. Perhaps the conventional categories of historical thought have helped to obscure the problem: the history of thought, for example, is generally interpreted as the history of invention and discovery, both physical and intellectual. Yet the history of the thought of the people is at least as potent a factor in the progress of the race. True, the popular thought may often represent a resisting force, and we need not marvel that the many movements of a poet's mind more readily capture the critic's attention than the few and uncertain movements of that Leviathan, the public mind. Nor is it surprising that the historians tend to be occupied with the acts and the motives of leaders. But those historians who find the spirit of an age in the total mass of its literary productions, as well as all who would tame Leviathan to the end that he shall not threaten civilization, must examine more thoroughly than they as yet have done the interactions of the inventive genius, the popularizing talent, and the public mind.

Lincoln's First Inaugural
by Marie Hochmuth Nichols

Part I

"Spring comes gently to Washington always," observed the poet-historian, Carl Sandburg. "In early March the green of the grass brightens, the magnolia softens. Elms and chestnuts burgeon. Redbud and lilac carry on preparations soon to bloom. The lovemaking and birthing in many sunny corners go on no matter what or who the blue-prints and personages behind the discreet bureau and departmental walls."[1] Spring of 1861 was little different from other springs in physical aspect. March 4th dawned as other March 4th's, no doubt, wavering between clearness and cloudiness. At daylight clouds hung dark and heavy in the sky. Early in the morning a few drops of rain fell, but scarcely enough to lay the dust. A northwest wind swept down the cross streets to Pennsylvania Avenue. The weather was cool and bracing, and on the

From *American Speeches* by Wayland Maxfield Parrish and Marie Hochmuth Nichols (New York: 1954). Used by permission of the David McKay Company, Inc. Mrs. Nichols is Professor of Speech at the University of Illinois.

[1] *Carl Sandburg,* Abraham Lincoln: The War Years (*Harcourt, Brace and Co., 1939*), *I, 120.*

whole, "favorable to the ceremonies of the day."[2] The sun had come out.

But if, on the whole, spring had come "gently" as usual, there was little else that bespoke the same rhythm. Out of the deep of winter had come the somewhat bewildered voice of President Buchanan asking, "Why is it . . . that discontent now so extensively prevails, and the union of the States, which is the source of all these blessings is threatened with destruction?"[3] Spiritually and morally, the city, indeed the nation, were out of tune, cacophonous, discordant.

Would there be a harmonizing voice today from the gaunt "orator of the West," about to take the helm of the nation? "Behind the cloud the sun is shining still," Abraham Lincoln had said three weeks before, as his train meandered across the Illinois prairies taking him on an "errand of national importance, attended . . . with considerable difficulties."[4] Trouble had not come suddenly to the nation, of course. Only a year previously the country had been "eminently prosperous in all its material interests."[5] Harvests had been abundant, and plenty smiled throughout the land. But for forty years there had been an undercurrent of restlessness. As early as 1820, an occasional voice had urged the necessity for secession. Again in 1850, with somewhat greater vehemence, voices were raised as the distribution of newly acquired Mexican territory took place. Then came the repeal of the Missouri Compromise in 1854, the civil war in Kansas and the Sumner-Brooks combat in the Senate in 1856, the Dred Scott decision in 1857, and the spectacular John Brown's raid at Harper's Ferry in 1859, all giving rise to disorder, unrest, and threats of secession as abolition sentiment mounted. Finally, came the election of 1860, and the North appeared to have "capped the mighty pyramid of unfraternal enormities by electing Abraham Lincoln to the Chief Magistracy, on a platform and by a system which indicates nothing but the subjugation of the South and the complete ruin of her social, political and industrial institutions."[6] It was not merely that Lincoln had been elected president, but the "majorities" by which he was elected were "more significant and suggestive than anything else—more so than the election itself—for they unmistakably indicate the hatred to the South which animates and controls the

2 New York Times, *March 5, 1861, p. 1, col. 1.*

3 *James Buchanan, "Fourth Annual Message, December 3, 1860,"* The Works of James Buchanan, *collected and edited by John Bassett Moore (Philadelphia: J. B. Lippincott Co., 1910), XI, 7.*

4 *Speech at Tolono, Illinois, February 11, 1861, as reported in* New York Daily Tribune, *February 12, 1861, p. 5, col. 3.*

5 *Buchanan, loc. cit.*

6 New Orleans Daily Crescent, *November 13, 1860, as quoted in* Southern Editorials on Secession, *edited by Dwight Lowell Dumond (New York and London: The Century Co., 1931), p. 237.*

masses of the numerically strongest section of the Confederacy."[7] Senator Clingman of North Carolina found the election a "great, remarkable and dangerous fact that has filled my section with alarm and dread for the future," since Lincoln was elected *"because he was known to be a dangerous man,"* avowing the principle of the "irrepressible conflict."[8] Richmond observers commented that a party "founded on the single sentiment, the exclusive feeling of hatred of African slavery," was "now the controlling power in this Confederacy," and noted that the question "What is to be done . . . presses on every man."[9] In Charleston, South Carolina, the news of Lincoln's election was met with great rejoicing and "long continued cheering for a Southern Confederacy."[10]

Scarcely more than a month had passed when South Carolina led off in the secession movement. Her two senators resigned their seats in the United States Senate on November 10, 1860, and on December 20 an Ordinance of Secession was adopted,[11] bringing in its wake secessionist demonstrations throughout the South.[12] By the first of February of the new year, Mississippi, Florida, Alabama, Louisiana, Texas, and Georgia had "repealed, rescinded, and abrogated" their membership in the Union by adopting secession ordinances, standing "prepared to resist by force any attempt to maintain the supremacy of the Constitution of the United States."[13] The other slaveholding states held a position of "quasi neutrality," declaring that their adhesion to the Union could be secured only by affording guarantees against wrongs of which they complained, and dangers which they apprehended.[14] Already by the end of 1860, secessionists at Charleston were in possession of the post office, the federal courts, the customhouses, and forts Castle Pinckney and Moultrie.[15]

It was not without clamor and fanfare that senators took their leave from familiar places. When, on December 31, Senator Judah Benjamin

---

[7] New Orleans Daily Crescent, *November 12, 1860, as quoted in* Southern Editorials on Secession, *p. 228.*

[8] *Speech of Senator Thomas L. Clingman of North Carolina in the Senate, December 3, 1860,* The Congressional Globe, *Second Session, 36th Congress, Vol. 30, p. 3.*

[9] Richmond Semi-Weekly Examiner, *November 9, 1860, as quoted in* Southern Editorials on Secession, *p. 223.*

[10] The Daily Herald, *Wilmington, N. C., November 9, 1860, as quoted in* Southern Editorials on Secession, *p. 226.*

[11] *Daniel Wait Howe,* Political History of Secession *(New York: G. P. Putnam's Sons, 1914), p. 449.*

[12] *J. G. Randall,* Lincoln the President *(New York: Dodd, Mead and Co., 1945), I, 215.*

[13] New York Times, *February 11, 1861, p. 4, col. 2.*

[14] Ibid.

[15] *Randall,* loc. cit.

of Louisiana reported that he would make a parting secession speech, "every corner was crowded"[16] in the Senate galleries. His closing declaration that "you can never subjugate us; you never can convert the free sons of the soil into vassals . . . never, never can degrade them to the level of an inferior and servile race. Never! Never!"[17] was greeted by the galleries with "disgraceful applause, screams and uproar."[18] As the galleries were cleared because of misbehavior, people murmured in departing, "Now we will have war," "D—n the Abolitionists," "Abe Lincoln will never come here."[19] Critics observing the national scene remarked, "The President . . . enters upon one of the most momentous and difficult duties ever devolved upon any man, in this country or any other. No one of his predecessors was ever called upon to confront dangers half as great, or to render a public service half as difficult, as those which will challenge his attention at the very outset of his Administration."[20]

January of 1861 came without hope, and with little possibility of the cessation of unrest. Occasionally the newspapers scoffed at the recommendation of the *Richmond Inquirer* that an armed force proceeding from Virginia or Maryland should invade the District of Columbia and prevent the peaceful inauguration of Abraham Lincoln, dismissing it as the "exaggeration of political rhetoric."[21] The capital of the nation was beset by rumor, clamor, occasional attempts at compromise, and general misbehavior. "I passed a part of last week in Washington," observed a Baltimore reporter, "and never, since the days of Jerico [sic], has there been such a blowing of rams' horns as may now be heard in that distracted city. If sound and clamor could overthrow the Constitution, one might well expect to see it go down before the windy suspirations of forced breath that shock and vibrate on all sides." Almost everywhere he met "intemperate and alarming disciples of discord and confusion." "War, secession, and disunion are on every lip; and no hope of compromise or adjustment is held out by any one. The prevailing sentiment in Washington is with the South."[22]

As secession went on apace in the South, Wendell Phillips declared in Boston's Music Hall that he hoped that all the slave states would leave the Union.[23] Horace Greeley, impatient after forty years of Southern threat, disclaimed a "union of force,—a union held together by

[16] New York Times, *January 1, 1861, p. 1, col. 1.*
[17] Congressional Globe, *Second Session, 36th Congress, Vol. 30, p. 217.*
[18] New York Times, *January 1, 1861, p. 1, col. 1.*
[19] Ibid.
[20] New York Times, *February 11, 1861, p. 4, col. 2.*
[21] The National Intelligencer (*Washington*), *January 3, 1861, p. 3, col. 2.*
[22] New York Times, *January 15, 1861, p. 1, col. 5.*
[23] New York Times, *January 21, 1861, p. 1, col. 4; see also, complete text of speech in* ibid., *p. 8, cols. 5, 6 and p. 5, cols. 1, 2.*

bayonets," and would interpose "no obstacle to their peaceful with-drawal."[24] Meanwhile, however, a few held out for compromise. On December 18, Senator Crittenden of Kentucky introduced a series of compromises in the Senate,[25] but action seemed unlikely. And when, on January 7, Senator Toombs of Georgia made a "noisy and ranting secession speech, and at the close was greeted with a storm of hisses and applause, which was continued some time," Crittenden's "appeal to save the country," presented in "good taste," created "little or no additional favor for his compromise measure."[26] While Crittenden appealed in the Senate, a peace conference met in Washington at the invitation of Virginia, with its announced purpose "to afford to the people of the slaveholding States adequate guarantees for the security of their rights."[27] Although delegates assembled and conducted business, ultimately submitting to the Senate a series of resolutions, it appeared from the beginning that "no substantial results would be gained."[28] It was clear that the sympathies of the border states which had not yet seceded "were with those which had already done so."[29] Ultimately, the propositions were rejected by the Senate, just as were the Crittenden resolutions, in the closing days of the Congress. In all, it appeared to be an era of "much talk and small performance," a dreary season of debate, with "clouds of dusty and sheety showers of rhetoric," a nation trying to live by "prattle alone," a "miserably betalked nation."[30]

When Lincoln left Springfield, February 11, to wend his way toward Washington, another President, Jefferson Davis, elected on February 9 to head the newly organized Southern Confederacy, was traveling from Mississippi to the Montgomery Convention of slaveholding states to help complete the act of secession, his trip being "one continuous ovation."[31] "The time for compromise is past," observed Davis, as he paused at the depot at Montgomery to address the crowd, "and we are now determined to maintain our position, and make all who oppose us smell Southern powder, feel Southern steel."[32] Clearly, people could agree that Lincoln was to inherit "a thorny wilderness of perplexities."[33] Would he "coerce" the seceded states and ask for the restoration of

---

[24] Horace Greeley, Recollections of a Busy Life (New York: J. B. Ford and Co., 1868), p. 398.

[25] Congressional Globe, Second Session, 36th Congress, Part I, Vol. 30, pp. 112–14.

[26] New York Times, January 8, 1861, p. 1, col. 1; see also, Congressional Globe, Second Session, 36th Congress, Part I, Vol. 30, pp. 264–71.

[27] Howe, op. cit., p. 465.

[28] Ibid., p. 467.

[29] Ibid., p. 467.

[30] New York Daily Tribune, March 13, 1861, p. 4, col. 4.

[31] New York Daily Tribune, February 18, 1861, p. 5, col. 6.

[32] Ibid., p. 5, col. 6.

[33] Ibid., March 4, 1861, p. 4, col. 2.

federal properties in possession of the secessionists? Would he respond to pressure "from all sides" and from a "fraction of his own
party" to consent to "extension" of slavery, particularly below the line
36° 30′? Would he listen to "compromise" Republicans in Congress
and only *"seem"* to compromise, "so as not to appear obstinate or
insensible to the complaints of the Slaveholders"?[34] Would he stand
by the Chicago Republican platform, severe in its strictures on the in-
cumbent Democratic administration's acceptance of the principle that
the personal relation between master and slave involved "an unquali-
fied property in persons"?[35] Would he stand by the part of the platform
which pledged "the maintenance inviolate of the rights of the States,
and especially the right of each State to order and control its own domestic institutions according to its own judgment exclusively"?[36] Was
the belief that he had so often uttered representative of the true Lincoln: "A house divided against itself cannot stand"?[37]

On March 4 as the newspapers gave advance notice of what was to
transpire during the day, there was a note of fear and uncertainty in
regard to the safety of the President-elect, along with the general
eagerness about the outlines of Lincoln's course of action to be announced in the Inaugural. "The great event to which so many have
been looking forward with anxiety—which has excited the hopes and
fears of the country to an extent unparalleled in its comparatively brief
history—will take place to-day," observed the *New York Times*. "The
occasion has drawn to the Federal Capital a greater crowd, probably,
than has ever been assembled there on any similar occasion. . . .
Whether the ceremonies will be marred by any untoward event is, of
course, a matter of conjecture, though grave fears are expressed on the
subject."[38] While visitors to Washington were seeking to get a glimpse
of the tumultuous Senate in all-night session, General Scott and his
advisers were together planning to take the "greatest precaution" for
preventing "any attack upon the procession or demonstration against
Mr. Lincoln's person."[39] Rumors of the presence of a "large gang of
'Plug Uglies' who are here from Baltimore,"[40] circulated freely. Whether
they were in Washington to make an attack on the person of the Presi-

---

[34] New York Daily Tribune, *February 18, 1861, p. 6, col. 1.*
[35] *M. Halstead,* A History of the National Political Conventions of the Current
Presidential Campaign (*Columbus, Ohio: Follett, Foster and Co., 1860*); *p. 138.*
[36] Ibid.
[37] *"A House Divided: Speech Delivered at Springfield, Illinois, at the Close
of the Republican State Convention, June 16, 1858," in* Abraham Lincoln: His
Speeches and Writings, *edited with critical and analytical notes by Roy P.
Basler (Cleveland, Ohio: The World Publishing Co., 1946), p. 372.*
[38] New York Times, *March 4, 1861, p. 4, col. 1.*
[39] New York Times, *March 4, 1861, p. 1, col. 2.*
[40] Ibid.

dent or to "create a disturbance, and plunder private persons"[41] was a matter for general speculation. Whatever the purpose, General Scott and his advisers had decided to leave nothing undone to secure the safety of the President-elect. Riflemen in squads were to be placed in hiding on the roofs commanding buildings along Pennsylvania Avenue. Orders were given to fire in the event of a threat to the presidential carriages. There were cavalry regulars to guard the side-street crossings, moving from one to another as the procession passed. From the windows of the Capitol wings riflemen were to watch the inauguration platform. General Scott would oversee the ceremonies from the top of a slope commanding the north entrance to the Capitol, ready to take personal charge of a battery of flying artillery stationed there. District militia in three ranks were to surround the platform to keep back the crowd. Armed detectives in citizen's clothing were to be scattered through the great audience.[42]

The occasion must have seemed strange to the man who had been accustomed to being carried on the shoulders of admirers on speaking occasions in his years as a stump orator in the West, and to being the idol of many a torchlight procession during the combats with the "Little Giant" in the tumultuous debates of 1858. Even the Capitol grounds where the crowds had begun to assemble had a strangely unfamiliar look in contrast to its fixity during his years as congressman in 1847 and 1848. "The old dome familiar to Congressman Lincoln in 1848 had been knocked loose and hauled down," noted Sandburg. "The iron-wrought material on the Capitol grounds, the hammers, jacks, screws, scaffolds, derricks, ladders, props, ropes, told that they were rebuilding, extending, embellishing the structure on March 4, 1861." "On the slope of lawn fronting the Capitol building stood a bronze statue of Liberty shaped as a massive, fertile woman holding a sword in one hand for power and a wreath of flowers in the other hand for glory. Not yet raised to her pedestal, she looked out of place. She was to be lifted and set on top of the Capitol dome, overlooking the Potomac Valley, when the dome itself should be prepared for her."[43] The carpenters had set up a temporary platform fronting the Senate wing for the occasion, with a small wooden canopy covering the speaker's

[41] Ibid.

[42] Ibid.; see also, Sandburg, The War Years, I, 120–21; Randall, Lincoln the President, I, 293, 294; William E. Baringer, A House Dividing (Springfield, Ill.: Abraham Lincoln Association, 1945), pp. 331–34; The Diary of a Public Man, Prefatory notes by F. Lauriston Bullard, Foreword by Carl Sandburg (Chicago: Privately printed for Abraham Lincoln Book Shop, 1945), pp. 73, 74; Clark E. Carr, Stephen A. Douglas, His Life and Public Services, Speeches and Patriotism (Chicago: A. C. McClurg and Co., 1909), p. 123.

[43] Sandburg, The War Years, I, 120.

table.[44] "The crowd swarmed about all the approaches leading to the capitol grounds," observed a witness, "while the spacious level extending from the east front of the capitol was one vast black sea of heads."[45] There were between 25,000 and 50,000 people there, waiting with expectancy.[46] "Every window in the north front of the Capitol was filled with ladies. Every tree top bore its burden of eager eyes. Every fence and staging, and pile of building material, for the Capitol extension was made a 'coyn of vantage' for its full complement of spectators."[47] It was noticeable that "scarce a Southern face is to be seen"[48] in the crowd, "judging from the lack of long-haired men."[49] While the crowd waited for the administration of the oath of the Vice-President, which took place in the Senate chambers, it was entertained with martial music, and "by the antics of a lunatic, who had climbed a tall tree in front of the capitol and made a long political speech, claiming to be the rightful President of the United States." Policemen were detached to bring him down, but he merely climbed higher and "stood rocking in the wind, and made another speech."[50] The ceremonies over indoors, the major figures of the occasion were seen emerging, Abraham Lincoln with James Buchanan by his side.

As Lincoln and Buchanan took places on the right side of the speaker's stand, Chief Justice Taney, who soon would administer the oath of office, took a seat upon the left. Many in the audience were seeing Lincoln for the first time. "Honest Abe Lincoln," the folks back home called him, or just "Old Abe" was the affectionate cry at the Chicago "Wigwam" as thousands cheered and shook the rafters "like the rush of a great wind, in the van of a storm,"[51] when he was nominated. Walt Whitman thought "four sorts of genius, four mighty and primal hands, will be needed to the complete limning of this man's future portrait—the eyes and brains and finger-touch of Plutarch and Eschylus and Michel Angelo, assisted by Rabelais."[52] "If any personal description of me is thought desirable," Lincoln had written two years before, "it may be said I am, in height, six feet four inches, nearly; lean in flesh, weighing on an average one hundred and eighty pounds;

[44] *Baringer*, op. cit., *p. 333.*

[45] *Correspondence of the* Cincinnati Commercial, *as quoted in* The Chicago Daily Tribune, March 8, 1861, p. 2, col. 4.

[46] New York Daily Tribune, *March 5, 1861, p. 5, col. 4.*

[47] Chicago Daily Tribune, *March 9, 1861, p. 3, col. 2.*

[48] New York Times, *March 4, 1861, p. 1, col. 2.*

[49] Chicago Daily Tribune, *March 5, 1861, p. 1, col. 2.*

[50] *Correspondence of the* Cincinnati Commercial, *as quoted in* The Chicago Daily Tribune, *March 8, 1861, p. 2, col. 4.*

[51] *Halstead,* op. cit., *pp. 149–51.*

[52] The Complete Writings of Walt Whitman (*New York: G. P. Putnam's Sons, 1902*), *II, 244.*

dark complexion, with coarse black hair and gray eyes. No other marks or brands recollected."[53] He was "not a pretty man," his law partner, Herndon, thought, "nor was he an ugly one: he was a homely man, careless of his looks, plain looking and plain acting." But he had that "inner quality which distinguishes one person from another."[54] "I never saw a more thoughtful face," observed David Locke, "I never saw a more dignified face, I never saw so sad a face."[55] Emerson had found in him the "grandeur and strength of absolute simplicity," when, on occasion, he had heard him speak, seen his small gray eyes kindle, heard his voice ring, and observed his face shine and seem "to light up a whole assembly."[56] "Abraham Lincoln: one of nature's noblemen," he was sometimes toasted.[57]

"It was unfortunate," says the noted Lincoln scholar, J. G. Randall, "that Lincoln was not better known, North and South, in March of 1861. Had people more fully understood his pondering on government, reverence for law, peaceful intent and complete lack of sectional bitterness, much tragedy might have been avoided."[58] "Gentle, and merciful and just!"[59] William Cullen Bryant was eventually to write. But now, in 1861, there was something unknown about Lincoln to many. It is true that after the Lincoln-Douglas debates he had gained recognition beyond the limits of his state. The Chicago *Democrat* called attention to the fact that "Mr. Lincoln's name has been used by newspapers and public meetings outside the State in connection with the Presidency and Vice Presidency, so that it is not only in his own State that Honest Old Abe is respected." "Even his opponents profess to love the man, though they hate his principles," it observed.[60] Again the *Illinois State Journal* took pride in reporting his growing fame. In "other states," it said, he had been found "not only . . . an unrivalled orator, strong in debate, keen in his logic and wit, with admirable powers of statement, and a fertility of resources which are equal to every occasion; but his truthfulness, his candor, his honesty of purpose, his magnanimity . . . have stamped him as a statesman whom the Republicans throughout the

[53] *Lincoln to J. W. Fell, Springfield, Illinois, December 20, 1859,* Complete Works of Abraham Lincoln, *edited by John G. Nicolay and John Hay (New York: The Tandy-Thomas Co., 1905), V, 288, 289.*

[54] *Herndon MS fragment, quoted in Randall, op. cit., p. 28.*

[55] Remembrances of Abraham Lincoln by Distinguished Men of His Time, *collected and edited by Allen Thorndike Rice (8th ed.; New York: Published by the* North American Review, *1889), p. 442.*

[56] *John Wesley Hill,* Abraham Lincoln, Man of God *(4th ed.; New York: G. P. Putnam's Sons, 1930), p. 306.*

[57] *Carl Sandburg,* Abraham Linclon, The Prairie Years *(New York: Harcourt, Brace and Co., 1926), 1, 199, 200.*

[58] New York Times Magazine, *February 6, 1949, p. 11.*

[59] *"Abraham Lincoln," in* The Poetical Works of William Cullen Bryant, *edited by Parke Godwin (New York: D. Appleton and Co., 1883), II, 151.*

[60] *Quoted in* Daily Illinois State Journal, *November 15, 1858, p. 1, col. 1.*

Union may be proud of."[61] In 1860, in New York, the "announcement that Hon. Abraham Lincoln, of Illinois, would deliver an address in Cooper Institute . . . drew thither a large and enthusiastic assemblage," and William Cullen Bryant thought that he had only "to pronounce the name of Abraham Lincoln" who had previously been known "only by fame" in order to secure the "profoundest attention."[62] Lincoln had faced thousands of people along the way to Washington, at Indianapolis, Cleveland, Philadelphia, Albany, Harrisburg, and elsewhere, being greeted enthusiastically. Still, "in general," observed Randall, "it cannot be said that he had a 'good press' at the threshold of office. Showmanship failed to make capital of his rugged origin, and there faced the country a strange man from Illinois who was dubbed a 'Simple Susan,' a 'baboon,' or a 'gorilla.' "[63] "Our Presidential Merryman," *Harper's Weekly* had labeled him,[64] later carrying a caricature recounting the fabricated story of his incognito entry into Washington. "He wore a Scotch plaid Cap and a very long Military Cloak, so that he was entirely unrecognizable," the caption read.[65] Men like Stanton thought of him as a "low, cunning clown."[66] And the Associated Press reporter, Henry Villard, remembered his "fondness for low talk," and could not have persuaded himself "that the man might possibly possess true greatness of mind and nobility of heart," admitting to a feeling of "disgust and humiliation that such a person should have been called upon to direct the destinies of a great nation."[67]

In the South, there had been little willingness to know the Lincoln they "should have known," the Lincoln who "intended to be fair to the Southern people, and, as he had said at the Cooper Union in February of 1860, 'do nothing through passion and ill-temper,' 'calmly consider their demands, and yield to them' where possible."[68] The South had made up its mind that whatever the North did to ingratiate Lincoln with them was done in deceit. "Since the election of Lincoln most of the leading Northern Abolition papers have essayed the herculean task of reconciling the Southern People to his Presidential rule," observed the *New Orleans Daily Crescent*. "Having succeeded to their heart's content in electing him—having vilified and maligned the South through a long canvass, without measure or excuse—they now tell us that Mr. Lincoln is a very good man, a very amiable man; that he is not at all violent in his prejudices or partialities; that, on the contrary, he is a

[61] Ibid., *November 12, 1858, p. 2, col. 1.*
[62] New York Times, *February 28, 1860, p. 1, col. 1.*
[63] *Randall, op. cit., I, 292.*
[64] *Vol. V (March 2, 1861), p. 144.*
[65] Ibid. *(March 9, 1861), p. 160.*
[66] The Diary of a Public Man, *pp. 48, 49.*
[67] Memoirs of Henry Villard *(Boston: Houghton, Mifflin Co., 1904), I, 144.*
[68] *J. G. Randall, "Lincoln's Greatest Declaration of Faith,"* New York Times Magazine, *February 6, 1949, p. 11.*

moderate, kindly-tempered, conservative man, and if we will only submit to his administration for a time, we will ascertain that he will make
one of the best Presidents the South or the country ever had! 'Will you
walk into my parlor said the spider to the fly.' " "Mr. Lincoln may be all
that these Abolition journals say he is. But, we do not believe a word
they say," the *Crescent* continued. "We are clearly convinced that they
are telling falsehoods to deceive the people of the South, in order to
carry out their own selfish and unpatriotic purposes the more easily.
They know that, although Lincoln is elected to the Presidency, he is
not yet President of the United States, and they are shrewd enough to
know that grave doubts exist whether he ever will be. The chances are
that he will not, unless the South is quieted. . . ."[69]

The South found it easier to view Lincoln as a stereotype, a "radical Abolitionist," an "Illinois ape," a "traitor to his country." Then, too,
the escape through Baltimore by night could "not fail to excite a most
mischievous feeling of contempt for the personal character of Mr. Lincoln throughout the country, especially at the South."[70]

Thus appeared Lincoln, who "without mock modesty" had described
himself en route to Washington as "the humblest of all individuals that
have ever been elevated to the presidency."[71]

Senator Baker of Oregon advanced to the platform and announced,
"Fellow-Citizens: I introduce to you Abraham Lincoln, the President-
elect of the United States of America."[72]

Mr. Lincoln had the crowd "matched"[73] in sartorial perfection. He
was wearing a new tall hat, new black suit of clothes and black boots,
expansive white shirt bosom. He carried an ebony cane with a gold
head the size of a hen's egg. He arose, "walked deliberately and com-
posedly to the table, and bent low in honor of the repeated and enthusiastic cheering of the countless host before him. Having put on his
spectacles, he arranged his manuscript on the small table, keeping the
paper thereon by the aid of his cane."[74] In a clear voice he began:[75]

Fellow-citizens of the United States:

*In compliance with a custom as old as the government itself, I appear
before you to address you briefly, and to take, in your presence, the
oath prescribed by the Constitution of the United States, to be taken by
the President "before he enters on the execution of his office."*

[69] Southern Editorials on Secession, *p. 229.*
[70] The Diary of a Public Man, *p. 46.*
[71] *"Address to the Legislature of New York, at Albany, February 18, 1861,"*
in Complete Works of Abraham Lincoln, *VI, 140.*
[72] New York Times, *March 5, 1861, p. 1, col. 3.*
[73] *Sandburg,* The War Years, *I, 122.*
[74] New York Times, *March 5, 1861, p. 1, col. 3.*
[75] *The text of the Inaugural being used is that contained in* Abraham Lincoln:
His Speeches and Writings, *edited by Roy P. Basler, pp. 579–90.*

I do not consider it necessary at present for me to discuss those matters of administration about which there is no special anxiety or excitement.

Apprehension seems to exist among the people of the Southern States, that by the accession of a Republican Administration, their property, and their peace, and personal security, are to be endangered. There has never been any reasonable cause for such apprehension. Indeed, the most ample evidence to the contrary has all the while existed, and been open to their inspection. It is found in nearly all the published speeches of him who now addresses you. I do but quote from one of those speeches when I declare that "I have no purpose, directly or indirectly, to interfere with the institution of slavery in the States where it exists. I believe I have no lawful right to do so, and I have no inclination to do so." Those who nominated and elected me did so with full knowledge that I had made this, and many similar declarations, and had never recanted them. And more than this, they placed in the platform, for my acceptance, and as a law to themselves, and to me, the clear and emphatic resolution which I now read:

"Resolved, *That the maintenance inviolate of the rights of the States, and especially the right of each State to order and control its own domestic institutions according to its own judgment exclusively, is essential to that balance of power on which the perfection and endurance of our political fabric depend; and we denounce the lawless invasion by armed force of the soil of any State or Territory, no matter under what pretext, as among the gravest of crimes."*

I now reiterate these sentiments: and in doing so, I only press upon the public attention the most conclusive evidence of which the case is susceptible, that the property, peace and security of no section are to be in any wise endangered by the now incoming Administration. I add too, that all the protection which, consistently with the Constitution and the laws, can be given, will be cheerfully given to all the States when lawfully demanded, for whatever cause—as cheerfully to one section as to another.

There is much controversy about the delivering up of fugitives from service or labor. The clause I now read is as plainly written in the Constitution as any other of its provisions:

"No person held to service or labor in one State, under the laws thereof, escaping into another, shall, in consequence of any law or regulation therein, be discharged from such service or labor, but shall be delivered up on claim of the party to whom such service or labor may be due."

It is scarcely questioned that this provision was intended by those who made it, for the reclaiming of what we call fugitive slaves; and the intention of the law-giver is the law. All members of Congress swear their support to the whole Constitution—to this provision as much as to any other. To the proposition, then, that slaves whose cases come within the terms of this clause, "shall be delivered up," their oaths are unanimous. Now, if they would make the effort in good temper, could they not, with nearly equal unanimity, frame and pass a law, by means of which to keep good that unanimous oath?

There is some difference of opinion whether this clause should be enforced by national or by state authority; but surely that difference is not a very material one. If the slave is to be surrendered, it can be of but little consequence to him, or to others, by which authority it is done. And should any one, in any case, be content that his oath shall go unkept, on a merely unsubstantial controversy as to how it shall be kept?

Again, in any law upon this subject, ought not all the safeguards of liberty known in civilized and humane jurisprudence to be introduced, so that a free man be not, in any case, surrendered as a slave? And might it not be well, at the same time to provide by law for the enforcements of that clause in the Constitution which guarantees that "the citizens of each State shall be entitled to all privileges and immunities of citizens in the several States"?

I take the official oath to-day, with no mental reservations, and with no purpose to construe the Constitution or laws, by any hypercritical rules. And while I do not choose now to specify particular acts of Congress as proper to be enforced, I do suggest that it will be much safer for all, both in official and private stations, to conform to, and abide by, all those acts which stand unrepealed, than to violate any of them, trusting to find impunity in having them held to be unconstitutional.

It is seventy-two years since the first inauguration of a President under our national Constitution. During that period fifteen different and greatly distinguished citizens, have, in succession, administered the executive branch of the government. They have conducted it through many perils; and, generally, with great success. Yet, with all this scope for [of] precedent, I now enter upon the same task for the brief constitutional term of four years, under great and peculiar difficulty. A disruption of the Federal Union, heretofore only menaced, is now formidably attempted.

I hold, that in contemplation of universal law, and of the Constitution, the Union of these States is perpetual. Perpetuity is implied, if not expressed, in the fundamental law of all national governments. It is safe to assert that no government proper, ever had a provision in its organic law for its own termination. Continue to execute all the express provisions of our national Constitution, and the Union will endure forever—it being impossible to destroy it, except by some action not provided for in the instrument itself.

Again, if the United States be not a government proper, but an association of States in the nature of contract merely, can it, as a contract, be peaceably unmade, by less than all the parties who made it? One party to a contract may violate it—break it, so to speak; but does it not require all to lawfully rescind it?

Descending from these general principles, we find the proposition that, in legal contemplation, the Union is perpetual, confirmed by the history of the Union itself. The Union is much older than the Constitution. It was formed in fact, by the Articles of Association in 1774. It was matured and continued by the Declaration of Independence in 1776. It was further matured and the faith of all the then thirteen States expressly plighted and engaged that it should be perpetual, by the Articles of Confederation in 1778. And finally, in 1787, one of the declared objects for ordaining and establishing the Constitution, was "to form a more perfect Union."

But if [the] destruction of the Union, by one, or by a part only, of the States, be lawfully possible, the Union is less perfect than before the Constitution, having lost the vital element of perpetuity.

It follows from these views that no State, upon its own mere motion, can lawfully get out of the Union,—that resolves and ordinances to that effect are legally void, and that acts of violence, within any State or States, against the authority of the United States, are insurrectionary or revolutionary, according to the circumstances.

I therefore consider that in view of the Constitution and the laws, the Union is unbroken; and to the extent of my ability I shall take care, as the Constitution itself expressly enjoins upon me, that the laws of the Union be faithfully executed in all the States. Doing this I deem to be only a simple duty on my part; and I shall perform it, so far as practicable, unless my rightful masters, the American people, shall withhold the requisite means, or, in some authoritative manner, direct the contrary. I trust this will not be regarded as a menace, but only as the declared purpose of the Union that it will constitutionally defend and maintain itself.

In doing this there needs to be no bloodshed or violence; and there shall be none, unless it be forced upon the national authority. The power confided to me will be used to hold. occupy, and possess the property and places belonging to the government, and to collect the duties and imposts; but beyond what may be necessary for these objects, there will be no invasion—no using of force against or among the people anywhere. Where hostility to the United States, in any interior locality, shall be so great and so universal, as to prevent competent resident citizens from holding the Federal offices, there will be no attempt to force obnoxious strangers among the people for that object. While the strict legal right may exist in the government to enforce the exercise of these offices, the attempt to do so would be so irritating, and so nearly impracticable with all, that I deem it better to forego, for the time, the uses of such offices.

The mails, unless repelled, will continue to be furnished in all parts of the Union. So far as possible, the people everywhere shall have that sense of perfect security which is most favorable to calm thought and reflection. The course here indicated will be followed, unless current events and experience shall show a modification or change to be proper; and in every case and exigency my best discretion will be exercised according to circumstances actually existing, and with a view and a hope of a peaceful solution of the national troubles, and the restoration of fraternal sympathies and affections.

That there are persons in one section or another who seek to destroy the Union at all events, and are glad of any pretext to do it, I will neither affirm nor deny; but if there be such, I need address no word to them. To those, however, who really love the Union, may I not speak?

Before entering upon so grave a matter as the destruction of our national fabric, with all its benefits, its memories and its hopes, would it not be wise to ascertain precisely why we do it? Will you hazard so desperate a step, while there is any possibility that any portion of the ills you fly from have no real existence? Will you, while the certain ills you fly to, are greater than all the real ones you fly from? Will you risk the commission of so fearful a mistake?

All profess to be content in the Union, if all constitutional rights can be maintained. Is it true, then, that any right, plainly written in the Constitution, has been denied? I think not. Happily the human mind is so constituted, that no party can reach to the audacity of doing this. Think, if you can, of a single instance in which a plainly written provision of the Constitution has ever been denied. If, by the mere force of numbers, a majority should deprive a minority of any clearly written constitutional right, it might, in a moral point of view, justify revolution—certainly would, if such a right were a vital one. But such is not our case. All the vital rights of minorities, and of individuals, are so plainly assured to them, by affirmations and negations, guarantees and prohibitions, in the Constitution, that controversies never arise concerning them. But no organic law can ever be framed with a provision specifically applicable to every question which may occur in practical administration. No foresight can anticipate, nor any document of reasonable length contain express provisions for, all possible questions. Shall fugitives from labor be surrendered by national or by State authority? The Constitution does not expressly say. May Congress prohibit slavery in the territories? The Constitution does not expressly say. Must Congress protect slavery in the territories? The Constitution does not expressly say.

From questions of this class spring all our constitutional controversies, and we divide upon them into majorities and minorities. If the *minority will not acquiesce, the majority must, or the government must cease. There is no other alternative; for continuing the government, is acquiescence on one side or the other. If a minority, in such case, will secede rather than acquiesce, they make a precedent which, in turn, will divide and ruin them; for a minority of their own will secede from them whenever a majority refuses to be controlled by such minority. For instance, why may not any portion of a new confederacy, a year or two hence, arbitrarily secede again, precisely as portions of the present Union now claim to secede from it? All who cherish disunion sentiments, are now being educated to the exact temper of doing this.*

Is there such perfect identity of interests among the States to compose a new Union, as to produce harmony only, and prevent renewed secession?

Plainly, the central idea of secession, is the essence of anarchy. A majority, held in restraint by constitutional checks and limitations, and always changing easily with deliberate changes of popular opinions and sentiments is the only true sovereign of a free people. Whoever rejects it, does, of necessity, fly to anarchy or to despotism. Unanimity is impossible; the rule of a minority, as a permanent arrangement, is wholly inadmissible; so that, rejecting the majority principle, anarchy or despotism in some form is all that is left.

I do not forget the position assumed by some, that constitutional questions are to be decided by the Supreme Court; nor do I deny that such decisions must be binding in any case, upon the parties to a suit, as to the object of that suit, while they are also entitled to very high respect and consideration in all parallel cases by all other departments of the government. And while it is obviously possible that such decision may be erroneous in any given case, still the evil effect following it, being limited to that particular case, with the chance that it may be overruled, and never become a precedent for other cases, can better be borne than could the evils of a different practice. At the same time, the candid citizen must confess that if the policy of the government upon vital questions, affecting the whole people, is to be irrevocably fixed by decisions of the Supreme Court, the instant they are made, in ordinary litigation between parties, in personal actions, the people will have ceased to be their own rulers, having to that extent practically resigned their government into the hands of that eminent tribunal. Nor is there in this view any assault upon the court or the judges. It is a duty from which they may not shrink, to decide cases properly brought before them; and it is no fault of theirs if others seek to turn their decisions to political purposes.

One section of our country believes slavery is right, and ought to be extended, while the other believes it is wrong, and ought not to be extended. This is the only substantial dispute. The fugitive slave clause of the Constitution, and the law for the suppression of the foreign slave trade, are each as well enforced, perhaps, as any law can ever be in a community where the moral sense of the people imperfectly supports the law itself. The great body of the people abide by the dry legal obligation in both cases, and a few break over in each. This, I think, cannot be perfectly cured; and it would be worse in both cases after the separation of the sections, than before. The foreign slave trade, now imperfectly suppressed, would be ultimately revived without restriction, in one section; while fugitive slaves, now only partially surrendered, would not be surrendered at all, by the other.

Physically speaking, we cannot separate. We cannot remove our respective sections from each other, nor build an impassable wall between them. A husband and wife may be divorced, and go out of the presence, and beyond the reach of each other; but the different parts of our country cannot do this. They cannot but remain face to face; and intercourse, either amicable or hostile, must continue between them. Is it possible, then, to make that intercourse more advantageous or more satisfactory, after separation than before? Can aliens make treaties easier than friends can make laws? Can treaties be more faithfully enforced between aliens than laws can among friends? Suppose you go to war, you cannot fight always; and when, after much loss on both sides, and no gain on either, you cease fighting, the identical old questions, as to terms of intercourse, are again upon you.

This country, with its institutions, belongs to the people who inhabit it. Whenever they shall grow weary of the existing government, they can exercise their constitutional right of amending it, or their revolutionary right to dismember or overthrow it. I cannot be ignorant of the fact that many worthy and patriotic citizens are desirous of having the national Constitution amended. While I make no recommendation of amendments, I fully recognize the rightful authority of the people over the whole subject to be exercised in either of the modes prescribed in the instrument itself; and I should under existing circumstances favor rather than oppose a fair opportunity being afforded the people to act upon it.

I will venture to add that to me the Convention mode seems preferable, in that it allows amendments to originate with the people themselves, instead of only permitting them to take or reject propositions, originated by others, not especially chosen for the purpose, and which might not be precisely such as they would wish to either accept or refuse. I understand a proposed amendment to the Constitution, which amendment, however, I have not seen, has passed Congress, to the effect that the federal government shall never interfere with the domestic institutions of the States, including that of persons held to service. To avoid misconstruction of what I have said, I depart from my purpose not to speak of particular amendments, so far as to say that holding such a provision to now be implied constitutional law, I have no objection to its being made express and irrevocable.

The Chief Magistrate derives all his authority from the people, and they have conferred none upon him to fix terms for the separation of the States. The people themselves can do this also if they choose; but the executive, as such, has nothing to do with it. His duty is to administer the present government, as it came to his hands, and to transmit it, unimpaired by him, to his successor.

Why should there not be a patient confidence in the ultimate justice of the people? Is there any better or equal hope, in the world? In our present differences, is either party without faith of being in the right? If the Almighty Ruler of nations, with his eternal truth and justice, be on your side of the North or on yours of the South, that truth, and that justice, will surely prevail, by the judgment of this great tribunal, the American people.

By the frame of the government under which we live, this same people have wisely given their public servants but little power for mischief; and have, with equal wisdom, provided for the return of that little to their own hands at very short intervals.

While the people retain their virtue and vigilance, no administration, by any extreme of wickedness or folly, can very seriously injure the government in the short space of four years.

My countrymen, one and all, think calmly and well, upon this whole subject. Nothing valuable can be lost by taking time. If there be an object to hurry any of you, in hot haste, to a step which you would never take deliberately, that object will be frustrated by taking time; but no good object can be frustrated by it. Such of you as are now dissatisfied, still have the old Constitution unimpaired, and, on the sensitive point, the laws of your own framing under it; while the new administration will have no immediate power, if it would, to change either. If it were admitted that you who are dissatisfied, hold the right side in the dispute, there still is no single good reason for precipitate action. Intelligence, patriotism, Christianity, and a firm reliance on Him, who has never yet forsaken this favored land, are still competent to adjust, in the best way, all our present difficulty.

In your hands, my dissatisfied fellow countrymen, and not in mine, is the momentous issue of civil war. The government will not assail you. You can have no conflict, without being yourselves the aggressors. You have no oath registered in Heaven to destroy the government, while I shall have the most solemn one to "preserve, protect and defend" it.

I am loth to close. We are not enemies, but friends. We must not be enemies. Though passion may have strained, it must not break our *bonds of affection. The mystic chords of memory, stretching from every battle-field, and patriot grave, to every living heart and hearth-stone, all over this broad land, will yet swell the chorus of the Union, when again touched, as surely they will be, by the better angels of our nature.*

With "more of Euclid than of Demosthenes"[76] in him, his delivery was not that of the spellbinder, agitator, or demagogue. His voice was a tenor that "carried song-tunes poorly but had clear and appealing modulations."[77] Habitually a little "scared"[78] when he spoke, he was "pale and very nervous"[79] on this occasion, but his "cheerfulness was marked."[80] "Compelled by nature, to speak slowly,"[81] his manner was "deliberate and impressive"[82] and his voice "remarkably clear and penetrating."[83] There was little evidence in his voice of the fear that might have come as the result of knowing that there were "heavy bets" about his safety.[84] Some of the spectators noted a "loud, and distinct voice, quite intelligible by at least ten thousand persons below him";[85] others found it a "clear, ringing voice, that was easily heard by those on the outer limits of the crowd";[86] still others noted his "firm tones of voice," his "great deliberation and precision of emphasis."[87] Sandburg might have remarked that it gave out "echoes and values."[88]

As Lincoln read on, the audience listened respectfully, with "intense interest, amid a stillness almost oppressive."[89] In the crowd behind the speaker sat Horace Greeley, momentarily expecting the crack of rifle fire.[90] At one point he thought it had come. The speaker stopped. But it was only a spectator crashing down through a tree.[91] Otherwise, the

---

[76] *Randall*, op. cit., *I, 49.*

[77] *Sandburg, The Prairie Years, I, 305.*

[78] [*W. H. Herndon and J. W. Weik*], Herndon's Life of Lincoln, *with an intro-duction and notes by Paul M. Angle (Cleveland: The World Publishing Co., 1949), p. 220.*

[79] The Diary of a Public Man, *p. 74.*

[80] *Correspondence of the* Cincinnati Commercial, *as quoted in* Chicago Daily Tribune, *March 8, 1861, p. 2, col. 4.*

[81] *Herndon and Weik*, op. cit., *p. 273.*

[82] New York Tribune, *March 5, 1861, p. 5, col. 4.*

[83] Ibid.

[84] New York Times, *March 4, 1861, p. 1, col. 2.*

[85] National Intelligencer, *March 5, 1861, p. 3, col. 3.*

[86] New York Times, *March 5, 1861, p. 1, col. 3.*

[87] *Correspondence of the* Cincinnati Commercial, *quoted in* Chicago Daily Tribune, *March 8, 1861, p. 2, col. 4.*

[88] *Sandburg, The Prairie Years, I, 306.*

[89] *Frederick W. Seward, Seward at Washington, as Senator and Secretary of State (New York: Derby and Miller, 1891), I, 516.*

[90] *Greeley*, op. cit., *p. 404.*

[91] Diary of a Public Man, *p. 74.*

crowd in the grounds "behaved very well."[92] Buchanan sat listening, and "looking as straight as he could at the toe of his right boot."[93] Douglas, close by on Lincoln's right, listened "attentively," showing that he was "apparently satisfied" as he "exclaimed, *sotto voce*, 'Good,' 'That's so,' 'No coercion,' and 'Good again.' "[94]Chief Justice Taney "did not remove his eyes from Mr. Lincoln during the entire delivery."[95] Mr. Cameron stood with his back to the President, on the opposite side to Mr. Douglas, "peering off into the crowd."[96] Senator Seward and the other Cabinet officers-elect "kept themselves in the background."[97] Senator Wigfall of Texas, with folded arms "leaned conspicuously in a Capitol doorway," listening to the Inaugural, plainly wearing "contempt, defiance, derision, on his face, his pantomimic posture saying what he had said in the Senate, that the old Union was a corpse and the question was how to embalm it and conduct the funeral decently."[98] Thurlow Weed moved away from the crowd, reporting to General Scott at the top of the slope "The Inaugural is a success," as the old general exclaimed, "God be praised! God in his goodness be praised."[99] To a newspaper reporter surveying the scene, there was a "propriety and becoming interest which pervaded the vast assembly" and "impressed every spectator who had the opportunity of overlooking it."[100] The crowd "applauded repeatedly" and "at times, rapturously,"[101] particularly at points where he "announced his inflexible purpose to execute the laws and discharge his whole constitutional duty."[102] When Lincoln declared, "I hold that in the contemplation of international law, and of the Constitution, the Union of these States is perpetual," the "cheers were hearty and prolonged."[103] When he said, "I shall take care that the laws of the Union be faithfully executed in all the States," he was met with a "tremendous shout of approval."[104] But the "greatest impression of all was produced by the final appeal,"[105] noted one of the

[92] Ibid.

[93] New York Times, *March 5, 1861, p. 1, col. 3.*

[94] Ibid.

[95] Ibid.

[96] *Correspondence of the* Cincinnati Commercial, *as quoted in* Chicago Daily Tribune, *March 8, 1861, p. 2, col. 4.*

[97] Ibid.

[98] *Sandburg, The War Years, I, 123.*

[99] *Seward, op. cit., pp. 516, 517.*

[100] New York Daily Tribune, *March 5, 1861, p. 5, col. 4.*

[101] Chicago Daily Tribune, *March 8, 1861, p. 2, col. 4, quoted from Cincinnati Commercial.*

[102] New York Daily Tribune, *March 5, 1861, p. 5, col. 4.*

[103] Chicago Daily Tribune, *March 8, 1861, p. 2, col. 4, quoted from Cincinnati Commercial.*

[104] Chicago Daily Tribune, *March 8, 1861, p. 2, col. 4, quoted from Cincinnati Commercial.*

[105] Ibid.

reporters. "With great solemnity of emphasis, using his gestures to add significance to his words," Lincoln remarked "You have no oath registered in Heaven to destroy this Government, while I shall have the most solemn one to preserve, protect and defend it," and the crowd responded with "round after round of cheering."[106] Finally, after Lincoln had addressed his "words of affection" to the audience, ending his address, "men waved their hats, and broke forth in the heartiest manifestations of delight. The extraordinary clearness [sic], straightforwardness and lofty spirit of patriotism which pervaded the whole address, impressed every listener, while the evident earnestness, sincerity and manliness of Mr. Lincoln extorted the praise even of his enemies."[107] "The effect of the Inaugural on the country at large remains to be awaited and to be gathered from many sources," observed a reporter, "but it is conceded on all hands that its effect, already noticeable on the vast gathering here, upon the city, and the tone of feeling here is eminently happy, and the source of great gratulation on every side."[108]

Chief Justice Taney stepped forward, shrunken, old, his hands trembling with emotion, and held out an open Bible. Lincoln laid his left hand upon it, raised his right hand, and repeated with a "firm but modest voice"[109] the oath: "I do solemnly swear that I will faithfully execute the office of President of the United States, and will, to the best of my ability, preserve, protect, and defend the Constitution of the United States." Lincoln was now President. Below, the crowd "tossed their hats, wiped their eyes, cheered at the tops of their voices, hurrahed themselves hoarse," and "had the crowd not been so very dense, they would have demonstrated in more lively ways, their joy, satisfaction and delight."[110] Over on the slope the artillery boomed a salute to the sixteenth President of the United States.[111] The crowd ebbed away, and Lincoln rode down Pennsylvania Avenue with Buchanan, bidding him good-bye at the Presidential mansion.[112]

The address had taken thirty-five minutes in delivery, and now it was all over, at least until the nation in general turned in its response. Lincoln had spent six weeks in preparing it—six weeks and many years of lonely thought, along with his active experience on the circuit and the stump. Like the "House Divided Speech" and the "Cooper Union Address" it was deliberately and cautiously prepared, undergoing revision up to the moment of delivery. "Late in January," he told his law

[106] Ibid.
[107] Chicago Daily Tribune, March 8, 1861, p. 2, col. 4, quoted from Cincinnati Commercial.
[108] Chicago Daily Tribune, March 9, 1861, p. 3, col. 2.
[109] New York Times, March 5, 1861, p. 1, col. 3.
[110] Ibid.
[111] Sandburg, The War Years, I, 122.
[112] Baringer, op. cit., p. 334.

partner, Herndon, that he was "ready to begin"[113] the preparation of the Inaugural. In a room over a store, across the street from the State House, cut off from all intrusion and outside communication, he began the preparation. He had told Herndon what works he wanted to consult and asked to be furnished "Henry Clay's great speech delivered in 1850; Andrew Jackson's proclamation against Nullification; and a copy of the Constitution." He "afterwards" called for a copy of Webster's reply to Hayne, a speech which he regarded as "the grandest specimen of American oratory."[114] "With these few 'volumes,' and no further sources of reference,"[115] he began his work on the address.

On February 2, 1861, he wrote a friend, George D. Prentice,[116] editor of the *Louisville Journal,* "I have the document blocked out; but in the now rapidly shifting scenes I shall have to hold it subject to revision up to the time of delivery."[117] He had an original draft printed by one of the proprietors of the *Illinois State Journal* to whom he entrusted the manuscript.[118] "No one else seems to have been taken into the confidence of Mr. Lincoln as to its contents until after he started for Washington on February 11."[119] Upon reaching Indianapolis, he presented a copy to O. H. Browning who had accompanied him from Springfield. According to Browning, "before parting with Mr. Lincoln at Indianapolis, Tuesday, he gave me a copy of his inaugural address, and requested me to read it, and give him my opinion, which I did. I thought it able, well considered, and appropriate, and so informed him. It is, in my judgment, a very admirable document. He permitted me to retain a copy, under promise not to show it except to Mrs. Browning."[120]

Upon arriving in Washington, Lincoln submitted a copy to Secretary Seward with the same invitation to criticize it.[121] According to Louis A. Warren, "As far as we know these two men are the only ones who made any suggestions about certain revisions in the original copy,"[122] even though a few others may have seen it.[123]

Reporters showed an avid interest in the preparation of the Inaugural,

---

[113] *Herndon and Weik,* op. cit., *p. 386.*

[114] Ibid.

[115] Ibid.

[116] Lincoln Lore, *No. 308 (March 4, 1935).*

[117] *Louis A. Warren, "Original Draft of the First Inaugural,"* Lincoln Lore, *No. 358 (February 17, 1936).*

[118] Ibid.

[119] Ibid.

[120] The Diary of Orville Hickman Browning, *edited with an introduction and notes by Theodore Calvin Pease and James G. Randall (Springfield, Ill.: Illinois State Historical Library, 1925), I, 1850–1864, 455, 456.*

[121] *Seward,* op. cit., *p. 512.*

[122] Lincoln Lore, *No. 358.*

[123] *John G. Nicolay and John Hay,* Abraham Lincoln, A History *(New York: The Century Co., 1914), III, 319. Nicolay and Hay observe that "Judge David Davis read it while in Springfield," and "Francis P. Blair, Sr., read it in Washington, and highly commended it, suggesting no changes."*

sometimes reporting inaccurately on the various stages of its preparation. Recording the activities of the President on Saturday night, March 2, one reporter erroneously observed: "Mr. Lincoln sent for Senator Seward, and at 11½ o'clock that gentleman reached the hotel. Mr. Lincoln read to him the Inaugural for the first time, and then asked his advice. Senator Seward took it up section after section and concurred heartily in a great part of it. He suggested a few modifications, an occasional emendation and a few additional paragraphs, all of which were adopted by Mr. Lincoln, and the Inaugural was declared complete and perfect by Senator Seward, who then retired."[124] On Sunday, the reporter remarked, "Mr. Lincoln stated this evening that the Inaugural could not be printed, as some points might require modifying or extending, according to the action of the Senate to-night. His son is now writing copies of what is finished, one of which will be given to the Associated Press when he commences reading it."[125] On the same day there were "reports of efforts in high quarters to induce the president to tone down his inaugural, but it is not affirmed that they were successful."[126]

A final report on the preparation of the Inaugural records the activities on the morning of March 4th: "Mr. Lincoln rose at 5 o'clock. After an early breakfast, the Inaugural was read aloud to him by his son Robert, and the completing touches were added, including the beautiful and impassioned closing paragraph."[127]

As J. G. Randall has observed, "if one would justly appraise Lincoln's first presidential state paper, this inaugural of 1861 deserves to be read as delivered and to be set over against the alternative statements that Lincoln avoided or struck out in revision. Statements pledging maintenance of Federal authority were toned down and shorn of truculence, while promises of conciliation were emotionally underlined."[128] Mr. Browning advised "but one change," supposed by some authorities to be "the most important one in the entire document."[129] "Mr. Seward made thirty-three suggestions for improving the document and nineteen of them were adopted, eight were used after Mr. Lincoln had modified them, and six were discarded *in toto.*"[130] Finally, Lincoln, "without suggestion from any one made sixteen changes in the original draft."[131]

And so, however much the country might criticize as it scanned the

[124] New York Times, *March 4, 1861, p. 1, col. 1.*
[125] New York Times, *March 4, 1861, p. 1, col. 2.*
[126] New York Daily Tribune, *March 4, 1861, p. 5, col. 1.*
[127] New York Times, *March 5, 1861, p. 1, col. 1.*
[128] *Randall,* op. cit., *I, 309.*
[129] *Warren,* loc. cit.
[130] Ibid.
[131] Ibid.

Inaugural, Lincoln could respond, as he did to the Douglas taunt in 1858, that the "House Divided Speech" had been "evidently well prepared and carefully written."[132] "I admit that it was. I am not master of language; I have not a fine education; . . . I know what I meant, and I will not leave this crowd in doubt. . . ."[133]

Lincoln did not have to wait long for a response from the country at large. As he delivered the address, little audiences unseen by the speaker dotted the land, clustering around newspaper offices and waiting for telegraphic reports of what was in the Inaugural. Between Washington and New York, the American Telegraph Company had placed at the disposal of the Associated Press three wires for the communication of the address.[134] Similar arrangements had been made with other key cities. The delivery of the Inaugural commenced at 1:30 P.M., Washington time, and the "telegraphers promptly to the minute" began its transmission. "The first words of the Message were received by the agents of the Press at 1:45, and the last about 3:30," observed the *New York Times*.[135] "Such rapidity in telegraphic communication has never before been reached in this country."[136] By four o'clock, "the entire document was furnished to the different newspapers,"[137] and special editions of the press were in the hands of readers within an hour. "People of all parties in this city, as elsewhere, were on tip-toe all day to know what was going on at Washington, and especially to hear what President Lincoln would say in his Inaugural," observed the *New York Times*.[138] "At length it was announced that the procession had reached the Capitol, and then, while the President was delivering his speech and the reporters were transmitting it by telegraph, there was a long period of unalloyed expectancy. Meantime, men given to talking, in the many crowds, discussed all sorts of topics, connected with the questions of the day, before little groups of gaping listeners. There was many a prophet among them, not without honor, before the Message was received, who knew exactly what it was going to contain, and foretold with marvelous preciseness the points which Mr. Lincoln would dwell on.

"It was nearly 5 o'clock when the eloquence of these worthies was

[132] *Speech of Senator Douglas, delivered in Chicago, July 9, 1858, in* The Political Debates between Abraham Lincoln and Stephen A. Douglas, *with an introduction by George Haven Putnam (New York: G. P. Putnam's Sons, 1913), p. 24.*

[133] *Speech in reply to Douglas at Chicago, Illinois, July 10, 1858, in* Abraham Lincoln, His Speeches and Writings, *edited by Roy P. Basler, p. 392.*

[134] New York Times, *March 5, 1861, p. 8, col. 5.*

[135] Ibid.

[136] Ibid.

[137] Ibid.

[138] New York Times, *March 5, 1861, p. 8, cols. 4, 5.*

suddenly quenched as by a wet blanket, and the wet sheets of the latest edition, with the President's Inaugural in black and white, leaped forth from the presses into the hands of all who could get copies. Then there was wild scrambling around the counters in publication offices, a laying down of pennies and a rape of newspapers, and the crowds began to disperse, each man hastening to some place remote from public haunt, where he might peruse the document in peace. The newsboys rushed through the city crying with stentorian lungs 'The President's Message!' 'Lincoln's Speech!' 'Ex-tray Times!' 'Get Lincoln's Inau-gu-ra-a-a-il!' And an hour later everybody had read the Message and everybody was talking about it."[139]

Out in Mattoon, Illinois, a similar scene was being enacted. A roving reporter, heading south from Chicago to observe the reactions of the crowds, made a "tour of the town" and stopped at hotel lobbies, where the speech, fresh from the press, was being "read and re-read, silently and aloud, to groups of ardent listeners . . . As the reading in a crowd progresses, when the reader comes to the place where Mr. Lincoln 'puts his foot down,' down goes likewise every foot in the circle."[140]

The home folks whom Lincoln had bade an affectionate farewell three weeks before were among the most anxious of the unseen audiences. Whereas they spoke only for themselves at the time of the tearful departure, they were now ready to speak for the nation. "The Inaugural Address of our noble Chief Magistrate has electrified the whole country," they said. "It has satisfied people of all parties who love the Union and desire its preservation. In this city it gives almost universal satisfaction."[141] In Quincy, the scene of one of the debates of 1858, the address was received with "much enthusiasm," and the Republican Gun Squad fired thirty-four guns;[142] in Peoria, "so great was the anxiety felt to see what Mr. Lincoln said, that people came forty miles to get copies of the message,"[143] reading it with "much enthusiasm."[144]

But occasionally there was a dissenting voice back home, particularly in the Democratic press, as there was generally throughout the North. While the *Chicago Daily Tribune* was "quite sure that no document can be found among American state papers embodying sounder wisdom and higher patriotism,—breathing kindlier feelings to all sections of the country,"[145] the Chicago *Times* denounced the Inaugural as "a loose, disjointed, rambling affair," concluding that the Union was

---

[139] Ibid.
[140] Chicago Daily Tribune, *March 8, 1861, p. 2, col. 3.*
[141] Illinois State Journal, *March 6, 1861, p. 2.*
[142] Chicago Daily Tribune, *March 6, 1861, p. 1, col. 3.*
[143] Ibid.
[144] Ibid.
[145] Chicago Daily Tribune, *March 5, 1861, p. 1, col. 1.*

now "lost beyond hope."[146] While the *New York Times* observed that "conservative people are in raptures over the Inaugural," and that "Its conciliatory tone, and frank, outspoken declaration of loyalty to the whole country, captured the hearts of many heretofore opposed to Mr. Lincoln,"[147] the New York *Herald* found that "the inaugural is not a crude performance—it abounds in traits of craft and cunning. It bears marks of indecision, and yet of strong coercion proclivities . . . It is neither candid nor statesmanlike; nor does it possess any essential dignity or patriotism. It would have caused a Washington to mourn, and would have inspired a Jefferson, Madison, or Jackson with contempt."[148] There were those in Maine who found it a "poor, weak, trashy affair, a standing disgrace to the country, and a fit commentary on the fanaticism and unreasonableness which made him President."[149] Some in Pennsylvania found it "one of the most awkwardly constructed official documents we have ever inspected," and "pitiably apologetical for the uprising of the Republican party, and his own election to the Presidency, by it."[150] And there were those in Ohio "who never expected to see a Black Republican peaceably inaugurated in this White Republican country . . . but now the Rubicon is passed," and the Inaugural, "like its distinguished author," is "flat-footed. It is more *magazinish* in *sound* than in *style,* smelling strongly of gunpowder, and is *'coercion' all over,* as the South understands that word."[151]

"It is an interesting study" said a Douglas journal, the Peoria *Daily Democratic Union,* on March 7th, "to look over the various journals that have come to our table since the delivery of President Lincoln's Inaugural Address, and notice the different manner in which they speak of it." "All of these criticisms of the Address cannot be correct, for they clash materially; and that fact demonstrates very plainly that some of them were either the offspring of prejudice, or were written by men incapable of judging of the merits of this first state paper of President Lincoln."[152]

Whereas there was difference of opinion in the North, much of it stopped short of vehement denunciation. However, the South saw little hope from Lincoln, and expressed itself accordingly. "Mr. Lincoln's

[146] *Quoted in Randall, op. cit., p. 306.*

[147] New York Times, *March 5, 1861, p. 1, col. 4.*

[148] *Quoted in the* New York Daily Tribune, *March 7, 1861, p. 6, col. 6.*

[149] The Bangor Union, *as quoted in* New York Daily Tribune, *March 8, 1861, p. 6, col. 5.*

[150] The Philadelphia Evening Journal, *as quoted in* New York Daily Tribune, *March 7, 1861, p. 7, col. 3.*

[151] Cleveland Plaindealer, *as quoted in* Chicago Daily Tribune, *March 9, 1861, p. 1, col. 3.*

[152] *Quoted in* Northern Editorials on Secession, *edited by Howard Cecil Perkins (New York: D. Appleton-Century Co., 1942), II, 643.*

Inaugural Address is before our readers," observed the *Richmond Enquirer*, "couched in the cool, unimpassioned, deliberate language of the fanatic, with the purpose of pursuing the promptings of fanaticism even to the dismemberment of the Government with the horrors of civil war . . . Civil war must now come. Sectional war, declared by Mr. Lincoln, awaits only the signal gun from the insulted Southern Confederacy, to light its horrid fires all along the borders of Virginia."[153] The *Richmond Dispatch* was equally strong: "The Inaugural Address of Abraham Lincoln inaugurates civil war, as we have predicted it would from the beginning . . . The sword is drawn and the scabbard thrown away . . . ere long Virginia may be engaged in a life and death struggle. . . ."[154] The *Baltimore Sun* observed, "The Inaugural, as a whole, breathes the spirit of mischief," and found "no Union spirit in the address."[155] "We presume nobody is astonished to hear that Secessionists regard the Inaugural as a 'declaration of war,' " noted one observer. "Before the Inaugural has been read in a single Southern State, it is denounced, through the telegraph, from every Southern point, as a declaration of war."[156] "I have heard but one construction of Mr. Lincoln's declaration of his intention to 'hold, occupy, and possess the property and places belonging to the Government, and to collect the duties and imposts,' " observed a special correspondent in Richmond. The Inaugural "is received with much disfavor," and "is regarded, if not as a declaration of war, as at least the expression of a determination to coerce the seceding States into compliance with the demands of the Federal Government."[157] Reporting from Charleston, South Carolina, another correspondent observed, "The part which, of course, attracted most attention and was read and re-read with deep interest, was that wherein Mr. Lincoln declares that to the best of his ability, he will take care, according to his oath and the Constitution, that 'the laws of the Union are faithfully executed in all the States,' and that he will use the power confided to him to 'hold, occupy and possess the property and places belonging to the Government, and to collect the duties and imposts.' " The verdict was, according to this correspondent, "that rebellion would not be treated tenderly by Mr. Lincoln, and that he was quite another sort of man from James Buchanan."[158]

At least a minority of the people of the South responded less vehemently. Occasionally a roving reporter, mingling among the crowds in

---

[153] *Quoted in* New York Daily Tribune, *March 7, 1861, p. 7, col. 2. See also, Southern Editorials on Secession, pp. 474, 475.*

[154] Southern Editorials on Secession, *p. 475.*

[155] *Quoted in* New York Daily Tribune, *March 7, 1861, p. 7, col. 1.*

[156] New York Times, *March 7, 1861, p. 4, col. 2.*

[157] New York Daily Tribune, *March 9, 1861, p. 6, col. 2.*

[158] New York Daily Tribune, *March 9, 1861, p. 6, col. 1.*

Southern cities, reported less fury. From Montgomery came word that Alexander Stevens had found the Inaugural "the most *adroit* State paper ever published on the Continent," and "a great moral impression has been produced"[159] in both Charleston and Montgomery. In Savannah, Georgia, "Not a word have we yet heard uttered against its tone," observed a reporter, predicting "a powerful and sweeping effect at the South."[160] Now and then a reporter noticed "a pretty general disappointment that the document contained so little 'blood and thunder.' "[161] "That the document should be calm and dignified in tone and style, logical in its conclusions, and plain and kind in its treatment of the great topic of the day, was annoying to the Rebels, who hoped to find in the address a provocation for extreme action."[162]

While the country at large read the speech and responded both favorably and unfavorably, Senator Clingman of North Carolina and Stephen A. Douglas engaged in debate over its meaning in the United States Senate. "If I understand it aright, all that is direct in it, I mean, at least, that purpose which seems to stand out clearly and directly, is one which I think must lead to war—war against the confederate or seceding State"[163] remarked Clingman. Douglas, on the other hand, who had "read it carefully" could not "assent to the construction" of the senator from North Carolina, believing he could "demonstrate that there is no foundation for the apprehension which has been spread throughout the country, that this message is equivalent to a declaration of war."[164]

Just as the country searched the Inaugural for the sentiments it contained, it also examined and appraised the language and style in which it was couched. The Toronto *Leader* could not admire the "tawdry and corrupt schoolboy style," even as it gave "credit" for its "good sense."[165] An Albany, New York, observer found it "useless to criticize the style of the President's Inaugural when the policy it declares is fraught with consequences so momentous." Nevertheless, he paused to describe it as a "rambling, discursive, questioning, loose-jointed stump speech." It consisted of "feeble rhetorical stuff."[166] While papers unfriendly to Lincoln were finding it "inferior in point of elegance, perspicuity, vigor, talent, and all the graces of composition to any other

[159] New York Daily Tribune, *March 12, 1861, p. 6, col. 1.*
[160] New York Daily Tribune, *March 11, 1861, p. 6, col. 2.*
[161] New York Daily Tribune, *March 9, 1861, p. 6, col. 1.*
[162] Ibid.
[163] Congressional Globe, *Second Session, 36th Congress, Vol. 30, Part II, p. 1436.*
[164] Ibid.
[165] *Quoted in* New York Daily Tribune, *March 7, 1861, p. 7, col. 3.*
[166] Albany Atlas and Argus, *as quoted in* Northern Editorials on Secession, *II, 628.*

paper of a like character which has ever emanated from a President of the Republic,"[167] papers that were friendly found the contrary to be the case. "It is clear as a mountain brook," commented a Detroit reporter. "The depth and flow of it are apparent at a glance."[168] In Boston, the *Transcript* reporter commented at length. "The style of the Address is as characteristic as its temper. 'Right words in their right places'; this is the requirement of good rhetoric. Right words at the right times, should be the test by which we try the speech of statesmen; and this test Mr. Lincoln's address will bear. It has not one flaming expression in the whole course of its firm and explicit statements. The language is level to the popular mind,—the plain homespun language of a man accustomed to talk with 'the folks' and 'the neighbors,' the language of a man of vital common sense, whose words exactly fit his facts and thoughts."[169] Occasionally, the concluding paragraph was singled out for praise. In Indianapolis, the reporter of the *Daily Journal* remarked: "The closing sentence, the only attempt at rhetorical display in the whole address, is singularly and almost poetically beautiful."[170]

Part II

Given the circumstances that brought forth the Inaugural Address, and removed in time from the passions which agitated the country, what may one say of Lincoln's address on March 4, 1861? The historian has often examined it for its effects, and has concluded that "Though not fully appreciated then, this was one of the great American inaugurals."[171] And the literary critic has sometimes observed its final passage, finding in it poetic beauty and enduring worth. Unlike the historian, we are not concerned merely with the Inaugural as a force in the shaping of American culture; nor are we concerned with its enduring worth as literature. The Inaugural was a speech, "meant to be heard and intended to exert an influence of some kind on those who heard it,"[172] or those who read it. We must, therefore, be concerned with evaluating the Inaugural as a speech, a medium distinct from other media, and with methods peculiarly its own. We must be concerned with discovering in this particular case "the available means of persuasion" and with evaluating their worth.

---

[167] Jersey City American Standard, *as quoted in* Northern Editorials on Secession, *II, 625.*

[168] Detroit Daily Tribune, *as quoted in* Northern Editorials on Secession, *II, 623.*

[169] *Quoted in* New York Daily Tribune, *March 7, 1861, p. 7, col. 1.*

[170] *Quoted in* Northern Editorials on Secession, *II, 619.*

[171] *J. G. Randall, "Lincoln's Great Declarations of Faith,"* New York Times Magazine, *February 6, 1949, p. 23.*

[172] *Wayland M. Parrish and Marie Hochmuth Nichols,* American Speeches, *New York, David McKay, 1954, p. 3.*

Let us view the Inaugural as a communication, with a purpose, and a content presumably designed to aid in the accomplishment of that purpose, further supported by skillful composition in words, and ultimately unified by the character and manner of the person who presented it.

We must not casually assume that Lincoln's purpose is easily discernible in the occasion itself. It is true, of course, that this was an inaugural ceremony, with a ritual fairly well established by fifteen predecessors, "Yet, with all this scope for [of] precedent," Lincoln was keenly aware that he entered upon the same task "under great and peculiar difficulty. A disruption of the Federal Union, heretofore only menaced, is now formidably attempted." If we are to discern the purpose that Lincoln had when he addressed the American people on March 4, 1861, we must recall the experiences of the nation between his election as President and the day of his inauguration. During that time, he had been made keenly aware of Southern resentment to a "sectional" President. The rapid movement of the Secessionists followed closely on the announcement of his election, and of the ascendancy of the Republican party to a position of power. The South viewed the Republican platform as an instrument for its "subjugation" and the "complete ruin of her social, political and industrial institutions."[173] By its acts of secession, and its establishment of a provisional government of its own, the lower South raised the very practical question: What is the authority of the federal government in regard to maintaining itself and in regard to reclaiming those federal properties possessed by retiring members?

Lincoln had also been made keenly aware of the doubts and skepticism that prevailed regarding his ability to lead his party and the nation. "I cannot but know what you all know," he had observed on his way to Washington, "that without a name, perhaps without a reason why I should have a name, there has fallen upon me a task such as did not rest even upon the Father of this Country . . ."[174] In addition, he was keenly aware of both Northern and Southern distrust of his moral character and integrity. Even to members of his party, he was a "funny man," given to stories in bad taste, and an Illinois wag. And to the South, he was at best thought to be as radical as the most rabid of the left-wing Republicans, hence a "dangerous man."[175] That he was aware of the prevailing sentiments regarding him as a man is reflected in his casual remark en route to Washington when, for a moment, his

---

[173] New Orleans Daily Crescent, *November 13, 1860, as quoted in* Southern Editorials on Secession, *p. 237.*

[174] *"Address to the Legislature of Ohio at Columbus, February 13, 1861,"* Complete Works, *VI, 121.*

[175] *Speech of Senator Clingman of North Carolina in the Senate, December 3, 1860,* The Congressional Globe, *Second Session, 36th Congress, Vol. 30, p. 3.*

address was misplaced. In a worried search, he described the Inaugural as "my certificate of moral character, written by myself."[176]

Although from the time of his election he was urged to state his views on the passing events, Lincoln had remained silent. That his silence was not due to a lack of anxiety is easily apparent. "Allusion has been made," he noted on his way to Washington, "to the interest felt in relation to the policy of the new administration. In this I have received from some a degree of credit for having kept silence, and from others some deprecation. I still think that I was right . . .

"In the varying and repeatedly shifting scenes of the present, and without a precedent which could enable me to judge by the past, it has seemed fitting that before speaking upon the difficulties of the country I should have gained a view of the whole field, being at liberty to modify and change the course of policy as future events may make a change necessary.

"I have not maintained silence from any want of real anxiety."[177]

What, then, was Lincoln's purpose? Clearly, he intended to take the occasion of the inauguration to declare the position of the Republican party in regard to the South, to announce his considered judgment in regard to the practical questions raised by the movement of secession, and, in all, to give what assurance he could of his personal integrity.

In evaluating the Inaugural, we must keep in mind its purpose, for the purpose of the speech controlled Lincoln's selection of materials, his arrangement, his style, and his manner.

Let us turn to the speech itself in order to note the materials and methods he employed to sustain his purpose. Considering the general predisposition of the South to view the incoming administration with suspicion, and considering the fact that Lincoln had not spoken for his own party since his nomination, he found it necessary to take a moment to "press upon the public attention the most conclusive evidence of which the case is susceptible," the idea of the integrity of the Republican party and his own integrity as its helmsman. Wise judgment could scarcely have dictated otherwise, for the lower South had gone out of the Union partly on the grounds that it expected no fair consideration from the newly born party, and the border states were contemplating similar measures. Lincoln attempted to conciliate his audience by assuring the country that "the property, peace and security of no section are to be in any wise endangered by the now incoming Administration." In order to do this he called attention to the fact that

---

[176] *Ward Hill Lamon*, Recollections of Abraham Lincoln, 1847–1865, *edited by Dorothy Lamon Teillard (Washington, D.C.: Published by the editor, 1911),* p. 36.

[177] "*Address to the Legislature of Ohio at Columbus, February 13, 1861,*" Complete Works, *VI, 121, 122.*

he was taking a solemn oath in "your presence"; he committed himself again to previously spoken words[178] that have "all the while existed, and been open to their inspection"; to the Republican platform pertaining to the "maintenance inviolate of the rights of the States, and especially the right of each State to order and control its own domestic institutions according to its own judgment exclusively";[179] and to the clause "plainly written in the Constitution," pertaining to delivering up "on claim of the party to whom such service or labor may be due"[180] the escaping fugitive. He concluded his opening remarks with a reiteration of the avowal that he took the "official oath to-day, with no mental reservations, and with no purpose to construe the Constitution or laws, by any hypercritical rules." This was neither the material nor the method of a "deceitful" or "dangerous" man. By it, Lincoln was attempting to touch off those favorable responses that accrue to the appearance of honesty, straightforwardness, and obedience to the Constitution. One must remember that Lincoln's pledge of faith could not have given satisfaction to the Abolitionist group within his own party with whom he was constantly identified by the South; it did, however, serve to differentiate him from the radical element and hence to reassure the states yet within the Union. From the standpoint of persuasiveness Lincoln was undoubtedly wise in taking the advice of Seward to omit the two paragraphs immediately following his opening statement in the original draft of the Inaugural:

The more modern custom of electing a Chief Magistrate upon a previously declared platform of principles, supercedes, in a great measure, the necessity of restating those principles in an address of this sort. Upon the plainest grounds of good faith, one so elected is not at liberty to shift his position. It is necessarily implied, if not expressed, that, in his judgment, the platform which he thus accepts, binds him to nothing either unconstitutional or inexpedient.

Having been so elected upon the Chicago Platform, and while I would repeat nothing in it, of aspersion or epithet or question of motive against any man or party, I hold myself bound by duty, as well as impelled by inclination to follow, within the executive sphere, the principles therein declared. By no other course could I meet the reasonable expectations of the country.[181]

178 *"Mr. Lincoln's Reply," First Joint Debate, at Ottawa, August 21, 1858,* The Political Debates between Abraham Lincoln and Stephen A. Douglas, *p. 209.*

179 *Halstead, op. cit., p. 138.*

180 *Article IV, Sec. 2.*

181 *For changes in the Inaugural, see MS of early printed version with secretarial reproductions of the changes, and accompanying letter of John Hay to Charles Eliot Norton, dated March 25, 1899, explaining the nature of the revi-*

To have used the paragraphs would undoubtedly have incited anew the suspicion that he was merely a "sectional" President and an "abolitionist" or "party man."

Having spent time in an attempt to gain a fair hearing for the rest of his address, Lincoln next took up the question for which the whole country awaited an answer, namely, What is the duty and the policy of the Republican administration in regard to Secession? Without delay, he laid down the proposition, "I hold, that in contemplation of universal law, and of the Constitution, the Union of these States is perpetual. Perpetuity is implied, if not expressed, in the fundamental law of all national governments"; hence "no State, upon its own mere motion, can lawfully get out of the Union,—that *resolves* and *ordinances* to that effect are legally void, and that acts of violence, within any State or States, against the authority of the United States, are insurrectionary or revolutionary, according to circumstances." Furthermore, "if the United States be not a government proper, but an association of States in the nature of contract merely, can it, as a contract, be peaceably unmade, by less than all the parties who made it?"

To the North, the mere assertion of the principle of perpetuity would have been sufficient; no further proof would have been necessary. But to the lower South, already out of the Union, and to the border states and upper South contemplating similar action, clearly assertion was not sufficient. Therefore, Lincoln found his proposition "confirmed by the history of the Union itself." The Union, he pointed out, was "much older than the Constitution"; it was "formed in fact, by the Articles of Association in 1774"; it was "matured and continued by the Declaration of Independence in 1776"; it was "further matured and the faith of all the then thirteen States expressly plighted and engaged that it should be perpetual, by the Articles of Confederation in 1778"; finally "in 1787, one of the declared objects for ordaining and establishing the Constitution, was *'to form a more perfect Union.'*" Although Lincoln's support of his proposition was factual, the facts themselves carried with them the respect and loyalty that had always attached to the founding fathers who were held in esteem for their vision and their wisdom.

Having stated the principle that guided him, Lincoln continued logically with its application, holding that "to the extent of my ability I

sions, in Widener Library of Harvard University. See also, John G. Nicolay and John Hay, Abraham Lincoln, III, 327–344; Louis A. Warren, "Original Draft of the First Inaugural," Lincoln Lore, No. 358 (February 17, 1936) and No. 359 (February 24, 1936). See, The Robert Todd Lincoln Collection of the Papers of Abraham Lincoln, Library of Congress. Microfilm in University of Illinois Library. This collection contains the most important source for the various working sheets of the Inaugural.

shall take care, as the Constitution itself expressly enjoins upon me, that the laws of the Union be faithfully executed in all the States." In discussing the policy of the government in enforcing the laws of the Union, Lincoln does not speak as the master or the mere advocate handing down a bloodless decision, but as a servant performing a "simple duty," the "American people" being "my rightful masters." As a skilled persuader, he was undoubtedly aware that lines of argument will often meet with varied responses according to whether they are put forward by those toward whom one feels sympathetic or antagonistic.[182] Nowhere in the Inaugural does Lincoln seek more earnestly to be conciliating and mild. He was aware that legalism alone would not sustain his purpose. He could have used the bold and confident assertion that appeared in the original draft of the Inaugural:

All the power at my disposal will be used to reclaim the public property and places which have fallen; to hold, occupy and possess these, and all other property and places belonging to the government and to collect the duties and imposts; but beyond what may be necessary for these objects, there will be no invasion of any State.

Even in the original draft, Lincoln had avoided the use of the names of specific forts to which he had reference. Pickens and Sumter were in a precarious position and were peculiarly explosive topics of discussion. However, Lincoln yielded even further in tempering his remarks, accepting the suggestion of O. H. Browning, and finally choosing only to say:

The power confided to me will be used to hold, occupy, and possess the property and places belonging to the Government, and to collect the duties and imposts; but, beyond what may be necessary for these objects, there will be no invasion, no using of force against or among the people anywhere.

Furthermore, "Where hostility to the United States, in any interior locality, shall be so great and so universal, as to prevent competent resident citizens from holding the Federal offices," he would make "no attempt to force obnoxious strangers among the people for that object," even though the "strict legal right may exist." And, the mails "unless repelled" would continue to be furnished. In doing this, "there needs to be no bloodshed or violence," he assured the country, and promised that "there shall be none, unless it be forced upon the na-

---

[182] *Robert K. Merton,* Mass Persuasion *(New York: Harper and Brothers, 1946), p. 109.*

tional authority." Nowhere did Lincoln assert a power or a practice that he believed impossible of enforcement, or that he believed could be interpreted as "coercion" in its baldest and most belligerent form.

Having announced his specific policy, Lincoln turned to those "who really love the Union," neither affirming nor denying that there were those "who seek to destroy the Union at all events," being "glad of any pretext to do it." In his original draft, he had intended pointedly to observe "Before entering upon so grave a matter as the destruction of our national Union, would it not be wise to ascertain precisely why we do it?" In his final draft, however, he blotted out the word "Union" and substituted for it the unifying and figurative word "fabric," further inserting the words "with all its benefits, its memories and its hopes," thereby seeking to heighten feeling by suggesting appropriate attitudes.

Having passed the climax of his remarks, Lincoln moved, in the last half of the Inaugural, to a reasoned discussion of related topics. He denied that any right plainly written in the Constitution had been violated, observing that majorities and minorities arise as a result of that class of questions for which no specific constitutional answer has been provided. The alternative to accepting the "majority principle" was always either "anarchy or depotism." Not even the Supreme Court could serve as the final arbiter on questions "affecting the whole people," for unless it limited its activity to making decisions on specific "cases properly brought before them," the "people will have ceased to be their own rulers." He argued the impracticability of secession, contrasting it with the simple act of divorce between husband and wife who may remain "beyond the reach of each other," and concluded that "Physically speaking, we cannot separate." Not even war was a satisfactory solution to difficulties, for "you cannot fight always," and after much "loss on both sides, and no gain on either," the "identical old questions" are again to be settled. "This country, with its institutions, belongs to the people who inhabit it," he insisted, urging that when the whole people "shall grow weary of the existing government, they can exercise their *constitutional* right of amending it, or their *revolutionary* right to dismember or overthrow it."

Lincoln's appeal throughout was to the "patient confidence in the ultimate justice of the people." "Is there any better or equal hope, in the world?" he asked, even as he noted the human tendency of parties in dispute to insist with equal confidence on being in the "right." Rising to the position of impartial leader, he sought faith in a higher law, and in a disinterested Ruler: "If the Almighty Ruler of nations, with his eternal truth and justice, be on your side of the North or on yours of the South, that truth, and that justice, will surely prevail, by the judgment of this great tribunal, the American people."

Lincoln ended his address with both a challenge and a declaration of faith. "In *your* hands, my dissatisfied fellow countrymen, and not in *mine,* is the momentous issue of civil war. The government will not assail *you.*" He was just about to take an oath, and to him an oath was a solemn pledge, not only in word, but in truth. It was an avowal of morality, binding him not only to duty to the people but to God, "the Almighty Ruler of nations." "*You* have no oath registered in Heaven to destroy the government," he pleaded in an attempt to secure the cooperation of all those who could help him in fulfilling the pledge he was to take, "while *I* shall have the most solemn one to 'preserve, protect and defend' it." His final appeal was to feeling rather than to reason. He undoubtedly realized that when men cannot achieve common ground through reason, they may achieve it through the medium of feeling. "I am loth to close," he observed. "We are not enemies, but friends. We must not be enemies. Though passion may have strained, it must not break our bonds of affection." No longer the advocate, or even the President performing official duties, Lincoln, taking the advice of Seward, became the affectionate father, the benevolent and hopeful counselor, trusting not only in reason, but calling on "memory," the "patriot grave," the "heart and hearth-stone," "the better angels of our nature" to "swell the chorus of the Union."

Whereas the disgruntled may have "found too much argumentative discussion of the question at issue, as was to have been expected from a man whose whole career has been that of an advocate,"[183] obviously others could not have failed to notice that Lincoln sought valiantly to employ all the "available means of persuasion." He had sought to reach his audience not only through reason, but through feeling and through the force of his own ethical ideals.

Any fair-minded critic, removed from the passions of the times, must find himself much more in agreement with those observers of the day who believed the Inaugural met the "requirements of good rhetoric" by having "right words in their right places" and "right words at the right times,"[184] than with those who labeled it "feeble rhetorical stuff," and found it "inferior in point of elegance, perspicuity, vigor, talent, and all the graces of composition to any other paper of a like character from a President of the Republic."[185] One who studies the revisions in phrase and word in the various drafts of the Inaugural must become aware that Lincoln was concerned not only with using the right argument, but with using words cautiously, and purposefully, to obtain a desired effect from his listeners and from his potential readers. To the

[183] The Diary of a Public Man, *p. 75.*
[184] The Boston Transcript, *as quoted in* New York Daily Tribune, *March 7, 1861, p. 7, col. 1.*
[185] Jersey City Standard, *as quoted in* Northern Editorials on Secession, *II, 625.*

rhetorician, style is not an aspect of language which can be viewed in isolation or judged merely by the well-attuned ear. Nor is it sufficient to apply such rubrics as clarity, vividness, elegance as absolute values, or as an adequate description of style. Words are an "available means of persuasion," and the only legitimate question is: Did Lincoln use words effectively to achieve his specific purpose?

Although Lincoln may have lamented that he did not have a "fine education" or that he was not a "master of language,"[186] he had a keen sensitiveness for language. He "studied to see the subject matter clearly," said an early teacher, "and to express it truly and strongly. I have known him to study for hours the best way of three to express an idea."[187] And when his partner, Herndon, attempted the grandiose in expression, Lincoln sometimes remarked, "Billy, don't shoot too high —aim lower and the common people will understand you. They are the ones you want to reach—at least they are the ones you ought to reach. The educated and refined people will understand you any way. If you aim too high your ideas will go over the heads of the masses, and only hit those who need no hitting."[188] Lincoln had become adept at stump speaking, and knew how to use language to make himself clear and to make a point. That he knew the power of language to fire passions and to cloud understanding is amply demonstrated in his remarks at Indianapolis when he was en route to Washington. "Solomon says there is 'a time to keep silence,'" he observed, "and when men wrangle by the month with no certainty that they mean the same thing, while using the same word, it perhaps were as well if they would keep silence. The words 'coercion' and 'invasion' are much used in these days, and often with some temper and hot blood. Let us make sure, if we can, that we do not misunderstand the meaning of those who use them. Let us get exact definitions of these words, not from dictionaries, but from the men themselves, who certainly deprecate the things they would represent by the use of words."[189] Lincoln was keenly aware that words themselves were often grounds for argument, systems of attitudes suggesting courses of action.[190] Then, too, Lincoln knew that his "friends feared" and "those who were not his friends hoped, that, forgetting the dignity of his position, and the occasion, he would descend

[186] *Speech in reply to Douglas at Chicago, Illinois, July 10, 1858, in* Abraham Lincoln: His Speeches and Writings, *edited by Roy P. Basler, p. 393.*

[187] *Herndon and Weik, op. cit., p. 99.*

[188] Ibid., *p. 262.*

[189] *"Address to the Legislature of Indiana at Indianapolis, February 12, 1861,"* Complete Works, *VI, 112, 113.*

[190] *Kenneth Burke, "Two Functions of Speech,"* The Language of Wisdom and Folly, *edited and with an introduction by Irving J. Lee (New York: Harper and Brothers, 1949), p. 40.*

to the practices of the story-teller, and fail to rise to the level of a statesman."[191]

The desire for clearness, the desire to subdue passion, the desire to manifest the integrity and dignity befitting a statesman in a responsible position—these are the factors that influenced Lincoln in his composition of the Inaugural, and to appraise his style without constant awareness of them is likely to lead the critic far afield. Let us consider Lincoln's style, then, as a system of symbols designed to evoke certain images favorable to the accomplishment of his purpose and, in so far as he could, to prevent certain other images from arising.

One of the most marked characteristics of Lincoln's style is its directness. By it he attempts to achieve the appearance of candor and honesty, traits that were eminently significant to the success of the Inaugural, considering the doubts and suspicions that were prevalent regarding his integrity. From the opening sentence to the conclusion one notes the unmistakable honesty and straightforwardness that reside in direct address. "I appear before you," he remarks, "to address you briefly, and to take, in your presence, the oath prescribed by the Constitution of the United States . . ." Again, he observes, "I have no purpose, directly or indirectly, to interfere with the institution of slavery in the States where it exists"; "I now reiterate these sentiments"; "I take the official oath to-day, with no mental reservations"; *"You* have no oath registered in Heaven to destroy the government, while *I* shall have the most solemn one to 'preserve, protect and defend' it." Direct and forthright throughout, he could scarcely have used words to better advantage in emphasizing his honesty and integrity.

What doubts there were pertaining to inadequacies traceable to his humble origins and his lack of formal education must in some wise have been dispelled by his clearness, his accuracy, and his freedom from the awkward expression or the simple idiom of the Western stump speaker. Lincoln had felt his inadequacies when he addressed an Eastern audience of educated men at Cooper Union and was uncomfortable. In his Inaugural, prepared for an audience representative of the whole country, he had been cautious and careful to use language that was sustained in its dignity. Seward, sometimes known for his polished expression, had given him some aid in the choice of the proper word. Lincoln accepted advice in such word changes as "acquiesce" instead of "submit," "constituted" instead of "constructed," "void" instead of "nothing," "repelled" instead of "refused," and he also accepted such a change of phrase as "imperfectly supports the law itself" for "is against the law itself." Although the changes are minor, they reflect Lin-

---

[191] *L. E. Chittenden,* Recollections of President Lincoln and His Administration *(New York: Harper and Brothers, 1904), p. 88.*

coln's desire for correctness and conciseness. On his own better judgment, he deleted the one extended metaphor that appeared in the original draft. "I am, rather for the old ship, and the chart of the old pilots," he had originally written, with some of the tang and flavor of his speech in addressing popular Western audiences. "If, however, the people desire a new, or an altered vessel, the matter is exclusively their own, and they can move in the premises, as well without as with an executive recommendation." The figure was not equal in elevation to the rest of his remarks. His final draft read simply, "I cannot be ignorant of the fact that many worthy and patriotic citizens are desirous of having the national Constitution amended. While I make no recommendation of amendments, I fully recognize the rightful authority of the people over the whole subject . . ." Such phrasing, simple in its dignity, undoubtedly was more appropriate and suited to his needs.

That Lincoln sought to control the behavior of his audience and the reader through the appropriately affective word is apparent throughout his address. There are times when even the level of specificity and concreteness, usually thought to be virtues of style, is altered in favor of the more general word or allusion. For instance, Lincoln had originally intended to say, "why may not South Carolina, a year or two hence, arbitrarily, secede from a new Southern Confederacy . . . ?" Finally, however, he avoided being specific, altering his remarks to read "why may not any portion of a new confederacy, a year or two hence, arbitrarily secede again . . . ?" Again, the ridicule in his assertion, "The Union is less perfect than before, which contradicts the Constitution, and therefore is absurd," is eliminated and reason is substituted: "The Union is *less perfect* than before the Constitution, having lost the vital element of its perpetuity." Lincoln sometimes chose the longer statement in preference to the sharp, pointed word or phrase, if by a longer expression he could avoid truculence or the pointing of an accusing finger. Such a phrase as "be on your side of the North or on yours of the South," aided considerably in creating an image of impartiality, and was to be preferred for the shorter, but divisive phrase, "be on our side or yours." The changes that Lincoln made in the direction of fullness rather than compression were designed to aid in clearness, exactness, and completeness, for the country expected him to express himself fully on the disturbing problems of the time.

The close of Lincoln's address, often cited for its poetic beauty, reflects not only his aesthetic sense, but perhaps more importantly, his power of using words to evoke images conducive to controlling response. As is very well known, Lincoln was not merely trying to be eloquent when he closed the address. He achieved eloquence and cadenced beauty through his direct attempt to be "affectionate,"

Seward having reminded him that perhaps feeling should supplement reason, and having suggested a possible conclusion:

> *I close. We are not we must not be aliens or enemies but ~~countrym~~ fellow countrymen and brethren. Although passion has strained our bonds of affection too hardly they must not ~~be broken they will not~~ I am sure they will not be broken. The mystic chords of memory which proceeding from ~~every bo~~ so many battle fields and ~~patriot~~ so many patriot graves ~~br~~ pass through all the hearts and hearths all the hearths in this broad continent of ours will yet ~~harmo~~ again harmonize in their ancient music when ~~touched as they surely~~ breathed upon again by the ~~better ange~~ guardian angel of the nation.*[192]

An image of great-heartedness, great humility, and great faith resulted when Lincoln rephrased Seward's suggestion in his own style. It was his final declaration of faith and had in it the emotional intensity that often accompanies the hoped-for but unknown. It was his final plea for a course of action befitting "friends."

Let us conclude our remarks on Lincoln's style by emphasizing that it reflected the same purposefulness that was characteristic of the arguments contained in the address. Through directness, clearness, dignity, and appropriately affective words, he sought to aid himself in achieving his ends.

One further means of persuasion may be noted, namely, that of his manner in oral presentation. Lincoln's delivery, of course, was significant chiefly to those who composed his immediate audience, and not to any great extent to the much larger audience throughout the country, except in so far as eyewitnesses and newspaper reports conveyed impressions pertaining to the character and personality of the speaker. It is undoubtedly true that Lincoln's manner contributed heavily to his effectiveness on this particular occasion. It may even be true that, had the whole country been immediately present, it would have found further grounds for trust. Ethical stature often shows itself not only in the selection of argument or the composition of words, but in those "echoes and values" that emanate from physical presence alone. "If I were to make the shortest list of the qualifications of the orator," Emerson once remarked, "I should begin with *manliness;* and perhaps it means here presence of mind."[193] It must be remembered that when Lincoln advanced to the platform to deliver his Inaugural, he did so in

---

[192] *Facsimile of the original suggestion of Seward as reprinted in* Abraham Lincoln: His Speeches and Writings, *edited by Roy P. Basler, pp. 589, 590.*

[193] "Eloquence," The Complete Works of Ralph Waldo Emerson (*New York: Sully and Kleinteich, 1875*), VIII, 123.

face of threats on his life. That he manifested little fear is apparent from practically all of the newspaper accounts of the day. The most usual observation indicated that "the great heart and kindly nature of the man were apparent in his opening sentence, in the tone of his voice, the expression of his face, in his whole manner and bearing."[194] In the judgment of many, he "gained the confidence of his hearers and secured their respect and affection."[195] Lincoln appears to have had a sense of communication, a complete awareness of what he was saying when he was saying it. His thought emerged clearly and appeared to be in no way obstructed by affectation or peculiarities of manner. With dignity and firmness coupled with mildness and humility he sought to enforce his plea by those powers that reside in personality. That they have stimulus value one can scarcely question.

Thirty-nine days after Lincoln delivered his Inaugural Address, Fort Sumter was fired upon. Civil war had begun. Lincoln had sought to save the Union by carefully reasoned argument, by regard for the feelings and rights of all the people, and by a solemn avowal of justice and integrity. That the Inaugural alone could not prevent the war is surely insufficient ground to condemn it for ineptness. "In speechmaking, as in life, not failure, but low aim, is crime."[196] There were many divisive forces, and these had gained great momentum by the time Lincoln addressed the American people. The South accepted the burden of his challenge, "In *your* hands, my dissatisfied fellow countrymen, and not in *mine,* is the momentous issue of civil war."

[194] *Chittenden,* loc. cit.
[195] Ibid., *p. 90.*
[196] *Parrish and Nichols,* op. cit., *p. 12.*

The Historical Approach

PUBLIC Address: A Study in Social and Intellectual History
by Ernest J. Wrage

In the title of a book, *Ideas Are Weapons,* Max Lerner gives to ideas a twentieth century connotation, for in this century all of the resources of man have twice comprised actual or potential materiel of warfare. The merit of the title lies in the emphasis it places upon function, although one must read beyond it to grasp the diversity of function which ideas perform. Man's capacities for thought somewhat resemble modern industrial plants which are capable of converting raw materials into either soap or bullets, of refining sugar into nutritive food or into alcohol for the manufacture of explosives. Similarly, from the biochemical processes of individual minds responding to environment may emerge ideas which serve to promote social conflict, while there are yet others, fortunately, which contribute to resolution of differences. Man's intellectual activities may result in ideas which clarify his relationships with his fellow men and to the cosmos, or in ideas which close minds against further exploration in favor of blind conformity to tradition and authority. It is axiomatic that the extant records of man's responses to the social and physical world as expressed in formulations of thought provide one approach to a study of the history of his culture. Whether we seek explanations for an overt act of human behavior in the genesis and moral compulsion of an idea, or whether we accept the view that men seek out ideas which promote their interests and justify their activities, the illuminating fact is that in either case the study of ideas provides an index to the history of man's values and goals, his hopes and fears, his aspirations and negations, to what he considers expedient or inapplicable.

The word *ideas,* therefore, is not restricted here to a description of the great and noble thoughts uttered by accredited spokesmen for the edification of old and young. It is employed in a more inclusive sense and refers widely to formulations of thought as the product and expression of social incentives, which give rise and importance now to one idea, then to another. They are viewed as the product of social environment, as arising from many levels of life, and as possessing social utility. Ideas are not here treated as entities which enjoy an independent existence and which serve as objects of contemplation by the self-avowed or occasional ascetic. While the history of ideas is un-

From *The Quarterly Journal of Speech,* XXXIII, 4 (December 1947), 451–457. Used by permission of Mrs. Naomi Wrage and the Speech Communication Association. Mr. Wrage was Professor of Speech at Northwestern University.

deniably concerned with major works in systematized thought, and with the influence of thinker upon thinker, exclusive devotion to monumental works is hopelessly inadequate as a way of discovering and assessing those ideas which find expression in the market place. Subtle intellectual fare may be very well for stomachs accustomed to large helpings of ideational substances rich in concentration; but there also is nutritional value in the aphoristic crumbs which fall into stomachs unaccustomed and unconditioned to large helpings of such fare, and the life sustained by the crumbs is not without historical interest. The force of Emerson's ideas upon the popular mind of his time, and even later, derives less from his intricate elaborations upon man and the cosmos than from his dicta on self-reliance. Moreover, ideas arise at many levels of human life and find expression in and attain force through casual opinion as well as learned discourse; and while the life span of many popularly-held ideas is admittedly short, often these "out-of-the-way" ideas thrive and emerge at higher levels of development. This extension in the conception of the history of ideas which includes more than monumental distillations of thought in philosophy, religion, literature, and science may be offensive to those of fastidious intellectual tastes, but there is increasing awareness that adequate social and intellectual history cannot be written without accounting for popular opinions, beliefs, constellations of attitudes, and the like.

I

Ideas attain history in process, which includes transmission. The reach of an idea, its viability within a setting of time and place, and its modifications are expressed in a vast quantity of documentary sources. Man's conscious declarations of thought are embodied in a mosaic of documents, in constitutions and laws, literature and song, scientific treatises and folklore, in lectures, sermons, and speeches. Of these, not the least either in quantity or value, as Curti points out, are the lectures, sermons, and speeches:

Historians of ideas in America have too largely based their conclusions on the study of formal treatises. But formal treatises do not tell the whole story. In fact, they sometimes give a quite false impression, for such writings are only a fraction of the records of intellectual history. For every person who laboriously wrote a systematic treatise, dozens touched the subject in a more or less casual fashion. Sometimes the fugitive essays of relatively obscure writers influenced the systematizers and formal writers quite as much as the works of better-known men. The influence of a thinker does not pass from one major writer to another without frequently being transformed or dissipated, or compressed in the hands of a whole series of people who responded to the thinker and his ideas. It is reasonably certain, moreover, that in the America of the early nineteenth century ephemeral writings, widely scattered as they were in pamphlets, tracts, and essays, reached a much wider audience and are often more reliable evidence of the climate of opinion than the more familiar works to which historians of ideas have naturally turned. The student of the vitality and modification of ideas may well direct his attention, then, toward out-of-the-way sermons, academic addresses, Fourth of July orations, and casual guides and essays.[1]

As a parenthetical comment, one recent study which makes extensive use of fugitive literature, particularly speeches, is Merle Curti's *The Roots Of American Loyalty,* published in 1946. But in the main, the rich vein of literature in speaking has hardly been tapped for this purpose except by the occasional prospector.

Curti's observations have germinal significance for the student of public address. They suggest an approach which is interesting for its freshness and fruitful in intellectual promise. If American life, to adopt his point of reference, is viewed through ideas historically viable, then ideas are to be studied as a body of intricate tissues, of differentiated yet related thought. While the establishment of macroscopic relationships provides the ultimate reasons for tracing out an American intellectual pattern, explorations of the parts is a necessary preliminary to this achievement. As an enterprise in scholarship, then, the first operation is one of collecting and classifying data within limited areas amenable to description and analysis. This accomplished, generalizations from the data become at once permissible and desirable, and provide a basis from which further exploration may be conducted.

It is at once apparent that the delineation of an American intellectual tradition calls for division of labor. It is not only the magnitude in task but diversity in data and in media of expression which invites specialization and varied technical skills in scholarship. There are, after all, appreciable and striking differences between the materials of hymnology and constitutional law. While students of philosophy, history, and literature are traditionally accredited as the official custodians and interpreters of intellectual history, it is the thesis of this paper that students of public address may contribute in substantial ways to the history of ideas. They possess credentials worthy of acknowledgment and interest in a type of materials germane to the object.

It has been amply treated and clearly said by others that the rhetoric

---

[1] *Merle Curti, "The Great Mr. Locke: America's Philosopher, 1783–1861,"* The Huntington Library Bulletin, *April, 1937, pp. 108–109.*

of public address does not exist for its own sake, that its value is instrumental, and that its meaning apart from an application to something is sterile. An endorsement of this doctrine leads us to an immediate recognition that the basic ingredient of a speech is its content. The transmission of this content is its legitimate function. It is a vehicle for the conveyance of ideas. It is a mode of communication by means of which something of the thought of the speaker is incorporated and expressed in language in ways which make for ready comprehension and acceptance by one or more audiences. It is for the very reason that public speeches and lectures are prepared with a listening audience in mind that they serve so admirably in a study of social thought. The full import of this point is disclosed by some comparisons.

When reporting the results of work to members of his guild, the physical scientist may confine himself to an exclusive concern with data, intricate operations, and complex thought. In preparation and presentation neither detail nor comprehensiveness needs to be sacrificed, for his discourse is not prepared with an eye to the limiting factors present in the differentiated audience. As distinguished from this highly specialized form of reporting, a public speech is a more distinctly popular medium which is useful for explaining the essence of an idea, for explaining the applicability of a particular, for establishing impressions and evoking attitudes, for direction in the more or less common affairs of men. Because speeches are instruments of utility designed in the main for the popular mind, conversely and in significant ways they bear the impress of the popular mind. It is because they are pitched to levels of information, to take account of prevalent beliefs, and to mirror tone and temper of audiences that they serve as useful indices to the popular mind.

This interaction between the individual mind of the speaker and the collective mind of the audience has long been appreciated, but for the most part this interaction has been considered in terms of its relationship to the speaker's techniques. What has happened to the ideas themselves under the impact of this interaction remains a field which is relatively unexplored in any systematic sense by students of public address. The techniques of the speakers are often highly individualized and perish with their bones; their ideas live after them. From the study of speeches may be gained additional knowledge about the growth of ideas, their currency and vitality, their modifications under the impress of social requirements, and their eclipse by other ideas with different values. Such a study of speeches belongs to what Max Lerner calls the "naturalistic approach" to the history of ideas, one which includes "not only the conditions of the creation of ideas but also the conditions of their reception, not only the impulsions behind the ideas, but also the uses to which they are put, not only the thinkers but also the popularizers, the propagandists, the opinion skill-groups, the final audience that believes or disbelieves and acts accordingly."[2]

Is not such scholarship properly confined to the professional historian? The question is dated and should be so treated. Squabbles over contested rights are hang-overs from an age of academic primogeniture. A study is to be judged by its merits, not by the writer's union card. But a more convincing argument for participation in scholarship of the history of ideas by students of public address is made apparent when we take another step in our thinking. The very nature and character of ideas in transmission is dependent upon configurations of language. The interpretation of a speech calls for complete understanding of what goes into a speech, the purpose of the speech and the interplay of factors which comprise the public speaking situation, of nuances of meaning which emerge only from the reading of a speech in the light of its setting. At this juncture a special kind of skill becomes useful, for the problem now relates directly to the craftsmanship of the rhetorician. The student who is sensitized to rhetoric, who is schooled in its principles and techniques, brings an interest, insight, discernment, and essential skill which are assets for scholarship in the history of ideas, as that history is portrayed in public speeches.

II

The prevailing approach to the history and criticism of public address appears to consist of a study of individual speakers for their influence upon history. If one may judge from studies available through publication, they fall short of that ambitious goal for reasons which are painfully apparent to anyone who has attempted to assess influence in history. Nevertheless, they do provide a defensible pattern in research which has yielded highly interesting data about prominent speakers, their speechmaking and speaking careers. Reference is made to this standard approach to public address simply as a means of establishing and clarifying some distinctions between it and the proposed method of study which concentrates upon the ideas in speeches. The differences are those of focus, of knowledge to be gained, and of procedure to be followed in investigation. While one approach is "speaker centered," the other is "idea centered." One focuses mainly upon the speaker and the speaking activity, the other upon the speech and its content. One seeks to explain factors which contributed to personal persuasion; the other yields knowledge of more general interest in terms of man's cultural strivings and heritage.

In point of procedure it should be at once apparent that there are differences involved in a study which centers, let us say, upon Henry

[2] *Max Lerner,* Ideas Are Weapons *(1940), p. 6.*

Clay as an orator and in a study which centers upon the ideas embodied in his speeches on the American System. To pursue the example, a study of the ideas in Clay's speeches is not committed to searching out the sources of his personal power with an audience, but is concerned with the doctrine of a self-contained economy as portrayed in his speeches in the perspective of that doctrine's history, from Hamilton to Matthew Carey's *Olive Branch,* to the congenial, nascent nationalism of Clay and contemporary speakers. Inasmuch as the American System is compounded of political and economic ideas, competence in handling the data of history is necessary; but it is also to be remembered that inasmuch as the ideas are projected through speeches, they are also the province of the rhetorician; that inasmuch as they are employed in speeches with the object of reaching and affecting a wide audience, the ideas are framed in a context of rhetorical necessities and possibilities. To adopt the rhetorical perspective is actually to approximate more closely a genuinely historical point of view when analyzing and interpreting speeches as documents of ideas in social history.

The possibilities for analysis in the rhetoric of ideas is illustrated in Roy P. Basler's essay on "Lincoln's Development As A Writer." The title of the essay should properly have included "And Speaker," for much of the brilliance of Basler's commentary arises from the treatment he gives the speeches.[3] Basler sets forth the basic ideas which are the essence of Lincoln's philosophy and links them to the dominant intellectual currents of Lincoln's age. He analyzes the rhetoric of Lincoln, not because he is interested in rhetoric *per se,* but because Lincoln's ideas were framed by his rhetoric, which, in turn, was profoundly affected by the exigencies present in the totality of social factors bearing upon the speaking situation. From an analysis of his rhetoric in this relationship, it is possible to come into a closer understanding of Lincoln's thought patterns and of the ideas he sought to lodge in the minds of his audiences. For instance, Basler recounts how the theme in the "House Divided" speech was carried through many stages of inference, that it underwent many modifications in order to achieve the nuances and implications which Lincoln desired. Basler concludes that "It would be difficult to find in all history a precise instance in which rhetoric played a more important role in human destiny than it did in Lincoln's speeches of 1858."[4] He speaks, of course, of the instrumental role of rhetoric as it served to crystallize the meanings which

[3] *Roy P. Basler,* Abraham Lincoln; His Speeches and Writings (*Cleveland and New York, 1946*), *pp. 1–49.*
[4] Ibid., *p. 28.*

Lincoln sought to convey. Through a masterful analysis of the rhetoric in the Gettysburg Address, Basler presents the underlying pattern of Lincoln's thought, as is suggested by a short excerpt from his treatment:

Lincoln's problem at Gettysburg was to do two things: to commemorate the past and to prophesy for the future. To do these things he took the theme dearest to his audience, honor for the heroic dead sons and fathers, and combined it with the theme nearest to his own heart, the preservation of democracy. Out of this double theme grew his poetic metaphor of birth, death, and spiritual rebirth, of the life of man and the life of the nation. To it he brought the fervor of devoutly religious belief. Democracy was to Lincoln a religion, and he wanted it to be in a real sense the religion of his audience. Thus he combined an elegiac theme with a patriotic theme, skillfully blending the hope of eternal life with the hope of eternal democracy.[5]

A speech is an agency of its time, one whose surviving record provides a repository of themes and their elaborations from which we may gain insight into the life of an era as well as into the mind of a man. From the study of speeches given by many men, then, it is possible to observe the reflections of prevailing social ideas and attitudes. Just as the speeches of Schwab and Barton, of Coolidge and Dawes (accompanied by the latter's broom-sweeping histrionics) portray the ethos of business and a negative view toward government intervention in social affairs, so do the speeches of Roosevelt and other New Dealers mark the break from the attitudes and conceptions which dominated the twenties. Both schools of thought express the social and economic values of the times. Both mirror the dominant moods of their respective audiences. The very structure, idiom, and tone of the speeches, moreover, play their parts in the delineation of those ideas. For example, the full import of Roosevelt's First Inaugural Address is not perceived without reference to the many nuances and imperatives of his rhetoric. It is in the metaphor of war and the image of the religious crusade, as well as in argument and statements of intention, that the speech articulates the inchoate feelings of the people on government's social responsibility. Similarly, from a wide investigation of sermons, lectures, and speeches related to issues, movements, and periods, might we not extend and refine our knowledge of social ideas portrayed in history? Such an attempt would constitute a kind of anthropological approach to a segment of cultural history.

[5] Ibid., p. 42.

III

Let the final argument be a practical one. Specifically, what applications may be made of this approach to public address in a university classroom? Experience has made it apparent to the writer that a course consisting only of successive case histories of individual speakers and speech-making leaves much to be desired. It certainly is open to question if an accidental chronology or arbitrary selection of orators provides a satisfactory focus and basic framework to warrant the label, "history of public address," or if it provides adequate intellectual and educational outcomes for the time expended. Interesting in its way as may be the study for its own sake of the personality, platform virtuosity, and career of an individual speaker, a mere progression of such more or less independent treatments is likely to be without secure linkage to historical processes. It is likely to result in an assortment of isolated, episodical, or even esoteric information which can make little claim to the advancement of the student's general culture.

There is more than a suggestion of antiquarianism in the whole business. We need, therefore, to provide a more solid intellectual residual. This may be realized when the focus of a course consists in the ideas communicated, in the ascertainable sources of those ideas, the historical vitality and force of the ideas, and of demonstrable refractions, modifications, or substitutions. As an adjunct to the materials of such a course, the study of the speaking careers and skills of individual speakers makes a valuable contribution. Such studies have supplementary value; but even more important is the study of the speeches themselves against a backdrop of history. Naturally, the exclusive study of speeches would result in historical distortion unless related to a larger framework of life and thought, to allied and competing ideas in the intellectual market place.

Seen against a broad and organized body of materials in intellectual and social history, the study of speeches both gives and takes on meaning in ways which contribute substantially to educational experience. Especially helpful as leads in providing background are such familiar works as Vernon L. Parrington, *Main Currents in American Thought;* Merle Curti, *The Growth of American Thought;* and Ralph H. Gabriel, *The Course of American Democratic Thought,* to mention but a few. Such literature supplies references and guidance to the main lines of thought which underlie movements and problems in American life; it brings into view not only tributaries which fed the main streams, but also rivulets of ideas which had a kind of independent existence. Speeches may be studied in relation to these movements. For example, intellectual turmoil and diluvial expression were provoked by the slavery controversy. Antislavery appeals, historians tell us, were couched in the language of personal liberty and Christian humanitarianism. Pro-slavery speakers, forced to compete upon an equally elevated plane, advanced arguments which derived from similar or equivalent ethical bases but which were interpreted in ways congenial to Southern institutional life and practice. True, the rhetoric of ideas fails to account for all the forces at work; yet a wide reading in sermons, lectures, and speeches does bring one into a deeper understanding of the basic ideational themes, variations upon the themes, and the dissonance which were a part of the controversy and contributed to ultimate settlement. When seen against a contextual backdrop, speeches become at once a means of illustrating and testing, of verifying or revising generalizations offered by other workers in social and intellectual history.

There is an implied recognition in what has been said, of a deficiency in the scholarship of public address. There is need for an organized body of literature which places speeches and speaking in proper relationship to the history of ideas. Quite apart from reasons of classroom utility, research in the ideas communicated through speeches needs doing as a means of contributing to knowledge and understanding generally. Adequate social and intellectual history cannot be written without reference to public speaking as it contributed to the ideas injected into public consciousness. But if research is to move forward, perhaps the time has arrived to explore in our individual and joint capacities the rationale, procedures, and materials by which it may be carried on. To this end, a symposium of papers which deals with these problems would help to clarify and stimulate research in public address in its relation to social and intellectual history.

The Little World of Barry Goldwater
by Ernest J. Wrage

You may wonder if this is a program on the rhetoric of contemporary politics or on the politics of contemporary rhetoricians. However provocative, I submit that my title for this paper is descriptively appropriate. For well over two years now, Barry Goldwater has made national news by riding the circuit, crying in the wilderness of contemporary complexity, recalling errant countrymen to the lost innocence of William McKinley—to a littler world spinning on a shortened axis of local government, a self-regulating economy, and a no-nonsense foreign policy that spells victory in big letters. All this for the enlargement of freedom which, he contends, has been whittled down by the welfare state and one-worldism.

From *Western Speech*, XXVII, 4 (Fall 1963), 207–215. Used by permission of Mrs. Naomi Wrage and the Western Speech Association. Mr. Wrage was Professor of Speech at Northwestern University.

In his biography of the Senator, Stephen Shadegg—the Senator's absolute alter-ego and ghoster—uses a subtitle to forge linkage between Goldwater and modernity. "Freedom is his flight-plan," says Shadegg,[1] to which I must add, into *un*reality. For surely, Barry Goldwater's world is Utopia fashioned out of nostalgia. It reminds me of a pertinent malapropism attributed to Mayor Richard Daley, hard-boiled Democratic boss of Chicago, who once exclaimed perfervidly, "What we have to do for Chicago is to restore to Chicago all those good things it never had!"[2]

Since November 6, 1962, Goldwater's little world seems to have become smaller, but for the moment, at least, he remains the most authentic popular spokesman for self-conscious conservatism in America. He must be accounted for as part of a renaissance of conservatism.

In 1949, in his presidential address to the Speech Association of America, Dean James H. McBurney, himself confessing a conservative bias, spoke critically of the disinclination of conservatives to test their credo in public forums, contenting themselves with "ceremonial chanting and cries of distress."[3] The same year, in his preface to *The Liberal Imagination,* Lionel Trilling remarked that ". . . Liberalism is not only the dominant but even the sole intellectual tradition." The impulses toward conservatism are strong, he acknowledged, but they express themselves not in ideas but in "irritable mental gestures." This is bad, he admonished prophetically for "it is just when a movement despairs of having ideas that it turns to force, which it masks in ideology."[4] Trilling wrote in December, 1949. Less than three months later, in a Lincoln Day speech at Wheeling, West Virginia, Joseph McCarthy exploited this despair by uncorking a demonology from which flowed the greatest witch hunt of our age.

The pleas of McBurney, Trilling, Clarence Randall and others, late in the 1940's, for well-articulated and responsible conservatism remain timely. But no longer does the voice of conservatism die in the throat, though it speaks in many accents. A thousand organizations promote the cause.[5] Its journals range from the scurrilous *The Cross and The Flag* to the popular *National Review* to *Modern Age* for the high-brows.

---

[1] *Stephen Shadegg,* Barry Goldwater: Freedom Is His Flight Plan (*New York, 1962*).

[2] *"Politician in Trouble: Richard Joseph Daley,"* The New York Times, *January 30, 1960, p. 11.*

[3] *James H. McBurney, "The Plight of the Conservative in Public Discussion,"* Vital Speeches of the Day, *XVI (March 1950), 343–345.*

[4] *Lionel Trilling,* The Liberal Imagination (*New York, 1950*).

[5] *Ralph E. Ellsworth and Sarah M. Harris,* The American Right Wing (*Washington, D.C.: Public Affairs Press, 1962), p. 2. This pamphlet, a report to the Fund for the Republic, contains a wealth of information about contemporary conservative groups.*

It enlists sophisticated writers such as Russell Kirk, Richard Weaver, Peter Vierek, Clinton Rossiter and others, and they have, seemingly, a guaranteed publishing outlet in the Regnery press. Frequently their thinking seems untouched by the Industrial Revolution and widespread democratization. They draw heavily on 18th Century archetypal conservatives such as Edmund Burke and John Adams and their doctrine, borrowing Burke's belief in the Divine Tactic or Providential Hand in History, ultimately turns into a mystique, largely unintelligible to a modern mind that is essentially secular and pragmatic. Even so, they are undeniably thinkers intent on fashioning a respectable conservative doctrine. But these are not the conservatives who command the Great Audience. That award goes to the politicos and pulpit pitchmen.

And what a variety on the popular spectrum! As classified by Clinton Rossiter, himself a worthy conservative, we have Robert Welch, the maladjusted conservative; Barry Goldwater, the non-adjusted; Eisenhower, the adjusted; and Rockefeller, the over-adjusted type.[6] You may play the game for yourself, pegging such names as Richard Nixon, George Romney, Ayn Rand, John Tower, Clarence Manion, J. Bracken Lee, John Flynn, Carl McIntire, Fred Schwarz, William F. Buckley, Jr., Ev and Charley of show fame, and others that come to mind.

How may we account for this flowering, or, in many instances, rank growth? The full explanation is complicated, to be sure, but I suggest three points that underscore a rhetoric of frustration.

1. For a generation, conservatives have stood largely discredited before the bar of public opinion. During the New Deal Era their cherished abstractions such as the Constitution, sanctity of contract, and the American way of life fell on deaf ears, and though they organized as "The American Liberty League," they were thumpingly rejected. Why? Before the touted "forgotten man" of the Hoover era stepped into the polling booth, FDR had only to take to the air waves and invite him to make the empirical test: "Are you better off than you were last year?" Roosevelt asked in his best man-to-man tones. "Have you lost any of your rights or Constitutional freedom of action and choice?"[7] The empiricism of these two questions goes far to explain both New Deal and Fair Deal successes and therefore the impotency of conservative inducements and rhetoric.

2. Two revolutions within a generation, from rugged individualism to the welfare state, from isolation to planetary involvements, have en-

---

[6] *Quoted on "Thunder on the Right," a CBS television documentary, February 22, 1962.*

[7] *For example, see Franklin D. Roosevelt, "Fireside Chat on the Accomplishments of the New Deal," in Ernest J. Wrage and Barnet Baskerville, eds., Contemporary Forum (New York, 1962), pp. 162–167.*

gulfed us. Both were responses to shock—to crisis in capitalism and to World War II and its aftermath. It's not easy to abandon deep-set convictions, values, and myths and to supplant them with improvisation as as a mode of life, particularly when a not-so-brave world keeps on trembling in ever deepening shadows of violence and extinction. Unrelieved tension and the inability of conservatives to achieve the power that confers responsibility made plausible the devil theory of history. Thus McCarthy exploited the moment, and with his theory of the great conspiracy—the twenty years of treason he so loudly alleged—succeeded for half a decade in misdirecting conservatism.

3. Contemporary conservatives remain perplexed on how to regain power. They regard the Republican Party, though not perfect, as the best vehicle for the return trip. But under whose theory of propulsion? Under Landon and his "New Frontier" (Landon's use of the caption antedated by a quarter of a century Kennedy's apparently unwitting appropriation of it), and more so under Willkie and Dewey, Republicans competed with Democrats on liberal, domestic and international fronts, inviting jeers of me-tooism. Robert Taft said flatly that the business of an opposition is to oppose, but Taft was jettisoned in favor of Ike, a war hero and popular president, but a political novice who proved unable to redeem his party. From an old-line conservative's angle of vision, the Republican record is one of bald opportunism which, to appropriate a line from one of Saroyan's characters, had "No foundations, all down the line."

More recently, Republicans have been guided by the Ev and Charlie formulas, which are essentially technical: Improve city organizations, find popular candidates, lift the party's face.[8] Still more recently, we have the Goldwater prescription—a dramatic, quasi-religious crusade with a broad-based ideological appeal highlighting ancient verities and immutable principles of the kind that are intended to send hearts soaring—in both parties.

An Arizona storekeeper, Barry Goldwater was first elected to the Senate in 1952, a Republican in a nominally Democratic state. He's a man of considerable substance and small learning. He flunked out of public high school in his freshman year, graduated from a military academy with distinction in military subjects only, and failed to complete his freshman year at the University of Arizona.[9] Evidently though, the Senator is not at all embarrassed in making *ex cathedra* pronouncements on the content and methods of contemporary education,

[8] For a perceptive analysis of the conservative's political plight in today's party struggles, see Russell Baker, "Growing Dilemma of the G.O.P.," The New York Times Magazine, April 8, 1962, p. 30 ff.

[9] Shadegg, op. cit., pp. 89–92.

publicly deploring as he does the domination of schools by the progressivism of John Dewey and his disciples.

Goldwater's early political capital consisted of a family name prominent in Arizona, a war record, and a wide acquaintance with Genus Arizonus gained through chatty talks while showing colored slides on Indians of the Southwest.[10] He came to national attention through televised hearings on labor racketeering, his bitter-ender speech on the Kennedy-Ervin Labor Bill, and his opposition to the Rockefeller-Nixon "New York Munich pact" at the time of the 1960 Republican Convention. The big reception accorded him by the Convention turned him into circuit rider in behalf of his brand of political fundamentalism and won for him the sobriquet of Mr. Conservative. Although he began to taper off shortly before the 1962 elections and expects to cut back drastically on his speaking in 1963, he has been averaging more than 35 speaking invitations per day at his peak.[11]

Regarded by the movie-minded as up to JFK's standards, Goldwater's matinee possibilities inspired Hubert Humphrey's quip: "Barry is under contract to 18th Century Fox." An authentic frontiersman—Arizona is our 48th state—Goldwater really sounds like just plain folks. His slightly twangy, dehydrated voice suggests that of cowboys on TV westerns. He is all reasonableness, even compassion as he urges private charity for the poor. Although the point is often made that he is no orator[12] (meaning no demagogue, I presume), as a speaker he succeeds in making an hour pass quickly, though the residue, in cool detachment of afterthought, seems skimpy and threadbare. With special attention to overtones and with benefit of analogues, let me suggest the affective components of his message that are calculated to stimulate and weld a community of conservative sentiment.

At bottom the Goldwater message is programmatic: A staged withdrawal of the federal government on the domestic front and an adventuresome foreign policy that he calls peace through victory. But however fundamental these hard elements of his credo, it is impossible to make a *crusade* today simply out of the materials of Social Darwinism, laissez-faire economics, and pre-nuclear military thinking. Surely then the *ultimate goal* must transcend mundane matters, and it does. In the Senator's words, "Conservatism holds the key to national salvation.

---

[10] Robert Sheehan, "Arizona Fundamentalist," Fortune, LXIII (May 1961), 137–140.

[11] For an interpretation of Goldwater's reduction in his speechmaking see Robert D. Novak, "Boost for Rocky Seen as Goldwater Curtails Nationwide Politicking," The Wall Street Journal, September 14, 1962, p. 1.

[12] Goldwater's most recent biographer is among those who downgrade his oratorical abilities. See Jack Bell, Mr. Conservative: Barry Goldwater (Garden City, N.Y., 1962).

. . ."[13] Now salvation is an eternal matter and nothing to trifle with. It is achieved by zealous pursuit of correct principles governing the nature of man, society, and the state. As the conservative sees things, the uniqueness of each individual refutes the liberal's passion for egalitarianism, since Nature and Nature's Author have made differentiation among the species a first principle. In the conservative philosophy, attention to economics is only a means to promote the individualism required for the development of the whole man; conversely, the liberal's ideal of a collectivized economy fosters gross materialism, wars with Nature, and ultimately destroys man's integrity and individuality. Says the conservative: The true role of the state is to extend freedom consonant with social order. The liberal, he contends, wittingly or not, propounds the ". . . first principle of totalitarianism; that the State is competent to do all things and is limited in what it actually does only by the will of those who control the State."[14]

If the polarities here seem distended and the conservative view somewhat rarefied, let me remind that the Senator is preaching salvation, and you don't equivocate about that. When pushed, in private interviews,[15] Goldwater can "er" and "ah" with the best of them, or back off with a "Well, damned if I know," but on the platform the choices before us emerge with the sharp clarity of copybook maxims: It's freedom or slavery; victory or appeasement. His impact, observers agree, derives basically from his reductionist views, his ability to make value judgments pass as facts, the simplicity and coherence of the whole presentation, and the religious cast of his rhetoric.

Goldwater offers sanctions. Conservatism, Emerson once remarked, is always plagued by a certain meanness. Goldwater offers a loftier version. The principles of conservatism, he asserts, piously echoing Burke and Kirk, ". . . are derived from the nature of man, and from the truths that God has revealed about His creation."[16] And to refute the charge that conservatism is an ill-concealed rationalization for acquisitiveness, the Senator insists that the ultimate object of individualism and competition is character-building. Which, of course, is the message of Andrew Carnegie, William Graham Sumner, Russell Conwell, and Horatio Alger —heroes all in the heyday of Social Darwinism.

As with all revealed Truths, those of conservatism are in contest with diabolism. Whereas McCarthy spoke darkly of traitors, Goldwater

[13] Barry Goldwater, The Conscience of a Conservative (*Shepherdsville, Kentucky, 1960*), Foreword. *This tract, which did so much to spread Goldwater's conservative philosophy, is largely derived from his speeches and broadcasts.*
[14] Ibid., p. 16.
[15] *For a brilliantly written account of his interview with Goldwater, see Gore Vidal, "A Liberal Meets Mr. Goldwater," Life, L (June 9, 1961), 106–118.*
[16] Goldwater, op. cit., Foreword.

speaks of dupes, pacificists, socialists, or whatever you call them—trailing off, as he does, into vagueness. Goldwater gives greater stress to the pervasive presence of insidious ideas, inveighing against those that sap our integrity—ideas like progressive education and welfare statism—and these must be countered by the special sanity of conservatives.

And Goldwater offers redemption for all. You and I, he says in effect, must accept our portion of guilt for abandoning traditional ways of thought, then hurries on to embrace extreme Arminianism.[17] Redemption is possible for Democrats (who vote too) as well as for Republican backsliders, and it can be achieved by returning to old-time political and economic thought of the post-Appomattox period.

If there is a theological cast to the Senator's political fundamentalism, as there is, what happens to the religious purity of conservatism on the campaign trail? Goldwater, like every practical politician, has been forced to come to terms with an illogical party system, based not on ideology, but on blocs of interest. "Let us be done with all this talk about hyphenated Republicans," I heard him say in the 1962 congressional campaign. "I don't care if he's a Rockefeller Republican, a Nixon Republican, or a Goldwater Republican. I don't care what his color is, as long as he is Republican, can get himself elected, and has strength enough to stand up in the Congress to shout 'here'!" This is purity of principle? Apparently, Goldwater relies heavily on the human will to believe, and on the theory that once the image of Mr. Conservative is set through headlines and speeches, it will safely weather compromises and changes of campaigns. And he may be right. I do know though that some rightists already despair of him.

As indeed, he despairs of them—at least the Far Right. From the Ultras—the men of fevered brain, hot eye, and spittle-caked lips—Goldwater seems to recoil aesthetically. But except for extreme spoilers and outriders, the conclusion is inescapable that Goldwater and the Ultras end up at approximately the same point and with the same program. Goldwater's problem then is to retain their support while escaping the opprobrium that attaches to them. He is edgy when questioned, but he struggles to speak well of many Birchers, especially Arizona Birchers, while opposing Robert Welch. In short, Goldwater stands staunchly for a decapitated Birch Society.

In this age of the personality cult, the problem of bucking and eventually displacing the Establishment, headed by a popular President, is

[17] *For an example of this pitch, see Goldwater's speech to the American National Cattlemen's Association, January 29, 1960, in A. G. Heinsohn, Jr., ed., Anthology of Conservative Writing in the United States, 1932–1960 (Chicago, 1962), pp. 205–210.*

a tough one for any critic even when aligned with Zeus and the cosmic forces. Interestingly, the popularity of Kennedy and Goldwater, though not to be equated, is the product of an "image" each has assiduously projected. But here the President has the advantage of exposure that goes with his office. Hence, Goldwater, with some modifications, has shrewdly resorted to a tactic of early British parliamentarians, in an age when critics of the monarch were understandably circumspect. His or her majesty can do no wrong, courtiers were wont to say, but he or she can be misled by scheming ministers. Goldwater seems wary when stalking Kennedy but confident and abandoned when cracking the skulls of men who surround and mislead the popular young president—Arthur Schlesinger, Jr., Ted Sorenson, Walter Heller, Adlai Stevenson—that crowd. And he can always extract a good laugh plus a round of applause from wisecracks about Robert Kennedy's "splashmanship."

But the greatest obstacle of all to Goldwater's success is the ever-accelerating pace of our age, the adaptations it demands, and the pragmatic philosophy of Americans. The instinct for survival is strong, and only a dolt will fail to roll with the punch. Mind you, I do not minimize the essential role of enlightened conservatives in our political life even in, or particularly because of this age of incredible flux; but Goldwater's "was-ism," his crusade to recover a lost world to which he assigns an illusory coherence and relevance, does seem a quixotic adventure in the extreme, though not without consequences however difficult they are to assess. What has been the feedback to his campaigning that has kept him relentlessly at it? Is the Presidency the inducement? Since Arizona is not a good presidential launching pad and since he has no strong urban support, this seems to be an unreasonable ambition for Goldwater to entertain. But then again, who knows the power of this lure on the Senator? Is he seeking to enhance his influence in Congress? A notorious absentee, the Senator hasn't had much time to give to congressional business, and by all accounts his colleagues remain unimpressed by his efforts. Unlike Robert Taft, who was skilled in the art of legislative action, Goldwater has made negligible contributions. Does he hope to found a new party or accomplish a realignment of old parties along ideological lines? There is no chance of either result in the foreseeable future, and he knows this.

Though they are unmeasurable, traces of Goldwater's influence are best perceived or sensed in a public mood that he has worked hard to develop through his speaking campaign. Hard core conservatives whose car bumpers carry stickers such as "I am a Conservative" or "Goldwater in 1964," offer the clearest indication of his catalytic influence. Apparently he has also had some success in stimulating a revival of conservatism among college students. But the full measure of Goldwater's impact on the public mind lurks in the lower levels of consciousness where we cannot probe. In what ways and to what extent has he enlarged the anxieties and guilt of those who, though not enrolled in the camp of the selfconscious conservatives, fear we are plunging down history's highway marked catastrophe? Uncertain, fearful, and frustrated, the public is understandably vulnerable to a message fashioned by an attractive United States Senator, out of primitive economics, folk mythology, and religiosity. Goldwater's sharp dichotomies put things on the line, offering a clean-cut choice and inducement for the unsophisticated listener. Even professing liberals have been known to voice grudging admiration that betrays their own uneasiness: "You have to admit you know where Barry stands." Who can say, for example, to what extent the widespread approval of Kennedy's essentially unilateral power play in the Cuban crisis is attributable to Goldwater's conditioning of the public mind?

Admittedly, we are groping as we try to fathom the depth of the Senator's impact on our times. We can point with confidence to him, however, as the most conspicuous, peripatetic spokesman of conservatism today, and we may safely credit him with being its foremost moodmaker by intensifying popular nostalgia for the world of yesteryear.

The Experiential Perspective

N the introductory essay to this book, we cited Thomas Kuhn's notions of paradigm and the breakdown of faith in paradigm as accounting for the historical pattern of science. We have adapted these notions to twentieth-century rhetorical criticism, and have described and illustrated a traditional perspective. Now we shall try to account for what appears to be a breakdown of faith in the paradigm.

In the 1940s and 1950s a few voices were raised decrying the traditional approach to rhetoric and communication. The General Semanticists were the most vocal early group of protesters.[1] However, not until the 1960s could one say that a serious break from traditional rhetoric and criticism had developed. Edwin Black's *Rhetorical Criticism: A Study in Method*[2] stands out as the book that announced the end of the neo-Aristotelian hegemony.

Interesting evidence of the shift can be derived from studying Barnet Baskerville's bibliographical essay "Selected Writings on the Criticism of Public Address." To the essay, first published in 1957, Baskerville added an "Addendum, 1967."[3] The contrast of the two essays is informative.

In 1957 Baskerville testified to "an abundance of critical literature on speaking" without "a corresponding interest in discussing the act of criticism itself." Throughout the essay he clearly implied that the traditional neo-Aristotelian and historical modes dominated criticism. But a decade later he wrote, "it is probably not inaccurate to observe that we have more distinguished essays *on* criticism than essays *in* criticism" [emphasis in the original].[4] The shift in emphasis was not brought about by a decrease in the number of essays in criticism but by an outpouring of articles on the shortcomings of existing work and recommendations for new directions. The shift in emphasis from the application of an accepted theory to speculation about acceptable theory is consistent with Kuhn's description of a breakdown of faith in a paradigm.

Reasons for a loss of faith are always complex, but perhaps we can identify a few of the interrelated causes of the break from a well-established tradition.

---

[1] See, for example, Irving Lee, "Four Ways of Looking at a Speech," The Quarterly Journal of Speech, XXVIII, 2 (April 1942), 148–155.

[2] Edwin B. Black, Rhetorical Criticism: A Study in Method, New York, Macmillan, 1965.

[3] Baskerville's essay first appeared in Western Speech (Spring 1957) and is reprinted together with the "Addendum, 1967" in Thomas R. Nilsen (ed.), Essays on Rhetorical Criticism, New York, Random House, 1968.

[4] Ibid., pp. 174 and 184.

First, providing a comprehensive rhetorical criticism as outlined by Wichelns is a challenge that few critics have met successfully. In practice, critics developed many shortcuts—providing only an historical analysis, focusing on a few Aristotelian topics, and being descriptive only—which reduced the satisfactoriness of the method. Many critics who have decried traditional criticism have objected actually to its incomplete application.

A second, and deeper, reason for the breakdown lies in a growing agreement that a speaker (or writer or publicist) is as much a result of cultural forces as he is an active participant in forming these forces. The critic, then, becomes interested in the cultural force itself, looking at discourse as something that permeates various sources yet is larger and more pervasive than any one of or all the sources. Thus, the traditional speaker orientation proves inadequate as the speaker recedes in the critic's interest and the socio-politico-economic environment as a source of rhetorical potency increases.

A third tendency of critics to break with the traditional perspective springs from the recognition that meaning is not inherent—put there through the intentions of sources—in messages; rather, meaning is interpreted from every response to the message and its concomitants. The critic, then, becomes aware of himself as an interpreter of events in which he is interested. Further, he is aware of the multitude of focuses possible. Any picture he presents will be but one of several possibilities. Such a line of reasoning does not imply that one interpretation is just as good as another; the question is not central to this tendency. Rather, the critic must ask himself what unique insight he can give into the phenomena that attract his concern. The result of his work must justify itself. In short, to borrow a phrase from the psychohistorian, Robert Jay Lifton, the critic becomes aware of "an ever expanding use of the self as one's research instrument."[5]

The fourth reason we shall give is simply an amalgam of the second and third: a greater concern for context and process. The complex interaction of speaker, audience, and context is what interests many critics today. Consistent with this range of interacting forces, since the critic views the rhetorical act as a continuing process, he is more likely to be interested in the extended campaign or political movement as a focus for his study. Initially, critics attempted to adapt the traditional method to their expanded interest, but soon many began to look elsewhere for more appropriate theory and a new perspective.

The break of faith in the traditional paradigm has been neither smooth nor complete. For several decades in fits and starts, but with increasing frequency, the field of rhetorical theory and criticism has

---

[5] History and Human Survival, *New York, Random House, 1970, p. 19.*

seemed chaotic, with many criticizing the traditional methods and few establishing sensible patterns as alternatives. However, we believe that a few central tendencies that describe fresh perspectives, have begun to emerge.

Roughly, we see the break with traditional criticism going in two directions. The direction we call experiential will be described in this chapter; the other direction, in the following chapter. The sequence is arbitrary and does not imply a temporal or a logical order. Both tendencies are general, but we believe they are distinct from traditional criticism and from one another.

Characteristics of the Experiential Perspective

Rejecting, consciously or unconsciously, traditional rhetorical criticism, many critics have taken themselves and their own perceptions as a basis for their work. The critic takes the interactions of the socio-politico-economic environment and the rhetorical forces as infinite and believes that the mind and experience must be drawn on creatively to form coherent views of the phenomena of discourse. Of course, this perspective entails assumptions that are different from those of traditional criticism.

First, from this perspective society is viewed as being in a continual state of process or change. Thus any statement the critic makes to describe or evaluate discourse must be quite tentative, since that discourse is a part of an ever-shifting reality. Interested in relationships, the experiential critic begins to understand that relationships are most subject to change. His tentativeness goes well beyond normal scholarly reserve; he holds no theory as absolute and believes that all rules can be disregarded if the circumstances warrant. The experiential critic does not see process simply as a cycle, which would imply that the discarded principles can be reclaimed. Instead, he is likely to see each day and its experiences as unique, requiring critical insight to understand the skein of passing phenomena and, especially, to act wisely in the face of changing circumstances.

Second, the experiential critic, in contrast to the traditional critic, believes that an infinite number of concepts, strategies, and perspectives are available for the study of the rhetorical act; and he believes that a close interaction between the critic and the act itself is necessary for the selection of the correct concepts, strategies, and perspectives for criticism. As the world is in a state of process, so is rhetorical theory. Thus fresh concepts and strategies, as well as different combinations of the old, must evolve if the critic is to do his work well.

A third assumption characteristic of the experiential critic follows from the understanding of both rhetoric and criticism as being interpretations of phenomena. This means that any critical vocabulary, in fact, any system of symbolizing, is arbitrarily established and does not reflect merely an external reality. Experiential critics are as likely as any others to be concerned about maintaining a close word-thought-thing relationship, because only through language can they communicate their interpretations and evaluations. However, they are especially sensitive to the impact that the arbitrary process of selecting a symbol can have on the perceptive process. The word-thought-thing relationship is reciprocal. Not only does the referent influence the selection of the word but the word influences the understanding of what is referred to. Thus, the experiential critic is likely to stress the arbitrary nature of all interpretations of phenomena.

Clearly, the experiential stance obligates the critic to be eclectic in his method, and he is likely to respond warmly to statements such as the following by the movie critic Pauline Kael:

I believe we respond most and best to work in any art form (and to other experience as well) if we are pluralistic, flexible, relative in our judgments, if we are eclectic. But this does not mean a scrambling and confusion of systems. Eclecticism is not the same as a lack of scruple; eclecticism is the selection of the best standards and principles from various systems of ideas. It requires more orderliness to be a pluralist than to apply a single theory . . . criticism is exciting because you must use everything you are and everything you know that is relevant. . . .[6]

The ideal eclecticism may seldom be attained, but then ideals generally are strived for rather than reached.

We believe that the experiential perspective manifests two subordinate strains. One we call simply the "eclectic"; the other is a special sort of eclecticism, which we call the "sociocultural-psychological." Because uses of the eclectic approach are so varied, we have chosen two pairs of essays to illustrate it.

The first pair is by Lawrence W. Rosenfield. In his theoretical essay, "The Anatomy of Critical Discourse," Rosenfield responds to the "ferment in rhetorical criticism" by challenging "critics to formulate more carefully their goals and methods." In his attempt at such a formulation, he establishes the critic as an "expert-spectator" who has numerous methodological alternatives open to him; it is the critic's responsibility to bring order out of the confusion of critical methods.

In "A Case Study in Speech Criticism: The Nixon-Truman Analog," Rosenfield demonstrates one way in which the eclectic critic may apply his art and, at the same time, develop rhetorical theory through its ap-

[6] *I Lost It at the Movies, Boston, Little, Brown, 1964, p. 309.*

plication. He analyzes Nixon's "Checkers Speech" and Truman's defense of his decisions in the Harry Dexter White case in an effort to develop a theory of effective strategies for speeches of apology. This inductive approach to theory building requires the critic's experience and judgment as the starting points in the analysis of the rhetorical act.

The second pair of essays illustrating the theory and application of eclecticism includes Wayne Brockriede's "Dimensions of the Concept of Rhetoric" and Wayne Brockriede and Robert L. Scott's "Khrushchev's 1959 American Tour." Brockriede's essay parallels Rosenfield's theoretical work in that it is concerned with a system of dimensions for the study of rhetorical communication. In the process of setting forth five assumptions implicit in establishing a system and discussing their implications, he identifies major elements that an eclectic critic may treat, but he recognizes, at least implicitly, the uniqueness of each criticism and the importance of the critic's task in selecting a specific focus. The essay by Brockriede and Scott demonstrates one application of the pattern.

What we call the sociocultural-psychological approach (a special case of eclecticism) is typified by the critical decision to communicate an insight into a given rhetorical act through the use of a nonrhetorical concept or theory as the organizing feature of the criticism. Many rhetorical critics have used Freudian psychology or Hegelian dialectic as a basis for the organization and analysis of their criticism. Almost any theory, for example, Toynbee's theory about the stages of civilization or Turner's "frontier thesis," might offer possibilities to such a critic. Essentially, the sociocultural-psychological critic develops an extended analogy, which he finds heuristic in a given case.

Two essays by Kenneth Burke are used to illustrate the theory and application of a sociocultural-psychological approach. Burke's critical career illustrates an astounding variety of approaches, and his "dramatistic" approach, familiar to many rhetoricians, will be presented later in this book. His essays, "Mind, Body, and the Unconscious" and "The Rhetoric of Hitler's 'Battle,' " are excellent examples of Freudian theory and application in rhetorical criticism.

We have argued that what we call experiential criticism represents a break with the traditional paradigm, and we believe that the essays that follow will help clarify the nature and potentialities of the experiential perspective. In Chapter 4 we shall explain and illustrate with further essays another direction in the break of faith in the traditional perspective.

The Eclectic Approach

THE Anatomy of Critical Discourse
by Lawrence W. Rosenfield

The recent ferment in rhetorical criticism generated by Professor Black's provocative *Rhetorical
Criticism: A Study in Method* challenges critics to
formulate more carefully their goals and methods.
The attempt to raise critical procedures from an *ad
hoc* status to something more systematic is not
new,[1] but, at least among rhetorical critics, it seems
today to hold a place of special interest.

The discussion of some of the logical features of criticism contained
in this essay responds to the call for a more formal understanding of
the critical act. It is an effort to abstract the implicit assumptions of
those whom we would clearly want to call critics, to consider the ways
in which it would make sense for an ordinary but responsible user of
the English language to talk about the behavior of critics and about
their products (criticism).

It is the contention of this essay that criticism is most sensibly conceived of as a special form of reason-giving discourse. The nature of
reason-giving in criticism becomes intelligible if we treat four particular questions concerning criticism: (1) What do we commonly mean
when we call someone a "critic"? (2) What features of criticism distinguish it from other intellectual endeavors? (3) What kinds of questions does criticism seek to answer? (4) By what modalities (formulae)
are reasons produced in criticism? Answers to these four questions,
and hence support for the central assertion, constitute the bulk of this
study.[2] Let us begin by raising the first question and asking of whom
we are talking when we speak of "the critic."

Whenever the word "critic" comes up in conversation, a variety of
images is liable to come to mind. Some think of the book reviewer or
the drama critic for a newspaper. Others, who equate "critic" with
"carper," are reminded of a sour, negative individual who cannot be
pleased. Still others (particularly if they are conversant with too many

From *Speech Monographs*, XXV, 1 (March 1968), 50–69. Used by permission of the author and the Speech Communication Association. Mr. Rosenfield is Professor of Speech at the University of Wisconsin, Madison.

[1] *Cf. L. H. Levy,* Psychological Interpretation *(New York, 1963), p. 30; R. Mc-
Keon, "The Philosophic Bases of Art and Criticism,"* Critics and Criticism,
Ancient and Modern, *ed. R. S. Crane (Chicago, 1952), pp. 147–175; L. Thons-
sen and A. C. Baird,* Speech Criticism *(New York, 1948).*

[2] *The reader should beware of confusing the remarks made in this essay
about the nature of criticism with handbook directions on how to do criticism
or with empirical descriptions of how criticism is done. The aim here is simply
to offer a topology which suggests the characteristic formal relationships
normally encountered by critics.*

Master's theses in public address) may imagine that "the speech critic" is a kind of reporter of public address in history.[3] Clearly, common usage has made the term so vague as to be practically meaningless. Is it possible to restrict the meaning of "critic" by adopting semantic boundaries which enable us to distinguish the legitimate critics from those for whom the label represents simply encomium (or invective)? To do so we would need to ascertain what actions we may ordinarily expect of one who is fulfilling the office of critic. If we investigate what I have chosen to call the "critical posture," or the stance habitually assumed by one who is fulfilling the logical requirements of critic, we can reach some consensus as to the behavior of the critic; we will then be in a better position to understand "criticism" itself. In order to clarify what is meant here, it may be helpful to draw a rough comparison between events discussed by critics and those events we commonly call "athletic." We shall discover that in the main the critical posture resembles the "spectator" half of an agent-spectator dichotomy.[4]

First of all, it is easy enough to understand that some sporting events are not only played but are observed as well—by individuals we call "spectators." And it is common that these spectators, if they are genuine fans, do more than simply purchase a ticket of admission so that they may sit in proximity to the athletic activity. They will also devote a certain time and effort to contemplating and discussing the events they observe. That is to say, the role of the spectator often entails reflection and communication about the athletic events. For instance, the baseball fan may attend winter Hot Stove meetings where particular plays will be recalled and mulled over; likewise, the Monday Morning Quarterbacks derive a certain satisfaction from assembling to debunk the maneuvers executed in recent football games.

This same quality of spectatorship seems to be common among those whom we might call fans of aesthetic events, whether their particular "sport" be painting or public communication.[5] One characteristic

---

[3] *Cf. E. G. Bormann,* Theory and Research in the Communicative Arts *(New York, 1965), pp. 227–238, for a discussion of the confusion which often arises between the role of historian and that of critic.*

[4] *Cf. N. Smart, "Sense and Reference in Aesthetics,"* British Journal of Aesthetics, *III (October 1963), 363–366; L. W. Beck, "Agent, Actor, Spectator and Critic,"* The Monist, *XLIX (April 1965), 167–182; D. Van de Vate, Jr., "Disagreement as a Dramatic Event,"* The Monist, *XLIX (April 1965), 248–261.*

[5] *Nothing esoteric is meant by "aesthetic." I intend only to convey the notion that the logical conditions mentioned here apply to the full range of interests open to the critic: dramatic productions, musical performances, traditional "fine art," as well as to orations and political dialogues. "Aesthetics" is derived from the Greek* aisthetikos *(of sense perception), and I use the term to suggest that the phenomena which provoke discussion by spectators are of the order which manifest themselves to the perceptions.*

of the rhetorical critic, then, is his interest in observing and discussing instances of rhetorical discourse, be they speeches, essays, or advertisements, from the vantage of the spectator.

Another characteristic which critics share with at least some sports fans is that both show an appreciation for the execution of the event or object.[6] The involvement of some fans is limited to being loyal followers of a favorite team; they are mainly concerned to share in the exaltation of the home team's victories. For such "part-time" fans, the outcome of a contest is of paramount interest. True enthusiasts, however, seldom gather merely to report the results of games; they do not confine their comments to the immediate, utilitarian aspects of athletic events. Such fans derive satisfaction from watching a film replay of a game whose final score they already know, a satisfaction we may label as appreciation. This appreciation, whether in the fan or the critic, is not inherently related to enthusiasm or suspense over outcome.

A third similarity between the posture of the critic and that of the athletic fan is that heightened appreciation (and hence increased satisfaction or pleasure) accompanies increased knowledge of the events or objects observed. The football fan who knows more than the formal rules of the game (e.g., understands the tactics of blocking assignments and the relative merits of the T-formation and the single wing) derives a satisfaction from second-guessing the coach which the less informed "rooter for the home team" misses. In other words, consciousness of artistic principles contributes to appreciation.

A final commonality follows from the notion of heightened appreciation. Some spectators, because of especially fine training or acute sensitivity, attain the status of "experts." In the athletic sphere such persons are often hired to act as sportscasters and sports-writers, and in the aesthetic realm they may be called upon to act as "critics" in giving reviews of books, plays, and the like. However, their titles do not derive from the fact that they are appointed or paid to perform these tasks. Rather, it is because of their competence that they are asked to assume the critic's office. An expert can be an amateur and still be a fine sports analyst or critic. What matters is exceptional understanding. Accordingly, "critical posture" refers to *the capacity a person has to act as an expert commentator,* and the critic, if he is nothing else, must be one who is capable of fulfilling this role.

Simple *capacity* to render commentary is not yet criticism. The

[6] *The notion of execution should not be confused with the idea of intent. The football pass may have been an accident and still have been well executed. "Skill in execution" is not synonymous with "doing what the creator intended." Cf. M. Eshleman, "Aesthetic Experience, The Aesthetic Object and Criticism," The Monist, L (April 1966), 281–291.*

expert-spectator who relishes the events he observes but does not relate his appreciation to others is not a critic, for "criticism" normally refers to the critic's verbal commentary on the event. Criticism is therefore the special variety of discourse which results when a person who has adopted a critical posture makes assertions, i.e., statements by an expert about "the way things are."[7] How then may we distinguish critical discourse from the general range of assertive discourse?

One procedure would be to examine several instances of discourse which we would definitely wish to call criticism and seek to discover its typical features. I refer the reader to two short essays dealing with a speech delivered by General Douglas MacArthur to a joint session of Congress (and through direct broadcast, to the nation) on April 19, 1951. The first essay is by journalist Richard Rovere, the second by Herbert Wichelns, a professor of speech.[8] Let them represent clear cases of discourse we would ordinarily consider rhetorical criticism. What characteristics make them intuitively admissible as criticism?

Richard H. Rovere

As a literary critic and political observer, I view the speech solely from the literary and political points of view. I am not qualified to criticize oratory or elocution.

As a piece of composition, the speech seemed to me a good deal but not a great deal better than the general run of public prose in the United States today. MacArthur has eloquence of a kind, but it strikes me as a rather coarse eloquence. He never shades his meanings, never introduces a note of humor, never gives the feeling that he is one man, only one, addressing himself to other men. His language is never flat and bloodless; neither is it flabby and loose-jointed, as so much writing of this sort is. But to me there is rather a fetid air about it. It does not leave me with the impression that a cool and candid mind has been at

---

[7] *This places literary and rhetorical critics in the peculiar position of producing verbal objects as comment on other verbal objects (e.g., novels, plays, speeches, etc.), so that both types of critic are in fact engaged in producing discourse about discourse. Cf. A. Hillbruner, "Criticism as Persuasion," The Southern Speech Journal, XXXVIII (Summer 1963), 260–267; E. Black, "Moral Values and Rhetorical Criticism," lecture delivered at University of Wisconsin, July 12, 1965; Thonssen and Baird, pp. 13–14.*

[8] *Both essays are drawn from F. W. Haberman, "General MacArthur's Speech: A Symposium of Critical Comment," Quarterly Journal of Speech, XXXVII (October 1951), 321–331. They are reprinted in C. C. Arnold, D. Ehninger, and J. C. Gerber, The Speaker's Resource Book (Chicago, 1961), pp. 283–286. Cf. also P. Wylie, "Medievalism and the MacArthurian Legend," ibid., XXXVII (December 1951), 473–478; P. R. Beall, "Viper-Crusher Turns Dragon-Slayer," ibid., XXXVIII (February 1952), 51–56; K. R. Wallace, "On the Criticism of the MacArthur Speech," ibid., XXXIX (February 1953), 69–74; M. H. Nichols, Rhetoric and Criticism (Baton Rouge, La., 1963), pp. 68–69.*

work on difficult matters of universal concern. Instead, it leaves me with the impression that a closed and in a sense a rather frantic mind has been at work to the end of making an appeal to history—not neglecting to use any of the rulebook hints on how to do it. I think not of history but of second-rate historian as I read the speech.

Form and content are, if not inseparable, very closely related. Politically, MacArthur's speech seemed extremely weak to me. This is not, I think, because I am opposed to his politics; I believe he could have made out a much stronger case for himself. But he never came to grips with the issues. For example, he wanted to have it that he was being persecuted for "entertaining" his particular views. This, of course, is rubbish. He got into trouble not for the political and military views he entertained (no doubt he was right in saying they were entertained by many of his colleagues) but for seeking to usurp the diplomatic function. He never sought to answer the objections to his position that rest on political and economic facts recognized by both sides; that if we followed him, we would be abandoned by several allies; that if Russia invaded Europe, which he has admitted might be an early consequence of his policy, the industrial balance would favor the Communist world; that, like it or not, American power does have its limitations. MacArthur's policy may be sounder than Truman's. But the contention cannot be sustained without facing these stubborn facts about the world today. MacArthur, in his speech, never faced them.

Herbert A. Wichelns

Demosthenes had the problem too; how much to spell out, how formal and explicit to make his proposals. At times Demosthenes judged it best not to "make a motion" but merely to offer comment and advice at large. MacArthur made a similar choice. In the main he chose not to debate, in the sense of formulating proposals and defending them in full. Instead he indicated the heads for debate, leaving no doubt as to the direction of his policy. Definite proposals were few, and sharply limited to Formosa and Korea. Supporting reasons were very sparingly given, and sometimes confined to bare assertions (as on the extent of China's present military commitment and Russia's probable course). But the call for a harder and more aggressive policy is plain from the beginning ("no greater expression of defeatism"). The chief support for that policy is neither logical argument nor emotional appeal, but the self-portrait of the speaker as conveyed by the speech.

It is an arresting portrait. Certain colors are of course mandatory. The speaker respects Congress and the power of this nation for good in the world. He is free from partisanship or personal rancor. He sympathizes with the South Koreans and with his embattled troops. He prefers victory to appeasement. He seeks only his country's good. He hates war, has long hated it. If these strokes are conventional, they take little time, except for the last, on which the speaker feels he must defend himself.

More subtle characterizing strokes are found in the "brief insight into the surrounding area" which forms a good half of the speech. Here the General swiftly surveys the nature of the revolution in Asia, the island-frontier concept and Formosa's place in the island-chain, the imperialistic character of the Chinese communities, the regeneration of Japan under his auspices, the outlook for the Philippines, and the present government of Formosa. All this before reaching Korea. Most of these passages have no argumentative force. But all together they set up for us the image of a leader of global vision, comprehending in his gaze nations, races, continents. The tone is firmest on Japan ("I know of no nation more serene, orderly and industrious"), least sure on the Philippines, but always positive.

Rarely indeed have the American people heard a speech so strong in the tone of personal authority. "While I was not consulted . . . that decision . . . proved a sound one." "Their last words to me"—it is the Korean people with whom the General has been talking. "My soldiers." The conduct of "your fighting sons" receives a sentence. A paragraph follows on the General's labors and anxieties on their behalf. The pace at which the thought moves, too, is proconsular; this is no fireside chat. Illustration and amplification are sparingly used; the consciously simple vocabulary of the home-grown politician is rejected. The housewife who "understood every word" was mistaken; she missed on epicenter and recrudescence and some others. But having by the fanfare been jarred into full attention, she understood quite well both the main proposition of the speech—a harder policy—and the main support offered—the picture of a masterful man of unique experience and global outlook, wearing authority as to the manner born.

One feature these comments display, which is often noted as an essential of critical discourse, is that both contain verdicts (sometimes called judgments or evaluations). Not all assertive discourse contains appraisal as criticism does. Scientific reports, for instance, display an exploratory impulse rather than an evaluative one.[9] Nor is this to say that critical essays must reach a settled and final verdict, for clearly Wichelns is at pains to avoid assessing MacArthur's speech as good or bad. But criticism does eventuate in, or at least has as an ultimate objective, assessment. Professor Black has put it most succinctly:

---

[9] *Bormann, pp. 227–229; E. Black,* Rhetorical Criticism: A Study in Method *(New York, 1965), p. 4.*

At the culmination of the critical process is the evaluation of the discourse or of its author; a comprehensive judgment which, in the best of criticism, is the fruit of patient exegesis. . . . Even the purely technical objective of understanding how a discourse works carries the assumption that it does work, and that assumption is an assessment. Similarly, to understand why a thing has failed is at least to suspect that it has failed, and that suspicion is an assessment. There is, then, no criticism without appraisal; there is no "neutral" criticism. One critic's judgment may be absolute and dogmatic, another's tentative and barely committal; but however faint the judicial element in criticism may become, it abides.[10]

If Black is correct, we ought seldom to find a critic engaging in description of a rhetorical event for its own sake; and if we do, we ought perhaps proceed most cautiously in determining whether to label the product "criticism."[11]

Clearly our two samples of criticism meet the criterion of making assessments. Rovere is explicit:

. . . the speech seemed . . . a good deal but not a great deal better than the general run of public prose . . . there is a rather fetid air about it. . . . Politically [the] speech seemed extremely weak. . . .

Wichelns' appraisal is more complex. Avoiding any "good-bad" evaluation, he invites us to accept his verdict on how the speech was executed (i.e., what made it work as it did). In Wichelns' judgment the speech called for a harder policy and this call was supported by the speaker's self-portrait. Both Rovere and Wichelns present us with settled, though not necessarily final or definitive, assertions as to the character and/or worth of the speech; their critical comments betray momentary terminations (benchmarks) in their thought processes, terminations which are expressed in the form of verdicts.

Once we grant that the assertive discourse of criticism strives for appraisal, we should concurrently examine the "reasons" offered to

---

[10] *Black, "Moral Values. . . ." Cf. Hillbruner, pp. 264–266; P. W. Taylor,* Normative Discourse *(Englewood Cliffs, N.J., 1961), p. 52; W. Righter,* Logic and Criticism *(New York, 1963), pp. vii–3; Bormann, p. 229; J. Holloway, "Symposium: Distinctive Features of Arguments Used in Criticism of the Arts,"* Proceedings of the Aristotelian Society *(supplement), XXIII (1949), 173.*

[11] *A. Isenberg, "Critical Communication,"* Philosophical Review, *LVIII (April 1949) 331. See also the following articles in* The Monist, *L (April 1966): M. Scriven, "The Objectivity of Aesthetic Evaluation," 159–187; H. Osborne, "Reasons and Description in Criticism," 204–212; H. Morris-Jones, "The Logic of Criticism," 213–221; P. Wilson, "The Need to Justify," 267–280.*

justify the verdicts. The bulk of both critical essays consists of reasons justifying the judgments. Notice, for example, Wichelns' assertion that MacArthur's main form of proof was his own self-portrait. It is supported by three contentions: that it was an arresting portrait, employing both "mandatory colors" and "subtle . . . strokes"; that the speech otherwise is lacking in argument and abounding in assertion; and that the speech was couched in the language of personal authority. From these Wichelns is enabled to conclude that the speech offered "the picture of a masterful man of unique and global outlook" as support for MacArthur's claims.

Dealing as we are with evaluative discourse, it is only natural to speculate further about the relationship linking verdicts and reasons. Imagine for instance the following situation: a friend says, "I read the novel *Tom Jones* last week." You treat this statement as a factual report. But were your friend to co-append, "It struck me as a rather shallow book," there is an immediate change in conditions. You may then decide to treat the combined statements as criticism, with the second sentence serving as an appraisal and the first now transformed from a report into part of the justification for the judgment. Furthermore, it would be extremely odd if your friend were to utter the second statement and at the same time deny having ever read the novel, having had any contact with anyone who had read it, or having had access to any critical comments about it. Obviously, we expect a critical verdict to be in some way conditional upon the reasons offered in its support. We are not yet in a position to see why reasons are expected or to determine how they function as support, but that they do so function to make criticism a reason-giving activity is evident.[12]

A valuable first step in grasping the logical structure underlying this conditional relation of reasons-and-verdict is to realize that criticism is an exercise in forensic reasoning. The critic's commentary is analogous to that of the trial lawyer who bases claims as to the proper verdict in a case on his interpretation of the facts in the light of some legal code. What tactics are open to the legal advocate? He may in some circumstances accept a set of legal standards (canons or laws) and apply them rigorously to the facts in the case. He may on the other hand feel

---

[12] *Let us momentarily disregard a related problem, whether one's verdicts must follow inevitably from one's reasons, as in a valid syllogism, or whether there is some looser connection between the evaluations and the justificatory reasons, perhaps a relation of appropriateness instead of one of correctness. What matters here is that both components are inseparable parts of the critic's assertions, no matter what their bearing on each other. Cf. Righter, pp. 74–84;* M. Weitz, "Reasons in Criticism," *Journal of Aesthetics and Art Criticism, XX (Summer 1962), 427–437; B. C. Heyl, "The Critic's Reasons," ibid., XVI (Winter 1957), 169–179.*

that the laws as they are commonly interpreted hurt his case. In that event he could propose a new interpretation of the laws which does more justice to the position he is defending; or if his mind functions after the fashion of an Erskine, he could seek to "make law" by questioning the established norms and attempting either to amend them or to substitute a code of his own choosing as the standard of evaluation. Again, some circumstances may be such that the counsel will accept a verdict contrary to his position but then go on to try to mitigate the thrust of the verdict by showing how special factors in the case deserve attention. Or perhaps there is a conflict in the legal code such as a contradiction between two laws. In the case of such an overlap, the advocate may argue for the priority of one law over another. In each of these instances the essential forensic tactic is to measure facts or observations against a code or canon.

A similar juxtapositioning of observations and normative standards constitutes the essence of critical activity:

The code may be the law of the land, the theory of probabilities, the standards of historical research, the canons of artistic excellence [*my italics*], *or their own standards for distinguishing truth from error. Whoever judges in these ways, then, needs two distinct kinds of knowledge: (1) knowledge about the facts or events he is to judge and (2) knowledge about the standards against which he is to measure the facts or events.*[13]

We may thus expect that reasons offered in critical discourse will lay claim to being the product of a "measurement" (comparison of data observed and norm). This does not mean that the verdict need follow inevitably from the comparison, only that it will claim such a juxtapositioning as a warrant for its own worth.

If the notion of forensic reasoning as the foundation of critical strategy is plausible, we have further grounds for rejecting some evaluations which are offered as specimens of criticism. Though tradition recognizes as "movie reviews" the placement of stars next to film titles in newspapers (four stars equivalent to "excellent," one star meaning "terrible"), we need not accept such markings as criticism (or if we do, as more than decapitated criticism). Again, what should one make of an argument which runs, "I feel that MacArthur's speech was unsatisfactory because the General once insulted me"? Such a remark is ordinarily disturbing. In part this is because the comment does not

[13] *J. F. Wilson and C. C. Arnold,* Public Speaking as a Liberal Art (*Boston, 1964*), *p. 97. Cf. Weitz; Isenberg, pp. 330–335; Taylor, pp. 9–14.*

fulfill forensic requirements: the reason offered, although it explains why the commentator holds the position he does, is not admissible as a justification for the verdict. In this case the norm (such as it is) violates the critical posture, and there is in addition a failure to juxtapose the norm to facts about the speech.

Observe how Wichelns illustrates the forensic pattern. He opens his essay by distinguishing between speeches which offer advice and those which join a debate. He thereby establishes the norm. He then spends the remainder of his first paragraph drawing attention to those facts about the speech which place it in the category of speeches of advice. In his next paragraph Wichelns formulates the principle that some remarks are mandatory on this kind of occasion—and then observes the extent to which MacArthur met those demands. In his third paragraph the critic implies that some rhetorical tactics reveal a proconsular image and then presents facts which enable him to ascribe such an image to MacArthur. The forensic pattern is evident throughout Wichelns' essay.

But the notion of forensic reasoning highlights one curious feature of criticism: although both norms and observations are logically essential, they need not be expressed separately. This aspect of criticism is illustrated in the dialogue concerning *Tom Jones*. When your friend justifies his evaluation of the novel with "I read the novel last week," where is the standard of judgment? Clearly, if it exists at all it is only implicit. One might suspect that your friend really meant, "I read the novel, and it did not measure up to my taste in novels," but that would only be speculation. Or take Rovere as a case in point. True, he announces at the outset that his standards will be "literary" and "political" ones. But then he goes on to call MacArthur's eloquence "coarse" and to say that MacArthur's language is neither "flat and bloodless" nor "flabby and loose-jointed." Are these observations or verdicts? And what are Rovere's standards for eloquence? Apparently, Rovere demands that the reader accept the existence and the excellence of the norms on faith. The norms do not appear in the criticism, though they are presupposed by Rovere's comments.

This fusion of otherwise distinct components is not an accident of composition. When Rovere condemns MacArthur's prose for its unshaded meanings, its lack of humor, its fetid language, is he hypothesizing that "the occurrence of these three elements results in coarse eloquence" after the fashion of the experimental scientists? Or is he calling to attention these particular observable features which, in these particular rhetorical circumstances, lend an air of coarseness to this particular speech? Rovere is obviously affirming his possession of standards of eloquence; but the application of the standards to a particular aesthetic event is, as we shall discover when we treat the modalities of analysis, far more complex than the measurement of the length of a metal pipe. In aesthetic judgments the standards often defy expression as general propositions for any but the most gross (and hence, trivial) features. And the standards applied are bound to the particulars of the single event because the events are too diverse and complicated to be comprehended by universal precepts. Such is the case of Rovere seeking to illuminate the coarseness of MacArthur's prose. He would be unable to provide general rubrics for what makes prose coarse because too many factors enter in; but he is able to account for the "coarse eloquence" in this case, and he does so.[14]

To answer what features of criticism distinguish it from other types of reason-giving discourse, we have so far maintained that the term "criticism" is most sensibly reserved for that assertive discourse produced by expert-spectators whose judgments as to the execution of (in this case) rhetorical phenomena are supported by forensic arguments. We may now consider the two remaining questions posed at the beginning of this essay. Let us for present purposes exclude from attention questions concerning the goals of rhetorical criticism or the origin and validity of rhetorical canons, interesting as these questions may be. In this essay we shall take for granted that the rhetorical critic possesses certain *a priori* objectives; he engages in the critical act for the sake of some preestablished end(s) which need not be specified here. We shall also presume that if called upon to do so, the critic could vindicate by means extrinsic to the realm of criticism (e.g., by metaphysical justification of some sort) his adoption of whatever rhetorical concepts he employs in his criticism.[15] Our interest is not in why he acts and believes as he does, but in how he exploits the critical opportunities available to him.

We are consequently obliged to examine the array of methodological options open to the rhetorical critic. At least two method-related questions invariably confront the critic in the exercise of his office: 1) what shall be the major focus of his critical analysis (what data will he find primarily relevant)? 2) what sorts of measurements or readings shall he take on the rhetorical transactions under investigation (in what fashion shall he transpose and describe the data he chooses to fix upon)? How he elects to answer these questions will in part influence both the nature and function of the critical reasons produced. Let us first ad-

---

[14] *Righter, p. 22.*
[15] *Cf. Taylor, pp. 128–138; McKeon, pp. 489–490; K. Burke,* A Grammar of Motives *(New York, 1945), p. 472; E. Olson, "The Poetic Method in Aristotle: Its Powers and Limitations,"* Aristotle's Poetics and English Literature, *ed. E. Olson (Chicago, 1965), pp. 187–191.*

dress ourselves to the alternative foci open to the critic of "public address."

If we schematize an instance of public communication encountered by the critic, we intuitively recognize four gross variables: the source(s) or creator(s) of the message, the message itself, the context or environment in which the message is received (including both the receivers and the social "landscape" which spawns the message), and the critic himself (who, especially in the study of public address of the past, is in a sense a unique receiver). For the sake of convenience, let us label the variables "S" (source), "M" (message), "E" (environment), and "C" (critic). Obviously, in a total interpretation of the communicative act all four variables are relevant. But equally obvious from past critical practice, such all-encompassing analysis will be rare if not impossible for the single critic. Perhaps the two most thoroughly examined messages in the English language are Shakespeare's *Hamlet* and Lincoln's *Gettysburg Address;* the very fact that criticism of these two is not yet exhausted attests to the impracticality of completely enveloping one verbal act with another. We are therefore forced to recognize that critics will have to concentrate on some permutation of the four variables as a means of making their critical tasks manageable.

For the rhetorical critic the one indispensable factor is M, the message. Exclusive concern for S, the source, is the biographer's business; study of E, the environment, is the historian's; studies relating speakers to audience apart from the substance of the message (as in explorations of the role of status or leadership in public affairs) are performed mainly by sociologists. The rhetorical critic sees the entire communicative transaction as somehow "suspended" from the language of the message under examination. For the rhetorical critic the verbal utterance constitutes a kind of linguistic architecture which supports and gives form to the total rhetorical act. In this belief the critic differs from the historian and sociologist, who may choose to treat the verbal factors as mere artifacts of the event. The rhetorical critic not only fastens his observation to M; he does so in the conviction that the message is fundamental to an appreciation of the entire event.[16]

The critic therefore occupies himself with some combination of variables which focus on the message: S-M, M-E, M-C, S-M-E, S-M-C, or M-E-C. These are combinations which constitute genuine critical options. It is not the critic's task to inspect these variables in isolation; neither is it sufficient for him to report that they all converged in a particular instance of public discourse.

Consider first the nature of the M-C focus, which represents an un-

[16] *Cf. T. Clevenger, Jr., "Research Opportunities in Speech,"* Introduction to the Field of Speech, ed. R. F. Reid (*Chicago, 1965*), *pp. 222–224.*

ashamedly introspectionist stance. This focus seeks to gauge the critic's personal response to the aesthetic object.[17] The critic who directs his attention to the M-C relationship will conceive of himself as a kind of sensitive instrument, and his analysis will be comprised primarily of reports of his own reactions to the work apart from any impact the work may have had on any particular "public." In this vein, Anatole France remarked that the good critic:

> . . . *is he who relates the adventures of his soul among masterpieces. . . . The truth is that one never gets out of oneself.*[18]

Rovere's commentary suggests that he adopted a focus such as the one described by France.

The M-C orientation grounds its validation on the premise that communication is essentially a unique event, a private transaction between message and receiver which can never be known to a third party. The critic is simply one more receiver of the message, albeit more sensitive than the typical, untrained receiver. If one accepts the notion that critical interpretation is so uniquely personal, it then follows that no interpretation can expect to be more than a justification of the critic's own state of mind as he responds to the aesthetic object.

And if communication is inherently a private matter, then one's faith in the critic's explication and overall taste constitutes at least as important a means of support for the verdicts offered as do the critic's stated reasons for his evaluation. Hence, in the case of Rovere, we need to trust his sensitivity as much as we need to be persuaded by his analysis of the prose. It is even possible to imagine that the primary function served by reasons submitted by an observer with the M-C focus is to demonstrate to a reader the observer's competence as a critic, to "exhibit his credentials," to make authoritative judgments.[19]

---

[17] *Cf. Heyl, p. 170; R. Wellek and A. Warren,* The Theory of Literature *(New York, 1949); W. Embler, "The Language of Criticism," Etc., XXII (September 1965), 261–277. This cryptic account is obviously not the entire story. The critic is not privileged simply to report his pleasure and/or pain on confronting the discourse. He is in some manner obligated to explain how and why the work justifies his particular response. It is also important to note that contemporary literary critics who claim to focus entirely on the work itself are in fact often employing the M-C paradigm; their failure to recognize the implications of their critical orientation results occasionally in rather odd exigeses.*

[18] *Anatole France, "The Literary Life,"* The Book of Modern Criticism, *trans. and ed. L. Lewisohn (New York, 1919), pp. 1–3. Cf. I. A. Richards,* Principles of Literary Criticism *(New York, 1925), pp. 5–24.*

[19] *Embler, p. 265; M. Beardsley,* Aesthetics: Problems in the Philosophy of Criticism *(New York, 1958), pp. 129–134.*

Such a conception of M-C analysis may account for the propensity of prominent critics to set forth lists of their favorite books, or of the best plays or speeches of all time. Having achieved eminence, they need no longer justify their selections, but are able to telescope or even abort their arguments in favor of short explications of why a particular book, play, or novel pleased them personally.

The next three foci are related to each other in their denial of an introspectionist critical stance and their advocacy of greater detachment. The S-M focus concentrates on understanding discourse as an expression of its creator. Most often the critic attempts to trace out the creative process by which the speaker externalized and structured the feelings, thoughts, and experiences contained within himself. The relation of source to message has prompted two general schools of criticism. One (which actually concentrates on the S$\rightarrow$M relationship) seeks to account for the rhetor's behavior as a function of the factors which influenced him: his education, the books he read, the persons who inspired him, and the like.[20] The other variation of the S-M focus, S$\leftarrow$M, is best typified by neo-Freudian critics who treat the aesthetic event as symptomatic of the artist's personal life and psychodynamics. The critic, in other words, acts as a kind of lay psychoanalyst, using the message as a key to understanding and evaluating the creator of the message.[21]

The M-E focus also incorporates two divergent streams of critical practice. In the one instance (M$\leftarrow$E), "environment" is interpreted broadly (as by historians and literary critics) to encompass the age and the civilization in which the message originated. The historian of ideas attempts to set the historical background in which particular works or clusters of works were produced, showing how the messages are themselves a reflection of their era. This emphasis finds its rationale in the assumption that to the extent that an aesthetic event can be considered typical of its age it will provide valuable insight into the intel-

[20] Cf. M. H. Abrams, The Mirror and the Lamp: Romantic Tradition (*New York, 1953*), pp. 21–25; J. Thorp, "The Aesthetics of Textual Critcism," PMLA, LXXX (*December 1965*), 465–482; L. D. Reid, "Gladstone's Training as a Speaker," The Quarterly Journal of Speech, XL (*December 1954*), 373–380; L. Crocker, "The Rhetorical Training of Henry Ward Beecher," The Quarterly Journal of Speech, XIX (*February 1933*), 18–24.

[21] Cf. H. D. Duncan, Communication and Social Order (*New York, 1962*), pp. 3–16; M. Maloney, "Clarence Darrow," in A History and Criticism of American Public Address, ed. M. K. Hochmuth, III (*New York, 1955*), 262–312; H. M. Ruitenbeek (ed.), Psychoanalysis and Literature (*New York, 1964*); N. Kiell (ed.), Psychological Studies of Famous Americans (*New York, 1964*); W. S. Scott, Five Approaches of Literary Criticism (*New York, 1962*), pp. 69–73; R. L. Bushman, "On the Uses of Psychology: Conflict and Conciliation in Benjamin Franklin," History and Theory, V (*#3, 1966*), 225–240.

lectual and social trends of that age.[22] Another direction which critics with an M-E focus have chosen to follow, one which has gained its widest acceptance among critics with a bent toward social science, interprets "environment" in a more prescribed sense, referring to the specific audience which the message had. These critics consider the "functional" relationship which existed between the discourse and its receivers. They seek to determine how the receivers used the messages presented to them as stimuli. The assumption underlying the functional (M→ E) approach to the M-E relationship is that, whatever the speaker's intention, the auditor attends to a speech in a manner which fulfills his own personal needs. An old man may attend a July 4th celebration, not prepared to be persuaded or inspired to increased patriotism, but simply because the ceremonial oratory reminds him of the speeches he heard on similar occasions in his youth. Similarly, the daily newspaper may function for some readers as a means by which they maintain an intimate contact with their favorite celebrities. For such readers, news of a Hollywood scandal is as welcome as a letter from home. In cases such as these, the M-E critic might concern himself with determining expectations of the audience as well as the extent to which those expectations were fulfilled by the discourse.[23]

Although it is possible for a rhetorical critic to employ any of the three foci so far mentioned, the bulk of traditional speech criticisms has not explored dyadic relationships but the triadic formulations of S-M-E. Essentially, this "pragmatic" orientation treats the message as an effort at persuasion and ventures to assess the artistic skill of the speaker in achieving his persuasive goals with his audience.[24] The extensive use of the S-M-E framework can be justified if we accept the notion that public address is, literally, discourse addressed to a public by a speaker who is carrying on public business by his act of communication. Because the critic takes for granted the Janus-like quality of public

[22] *For example, V. L. Parrington,* Main Currents in American Thought (*New York, 1927*), *3 vols.; R. T. Oliver,* History of Public Address in America (*Boston, 1965*); *M. Meyers,* The Jacksonian Persuasion (*New York, 1960*); *A. O. Lovejoy,* The Great Chain of Being (*Cambridge, Mass., 1936*); *D. M. Chalmers,* The Social and Political Ideas of the Muckrakers (*New York, 1964*); *G. Orwell,* "Boys' Weeklies," *in* A Collection of Essays *by George Orwell* (*Garden City, N.Y., 1954*), *pp. 284–313; Scott, pp. 123–126.*

[23] *Cf. Heyl, p. 169; D. Katz, "The Functional Approach to the Study of Attitudes,"* Public Opinion Quarterly, *XXIV (Summer 1960), 163–204; J. K. Galbraith,* Economics and the Art of Controversy (*New York, 1955*), *pp. 3–31; L. W. Lichty, "The Real McCoys and It's (sic) Audience: A Functional Analysis,"* Journal of Broadcasting, *IX (Spring 1965), 157–165; B. DeMott, "The Anatomy of Playboy,"* Commentary, *XXIV (August 1962), 111–119.*

[24] *Abrams, pp. 16–21; W. N. Brigance, "What is a Successful Speech?"* The Quarterly Journal of Speech Education, *XI (April, 1925), 272–277; Black,* Rhetorical Criticism, *pp. 36–58; Thonssen and Baird, pp. 448–461.*

address, revealing simultaneously the communicator and the social environment to which he seeks to adapt himself, the S-M-E critic emphasizes in his study the mediating nature of the message in moving (or failing to move) the audience toward the speaker's vision of how the demands of occasion ought to be met and resolved.[25]

The three foci—S-M, M-E and S-M-E—comprise a set because they share one quality which distinguishes them from the introspectionist reports of the M-C focus. This shared quality is a stress on objective, verifiable, critical statements. By placing the spectator outside the critical equation, each method attempts to make of criticism a dispassionate report of what actually "is," a judicious, unbiased account of properties which inhere in the communicative event itself. In so doing they imply that the critic should strive to produce an analysis of the essential nature of the phenomenon apart from any idiosyncrasies in his personal responses.[26]

None of the three "impersonal" approaches so far mentioned can serve the ends of the introspectionist, and hence, none of the three finds encourages critical reasons employed mainly to establish the critic's own credentials as a sensitive observer. Instead, the critic who strives for a dispassionate and reliable report of the rhetorical act will find that the reasons he gives in support of his verdicts function primarily to call to the attention of others those characteristics of the original communication which merit their further contemplation. The method is similar to that of the football announcer who uses an instant replay camera. A team scores a touchdown, and seconds later the television commentator says, "As we play back the scoring play, notice the excellent footwork of the man with the ball." The listener-viewer is thus primed to observe for himself a feature of the event which the expert-commentator feels merits attention. The same ostensive function applies to the selection of reasons by the impersonal, rhetorical critic; his reasons do not report, nor do they simply support a conclusion—they call on the reader to observe for himself.

The last two foci available to the critic, S-M-C and M-E-C, reject the cleavage between introspection and impersonal functions of critical discourse. Justification for these two foci stems from the recognition of contemporary science that the very act of observation alters the event observed and so distorts the information one is able to obtain about the event. The distortions can never be overcome by more precise ob-

[25] D. C. Bryant, "Rhetoric: Its Scope and Function," Quarterly Journal of Speech, *XXXIX (December 1953)*, 401–424.
[26] B. Harrison, "Some Uses of 'Good' in Criticism," Mind, *LXIX (April 1960)*, 206; A. H. Hanney, "Symposium: Distinctive Features of Arguments Used in Criticism of the Arts," p. 169.

servations or measurements, but can only be acknowledged by specifying a degree of uncertainty and looseness in one's formulations.

As applied to the critical act, such a position holds that criticism is inevitably the product of the critic's encounter with the rhetorical event, that the locus of criticism is neither critic nor ontic event but the critic's intrusion upon the event. Such an intrusion may not directly influence the agents involved in the communication; we may wish to admit, for instance, that as he prepared his first inaugural address Thomas Jefferson probably did not significantly alter his behavior in conscious anticipation of twentieth-century rhetorical critics. But neither should we misconstrue the dilemma faced by the critic who would do more than resurrect the data of the past. His problem is less one of succumbing to personal bias than it is of taking and formulating precise measurements on the event under investigation.[27] Our final two foci suit the critic who has reconciled himself to the inevitable impossibility of making meticulously accurate statements about the events he observes, who wishes instead the maximum fidelity possible within the limits imposed on his by the nature of perception and critical language. His framework for observation indexes neither the event *in vacuo* nor his own response to the event, but the relation which joins him to the rhetorical act.

The critic who adopts the S-M-C focus assumes that a speech will no more exist "out there" in some ontic world than does a symphony reside "in" a musical score or a drama "in" a manuscript.[28] Instead, he believes that we can discern an artistic intention in a work of art; and the aesthetic experience, be it to speech or symphony, is the experiencing and articulation of that artistic intention. Artistic intention is understood as the peculiar way in which the elements of the message cohere in the movement of confrontation with the observer-critic.

There are objective clues in the messages as to the meaning which will be actualized by the interaction of observer and thing observed. It

[27] A. G. Van Melsen, The Philosophy of Nature (*New York, 1953*), p. 226; L. Brillouin, Science and Information Theory (*New York, 1962*), p. 232; F. C. Frick, *"Some Perceptual Problems from the Point of View of Information Theory,"* Psychology: A Study of a Science, *II* (*New York, 1959*), 77; J. Rothstein, *"Information and Organization as the Language of the Operational Viewpoint,"* Philosophy of Science, *XXIX* (*October 1962*), 406–411; J. Ruesch, *"The Observer and the Observed: Human Communication Theory,"* Toward a Unified Theory of Human Behavior, *ed. R. R. Grinker* (*New York, 1956*), pp. 36–54; M. Bunge, Causality: The Place of the Causal Principles in Modern Science (*New York, 1963*), pp. 348–349; P. Frank, Philosophy of Science (*Englewood Cliffs, N.J., 1957*), pp. 207–231; A. Moles, Information Theory and Esthetic Perception (*London, 1958*).

[28] Cf. A. G. Pleydell-Pearce, *"On the Limits and Use of 'Aesthetic Criteria,' "* Philosophical Quarterly, *IX* (*January 1959*), 29–30.

becomes the critic's task to investigate that cooperation of elements and ratios in the message which gives rise to the artistic meaning-as-experienced. In other words, speaker, speech, and observer momentarily coalesce as the elements of the rhetorical event unite to move toward some terminal condition. The critic's objective is to explicate that condition and the communication factors which contribute to or retard the transaction. The critic seeks to determine the nature of the demands made by the rhetorical event upon the beholder of the event. He is of course obligated to be alert to his own predilections as an instrument of observation, but his attention is focused outward upon artistic intention rather than inward as with introspection.[29]

The source enters into this equation because it is posited that the artist's intention(s) in creating the message may provide a key to understanding the artistic intention embodied in the message. The critic assumes that the speaker, by virtue of his close connection with the message, is something of an authority on the event; that is, the speaker often possesses special knowledge about the speech which adds depth to the critic's own interpretation. Hence, a comparison of artist's intentions with artistic intentions may prove a valuable aid in centering interest on the decisive qualities of the work of art.

Consider, for example, John Kennedy's television address to the nation on the Cuban missile crisis in 1962: we might regard the policy enunciated on that occasion as rhetorically inappropriate. However, if we knew that Kennedy was privy to secret information indicating that the Russians would withdraw their missiles if we took a strong line, this knowledge would help clarify the forceful posture Kennedy chose to adopt and possibly alter our critical assessment of the artistic intention evidenced in the discourse. We might now see the message as primarily a warning to Russia rather than as a report to the nation.

Notice that the S-M-C focus does not obligate the critic to accept the artist's personal conception of his creation; the purpose of uncovering Kennedy's purpose in speaking is not to whitewash Kennedy but to understand the parameters within which his verbal behavior operated. We might still find that Kennedy chose an inappropriate rhetorical strategy. Or we might conclude that Kennedy was himself not fully aware of the real significance of the discourse he produced. Our search does not necessarily tell us anything about the ultimate character of the message for the artist's intentions are ancillary to our primary con-

---

[29] Cf. E. Berne, Transactional Analysis in Psychotherapy (New York, 1961); Ch. Perelman and L. Olbrechts-Tyteca, "Act and Person in Argument," Philosophy, Rhetoric and Argumentation, ed. M. Natanson and H. W. Johnstone, Jr. (University Park, Pa., 1965), pp. 102–125.

cern, which is artistic intention.[30] We seek to discover the speaker's point of view; the symptoms of artistic and intellectual choice thereby revealed may lend depth to our apprehension of the design of the message.

Like its S-M-C counterpart, M-E-C rests on a conception of the critical act as an encounter. And it also recognizes the importance of artistic intention, of the demands made by the work upon the recipient of the message. The primary distinction between the two frameworks is the emphasis that the M-E-C focus places on the rhetorical event as an act, a performance which is only fully consummated in that instant when message is apprehended by receiver. Just as a play is not theatre until it is being performed for an audience, so the rhetorical artifact (such as a speech manuscript) becomes discourse only when it is experienced in a public "arena" or forum.[31] The rhetorical critic therefore necessarily fastens his attention not on the moment of creation but upon the moment of reception, realizing all the while that by his intrusion he is mutilating the confrontation of message and audience.

One consequence of this shift in emphasis is that the M-E-C critic is less concerned with the speaker's influence on the message than is the S-M-C critic. As the French symbolist Paul Valéry has contended:

There is no true meaning to a text—*no author's authority. Whatever he may have* wanted to say, *he has written what he has written. Once published, a text is like an apparatus that anyone may use as he will and according to his ability: it is not certain that the one who constructed it can use it better than another.*[32]

Although there are important differences between symbolist literary criticism and the traits of M-E-C rhetorical analysis, they are in this respect similar.

Whereas the S-M-C focus concentrates on the aesthetic demands of

---

[30] Cf. R. Kuhns, "*Criticism and the Problem of Intention,*" Journal of Philosophy, *LVII (January 7, 1960),* 5–23; S. Gendin, "The Artist's Intentions," Journal of Aesthetics and Art Criticism, *XXIII (Winter 1964),* 193–196; E. Roma III, "*The Scope of the Intentional Fallacy,*" The Monist, *L (April 1966),* 250–266.

[31] M. O. Sillars, "Rhetoric as Act," The Quarterly Journal of Speech, *L (October 1964),* 277–284; H. Arendt, Between Past and Future (*Cleveland, 1963*), *pp. 143–172;* S. K. Langer, Problems of Art (*New York, 1957*), *pp. 1–58;* S. C. Petter, The Work of Art (*Bloomington, Indiana, 1955*); M. Natanson, "The Claims of Immediacy," in Philosophy, Rhetoric and Argumentation, *ed. M. Natanson and H. W. Johnstone, Jr. (University Park, Pa., 1965), pp. 10–19;* W. Sacksteder, "Elements of the Dramatic Model," Diogenes, *LII (Winter 1965),* 26–54; P. K. Tompkins, "*Rhetorical Criticism: Wrong Medium?*" Central States Speech Journal, *XIII (Winter 1962),* 90–95.

[32] Paul Valéry, The Art of Poetry (*New York, 1958*), p. 152.

the event upon *an* auditor (the potential interpretation which any sensitive recipient might make), M-E-C considers the aesthetic demands made by the event upon *the* auditors (the likely meaning of the message for a given public). To illustrate, the S-M-C critic would seek to assess the enduring worth of medieval morality plays, taking account of their original cast as inculcators of religious faith; the M-E-C critic, on the other hand, would distinguish between the meaning of a morality play for its original audience and its meaning (perhaps totally different) for a typical contemporary auditor. Constrained thus by context, the M-E-C critical focus is more particularized, with the critic acting as a kind of surrogate for the audience he projects into the communicative event.[33]

Nor is the M-E-C frame simply a variation of the more objective message-environment focus. M-E analysis offers a predominantly historical interpretation of "how it was" when the public confronted the speech. The M-E critic seeks to understand the nature of the transaction as it in fact originally occurred. He may even go so far as to evaluate the speech using the rhetorical norms of the period and society in which the speech was delivered. He has a tendency to work back from the context to the message as he engages in assessment.

In contrast, an historistic interpretation might be more appropriate to an M-E-C focus. The M-E-C critic would try to go beyond understanding the message *as* the original participants understood it and attempt also to understand it *better than* they did.[34] He would seek to determine "how it would have to be" if one were to derive the fullest significance implicit in the rhetorical event. It is likely that an observer with an M-E-C orientation would follow a course of action in which he first analyzed the message, then projected from his analysis a description of the public for whom the message would be most appealing, and finally compared the bulk of the actual audience with his composite ideal auditor.

It is suggestive for us to bear in mind that both frames originate in the physicist's efforts to accommodate his formulations to the inherent uncertainty of the cosmos. We might therefore expect S-M-C and

[33] *The problem of a possible shift in meaning for morality plays is raised in* F. J. Coleman, "A Phenomenology of Aesthetic Reasoning," Journal of Aesthetics and Art Criticism, XXV (Winter 1966), 197–203.

[34] *The distinction has been alluded to by R. L. Scott in his review of E. Black's* Rhetorical Criticism (The Quarterly Journal of Speech, LI [October 1965], p. 336). *Scott suggests that one may go to extremes in appealing to the immediate audience as a decisive measure of rhetorical merit, that in such instances the critic may be more concerned with direct measures of audience response such as shift-of-opinion ballots than with the speech itself. An extremist M-E critic might indeed tend to fit such a description, but an M-E-C critic would be unlikely to find himself in such a posture.*

M-E-C critics to be somewhat more heedful of the limitations of their investigations and less inclined to construct a brief for a particular interpretation. They might be somewhat more prone to employ their reasons as part of a calculation of the validity of particular rhetorical concepts. Their primary objective would then be to modify rhetorical theory to accommodate their clinical observations rather than to establish their own credibility or assist readers to derive increased satisfaction from the rhetorical event under discussion. We would expect critics with this cast to be more tentative in their reason-giving, since their comments would operate less in an advocative capacity and more as a special kind of scientific discourse. Such a critic might very well take the view that if his reasons are sound those to whom he reports will *probably* attach greater value to his judgments. He would therefore seek to determine the strength of his reasons.[35]

Let us conclude consideration of alternative critical foci by reminding ourselves that the focus adopted by the critic determines what kind of questions he will find most interesting. Insofar as the critic chooses to relate the rhetorical event to its creator he will ask: How did the message come to be? Is it symptomatic of the speaker? What are the capacities of the rhetor as an artist? How does the man shape the message? The critic who regards the message as the initial stimulus in his formula will ask himself a complementary set of questions: How does the message reflect its context? What evidence is there that the message as created was appropriate to the climate in which it was employed? How did the message serve to influence its environment? How and why does my experience with this message differ from the likely experiences of other recipients? These are all legitimate questions for a critic to ask; but his decision as to which shall occupy his attention will be at least partially influenced by the focus he has chosen to adopt.

Although many more problems pertaining to the logic of rhetorical criticism remain, this essay will treat only one more topic, the procedures available to the critic for relating norm and observation. This topic is essential since reason-giving has been shown to be the fundamental aspect of the logic of critical discourse.

We can imagine judgments which do not entail even the possibility of supporting reasons, but we ordinarily treat such evaluations as capricious remarks when uttered by critics. The manner in which a critic relates fact and criterion is of some moment if we hope to under-

---

[35] *E. H. Hutten, "Uncertainty and Information,"* Scientia, *IC (#9–10, 1964), 199–206; J. J. Kupperman, "Reasons in Support of Evaluations of Works of Art,"* The Monist, *L (April 1966), 222–236; J. Rothstein,* Communication, Organization, and Science *(Indian Hills, Colo., 1958). The problem we face at this point in the discussion is that no clear instances of this critical stance are available as of this date.*

stand the character of his reason-giving. For our purposes, the term "modality" will refer to any characteristic manner (or formula) for joining observations and norms so as to produce justificatory reasons in criticism. The term's meaning is thus roughly comparable to the sense of "function" as used in calculus.[36] To explain this special use of "modality" it is necessary to begin with a clarification of the term "juxtapose."

Earlier in this essay the critic was compared to the lawyer pleading a case. It was then suggested that a critic's primary task is to formulate justificatory bases for his verdicts by "juxtaposing" descriptions and norms. The term "juxtapose" is purposely vague, and it must be understood in light of John Dewey's observation that criticism:

. . . *is judgment engaged in discriminating among values. It is taking thought as to what is better and worse in any field at any time, with some consciousness of why the better is better and why the worse is worse.*[37]

Now determination of better-and-worse may take several forms. One might "grade" a speech according to various criteria or rank it with respect to other speeches and along designated scales, or he might simply classify it by type as part of a general act of recognizing features (when one labels a speech "epideictic," what he in fact does is provide a shorthand notation of several qualities we expect to find in epideictic oratory).[38]

Whatever the informative pattern evident in criticism, we expect that two related features of the critical act will remain constant. The critic will first have alternative speeches in mind as he approaches the object of study. Better-and-worse implies better-or-worse-than something else. To say that Adlai Stevenson was a great speaker suggests that the critic can discriminate between the speeches of Stevenson and those of some not-so-great speakers. To find fault with Lyndon Johnson's style suggests that the critic has in mind alternative stylistic tactics which Johnson might employ to improve his style.

The second implication to be drawn from Dewey's comment is that the alternative(s) the critic has in mind will take the form of particular speeches or aspects of speeches. To illustrate: suppose we feel that "good" speeches generally require transitions between main points.

[36] Cf. R. P. Agnew, Analytical Geometry and Calculus with Vectors (New York, 1962), pp. 111–117.

[37] Cited in M. K. Hochmuth (ed.), History and Criticism of American Public Address, III (New York, 1955), 4.

[38] Hanney. p. 170; Righter, pp. 64–69; Kupperman, pp. 229–233; Levy, p. 11.

Should we find a speech lacking transitions is it perforce a "bad" speech? Obviously not. Some speeches do not need transitions. Hence, the rubric "good speeches have transitions" is merely a guiding principle which serves to canalize critical observations; it is a reminder to consider the possibilities of an alternative speech containing transitions. To judge a discourse deficient in its use of transitions we need to have in mind how the addition of transitions might improve the speech; we must have an alternative image of a speech which is better, in particular ways, than the one we are observing. The "juxtaposition" called for in criticism is not straightforward application of rules to events in the manner by which we measure the length of an object against a yardstick. There is instead an oblique, two-step process by which the critic either generates or selects an appropriate alternative discourse and then compares that specific alternative to the discourse under analysis. The two modalities we shall consider represent general procedures for so joining observations and rhetorical norms.

A model modality is employed when the critic starts by generating some sort of paradigm which he will use as a basis of comparison. Laymen commonly speak of models in reference to airplanes, toy houses, or sets of blueprints. They tend to associate the term with miniatures, objects and/or plans drawn to scale.[39] However, the more appropriate sense of "model" in criticism is one which roughly corresponds to "prototype" or to "exemplar of a kind." Drawing on his rhetorical theory, the critic generates a model representing his conception of what would have constituted the ideal speech for the situation. He then compares his archetype with the speech which was actually delivered in order to determine the degree and the nature of the disparity between paradigm and actual speech. The comparison precipitates a kind of diagnosis; if the model conforms to the critic's rhetorical theory (as we must assume it does if it is to be regarded as a paradigm), then disparity between the norm-discourse and the actual one should provide some insight into both the aesthetic excellence and the rhetorical weaknesses evident in the discourse being inspected.

This notion of the norm as a model presupposes that the critic can himself create a prototype which is neither a stock image ("the speech for all occasions") nor yet a capricious whim. His model must be one which in its essentials conforms to his rhetorical theory. As we noted earlier, no rhetorical theory is so detailed that it can account for every aspect of every speech except in general outline. The well-wrought model requires a sensitive creator who can use his theory as a point of departure in developing in his imagination the model uniquely suited

[39] *M. Black*, Models and Metaphors (*Ithaca, N.Y., 1962*), *pp. 219–224.*

to assess a particular message. The search for an explanation for the extent and character of deviation from the paradigm model will then constitute the invention of critical reasons .

Both Rovere and Wichelns illustrate the model modality of reason-giving. Rovere contrasts MacArthur's speech by means of a treatment of issues demanded by the controversy; on that basis he decides Mac-Arthur's effort is inappropriate to the occasion. Wichelns, too, seems to reason from an implicit prototype insofar as he comments on attributes present and lacking, mandatory and optional in MacArthur's prose. If Wichelns is unwilling to discuss the appropriateness of Mac-Arthur's tone of authority (and his silence on this score is revealing), he is at least willing to address himself to MacArthur's skill in executing the tactic; and such comments, responsibly made, entail a theoretical conception of how public image is conveyed in a speech.

The essential feature of the second tactic of comparison, the analog modality, is that the norm employed is some actual discourse and not a theoretically derived prototype. Imagine the behavior of a critic who wished to characterize the rhetoric of Fidel Castro on those occasions when Castro justifies his failure to hold popular elections. The critic might use his rhetorical theory to generate a model of what would be appropriate for Castro to say; he might, on the other hand, be reminded of the rhetoric of another revolutionary in similar circumstances, say Cromwell dissolving Parliament. In the latter case, the critic might choose to juxtapose Castro's discourse to Cromwell's. His norm would no longer be paradigmatic, for he would have no *a priori* grounds for judging either Castro or Cromwell the more worthy rhetorician.

In lieu of such assessments, the critic would use Cromwell's speeches for topological purposes, much as he would a road map. Cromwell's discourse would serve to focus and guide the critic in his interpretation of Castro. Critical judgments would thus assume the form of statements of more-and-less or better-and-worse respecting particular qualities evident in the discourses. Perhaps Cromwell is more likely to engage in personal invective while Castro is more discursive in justifying his policies.

An illustration of the analog modality is found in Professor Laura Crowell's criticism of the speaking of John Pym, the English Parliamentarian. Crowell is contending that a distinctive feature of Pym's address is his interpretation of new events within the context of already-accepted materials and attitudes:

To people whose world was changing from medievalism to modernism under their feet, the words of a man who consistently saw events in larger context and who had details ready at hand on Biblical, philosophical, legal, financial, and parliamentary matters were extremely comforting. A cocksure age is ready for persuasion to new proposals, easily abandoning the present, not fearing the leap. But a skeptical age, such as Pym's, asks a persuasion that keeps its hold upon the present even while raising questions; it needs to feel the security of the past even while rising to meet new problems.[40]

The contrast between the debate of Pym's time and contemporary debate over, say, social welfare enables the critic in this case to highlight a quality in Pym's discourse which might not be readily evident were one to attempt to conceive the ideal rhetorical strategy for Pym solely on the basis of a rhetorical theory.

The analog relation of two particulars without direct recourse to a set of precepts entails a special role for rhetorical theory in the interpretative act. In the model modality the critic's norm is generated and constrained by theoretical precepts. In the analog situation rhetorical theory constitutes a shorthand account of those rhetorical categories which are typically helpful to the act of comparison. In the latter instance the critic is less concerned with creating a prototype than he is with "characterizing" an actual discourse.[41]

The analogical modality opens realms of critical analysis which have been for the most part neglected by rhetorical critics. Let us imagine that a critic, having assessed Castro in the light of the rhetorically similar Cromwell, decides to compare him with some apparently unrelated speaker, such as William Faulkner accepting the Nobel Prize for literature. There is no logical reason why such a comparison would be fruitless, yet it is clear that such a juxtaposing would yield results quite different from the comparison of Castro and Cromwell. Theoretically, the possibilities of analysis are infinite. Why not compare messages across cultures (say inaugural addresses of Presidents and coronation speeches of Kings), or across genres (John Adams the speaker and John Adams the writer of diaries)? Why not juxtapose various rhetorical forms, such as Ingersoll's witty ripostes at the Lotus Club and the cryptic visions of a religious mystic? Or why not contrast totally different rhetorical objects (Burke to the electors of Bristol and Martin Luther King to a college audience)?

The model modality finds its optimal use in confirming or qualifying rhetorical theory, where the analog modality, because of its factorial character, provides a point of departure which enables the critic to derive new categories and precepts from his investigation. The model-

---

[40] *L. Crowell, "The Speaking of John Pym, English Parliamentarian," SM, XXXIII (June 1966), 100.*
[41] *Levy, pp. 65–66.*

based critic is asking whether the rhetorician met certain criteria which were established by a given rhetorical system; the analog critic compares and contrasts, searching out theoretical explanations to accommodate his discoveries. In both instances theory assists the critic in his task and is in turn refined by the act of criticism. But it is clear that slatternly reliance on rhetorical canons to perform critical tasks is futile in either modality. Even where the canons suggest no obvious fault in a particular discourse, it is always possible that the astute critic could imagine a better speech or pamphlet, it is always possible that a felicitous comparison might expose qualities beyond the scope of the rhetorical theory at hand.[42]

Conclusion

This essay began by asserting that criticism is distinguished as a form of discourse by its peculiar reason-giving qualities. The ensuing discussion of this assertion holds two implications for speech scholars. The first is the suggestion, implicit in our analysis of the terms "critic" and "criticism," that rhetorical criticism does not operate *in vacuo.* Speech criticism can be best understood within the broader context afforded by a general conception of criticism's logical features. It has been argued that among the formal aspects which unite speech criticism with other varieties of critical discourse is the expert-spectator posture assumed by all critics. Another feature common to all criticism and setting it apart from the bulk of public discourse is its reliance upon forensic reasons-in-support-of-verdicts as its primary method for advancing contentions.

The second implication derives from our consideration of critical foci and modalities: it is possible to discern a finite set of relatively clearcut methodological options open to the critic. There is, in other words, a system of alternatives inherent in critical endeavor; criticism is not the "blooming, buzzing confusion" it may at times seem. Thus, for example, conceiving of the critical act as encompassing the four gross components of the communicative event enables us to specify in at least loose terms the kind of questions to which a given critic has addressed himself. Indeed, the recognition that various critics will give primary emphasis to particular combinations of S, M, E and C helps us to understand (although not necessarily to resolve) controversies which pit

---

[42] *In at least one instance the model-analog distinction breaks down and the modalities seem to fuse. That is where the critic relies on a touchstone as a standard of comparison. The touchstone, or "classic of its kind," at once represents an ideal and is at the same time an actual discourse which could conceivably be replaced in its role of prototype by some other discourse yet to be discovered. That the touchstone fulfills this dual role may explain its attraction for many critics as well as the rarity of its appearance as an effective critical tool. Cf. Wilson, pp. 272–276.*

critics of one focus against those of another. We are at least aware that the issue in the debate is often not so much the validity of the critics' arguments or the acuity of their observations as it is the importance each school attaches to particular relationships among the four communicative variables.

We have also considered the two fundamental modalities open to the critic as he relates his artistic criteria to the rhetorical event. We have seen that the common conception of the critic as one directly applying his canons in the manner of a measure applied to an object is overly simplified. The relation of criteria to object is oblique, entailing the critic's own conception of what the rhetorical work might have been. And this need for a one-to-one comparison again reminds us that the critic's selection from among the methodological options available will influence the character of his discourse.

Criticism, in sum, reveals itself to be a peculiarly open-ended, frustrating, but not incomprehensible endeavor. If the general condition of the critical act is diversity of substantive and methodological options, there are still reasonable limits to the range of those options. In the final analysis it is perhaps this vast complexity of opportunity that makes understanding the formal facets of critical method tenuous and difficult, yet at the same time renders understanding virtually indispensable to the student of criticism.

A Case Study in Speech Criticism:
The Nixon-Truman Analog
by Lawrence W. Rosenfield

One of the most controversial public addresses of modern American history is also one on which rhetorical scholars have remained strangely mute. I refer to the radio-television broadcast by the then vice presidential candidate Richard Nixon on September 23, 1952, the famous "Checkers" speech in which Nixon explained to the American public his use of a special campaign fund.[1] There also exists a remarkably similar address, a broadcast by ex-President Harry S. Truman on November 16, 1953 in which Truman answered charges that while president he had allowed a Communist agent, Harry Dexter White, to hold high governmental office. The generic resemblance of the two speeches (both may be classified as mass-media apologia) invites what may be called analog criticism—comparing the speeches in such ways

From *Speech Monographs*, XXXV, 4 (November 1968), 435–450. Used by permission of the author and the Speech Communication Association. Mr. Rosenfield is Professor of Speech at the University of Wisconsin, Madison.

[1] *The only formal scholarly reference to it is Professor Baskerville's sketch of the "Nixon affair" in F. W. Haberman (ed.), "The Election of 1952: A Symposium,"* Quarterly Journal of Speech, *XXXVIII (December 1952), 406–408.*

that each address serves as a reference standard for the other. The objective of such a method of comparison and contrast is two-fold: to specify the fundamental anatomical features which relate the two speeches (engage in a *factorial* analysis of the category of apologetic discourse exemplified by the messages) and to assess the relative artistic merit of each speech, còmpared to the other.[2]

Comparison of these particular speeches is fruitful on several counts. First, an element of objectivity (especially important when discussing contemporary partisans like Nixon and Truman) is introduced when the speeches are played off against each other in the critic's analysis. Second, the identification of similar qualities in the two messages suggests to the critic certain constants operating in an otherwise undefined form—use of instantaneous electronic media to answer accusations. In these two instances we have cases of relatively early efforts by public officials to cope with the rhetorical problems raised by the demands of apologiae nationally broadcast. Where we discover similarities in the messages, we have grounds for attributing those qualities to the situation or the genre rather than to the individual speaker. And should we at some future date find modified tactics in apologetic speeches, we would be in a position to determine whether an evolution occurred in the form itself. Finally, because the surface conditions of these two speeches are so similar, the critic will be alert to the distinctive qualities of each. And having recognized those differences, he will be justified in evaluating the configuration of unique features in each speech as evidence of the individual speaker's artistry in responding to the exigencies of the situation.

The remainder of this paper is divided into five sections. A brief sketch of the incidents surrounding the two speeches is followed by discussion of similarities in the rhetorical contexts which gave rise to the speeches, by specification of the common elements in the two addresses, by consideration of their divergent features, and by discussion of the critical and theoretical implications of the entire rhetorical analysis.

The Nixon fund affair occurred during the 1952 Eisenhower-Stevenson presidential race. On Thursday, September 18, the *New York Post* featured a story headlined "Secret Nixon Fund." It opened as follows:

The existence of a "millionaire's club" devoted exclusively to the financial comfort of Senator Nixon, GOP Vice Presidential candidate, was revealed today.[3]

---

[2] *For further discussion of the analog method as a tool for speech criticism see Rosenfield "The Logic of the Critical Act" in* Rhetorical Criticism, *ed. D. Burks and J. Cleary (in press).*

[3] *Richard M. Nixon,* Six Crises *(Garden City, 1962), pp. 80–81.*

Democratic National Chairman Mitchell, in a "great show of indignation over corruption," promptly demanded that all details of the fund, including contributors and expenditures, be made public, and he called on candidate Eisenhower to remove Nixon from the Republican ticket. The next morning the battle was joined when Nixon responded to the charges in a whistle-stop speech in Marysville, California, characterizing them as a smear by Communists and crooks.[4]

This puerile exchange might have been muffled in the campaign cacophony had not the Republicans been touchy on matters ethical. They had pinned their election hopes on a "crusade to clean up the corruption mess in Washington." Hence, they felt themselves being hoisted on their own petard as the charges against Nixon spread and as several prominent newspapers began to give editorial support to the proposal that Nixon be dropped from the ticket. Should they retain Nixon the "crusade" might take on the shabby appearance of a huckstering attempt to horn in on the proceeds of corruption. But dropping him would imply a plea of "no contest" on the corruption charge and would open them to scorn for having nominated a rook. In either event they would forfeit the corruption issue. The Republicans chose to skirt these painful alternatives and to throw the question of Nixon's future open to a national plebiscite—they purchased a half hour of national broadcast time and instructed Nixon to clear himself of the charges with the electorate.[5]

Thus it was that on September 23, a bare five days after the charges were leveled, Richard Nixon addressed in his own defense the largest television audience to that time, sixty million people. The speech had three sections: a denial of unethical conduct in maintaining a campaign fund, a revelation of Nixon's personal financial history, and a partisan counterattack on the ethical qualifications of the Democrats' nominees. The response to the speech was immediate and fantastic: the public was virtually unanimous in its support of Nixon. Within hours the Republican panic had turned to glee; the "crusade" issue was more vital than ever, and Democrat Stevenson was straining to account for his own personal campaign fund. With a single speech Richard Nixon had won a decisive initiative for his party.[6]

Ex-President Harry S. Truman's ordeal smacked somewhat less of Armageddon and more of a joust; and the outcome was for several reasons less distinct than in Nixon's case. On November 6, 1953, Republican Attorney General Brownell charged in a Chicago speech

---

[4] *Nixon, pp. 83–84;* New York Times, *September 20, 1952, p. 9.*
[5] *Nixon, pp. 95–112.*
[6] *Nixon, p. 118;* A. Hillbruner, Critical Dimensions: The Art of Public Address Criticism (*New York, 1966*), p. 60.

(some claimed it was a smokescreen to draw attention away from recent Republican congressional election losses) that one Harry Dexter White, an alleged Communist spy now dead, had been promoted to a sensitive position with the International Monetary Fund during the Truman administration despite knowledge of his spying activities by "those who appointed him."[7] Truman at first denied ever having seen such reports on White. In the verbal sparring of the next few days both parties hedged. As bits of evidence came to public attention, Truman acknowledged that an unfavorable report had been received concerning White but claimed that at the proper time he had "fired" White. Later Truman shifted again to claim that he had "forced White's resignation." For his part, Brownell watered his accusation to one of "laxity" by the Truman administration in meeting Communist infiltration.

The immediate stimulus for Truman's national broadcast was a subpoena served on November 10 by Representative H. H. Velde (Illinois Republican) directing Truman to testify before the House Un-American Activities Committee regarding the White controversy.[8] Truman rejected the subpoena as his "duty under the Constitution" and chose instead to make his broadcast to fifty million people on Monday, November 16.

Like Nixon, Truman divided his remarks into three parts. He explained his refusal to testify before the H.U.A.C., justified his handling of Harry Dexter White's promotion, and attacked Brownell for having raised the issue. There were no immediate political stakes in the Brownell-Truman clash, so reaction to the speech was undramatic. In the ensuing week F.B.I. Director J. Edgar Hoover's testimony before the Senate Internal Security Committee cast some doubt on the interpretations Truman had offered in his speech. But, by November 18, Eisenhower signalled an end to the confrontation when he expressed hope that the whole issue concerning Communist internal subversion would be history by 1954. Within a week public interest had waned as congressional investigators turned from the White case to other allegations of espionage. Editorials tended to scold both Brownell and Truman for intemperate statements; then most newspapers dropped the matter. In retrospect Truman's can be considered a qualified victory. Though not as conclusive in its effects as Nixon's, his speech served to clear him

[7] New York Times, *November 7, 1953, p. 1.*

[8] *Velde apparently acted in a fit of enthusiasm without consulting Republican congressional leaders. In any event the main effect of the subpoena, besides giving Truman an excuse to mount a national forum, was to embarrass the Eisenhower administration. During his November 11 press conference, President Eisenhower noted in typical fashion that he "personally wouldn't have issued a summons" to an ex-President. Cf.* New York Times, *November 12, p. 14.*

of the main accusations and ended public interest in the circumstances of White's advancement.

These sketches of the two controversies provide sufficient background to enable the reader to consider the rhetorical context from which the two speeches grew.

A prime resemblance between the two speaking situations can be found in the expectations of the two national broadcast audiences. The period 1952–1953 was not marked by any striking shifts in American public opinion on major political issues,[9] and virtually the same individuals comprised the bulk of the two audiences.

The reputations of the two speakers were also such that the public would probably expect much the same rhetorical posture of each. With careers punctuated by flamboyant partisan utterance, there was little hint in the political biographies of Nixon and Truman that either was disposed to seek bipartisan consensus of the sort made popular by Dwight Eisenhower or Lyndon Johnson. Each stood in the public mind as a partisan "slugger," a staunch, uncompromising combatant for his party. As often as not it had been Truman's and Nixon's public remarks that had caused each to perform in the limelight of controversy. Richard Nixon was blessed with a kind of notoriety for pugnacious campaign tactics and for his role in the Alger Hiss investigations. "Irascible" is perhaps the most apt description of Harry Truman's prior public address. It was not without reason that the rallying cry of his 1948 presidential campaign had been, "Give 'em Hell, Harry!" And a public which remembered Mr. Truman's threat to punch the nose of a music critic who had panned daughter Margaret's singing would presumably expect the ex-President to deliver some pungent remarks in any address of self-defense.

Subjected to a personal attack centering on charges of past misconduct in public office, each speaker was placed in a Demosthenic posture; he must go before the citizenry to clear himself of accusations leveled by political assailants. The appropriate argumentative strategy was clearly forensic. The listeners could expect arguments of accusation and defense relating primarily to the interpretation of past facts. To this extent one may say each speaker was propelled by the logic of his situation toward the same, overall rhetorical strategy.

Though it was common practice in ancient Greece for the accused to speak directly to his judges, the use of electronic media for such a purpose was unorthodox in mid-century America. By their decisions to by-pass the customary medium of contemporary public dialog, the

[9] Cf. N.O.R.C. public opinion surveys 312, 315, 329, 334, 339, 348 for the period 1951–1953 (The Roper Public Opinion Research Center, Williamstown, Mass.); A. O. Hero, Jr., "The American Public and the United Nations, 1954–1966," The Journal of Conflict Resolution, X (December 1966), 436–475.

press, and to go instead directly to the people, Nixon and Truman tell us something about the intense character of their situations. Their choice may have been in part simply a symptom of things to come; we appear to rely more and more on the air waves for our contact with current affairs. But one cannot escape the feeling that in these two instances the central figures found the struggle so intense (if not climactic) that they felt it necessary to avoid the inevitable distortion of messages which results from the intervention of the newsprint channel.[10] At any rate, they chose to risk the outcome of their battles on single national broadcasts.

In retrospect a fourth similarity of context becomes apparent: both conflicts were short, sharp, and quickly resolved. The Nixon debate lasted from September 18 to September 24, the day Eisenhower announced that Nixon was vindicated. The Harry Dexter White affair merited headlines from November 7 to November 19.[11]

Finally, the broadcasts were in each case watersheds in the controversies. Nixon's speech caused the collapse of sniping at his campaign funds; Truman's speech was the last public mention of the possibility that a congressional committee might subpoena an ex-President. In view of their importance in each conflict, it is especially remarkable how brief the speeches were. Truman spoke for twenty-three minutes and Nixon's speech ran just under a half hour. One is reminded by contrast of the protracted, even leisurely paced, nineteenth-century oratorical struggles. These modern clashes seem abrupt in any such comparison.

We cannot with assurance attribute the differences between contemporary and former controversies either to qualities inherent in current issues or to the development of electronic media. The cost of air time limits the length of speeches, but it does not prevent continuance of debate by other means. But we can say that the contextual factors here mentioned—a forensic issue, use of broadcast facilities to carry a case directly to the public, relatively limited exposure time, and the sharp, decisive quality of the encounter—seem not coincidentally present in the two cases we are examining. If we as yet have no basis for determining which of the factors were antecedent and which were consequent, which were essential and which accidental, we can at least

---

[10] C. E. Swanson, J. Jenkins, and R. L. Jones, "President Truman Speaks: A Study of Ideas vs. Media," Journalism Quarterly, XXVII (Summer 1950), 251–262; J. Ericson, "The Reporting by the Prestige Press of Selected Speeches of Senator Goldwater in the 1964 Presidential Campaign," unpubl. diss. (University of Wisconsin, 1966).

[11] Although reverberations were felt afterward in connection with other congressional investigations, it is fair to say that Truman's role in it was a scant two weeks.

hypothesize that other contemporary apologiae are likely to display the same combination of attributes. The two speeches under investigation asked national audiences of roughly the same backgrounds to decide the guilt or innocence of two colorful political spokesmen. In choosing to risk defense on a single short speech transmitted directly to the public, the two speakers revealed something of the urgency they must have attached to their acts. What then, may we expect when men of such stripe find it necessary to speak as advocates in their own behalves under circumstances such as these? For a tentative answer we may turn to the messages actually presented by Nixon and Truman.

Both speeches adhered to classic forensic strategies, and both displayed martial overtones. In his denial of the charges, Nixon resorted to arguments of motive and fact (*quale sit* and *an sit*). At the outset he asserted that the appropriate standard for judging his acceptance of campaign contributions must be purity of motive:

I say that it was morally wrong—if any of that $18,000 went to Senator Nixon, for my personal use. I say that it was morally wrong if it was secretly given and secretly handled.[12]

Having demonstrated that these moral precepts were not violated in his use of the funds, Nixon proceeded to a factual iteration of personal financial affairs. These considerations ranged from his need to work in the family grocery store as a boy through the current unpaid balance on his home mortgage. The point of the narrative was clear: there was no evidence of campaign funds diverted to personal use. Nixon denied the accusation with facts.

For Harry Truman, argument by fact was not an option. The public already had reason to believe that at the time he was promoted Harry Dexter White was at least suspected by authorities of subversive activities. Truman employed forensic arguments of motive and value (*quale sit* and *quid sit*) in his defense. He contended that White's promotion was engineered so as to minimize the security risk while at the same time keeping secret an ongoing F.B.I. investigation of subversion. Hence, the motives for Truman's past acts were honorable. He justified his refusal to appear before Representative Velde's committee by ap-

---

[12] *This and all following quotes from the Nixon speech are from an official speech transcript prepared by four National Broadcasting Company stenographers and printed in the* New York Times *of September 24, 1952, p. 22. The* Times *text was verified by comparison with a text appearing in* Vital Speeches of the Day, *XIX (October 15, 1952), 11–15. A variant text can be found in* U.S. News and World Report, *XXXIII (October 3, 1952), 66–70. For a discussion of the problem of textual authenticity see E. G. Bormann,* Theory and Research in the Communicative Arts *(New York, 1965), pp. 173–191.*

pealing to a higher value—such an appearance would represent a threat to the constitutional separation of the three branches of government because it would subject past executive decisions to Congressional review. Implicit in Truman's argument was the premise that constitutional prerogatives take precedence over investigations of national security breaches.

Forensic strategy normally entails accusation as well as defense. Whether from habit or because they perceived that their situations demanded such tactics, both Nixon and Truman chose invective as their mode of attack. It seems more than coincidental that their speeches abound in *ad hominum* innuendoes concerning the moral qualities of their accusers, that in each case roughly the last third of the speech is almost entirely devoted to this kind of forensic offensive.

According to Truman, the Eisenhower administration was guilty of "shameful demagoguery"; Mr. Brownell degraded his office by engaging in political trickery and skullduggery, by lying to the American people, by smearing a defenseless and patriotic American (Chief Justice Fred Vinson, now dead), and by displaying "mealy-mouthed" cowardice. Truman also drew a red herring across the issue when he slipped in a reference to Senator Joseph McCarthy:

> It is now evident that the present administration has fully embraced, for political advantage, McCarthyism. I'm not referring to the senator from Wisconsin—he's only important in that his name has taken on a dictionary meaning in the world. And that meaning is the corruption of truth, the abandonment of our historical devotion to fair play. It is the abandonment of the "due process" of law. It is the use of the big lie and the unfounded accusation against any citizen in the name of Americanism and security. It is the rise to power of the demagogue. . . .[13]

[13] *The Truman text is from the transcript in the November 17, 1953* New York Times, *p. 26. Variant texts can be found in* U.S. News and World Report, *XXXV (November 27, 1953), 104–106 and the* Kansas City Times, *November 17, 1953, pp. 1–2. The* New York Times *version gives internal evidence of being the most accurate account of what Truman actually said except for its omission of the bracketed words in the following sentence (spoken in reference to the late Chief Justice Vinson): "But I deeply resent these cowardly in [sinuations against one who is] dead." Philip C. Brooks, Director of the Harry S Truman Library of Independence, Missouri, agrees that the selected text is the most accurate one available (there being no reading copy of the text); but in a personal letter he refers to the* New York Times *version as a "press release text," thus casting doubt on its accuracy. Since no tape recording seems to exist, close stylistic analysis which would demand the exact words uttered by Truman on the occasion has not been attempted. See J. Thorp, "The Aesthetics of Textual Criticism,"* PLMA, *LXXX (December 1965), 465–482; R. W. Smith, "The 'Second' Inaugural Address of Lyndon Baines Johnson: A Definitive Text,"* SM, *XXXIV (March 1967), 102–108.*

The excerpt intrigues. Was Truman accusing the administration of merely aping McCarthy, or was he suggesting that McCarthy exerted a substantial influence in the government? His meaning was conveniently vague. What stands out in Truman's attack is that it is unanswerable, for it substitutes name-calling for an assessment of motive. Brownell, for instance, could only reply to the charge of being mealy-mouthed by hurling a more insulting label at Truman; it was here, as always, futile to treat such an accusation as a "charge" in the traditional, legal sense.

Although not as explicit, Richard Nixon proved more adept than Truman in his use of innuendo. The ex-President pinned the label "liar" on Brownell outright; candidate Nixon was content with a telling sideswipe at his opposition. Twice, as if in tossing it off in passing, Nixon reminded the public that his Democratic counterpart, vice-presidential candidate Sparkman, had his wife on the Senate payroll. Nixon in both instances hastened (almost too quickly, one might feel)[14] to add, "I don't condemn him for that," "that's his business." The critic detects the swish of a matador's cape here. Nixon's nobility ("I'm for fair play") is deftly juxtaposed to the crass conduct of Sparkman. Nixon doesn't plunge the sword—he is content to draw blood. Standing aside, as it were, Nixon left the audience to judge who was in fact honorable in the use of Senate funds, but by means of the sharp contrast the auditor was offered only one option.

This distinctive habit of juxtaposing black and white distinguished Nixon's acrid invective from Truman's forthright smears. Consider the following passages:

> . . . *I love my country. And I think my country is in danger. And I think that the only man that can save America at this time is the man that's running for President on my ticket, Dwight Eisenhower. You say, why do I think it's in danger? And I say, look at the record. Seven years of the Truman-Acheson Administration and what's happened? Six hundred million people lost to the Communists, and a war in Korea in which we have lost 117,000 American casualties.*

*   *   *

> *You wouldn't trust a man who made the mess to clean it up. That's Truman. And . . . you can't trust the man who was picked by the man who made the mess to clean it up, and that's Stevenson.*
>
> *And so I say, Eisenhower, who owes nothing to Truman, nothing to the big-city bosses—he is the man that can clean up the mess in Washington.*

*   *   *

[14] *Nixon documents his deliberate intent in his book. See* Six Crises, *p. 118.*

> *I'm going to campaign up and down America until we drive the crooks and the Communists and those that defend them out of Washington, and remember, folks, Eisenhower is a great man. Believe me, he's a great man, and a vote for Eisenhower is a vote for what's good for America.*

What is striking is Nixon's habit of joining off-handed insults of the opposition with knight-in-shining-armor depictions of him and his. By this uneasy combination of dropped lines and stereotypes a Nixon insult was made at once more provocative—and more suspect—than the ingenuous efforts of Mr. Truman. For listeners there was the satisfaction of discerning the *act* of attack often tinged, one may believe, with distaste at being told so bluntly and sweepingly that untarnished good imbued Republicans and unrelieved corruption permeated the Democratic Party.

In addition to common forensic strategies and *ad hominum* ploys, a third general similarity characterized the two speeches: the manner in which documentation was employed to support arguments. Had this been an oratorical contest between Nixon and Truman, one might be tempted to ask which speaker displayed the better looking set of facts. Nixon's speech is of course best remembered for the section which began:

> *And I'd like to tell you this evening that just about an hour ago we received an independent audit of this entire fund . . . and I have that audit here in my hand. . . .*

The section ended with the famous anecdote which caused the speech to receive the popular title "the Checkers Speech": the story of how Nixon had accepted only one personal gift while in public office—the cocker spaniel, Checkers.[15] The section occupied the entire middle third of the address and contained all of the documentation used in the speech.

Is it only coincidental that all of Harry Truman's documentation, such as it was, was also located in the middle third of his speech? Truman did not have any records in his hands. Instead he announced his presentation of inartistic data in this way:

> *I have had my files examined and have consulted with some of my colleagues who worked with me on this matter during my term of office.*

[15] *Nixon admits that he planted this anecdote as another barb at the Democrats. The inspiration for the ploy was F.D.R.'s "Fala" speech during the 1944 presidential campaign.* Six Crises, *p. 103.*

Truman then "reported" his findings as a narration interwoven with interpretation; his evidence tended to uphold the assertion that his decisions were the most expedient under the circumstances. He ended his narration with the death of White in 1948, after White's appearance before H.U.A.C.

Why both speakers should lump all documentation in the middle of their speeches, and why both should assign the same relative space to presentation of evidence I am not sure. The simple enumeration of quasi-documentary data found in both cases might be taken as proof of the contention that ours is an age which puts its faith in facts rather than reason, and that contemporary rhetorical strategies often reflect that trust.[16] It is in any case somewhat beside the point for the critic to test by the traditional logical criteria the soundness of conclusions drawn from such selective, factual data as Nixon and Truman presented.

It seems clear that in one sense it was less important that the materials these speakers presented should provide absolute corroboration of their assertions than that the core of each case should contain a disclosure of new data. These data constituted artifacts; their presence lent an air of scientific proof (note the actuarial tone of Nixon's revelations) which could serve an important rhetorical end in and of itself. Professor Baskerville has argued that Senator Joseph McCarthy relied on an illusion of scientific proof to gain belief.[17] I suggest that if we leave aside matters of inferential soundness we can detect both Nixon and Truman benefitting from public acceptance of confirmation-by-a-heap-of-new-information.[18] And this interpretation gains plausibility when one recalls that the "charges" being answered alleged the *existence* of a fund and the motive of an act.

One final resemblance between the two apologiae is related to the use of documentation. Aside from the "good looking" new data presented, there were, strictly speaking, no new arguments in either speech. All the key ideas, and even the insults, can be found scattered in public statements made by the two speakers in the weeks prior to their television addresses. As early as September 19, for exam-

---

[16] Cf. W. S. Howell, "The Declaration of Independence and Eighteenth-Century Logic," William and Mary Quarterly, *XVIII (October 1961), 463–484;* R. Weaver, The Ethics of Rhetoric *(Chicago, 1953); Dwight Macdonald, "A Critique of the Warren Report,"* Esquire, LXIII *(March 1965), 59ff.*

[17] B. Baskerville, "The Illusion of Proof," Western Speech, XXV *(Fall 1961),* 236–242.

[18] This "faith in the fact" hearkens back in the American rhetorical tradition at least as early as the age of Muckraker journalism. Cf. D. M. Chalmers, The Social and Political Ideas of the Muckrakers (New York, 1964); G. Ashenbrenner, "The Rhetoric of the Muckrakers," unpubl. thesis (University of Wisconsin, 1967).

ple, Nixon was claiming that the charges against him were a "smear by Communists and crooks" intended to make him relent in his campaign. On that same day Nixon also made references to Mrs. Sparkman's drawing a Senate salary.[19]

The finding that major speeches grew out of series of minor speeches, that the act of rhetorical invention was in fact an act of *selection* from previously used ideas is not unusual in rhetorical criticism. Studies of the major speeches of Grady, Bryan, Martin Luther King, and many others reveal the same thing: the oratorical masterpiece delivered at a crucial juncture in history reveals the orator not so much rising to heights of inspiration as choosing judiciously from a repertory of past ideas an appropriate mix of materials.[20] If our small sample is at all typical, the speech in the moment of crisis is most likely to represent a climax, a summing up, of those rhetorical thrusts which seem to have been most effective with the public on previous dry runs.[21]

In the speeches under examination here, two possible implications seem to follow from the similar inventive processes. One is that under conditions of contemporary American public address little fresh adaptation of *content* is to be expected in a climactic message. Whether Nixon or Truman spoke to a whistle-stop crowd in Idaho, a group of reporters, or a national audience, the substance of the speaker's remarks remained the same. In either case adaptation was from the outset constantly directed to the American public as a whole rather than to the immediate audience.

The central place scholars have accorded speakers' adaptation of arguments to *specific* audiences may be somewhat less justified in explaining the characteristics of television apologiae than we might at first think. Indeed, the only original element in either of the speeches examined here was the inclusion of new facts. Disclosure of new information may be more significant as a rhetorical phenomenon in dis-

[19] New York Times, *September 20, 1952, p. 9.*
[20] *Cf. Baskerville, Q.J.S., p. 407; T. D. Harrison, "The 'New South' Revisited," paper presented at "debut" session of S.A.A. National Convention, December 1965; D. H. Smith, "Martin Luther King, Jr., Rhetorician of Revolt," unpubl. diss. (University of Wisconsin, 1964); R. T. Oliver, History of Public Speaking in America (Boston, 1965), pp. 484–485.*
[21] *The critic may, if he chooses, examine the process whereby Nixon and Truman "discovered" the materials they eventually used—but only if he reckons with the clusters of earlier minor statements made by both men. In limiting the scope of the critical study to the television addresses themselves, the rhetorical critic must perforce adjust his notion of invention to one which emphasizes the means each speaker employed in selecting materials already available rather than broadening the concept of invention to include research procedures the speaker may originally have used.*

course prepared for a mass audience than are specific tactics of adaptation to the immediate audience.

To the extent that this implication holds, it suggests another. What distinguished Nixon's television apologia from Nixon's remarks to the press during the week prior to his speech was not the substance but the form. The *manner* in which Nixon chose to array for a national audience the ploys he had by trial and error found successful on more limited platforms cannot alone account for the potentialities of his broadcast address. The elements of rhetorical artistry unique to apologiae will be better seen if we turn from consideration of overall strategies to individual differences Nixon and Truman manifested in their tactics of array and emphasis.

Close reading confirms that there were indeed fundamental differences in the fabrics of the two speeches. Three formal qualities become prominent when one undertakes to depict the artistic genius of each discourse: the inferential patterns, the foci of attack, and the relative emphases on public or personal affairs. These three elements seem to set Nixon apart from Truman as an apologist.

The first impression one draws on comparing the two speeches is that where Truman's message displays a kind of dynamic, structural progression, Nixon's is hortatory and reminds one of stone blocks cemented into an edifice. The instrument of Truman's kinetic coloration seems to be his tendency to fuse acceptable (from the point of view of the audience) universal principles and conditional propositions into short, direct, enthymematic inferences. In the following passage the first two sentences form the theoretical ground from which Truman, in the third sentence, drew the consequence. Let us assume that most auditors accepted the principle of maintaining the independence of the executive branch of government. By articulating that principle, Truman prepared them to accept the truth of his fourth and fifth sentences which extended the principle to cover his behavior as chief executive.

The separation and balance of powers between the three independent branches of government is fundamental in our constitutional form of government. A congressional committee may not compel the attendance of a President of the United States, while he is in office, to inquire into matters pertaining to the performance of his official duties. If the constitutional principle were otherwise, the office of the president would not be independent. It is just as important to the independence of the executive that the actions of the President should not be subjected to questioning by the Congress after he has completed his term of office as that they should not be questioned while he is serving as President. In either case, the office of President would be dominated by

Congress, and the Presidency might become a mere appendage of Congress.

There is a logical gap between premise and conclusion, but if we accept the notion of enthymematic inference it is not difficult to imagine that an auditor who fully granted the explicit major premise would be prepared to fill in for himself the implicit minor premise. Truman's "if" statement thus serves in this instance to intensify adherence to the basic principle and to prepare hearers to make the necessary logical leap.

A like inferential movement occurred in a section where Truman justified his disposal of the White case.

But following receipt of the F.B.I. report and the consultations with members of my cabinet, it was decided that he would be limited to membership on the board of directors of the International Monetary Fund. With his duties thus restricted, he would be subject to the supervision of the Secretary of the Treasury, and his position would be less important and much less sensitive—if it were sensitive at all—than the position then held by him as Assistant Secretary of the Treasury.

Tonight I want the American people to understand that the course we took protected the public interest and security and at the same time permitted the intensive F.B.I. investigation then in progress to go forward. No other course could have served both of these purposes.

Truman asked the audience to look to the consequences of his alternatives; he asked them to grant the worth of his dual objectives, and he devoted his verbal effort to convincing them (by mention of the F.B.I. report and cabinet consultations and by showing how the Secretary of the Treasury could better control White's activities) that the chosen policy was the most expedient.

It is no insult to Nixon to observe that his disposition suggests that of a catechism: he puts the question he wants the audience to consider and then he speaks to the question as if reading from a trial brief.

But then, some of you will say, and rightly, "Well, what did you use the fund for, Senator? Why did you have to have it?"

Let me tell you in just a word how a Senate office operates. . . .

* * *

But then the question arises, you say, "Well, how do you pay for these and how can you do it legally?"

And there are several ways that it can be done, incidentally, and it is done legally in the United States Senate and in the Congress. The first way is to be a rich man. I don't happen to be a rich man, so I couldn't use that.

And now I'm going to suggest some courses of conduct.

First of all, you have read in the papers about other funds, now. Mr. Stevenson apparently had a couple. . . .

These excerpts not only represent juncture points in Nixon's speech— they are also frames which shape the arguments. Given such over-powering lead-ins there is little room for an auditor's imagination to function. His mind remains riveted as the argument unfolds. Viewed as a performance-in-time, the inferences are pre-determined by the transi-tions, and the discourse stubbornly resists efforts by an auditor to par-ticipate independently in the communicative act. There are undoubted merits in such structure; but the organization does not permit enthy-mematic reasoning as did Truman's. It was perhaps this catechetical feature of Nixon's recital which lent that "harsh and boney" quality of pre-packaged argument, not fully digested by the speaker, which some respondents discerned in his address.

Opponents were for both men objects of scorn, but Nixon and Tru-man differed in the breadth with which they defined the enemy camp. For Truman the "enemy" was a single man—Herbert Brownell. At times, as in the opening words of the speech, he depicted Brownell as a tool of the administration, but for the most part his invective sought out Brownell alone.

There can't be any doubt that Mr. Brownell was talking about me. Now let me talk about Mr. Brownell and this phony charge he has made.

His charge is false, and Mr. Brownell must have known it was false at the very time he was making it.

Mr. Brownell has made a great show of detail. . . . As Mr. Brownell should have learned by this time. . . .

* * *

There is one aspect of this affair that should be clear to everyone. That is the obvious political motivations of this attack on me.

In the launching of this attack on me, the Republican attorney gen-eral worked hand in glove with the Republican National Committee. The manner and the timing of what has been done made it perfectly clear that the powers of the attorney general have been prostituted for hopes of political gain.

In all cases Truman's tactic was to *accuse* Brownell, thus using con-sistently an overall forensic strategy. The cumulative impact of Truman's strategy would leave one who took the ex-President's words at face value with the feeling that the confrontation was between Truman and Brownell alone. Both the partial and the neutral auditor were given grounds for believing that Brownell unjustly maligned Mr. Truman. The entire force of Truman's argument was thus channeled to turn the attack back upon his accuser.

The clear focus of Truman's invective can be seen from these figures: of 15 accusatory references in the speech, 7 concern Brownell's personal behavior (he lied, fooled the public, is the source of malicious charges); 3 accuse Brownell of cheapening his office; 4 charge that the administration used Brownell as its tool in this affair; 1 places Brownell in conspiracy with the Republican National Committee. Again, where Truman stated the charges against him, he invariably coupled those statements with counter-charges that Brownell lied in his accusation. Had he not been so consciously mounting an offensive against Brownell, Truman might have contented himself at those points with a simple denial of the charges, but roughly 45 percent of the Truman speech concentrated on the "sordid" role of Brownell. This is gross evidence of the sharp focus of Truman's invective.

The characteristics of Truman's attack are the more noteworthy because of the comparative diffusiveness of Nixon's invective. Where Truman carefully leveled his sights on a particular object of scorn, Nixon must appear to all but his most devoted listeners to be lashing out at a penumbral host of spectres. Consider the swath cut by the following excerpts.

My fellow Americans: I come before you tonight as a candidate . . . and as a man whose honesty and integrity has been questioned.

By whom? Nixon never makes clear who is accusing him.

I am sure that you have read the charge, and you've heard it. . . .

Again there is no recognition of a particular source for the charge.

And the record will show that [he had not exerted influence on behalf of fund contributors] the records which are in the hands of the Administration.

Is the source of the charges somehow in league with the Administration?

. . . and let me say that I recognize that some will continue to smear, regardless of what the truth may be. . . .

Here again, the sources of attack are everywhere; perhaps reasonably, Nixon seemed to see himself in a state of siege. Yet, however justified such a belief may have been, its expression could not contribute to a well-focused counterattack.

One other thing I probably should tell you, because if I don't they'll probably be saying this about me too. . . . [Nixon here employs the "Checkers" gambit.] And, you know, the kids love the dog, and I just want to say this, right now, that regardless of what they say about it, we're gonna keep it.

* * *

. . . I remember, in the dark days of the Hiss case, some of the same columnists, some of the same radio commentators who are attacking me now and misrepresenting my position, were violently opposing me at the time I was after Alger Hiss.

Is the squabble between Nixon and the press? Or is it the case that the unnamed columnists are joining forces with other sinister agents to destroy Nixon? No listener could tell *from the discourse,* for the last excerpt is as close as Nixon came to identifying his attackers.

Failure to name accusers would not be significant (it probably has certain redeeming features) were it not that a concomitant limitation must thereby be placed upon the impact of an apologia. Nixon could not thus control the vector of his counterattack as precisely as Truman. Hence the tone of Nixon's reply tended toward the petulant, as though the man were lashing out at unknown conspirators seeking to victimize him. A rough classification of approximately 20 attack-statements in Nixon's speech shows that one-third were references to unspecified opponents, another third were scattered digs at Mr. Sparkman, the State Department, Mr. Stevenson, etc., and the final third were epideictic magnifications of corruption in the Truman administration. There was, in short, no concerted effort on Nixon's part either to isolate the source of the accusations or to provide the audience an explanation for such attacks.

It may be objected that Nixon's two-fold goal of clearing himself and scoring election points would force him to employ this particular pattern in invective. But the pattern, it turns out, is a Nixon pattern, not one peculiar to the situation. As befits a campaigner, Nixon showed greater concern with the faults of his political opposition in 1952 than with the source and nature of accusations against him. But the consequences of this unfocused invective appear to have stretched beyond the political contest of 1952. Some years later Nixon was to refer to this apologia as the event which made possible his election as vice president and at the same time denied him the presidency in 1960.[22] It may be that the reputation for immaturity which attached itself to Nixon had its origins in the undisciplined, unfocused attacks found in this speech.

A third notable difference also distinguishes the two speeches. The tone of the public man doing public business pervades the Truman address, whereas Nixon offers a revelation of the personal morality of a private man. This difference in tone grew in part out of the exigencies of each speaker's self-defense; however, both men spoke as public officials, so the contrast may also be taken as in some degree an index to the habitual rhetorical postures of the men.

As Harry Truman dealt with it, Brownell's accusation concerned the conduct of a public official in the execution of his office; the official happened to be named Truman.

When I became President, I took an oath to preserve, protect and defend the Constitution of the United States. I am still bound by that oath and will be as long as I live. While I was in office, I lived up to that oath. . . . Now that I have laid down the heavy burdens of that office, I do not propose to take any step which would violate that oath or which would in any way lead to encroachments on the independence of that great office.

Was Truman using the office to shield himself from public scrutiny? Let us grant that he was not, that he was sincere in perceiving the demand that he testify as a genuine threat to the independence of chief executives. Corroboration for this interpretation is provided by Truman's other references to himself. Virtually all of the new data he provided, for example, were designed to show the calculated wisdom of the policy he eventually chose to follow. His mentions of himself served chiefly to enliven and personalize the image of an official struggling to arrive at a rational course of action. In the two instances where he mentioned himself as a person, it was to diminish his personal significance and to place the issue in the larger perspective of public affairs.

First, I would like to tell you, the people of America, why I declined to appear before that committee. On the surface, it might seem to be an easy thing to do, and smart politics, for Harry Truman, now a private citizen of Independence, Missouri, to use the committee as a forum to answer the scurrilous charges which have been made against me. Many people urged me to do that. It was an attractive suggestion and appealed to me.

But if I had done it, I would have been a party with the committee to

[22] *Nixon, Six Crises, pp. 125–129.*

an action which would have undermined the constitutional position of the office of President of the United States.

* * *

If this were a matter which merely involved the name and reputation of Harry S. Truman, private citizen of Independence, Missouri, I would not be as concerned as I am. I can take care of myself. I believe that the American people know me well enough from my service as captain of Battery D in World War I to my service as President of the United States to know that I have always acted with the best interests of my country at heart.

But Mr. Brownell knows that, in this matter, when the final decision was mine, I relied on my principal advisers. . . .

There is one aspect of this affair that should be clear to everyone. That is the obvious political motivations of this attack on me.

Clearly, Truman preferred the *persona* of the office, and he allowed it to slip for only the briefest, most stereotyped glimpses of the real man behind the mask.

Almost the reverse was the case with Richard Nixon. Let us grant to him, too, the sincerity of his utterance. It still remains that his self-references all highlight the human creature, Dick Nixon, not the United States Senator, a public figure seeking election to another office:

It was not a secret fund. As a matter of fact, when I was on "Meet the Press"—some of you may have seen it, last Sunday—Peter Edson came up to me, after the program, and he said, "Dick, what about this fund we hear about?" And I said. . . .

Nixon *could* have generalized his argument to a discussion of the dilemma faced by the public official who must avoid temptations to corruption even as he seeks campaign contributions. He began on this course when he briefly considered the difficulty of running a Senator's office on the meager funds allotted by Congress.[23] But in the main he chose to present an autobiographical recitation of The Life and Hard Times of Young Dick Nixon.

The baring of one's finances (Nixon called it baring his soul) is not lightly undertaken in our commercial society; it surely requires some self-sacrifice. Its spectacular quality leads one to wonder whether it was rhetorically essential to Nixon's apologia or whether it offers a special kind of reading on the speaker. A few, but only a few, public

[23] *Professor Baskerville argues in the Q.J.S. symposium that Nixon ought to have taken this tack. I would not go so far, but would simply point out the ultimate rhetorical consequences of the path Nixon chose to follow.*

figures publicly report the full details of their finances. My own inclination is to believe that the prominence of creature-Nixon in this discourse served dual ends. It would seem unlikely, for instance, that a struggling young couple renting an eighty-dollar-a-month apartment in Fairfax, Virginia could be benefitting from graft. The material presented is persuasive, even for the doubter; and it is touching. But at the same time the information offered is not entirely relevant, for it fails to address itself to the issue: "Was there a misuse of campaign funds?" Nixon had already treated that issue in his denial of dishonesty, in his description of the needs of a modern Senate office, and in his report of the audit. The impression remains that Nixon was more ready to display his personal self than is common among civic men.

This same impression is further confirmed when we notice that the homey tone pervaded Nixon's speech as thoroughly as the public tone colored Truman's address. In both cases there was, for example, the matter of justification for conduct. Nixon explained that he could have put his wife on his Senate payroll, as Sparkman had done:

> . . . *but I have never done that for this reason: I have found that there are so many deserving stenographers and secretaries in Washington that need the work that I just didn't feel it was right to put my wife on the payroll.*

Or consider Nixon's explanation of why he intended to continue to fight the smears:

> *Because, you see, I love my country. And I think my country is in danger.*

Nixon, it appears, persistently, as though habitually, accounted for his public behavior by reference to his personal sentiments. It seems reasonable to suggest that Harry Truman would probably have sought other, equally effective justifications and proofs had he been in Nixon's place. At any rate, his apologia was far less creature-centered than Nixon's.

It may be that this distinction between the image of a public figure and that of the private man accounts for the observer's subjective impression that Harry Truman's message all adds up to a public warning while Richard Nixon's message amounts to an extended claim: "They're out to get me." And this difference in the core of the messages may provide an additional clue as to why the "Checkers" speech, so effective with the immediate audience, could another day function as a barrier to Nixon's presidential ambitions.

The Nixon plea sacrificed the mystique of the public man. It displayed him as a living, breathing citizen—perhaps too suggestive of Dagwood Bumstead. News commentator, Eric Sevaried, may have expressed the long-range public judgment aptly when he tried to explain the defeat of homey though honest and capable candidates for office:

We say in a democracy that we like the ordinary man. But we don't like him that much.[24]

When Nixon spoke to 60,000,000 people of his desire to help one deserving steno rather than hire his wife, even his loyal followers must have wondered whether he expected to be believed totally and literally. With whatever sincerity, Nixon ensnared himself by his rhetorical choices: he portrayed himself as at least a touch too simple for a complex age and too insensitive to the demands of a national, public occasion. It seems even fair to say that not every listener's smirk was one of superiority, but some were smirks of embarrassment. Nixon's response to attack, though emotionally appealing, was not fully appropriate to the public man, at least in this century.

Let us now extrapolate from the foregoing analysis those characteristics which appear to shed light on the two speeches under investigation. Conceivably, these features may represent parameters which will define other apologiae presented via the mass media.

There are four similarities in the two discourses which I take, at this time, to represent constants in the apologetic equation. Recognizing that these similarities may be accidental, may reflect some underlying kinship of the two speakers, or may be genuine symptoms of the demands of the apologetic form, we may tentatively hypothesize that the broadcast apologia is likely to be a part of a short, intense, decisive clash of views. We may further predict that a speaker who chooses to argue in his own defense over the airwaves is unlikely to limit himself to defensive remarks. In all probability he will take the opportunity to engage in some form of invective. We may perhaps be more than ordinarily aware of the invective in these two addresses because of the speakers' reputations; therefore, future criticism ought to study the extent to which invective is a staple of the genre. A heaping of data without careful attention to their artistic use may or may not be unique to modern apologetics, but the lumping of facts in the middle third of both speeches seems more than coincidental. It may be that either the circumstances surrounding broadcasting or the forensic demands of apologiae exert particular influences in these connections. Finally, the apologists' tendency to reassemble previously used arguments for

[24] *Eric Sevareid, Columbia Broadcasting System election returns program, November 8, 1966.*

presentation from the national rostrum (as evidenced in the fact that these two speeches are simple composites of earlier remarks) may hold implications both for our conception of rhetorical invention and for the critic's selection of facets for interpretation.

Whether or not the similarities we have just reviewed represent constants in the apologetic equation, we may regard as variables the dimensions of individual difference which were observed. Here emerged three ways by which speakers may put their personal imprints on messages: the manner in which the inferential pattern controls the form of the address, the degree to which the speaker channels his attack and thereby directs his listeners' aggression, and the ratio of public-personal explanations which becomes prominent in messages employing otherwise intimate electronic media.[25] There may of course be other factors influencing the character of modern broadcast apologiae, and we cannot discount the probability that as men gain experience in the use of electronic media the forms and styles of apologiae will change. Be that as it may, the elements of form and style amplified here deserve further study in apologiae and other genres of rhetorical discourse.

Finally, we are in a position to draw some conclusions concerning specific qualities of the two speeches here analyzed. First, it seems patently unfair to hold either Mr. Nixon or Mr. Truman in contempt, as many have, because either "injected personalities" into his remarks. Even granting the mercurial nature of the two speakers, there is a possibility that resort to invective is virtually inevitable given the unique configuration of forces operating upon the apologist. Secondly, if we wish to judge the logical validity or weight of evidence in either speech, we shall need to distinguish formal standards (which are often drawn from the courtroom) from the relativistic norms inherent in apologetics or in the age. To accuse Mr. Nixon of inadequate support for his contentions is to overlook the impact of his evidence on his audience. If accusations are to be mounted in this connection they are better directed to a society which contents itself with piles of evidence in place of rigorous argument.[26]

Lastly, while recognizing the unfairness of many journalistic criticisms of Richard Nixon, it does seem reasonable to contend that the most curious short-coming of his "Checkers" speech, when compared with Truman's address, was its endurance in the public mind, its capacity to outlast the demands of the occasion. Whereas Harry Truman's discourse was totally relevant to specific rhetorical objectives, Nixon

[25] *Cf. J. M. Ripley, "Television and Recreational Patterns,"* Television Quarterly, *II* (*Spring 1963*), *31–36;* M. McLuhan, Understanding Media: The Extensions of Man (*New York, 1965*), *pp. 297–337.*

[26] *On this matter of loose standards of assessment in a given society see* Aristotle, Rhetoric, *1354a 15–24.*

in a single stroke demolished both the opposition's case and injured his own standing as a public man. "Checkers" resulted in immediate victory for the campaigner; yet its traces admittedly continue to plague the political figure.[27]

Dimensions of the Concept of Rhetoric
by Wayne Brockriede

During recent years a state of cold war has existed in the field of speech. Humanists who seek to understand rhetoric primarily through the use of historical scholarship and behavioral scientists who seek to develop a communication theory primarily through empirical description and experimental research have tended to see one another as threatening enemies. Yet members of these factions have the common objective of studying similar phenomena. The student of communication who conceives his study as focusing on pragmatic interaction of people and ideas is concerned with the rhetorical impulse within communication events.[1]

The purpose of this essay is to sketch the beginning and to encourage the further development of a system of dimensions for the study of rhetorical communication. Five assumptions implicit in this attempt should be stated explicitly from the outset.

First, the conception of rhetoric broadly as the study of how interpersonal relationships and attitudes are influenced within a situational context assumes the presence of the rhetorical impulse in such diverse acts as a speaker addressing an audience face to face or through mass media, a group of people conferring or conversing, a writer creating a drama or a letter to an editor, or a government or some other institution projecting an image.

Second, the concept of rhetoric must grow empirically from an observation and analysis of contemporary, as well as past, events.[2] The dimensions should be selected, developed, structured, and continuously revised to help explain and evaluate particular rhetorical acts.

[27] *Cf. E. Black,* Rhetorical Criticism *(New York, 1965), pp. 162–164.*

From *The Quarterly Journal of Speech,* LIV, 1 (February 1968), 1–12. Used by permission of the author and the Speech Communication Association. Mr. Brockriede is Professor of Communication and Drama at the University of Colorado.
[1] *Although my treatment differs from Dean C. Barnlund's excellent analysis in his "Toward a Meaning-Centered Philosophy of Communication,"* Journal of Communication, *XII (December 1962), 197–211, the scope of my conception of rhetoric seems similar to the scope of his conception of communication. Gerald R. Miller in his* Speech Communication: A Behavioral Approach *(Indianapolis, Ind., 1966), makes explicit (p. 12) his synonymous usage of the terms rhetoric and speech communication.*

[2] *An argument which supports this claim is developed in my essay "Toward a Contemporary Aristotelian Theory of Rhetoric,"* QJS, *LII (February 1966), 35–37.*

Third, although the theorist, critic, or practitioner may focus his attention on a rhetorical act, such an act must be viewed as occurring within a matrix of interrelated contexts, campaigns, and processes.

Fourth, the rubrics of a rhetorical act are best viewed as dimensional, each reflecting a wide range of possible descriptions and not as expressing dichotomies.

Fifth, the dimensions of rhetoric are interrelational: each dimension bears a relationship to every other dimension.

This essay, therefore, represents an attempt to sketch a contemporary concept of interrelated interpersonal, attitudinal, and situational dimensions of a broadly conceived rhetorical act.

1

Traditional rhetoric places much less emphasis on interpersonal relationships than does the model presented in this paper. Even the concept of *ethos* frequently has been conceived as personal proof functioning rationalistically as a message variable.[3]

What are here developed as interpersonal dimensions may indeed function in an instrumental way, having some influence on a rhetorical act which aims primarily at attitudinal influence or situational appropriateness. But interpersonal dimensions themselves often represent the principal goals; and the establishment, change, or reinforcement of such interpersonal relationships as liking, power, and distance may exercise a controlling influence on the other dimensions.

Liking. This interpersonal dimension poses the question: how attracted to one another are the people who participate in a rhetorical act? Liking differs qualitatively and may refer to such continua as spiritual adoration—hate, sexual attraction—repulsion, friendship—enmity, and compatibility—incompatibility. In a dyadic act the feelings may or may not be mutual. When many people are involved—as in hearing a public address, participating in a discussion, or reading a best-seller, a single relationship may be characteristic—as when an audience becomes polarized, or relationships may vary—as when some discussants feel affection for a leader whereas others are repelled. Liking also differs in degree of intensity and in degree of susceptibility to change.

The change or reinforcement of the liking dimension may function as the primary purpose of a rhetorical act; courtship, for example, aims principally at affecting this relationship. Or increasing, maintaining, or decreasing the degree people like one another may be a by-product of

---

[3] *For example, in Lester Thonssen and A. Craig Baird's* Speech Criticism *(New York, 1948), the chapter on* ethos *(pp. 383–391) is subtitled "ethical proof in discourse."*

a situation which has other chief aims. Or the liking relationship, though it remains essentially unchanged during a rhetorical act, may have a profound influence on whether other dimensions vary, as well as on how they vary.[4]

Power. Power may be defined as the capacity to exert interpersonal influence. Power may be the ultimate purpose or function, as in a power struggle, or it may be a by-product of or an influence on the controlling dimensions. The power dimension includes two primary variables.

First, what are the kinds of power? One is the influence a person has because others like him. The word *charisma* denotes this kind of power when it reaches a great magnitude. But personal magnetism exists also in lesser degrees. The power of personal attractiveness represents a kind of intersection of liking and power. A second type of power stems from position or role in the social system. By having control over the assignment of sanctions, the allocation of rewards and punishments in a social system, a man merely by virtue of his office or role may be powerful. A third type is the control over the communication channels and other elements of the rhetorical situation. This situational power corresponds to what some people call the gatekeeper function. A fourth kind of power is an influence over the sources of information, the norms and attitudes, and the ideology. Such an influence seems to depend on the extent to which other people trust one's ideational competence generally and his special expertise on matters relevant to the rhetorical act, on their perceptions of his general willingness to express himself honestly and accurately and of his special candor on the particular relevant topics, and on their feelings of confidence in their abilities to predict accurately the meaning and significance attached to his statements and actions.[5] Finally, one exercises indirectly a degree of power by having access to and influence on other people who can exercise the other kinds of power more directly. So a first general variable of the power dimension is the degree with which people participating in a rhetorical act can manifest these kinds of power.

[4] *Hugh D. Duncan stresses this dimension in his* Communication and Social Order (*New York, 1962*) *when he says (p. 170) that* "*the study of how men court each other . . . will tell us much about the function of rhetoric in society.*" *See also Kenneth Burke,* Rhetoric of Motives *in* A Grammar of Motives and a Rhetoric of Motives (*Cleveland, 1962*), *pp. 732–736. I make no attempt in this essay to catalogue the status of knowledge or to supply bibliographies concerning each of the dimensions discussed. I shall suggest, however, a source or two which will develop further each of the dimensions considered in this essay.*

[5] *Kenneth Andersen and Theodore Clevenger, Jr., provide an excellent synthesis of information on this kind of power in* "*A Summary of Experimental Research in Ethos,*" Speech Monographs, *XXX (June 1963), 59–78.*

A second variable is power structure. Knowing how much power of what kind each rhetorical participant has may be less immediately relevant than knowing the relationship among the power statuses of the people involved. That is, power is relative rather than absolute. The significance of the power of a writer, for example, regardless of the amount or kind he may possess, depends on how much power he has relative to that of his readers. Two questions especially are important in an analysis of the power structure. How disparate are the power positions of the various participants of an act, and does the act function to increase, maintain, or decrease the disparity? How rigid or flexible is the structure, and does the rhetorical act function to increase, maintain, or decrease the stability?[6]

Distance. The concept of distance is related to the other interpersonal dimensions. One generally feels "closer" to those persons he likes and "farther" from those he dislikes, but the greater the power disparity the greater the distance. Like all other dimensions, the establishment of an appropriate distance (whether decreasing, maintaining, or increasing it) may be a rhetorical act's primary function, an incidental outcome, or an influencing factor.

Two kinds of distance make up this dimension. One is an interpersonal distance between each two participants in a rhetorical act. The other is a social distance which exists within the structure of the group or groups within or related to the rhetorical act—such groups as audiences, committees, organizations, societies, and cultures. Although interpersonal and group distance are related closely and tend generally to covary, they are discrete variables in that two persons in a discussion group, for example, may move more closely together while the group structure is in the process of disintegrating.[7]

---

[6] *This dimension seems to have been ignored in the study of many rhetorical situations. It is only implied, partially, for example, in the public address doctrine of ethos. During recent years, however, under the headings of leadership and power structure, many small group specialists have emphasized it. See, for example, Dorwin Cartwright and Alvin Zander,* Group Dynamics: Research and Theory, *2nd ed. (Evanston, Ill., 1960), pp. 487–809. Among a number of useful works in the field of political sociology which are relevant to an understanding of the function of power in rhetorical acts, see* Class, Status, and Power, *ed. Reinhard Bendix and Seymour Martin Lipset, 2nd ed. (New York, 1966), pp. 201–352.*

[7] *One of the shortcomings of the concept of interpersonal distance is that the term is not readily operationalized into specifiable behaviors. Consciously or unconsciously, however, people seem to have a sense of closeness or distance from others; such a feeling can influence rhetorical interaction. The philosophical basis for Kenneth Burke's rhetoric is the view that men are fundamentally divided. His concepts of identification and consubstantiality suggest that one of rhetoric's functions is to reduce man's interpersonal*

Several questions about the role of interpersonal and group distance in rhetorical situations seem important. How much distance (of each type) is optimal in achieving certain kinds of interpersonal, attitudinal, and situational rhetorical functions? What conditions of the other dimensions are most likely to increase, maintain, or decrease the distance (of each type)?

2

Controversial ideas which involve a choice among competing judgments, attitudes, and actions form a necessary part of any rhetorical act. Very often, although not always, such a choice is the primary operation, and the various interpersonal and situational dimensions merely create the environment in which the choice is made and influence how the choice is made. Traditionally, rhetoric seems rather consistently to have made this sort of assumption. The principal function of some rhetorical acts is interpersonal interaction or situational appropriateness, however, and the influence on attitudes in the making of choices is secondary. Attitude may be defined as the predisposition for preferential response to a situation. Two kinds of attitudes have rhetorical significance: attitudes toward the central idea in a choice-making situation and the ideological structure of other related attitudes and beliefs.

Central Idea. Several features of attitudes toward the central idea of a rhetorical situation require study.

First, although attitudes customarily have been considered as a point on a scale, this view is inadequate. As Carolyn Sherif, Muzafer Sherif, and Roger E. Nebergall have pointed out, a person's attitude may be described more accurately by placing various alternative positions on a controversy within three latitudes—of acceptance, of rejection, and of non-commitment.[8] On the policy of the United States toward Vietnam, for example, a person may have one favored position but place other positions within his latitude of acceptance; such additional positions are tolerable. He may have one position that he rejects more strongly than any other but place other positions within his latitude of rejection. Finally, because he lacks information, interest, or decisiveness, he may place other positions within his latitude of non-commitment. To understand or predict the attitudinal interaction in a rhetorical situation one

---

distance from man. See, for example, Burke, pp. 543–51. Edward T. Hall treats distance literally as a variable in communication situations in his Silent Language (*Garden City, N. Y., 1959*), pp. 187–209. The concept of social distance is implied in such terms in small group research as group cohesiveness, primary groups, and reference groups.

[8] Attitude and Attitude Change: The Social Judgment-Ego Involvement Approach (*Philadelphia, 1965*), pp. 18–26.

must know whether its central idea falls within the participants' latitude of acceptance, rejection, or non-commitment.

Second, the degree of interest and the intensity of feeling with which the central idea confronted in a rhetorical act occupies a place in whatever latitude will influence potentially all other dimensions of that act.

Third, the way the various latitudes are structured is an influential variable. Sherif, Sherif, and Nebergall identify one such structure which they term ego-involvement. A person who is ego-involved in a given attitude tends to perceive relatively few discrete alternative positions, to have a narrow latitude of acceptance—sometimes accepting only one position, to have a broad latitude of rejection—lumping most positions as similarly intolerable, and to have little or no latitude of non-commitment.[9] The ego-involved hawk, for example, may accept only a strong determination to achieve a military victory, assimilating all positions close to that one; and he may reject all other stands, seeing little difference between unilateral withdrawal and attempts to negotiate that necessitate any genuine concessions to the adversary, and labeling anything less than total victory as appeasement.

Fourth, a person's persuasibility on the central idea of a rhetorical act is a relevant variable. How likely is a person to respond positively to attempts to change his attitude? This question suggests the superiority of the Sherif, Sherif, and Nebergall analysis. The question is not the simple one of how likely is a person to move from "yes" to "no" or from favoring a negotiated settlement in Vietnam which does not involve the possibility of a coalition government in South Vietnam to one which does. It is the far more complex question of whether positions which are now assigned to one latitude can be moved to another one. This concept recognizes, for example, that to move a person from a position of rejection to one of non-commitment is significant persuasion. A person's persuasibility is related, of course, to the nature, intensity, and structure of his attitude.[10] An ego-involved person who feels strongly about an idea is less likely to change his attitude than one who is less ego-involved or less intense.

What the preceding discussion suggests is that the nature, intensity, structure, or persuasibility of the attitude of any participant toward the central idea in a rhetorical transaction will influence the other dimensions and be influenced by them. In addition, the relationship of the attitudes of each participant to those of others in the situation will influ-

[9] Ibid., p. 233.

[10] In addition, an individual's personality may be one of the determinants of his persuasibility on controversial propositions. See Irving L. Janis, Carl I. Hovland, et al., Personality and Persuasibility (New Haven, Conn., 1959), and Milton Rokeach, The Open and Closed Mind (New York, 1960).

ence their interaction together. The issue here can be focused in a single question: how similar are the people in a rhetorical act with respect to the nature, intensity, structure, and changeability of their attitudes toward the idea under focus in the rhetorical act? Or, to put the question in a slightly different way: to what extent can people identify with the attitudes of one another?[11]

Ideology. An attitude does not exist in a vacuum. One idea does not occur by itself. Rather, attitudes have homes in ideologies. The ideologies evoked in a rhetorical act influence, and may sometimes dominate, the other dimensions.

Several ideological structures may be identified. Attitudes may relate to other attitudes, to systems of values and norms, to ethical codes, and to philosophic presuppositions about the nature of man, the nature of reality, the nature of language, and the nature of knowledge. About each of these contexts two questions may be raised: What is the nature of the ideological structures of each participant in the act? How similar or different are the ideologies of the various participants?

The central idea of any rhetorical transaction evokes not only attitudes toward that idea but attitudes toward related ideas. In recent years several theories and approaches have developed: balance theory, the theory of cognitive dissonance, the congruity hypothesis, and the social judgment approach.[12] Although these formulations differ and the differences are argued heatedly, one principle seems accepted by most attitude theorists: man has an urge to think himself consistent, to try to achieve homeostasis within his system of attitudes.

Although relatively few persons work out a careful formulation of an ideology which consciously monitors various attitudes, each person very likely has an implicit ideology which unconsciously affects the development of any attitude in the system. Anyone attempting to change one attitude of a person, therefore, will profit from the admittedly difficult task of identifying that person's other attitudes and of considering how they may facilitate or retard such an attempt and how the target-attitude will, if changed, affect other attitudes. In addition, to understand the rhetorical interaction on some central idea one must also consider how similar or different one person's attitudes toward related ideas are to those of other people in the rhetorical act.

---

[11] *Kenneth Burke's concept of identification seems to relate to the attitude dimension as well as to the dimension of interpersonal distance.*

[12] *See Fritz Heider, "Attitudes and Cognitive Organizations,"* Journal of Psychology, *XVL (April 1946), 107–114; Leon Festinger,* A Theory of Cognitive Dissonance *(Evanston, Ill., 1958); Charles E. Osgood, Percy Tannenbaum, and George Suci,* The Measurement of Meaning *(Urbana, Ill., 1957); and Sherif, Sherif, and Nebergall.*

A second ideological variable is the system of values and norms sub-scribed to by the people in a rhetorical act. Just as a person's atti-tudes relate to his other attitudes, they relate also to more fundamental principles which he values. Whereas the first relationship may be viewed as a sort of part-to-part analogical inference, the second is a part-to-whole (or whole-to-part) inference. General values both evolve from many particular attitudes, and they also structure new experience in the development of new attitudes toward new situations.[13]

One of the most important sources of each person's fundamental values is his membership in small groups, organizations, societies, and cultures. The argument can be made that all values can be traced gen-erally to a social origin, but some values especially can be associated closely with membership in a particular reference group—whether small group, organization, society, or culture. Such shared values are termed norms. When a rhetorical situation involves the actual or implied presence of such groups, the norms of those groups predictably are going to function as an ideology which will tend to set limits for at-titudes of group members.[14]

A third kind of ideology is the ethical variable which raises two questions: What personal morality or public ethic guides the interaction of attitudes? Is the code of conduct acceptable to others who partici-pate in the rhetorical act? A transaction of ideas viewed as unethical by someone with whom a person tries to interact will have adverse effects on many of the other dimensions.[15]

A fourth ideological variable consists of a person's philosophic pre-suppositions about the nature of man, the nature of reality, the nature of language, and the nature of knowledge. This variable probably func-tions relatively rarely as the primary goal of a rhetorical act, perhaps only when philosophers engage in dialogue, but it establishes a frame of reference within which attitudes interact. Is a man an object to be manipulated or a decision-maker in the process of making radical

[13] In their essay "The American Value System: Premises for Persuasion," Western Speech, XXVI (Spring 1962), 83–91, Edward D. Steele and W. Charles Redding state, "Values, as they exist psychologically in the mind of the audi-ence, have been generalized from the total experience of the culture and 'internalized' into the individual personalities of the listeners as guides to the right way to believe or act" (p. 84). Karl R. Wallace argues that general value premises function as the substance of rhetoric—as good reasons which support propositions or value judgments. See "The Substance of Rhetoric: Good Reasons," QJS, XLIX (October 1963), 239–249.

[14] See A. Paul Hare, Handbook for Small Group Research (New York, 1962), pp. 23–61.

[15] Edward Rogge, in his "Evaluating the Ethics of a Speaker in a Democ-racy," QJS, XLV (December 1959), 419–425, suggests that the standards used to evaluate a speaker's ethics be those established by the audience and the society of which it is a part.

choices? To what extent does he behave rationally? To what extent is his rhetorical behavior determined for him and to what extent does he exercise free will? Does one take an Aristotelian, a Platonic, or a phenomenalistic stance on the question of the nature of reality? How does man acquire knowledge? To what extent does he come to know through *a priori* intellection, through revelation, through intuition, through memory, through empirical observation, through existential experience, or through scientific analysis?[16] How each person in a rhetorical act answers these questions, and the degree to which the various answers are similar, will influence how attitudes interact.

3

A rhetorical act occurs only within a situation, and the nature of that act is influenced profoundly by the nature of the encompassing situation. Furthermore, on certain ceremonial occasions situational dimensions dominate the act. A speaker's function in a funeral oration, for example, may be merely to meet the expectations of the occasion. Six situational dimensions form a part of the conceptual framework advanced in this essay: format, channels, people, functions, method, and contexts.

Format. The essential concern of this dimension is how procedures, norms, and conventions operate to determine who speaks and who listens.

Formats fall into two general types which anchor the ends of the dimension. At one extreme is a polarized situation in which one person functions as speaker or writer and others function as listeners or readers. At the other extreme is a type of conference situation in which the functions of the various participants rotate freely between speaking and listening.

Formats vary with respect to the degree of flexibility permitted rhetorical participants. In some situations, for example in written and electronic discourse, a rhetorician has little opportunity to revise his original plans within the act, although he may utilize feedback in designing subsequent acts in a campaign. In other situations a rhetorician has maximum opportunity to observe the reactions of others and to make appropriate decisions accordingly.[17]

---

[16] *The importance of the philosophic dimension of rhetoric is well argued by Otis M. Walter in "On Views of Rhetoric, Whether Conservative or Progressive,"* QJS, *XLIX (December 1963), 367–382.*

[17] *See David K. Berlo,* The Process of Communication *(New York, 1960), pp. 111–116. Ironically, in public address, a format which offers considerable opportunity for communicative flexibility, the role of feedback has been analyzed very little.*

Channels. The role of channels in a rhetorical act is manifested in three variables. First, is the communication conveyed verbally, nonverbally, or through a mixture of the two modes? Radio speaking and written messages are instances of the verbal channel; a silent vigil and pictures employ the nonverbal channel; and face-to-face speaking, television, and books which feature graphic materials illustrate the mixed mode.[18]

Second, if language is employed, is it in oral or written form? Although the distinction between these two channels needs no clarification,[19] their modes of transmission require analysis. Traditional rhetoric has long studied delivery as one of the canons. Although students of written composition have paid far less attention to the study of transmitting messages, such features as the selection of paper, binding, cryptology, and the like may influence the interaction between writer and reader more than the persons playing either role recognize. Delivery, whether in oral or written channel, illustrates well the primary idea of this essay: that each dimension relates to every other dimension. Delivery will influence and be influenced by the interpersonal dimensions of liking, power, and distance; by the attitudes toward the central idea and toward those related to it; and by the other situational dimensions of format, people, functions, method, and contexts.

Third, is the rhetoric transmitted directly or indirectly? A direct channel is a system of communication in which one person relates to someone else without the interference or aid of a third person or a mechanical device. The oral interpretation act, the speaker who reaches the newspaper reader via a reporter, the tape recording, television, and the two-step flow of communication all illustrate the indirect channel.[20] But indirectness admits of degrees. Messages may be transmitted through only one intermediary person or agency, or they may follow a circuitous track, as in a typical rumor, between its originator and its ultimate, and perhaps indefinite, destination.[21]

---

[18] *Marshall McLuhan's* The Medium is the Massage *(New York, 1967) is a notable attempt to make the nonverbal code as important in a book as the verbal.*

[19] *Joseph A. DeVito's study of "Comprehension Factors in Oral and Written Discourse of Skilled Communicators,"* Speech Monographs, *XXXII (June 1965), 124–128, concluded that written discourse involved a more difficult vocabulary, simpler sentences, and a greater density of ideas than did oral discourse.*

[20] *The two-step flow of communication and the concept of opinion leadership has considerable applicability to rhetoric. See Elihu Katz and Paul F. Lazarsfeld,* Personal Influence *(Glencoe, Ill., 1955), and Elihu Katz, "The Two-Step Flow of Communication: An Up-to-Date Report on an Hypothesis,"* Public Opinion Quarterly, *XXI (Spring 1957), 61–78.*

[21] *The classic study of rumor is Gordon W. Allport and Leo Postman,* Psychology of Rumor *(New York, 1947).*

People. How rhetorical situations are populated forms six variables. One concerns the number of interacting people. Are they few or many?[22]

A second variable is the number of groups which function in the situation, whether as audiences or conferences. The range is from one to many. A speaker may address one particular audience or many audiences, either simultaneously or consecutively. A person may participate in a conference which operates virtually as a self-contained unit or in a conference involving multiple groups.

A third variable has to do with the degree to which the people are organized. The range is from a virtual absence of organization to the status of a highly structured and cohesive reference group.

A fourth variable, closely related to the third, involves the degree of homogeneity among the participating people. They may exhibit a high degree of homogeneity, they may be similar on some and different on other properties, or they may differ so much as to constitute essentially different groups even though they participate in the same situation.[23]

Fifth, participants in a rhetorical situation may vary widely in their degree of awareness of their roles and in their degree of involvement in the situation.

Sixth, those who people a rhetorical situation engage in a range of relationships to that situation. One, some, many, or all of the participants may regard themselves or be regarded by others as depersonalized stimulus objects; as members or agents of a culture, institution, or group; as performing a role; as projecting an image; as manifesting a set of properties or as selves with radical choices to make or commitments to uphold.

Functions. The functions of a rhetorical situation may be viewed from a general perspective or along interpersonal and attitudinal dimensions.

Some questions of situational function seem to apply both to the interpersonal and to the attitudinal aspects of a rhetorical act. To what extent are interpersonal relationships and/or attitudes to be reinforced or changed? What degrees of intensity of reinforcement or change does the situation call for? If change is to function, in what direction?

---

[22] *I am inclined to include the intrapersonal communication of self-address within the scope of rhetoric. An individual's roles may interact intrapersonally and attitudinally in a variety of situational contexts in ways closely analogous to the interpersonal and attitudinal interaction of two or more persons. For support of this position, see Barnlund, 199–201, and Burke, pp. 561–563.*

[23] *The effect of a group's homogeneity and receptivity on the integration and polarization of an audience is admirably discussed in Charles H. Woolbert's pioneer monograph "The Audience,"* Psychological Monographs, *XXI, No. 92 (June 1916), 37–54.*

Other questions relate directly to the interpersonal dimension. Are people trying primarily to relate, identify, disengage, or in other ways to interact with others in the situation, or are they trying to express their "selves" conjointly? Are they trying to court, please, satisfy, tolerate, dissatisfy, or derogate one another? Are they trying to change or reinforce the power disparity or power structure of the situation? Are they trying to increase, maintain, or decrease social or interpersonal distance? Is group maintenance or group cohesiveness a relevant situational function?

Still other questions relate directly to three kinds of attitude influence. First, a person may present a message with a designative function—to present information, describe, define, amplify, clarify, make ambiguous, obfuscate, review, or synthesize ideas. Second, someone may present a message with an evaluative function—to praise, make commentary, hedge, criticize, or blame some person, object, situation, judgment, or policy. Third, someone may present a message with an advocative function—to solve a problem, create indecision, reinforce a present choice, foster delay, choose a change [*sic*] alternative, resolve a conflict, propose a compromise, or stimulate action.

The functions of rhetorical situations appear far more complex than implied by the traditional categories of inform, entertain, and persuade.

Method. Any situational function is manifested instrumentally through a number of message variables. These constitute the methodological dimension of the rhetorical act. Method is less often than other dimensions the ultimate function of the act; typically it plays the instrumental role of facilitating whatever dimension is primary.

Method includes the materials presented, the form in which they are structured, and the style in which materials and form are communicated.

Three questions about the material to be presented seem important. How much data should be presented? What kinds of data should be employed? From what sources should they be derived? These questions, of course, have no simple answers universally applicable.

The form variable may be analyzed in two ways. A distinction can be made between a sort of form-in-the-large which permeates the rhetorical method and a more microscopic set of structures which develops. The rhetorical act may be transacted through some conventional medium like an essay, a play, or a speech. A rhetorician may fulfill expectations by using identifiable forms in typical ways, or he may create new forms or employ old forms in new ways. Whether forms are appropriately new or old and whether their development is appropriately conventional or eccentric, of course, depends on the experience and expectations of the other people in the rhetorical act. The method may represent a straightforward management of materials to develop a central idea directly, or reflect an indirect ordering—for example, through the use of irony.[24] How prominent the form-in-the-large is to be is an important issue. Should the form become clearly evident in the discourse, or should it fulfill its function unobtrusively and not call any special attention to itself?

The form variable may also be viewed microscopically. This level of analysis includes a consideration of the logical connection between the material presented and the ideas advanced—which calls for the student of rhetoric to understand the logic of rhetorical interaction and the modes of reasoning appropriate to such interaction.[25] It includes a recognition of the structure which joins the ideas advanced into a pattern which amplifies or supports the central idea—which calls for an understanding of the patterns of expository and argumentative discourse, the analysis of a controversy into its issues, and the methods of problem-solving and negotiation.[26]

Specific formal structures may be recognizable immediately to others in the act and utilized in predictable ways, or they may be new and less obvious. Furthermore, the two levels of form in a discourse, the macroscopic and the microscopic, may function harmoniously toward the same end or constitute incongruity. Form, whether large or small, may be designed to facilitate information transfer or to disrupt it; to create a relatively narrow range of meanings and attitudinal responses or to maximize ambiguity; to present an optimal amount of material efficiently or to aim at redundancy; to achieve identification or alienation; to reinforce meanings and attitudes or to change them; and to increase or decrease the intensity of feelings toward the ideas.

Style, like form, may be viewed macroscopically or microscopically. Rhetorical style may be looked at from the point of view of broad symbolic strategy, a style-in-the-large. I take this concern to be behind

[24] *For an excellent analysis of rhetorical irony, see Allan B. Karstetter, "Toward a Theory of Rhetorical Irony,"* Speech Monographs, *XXXI (June 1964), 162–178.*

[25] *If one accepts the central idea of this essay that rhetoric is a system of interrelated dimensions, he must conclude that a rhetorical logic must accommodate the function of dimensions other than the one concerned with formal relationships among propositions. Irrelevant to rhetorical analysis is any logical system which assumes that man is only rational and that men do not vary, that ideas can be divorced from their affective content and from their ideological contexts, and that the only situation is that of the logician talking to the logician.*

[26] *Rhetoricians have tended to treat these various organizational patterns, like logic, as invariant structures, without due regard for the totality of the rhetorical situation—its people, its functions, and its contexts.*

much of the writing of Kenneth Burke.[27] Or it may be analyzed by looking at smaller units of analysis—at the level of the phoneme, word, sentence, or paragraph. Perhaps the writing of modern linguists may provide better ways of analyzing style microscopically than rhetoricians have followed traditionally.[28]

Many of the questions raised about form appear to apply also to style. Whether looked at large or small, style, too, provokes such issues as efficiency of information transfer, clarity *vs.* ambiguity, conciseness *vs.* redundancy, confidence *vs.* uncertainty, and identification *vs.* alienation. The issues can be resolved only by studying the particular interaction of the other dimensions in each unique rhetorical act.

Contexts. The contexts of time and place may alter in various ways how other dimensions function in the act. In this regard context is typical of situational dimensions. The substance of a rhetorical act is rarely located in the situation: it more characteristically focuses on the interpersonal and attitudinal categories. Aspects of the situation, including context, although not fundamental or ultimate, however, can alter decisively the other categories and hence change the substance of the act.

In addition, time functions in another way. Each rhetorical act has some larger setting and fits into one or more ongoing processes.[29] For example, a novel may be a part of a movement or of several movements, a representation of an ideology or several ideologies, a moment in the career of the writer, a specimen of some formal or stylistic tendency, a phase in some long-term interpersonal relationship with a set of readers, *et cetera.* Several questions may suggest some of the ways a rhetorical act may relate to its contexts. Does an act occur relatively early or relatively late in one or more processes? To what extent is the act congruous with its larger framework? Does the act play one role in one context and a different, and perhaps conflicting, role in another?

[27] *Burke, for example, says (p. 567) that rhetoric "is rooted in an essential function of language itself, . . . the use of language as a symbolic means of inducing cooperation in beings that by nature respond to symbols." For Burke, rhetorical analysis is an attempt to unearth the essential linguistic strategies of the rhetorical agent.*

[28] *In "A Linguistic Analysis of Oral and Written Style," QJS, XLVIII (December 1962), 419–422, Jane Blankenship applied the system of analysis which Charles C. Fries described in his book* The Structure of English *(New York, 1952).*

[29] *Two recent books which display a contextual orientation to rhetoric are Wallace Fotheringham,* Perspectives on Persuasion *(Boston, 1966), and Huber W. Ellingsworth and Theodore Clevenger, Jr.,* Speech and Social Action *(Englewood Cliffs, N. J., 1967).*

4

Important to the student of rhetoric is the question of points of view. A rhetorical act will be perceived quite differently by each person who participates in it, and still differently by each person who observes and criticizes it from "the outside." Here, as elsewhere, "meanings are in people," not in discourses. Students of rhetoric must try to determine how the various participants and observers have perceived the dimensions of the act and to discover the extent to which such perceptions differ. The points of view of the relevant people become part of an important dimension of the act.

The consideration of point of view may have different implications for theorists, as compared with participants and critics. The theorist tends to be interested in generalizations at the highest level of abstraction he can achieve, whereas participants and critics tend to be interested in making decisions or judgments about one very particular and unique act.

Perhaps the most important single characteristic of rhetoric is that it is a matrix of complex and interrelated variables of the kind discussed in this paper. The theorist cannot meaningfully pluck from the system any single variable and hope to understand it apart from the others. How can one understand style, for example, without knowing how it interrelates with power structure, with distance, with attitudes and ideologies, with the demands of format and context—in short, with every other dimension of the act? Gross generalizations about stylistic characteristics which ignore the assumption that style functions very differently when placed in different combinations with the other variables simply will not do. Unfortunately for the prognosis of theoretical advances in rhetoric, the combinations and permutations of the alternatives afforded by the various dimensions are so many as to approach infinity. But methods will have to be developed to pursue the sort of interrelational kind of analysis which an adequate theory of rhetoric requires.[30]

The practitioner may use such an interrelational analysis before, during, and after a transaction as a guide to the decisions he must make to give himself the best chance of interacting with others as he wishes.

The critic may profitably identify the single most compelling dimen-

---

[30] *Warren Weaver has argued that science must "make a third great advance which must be even greater than the nineteenth-century conquest of problems of simplicity or the twentieth-century victory over problems of disorganized complexity. Science must, over the next fifty years, learn to deal with these problems of organized complexity." See "Science and Complexity," in* The Scientist Speaks, *ed. Warren Weaver (New York, 1945), p. 7. Implicit in my essay is the belief that rhetoric represents a problem of "organized complexity."*

sion of a rhetorical act under consideration and then investigate how that dimension interrelates with others which appear to be relevant. For example, a critic studying Nikita Khrushchev's interaction with the American public during his 1959 visit to this country might focus primary attention on Khrushchev's reduction of interpersonal distance between himself and his hosts in order to see how his distance-reducing rhetoric related to new American images of Khrushchev personally along liking and power dimensions; to his attempts to make attitudes and ideologies consubstantial; and to his use of various rhetorical situations for these functions. If a critic accepts the fundamental premise that each rhetorical act or process is unique, that dimensions interrelate in a way to create a unity never achieved in the past or in the future, then he commits himself to a search for a new way to select, structure, and weigh dimensions for each new act he criticizes.

My hope is that the dimensions described in this essay may provide a framework for theoretical development, practical decision-making, and critical analysis.

Reducing Rhetorical Distance:
Khrushchev's 1959 American Tour
by Wayne Brockriede and Robert L. Scott

The 1950s were tense years of policy disputes between the United States and the Soviet Union. For example, the Soviet Union pressed hard for a change in the status of Germany, especially Berlin, which Nikita Khrushchev described as "abnormal" and "a bone in my throat" but the United States was determined not to leave Berlin. From the point of view of policy, the status quo was frozen.

Beneath the surface of such a stalemate, however, existed a tacit agreement concerning how policy issues of the Cold War were to be disputed. Principal among these agreements was the recognition that neither side was willing to initiate a nuclear war. Since the Korean War both sides had cautiously refrained from taking action that would broaden the conflict to include an American-Soviet confrontation. The 1955 Geneva Conference made the understanding explicit. In spite of a rhetoric of liberation during the Dulles era, the United States did not intervene in the Hungarian revolt of 1956. The ultimatum Khrushchev had issued concerning Berlin was lifted in 1959. Although disputes were not immediately negotiable, any alteration of the status quo had to be attempted without risking nuclear war between the major powers.

No limitation existed on the rhetorical level. The leadership and the people on both sides had conditioned one another to engage in what Adlai Stevenson called "massive verbal retaliation." Charles O. Lerche claimed that "the Soviet Union has raised the art of vituperative propaganda to new heights of excess in language and vulgarity in presentation" (p. 47), but a Soviet observer could have evaluated United States verbal abuse toward the Soviet Union similarly. Urie Bronfenbrenner argues persuasively that both sides developed a "mirror image" of the other (see also Lerche and Osgood). Full scale verbal assaults were the order of the day.

On August 4, 1959, the two governments issued an announcement that Premier Khrushchev would make an official visit to the United States in September and that President Dwight D. Eisenhower would make a return visit to the Soviet Union later that autumn. Premier Khrushchev's visit, September 15–27, is a complex and rewarding phenomenon for rhetorical analysis. Although neither government seemed to expect any major policy settlements, the joint announcement of the visit expressed "the hope that the forthcoming visits will contribute to better understanding between the USA and USSR, and promote the cause of peace" (quoted in *Khrushchev in America,* p. 9). Although policies were to remain frozen, the agreement to keep the peace was to be reinforced, and the rhetorical distance between the two countries was to be reduced.

Before the Tour

What were the prevailing attitudes of Americans toward Premier Khrushchev and the Soviet Union, the hopes and fears of the American hosts, and the possible goals of the Soviet guest on the eve of the rhetorical transaction?

Some Americans had reacted negatively to the announcement of the exchange of visits. Boston's Cardinal Richard Cushing "denounced all Russians as spies, urged Catholics to recite the rosary and pray during Khrushchev's twelve-day visit" (*Time,* 8–31–59, p. 12). On August 13, 1959, Senator Thomas J. Dodd of Connecticut told the Senate:

I hope that during Khrushchev's visit we shall hear church bells in the land, tolling their remembrance for the murdered millions behind the Iron Curtain. . . . Let there be no cheers for the Red Dictator, no crowds assembled to greet him, no flattery or flowers. Let our people be civil but silent ("Khrushchev's Visit," p. 712).

Most people approved the visits, however. *Newsweek* reported that thirteen of Premier Khrushchev's recent American callers "were unanimous in the belief that President Eisenhower's invitation . . . [held] out more promise of improving international relations than risk of impairing them" ("How to Handle Khrushchev," p. 22). Surely the war-hero President would not become soft on communism and surely he could "take care of himself, and the cause of the free world" ("What Americans Think," p. 40).

Although Americans favored the visits, they viewed the Soviet Union and its Premier with suspicion and hostility. They saw the Soviet Union not merely as an opponent, but as the enemy with whom one must regard "the struggle as one of life or death" (Morris, pp. 160–161). "After 14 years of the Cold War," William V. Shannon observes, "any Russian ruler would be received with suspicion and reserve." Although Merle Fainsod in 1956 had recognized that Khrushchev was able to "project an image of personalized and humanized leadership" (p. 35), most Americans in 1959 viewed him as "an abstract concept," as "embodied evil" ("Without Horns or Tails," p. 43). The only personal characteristics of Premier Khrushchev that had come into reasonably clear focus were essentially negative—such pictures as "the monster of deceit and treachery, the drunken peasant, the mass killer" ("The Visit"), a "vodka-drinking, musical comedy clown" (Sheerin, "What We Learned," p. 80).

Yet many people looked forward hopefully to the visit. One cause for hope was the belief, as Howard K. Smith expressed it, that "something new must be tried to break the log-jam and ease tension" (*Images of Peace*, p. 51). Senator Everett M. Dirksen of Illinois explained that

if there can come some end to the tensions which now exist between nations, and some relief from the costly armament burden which sits so heavily on people in all parts of the world, I believe history will rank President Eisenhower as the boldest peacemaker in many generations ("The Range of Reaction in Congress," pp. 69–70).

A second cause for hope was the idea that the Premier's experience in the United States would give him a better understanding of this country and its purposes. Before the visit had been announced, Vice President Richard M. Nixon argued that Khrushchev has "some real misconceptions with regard to both our policies and our people. And I think that by going to the United States and seeing first hand our country and people, this will serve to reduce those misconceptions" (Caruthers, p. 1). On several occasions President Eisenhower stressed his hope that a visit would increase Premier Khrushchev's understanding of the United States.

Some people minimized this hope by declaring that Mr. Khrushchev already knew a great deal about the United States and was not re-markably well motivated to learn more. After the tour, one observer noted that "he seems to have come to America more in a spirit of national self-assertion than of genuine inquiry; and in some respects the tour may have confirmed his prejudices rather than removed them" ("The Glacier Moves"). Stevenson, who was an early and staunch ad-vocate of the exchange of visits, nevertheless recognized and was im-pressed by Khrushchev's grasp of American affairs:

I don't think Khrushchev is so abysmally ignorant of us as the Soviet press, with its distorted image of America, would lead one to suppose. For he is one of the privileged minority in Russia not dependent on Pravda for the truth or Izvestia for the news. . . . I was struck by his grasp of many details of the international situation and of our policy (p. 5).

Interestingly, few persons voiced the hope that the government or the people of the United States might learn to know Premier Khrushchev or his purposes better.

Those who feared or opposed the trip believed that the Soviet Pre-mier had gained by the fact of the invitation a tremendous increase in international prestige, especially among peoples in the Soviet satellites and in the uncommitted nations. Daniel Schorr observed that in Poland, for example, "there was a feeling that Khrushchev's visit . . . was a public relations coup before it ever started" ("Khrushchev's 'Hard Sell,' " p. 6; see also *The Crimes of Khrushchev,* p. 13). The one coun-try for which the visit did not enhance Soviet prestige was China. Sev-eral observers argued that "Premier Khrushchev's decision to visit the United States represented the point of no return in the deepening schism between the Soviet Union and China" (Slusser, p. 200; see also Morris, p. 151).

What were Premier Khrushchev's motives for seeking and accepting an invitation to tour the United States? First, no doubt, he hoped that the visit would provide a "propaganda opportunity to project a more favorable impression of himself and of Soviet strength," by having a "sounding board in a country with the world's most highly developed system of mass communication" ("Questions of the Week," p. 39).

Second, he may well have hoped to enhance his power in the Soviet government and his popularity among his own people. Contrary to a widespread belief in 1959 that Khrushchev was an absolute dictator, today many historians argue that Khrushchev's power was never un-limited and that some of his initiatives were designed to maintain and increase his status as leader of an oligarchy. Richard Lowenthal expresses this point of view: "Khrushchev disposes of all the levers of command, but he is not yet regarded as infallible within the inner circle. . . . Khrushchev's lack of historical achievements . . . [induces him to] hunt for spectacular prestige successes abroad" (p. 122).[1] Presumably, the Soviet Premier hoped that he could gain a "spectacular prestige success" in the United States.

Contrary to another widespread belief in 1959 that the opinion of the Soviet people was essentially irrelevant to policy determination, many Kremlinologists recognized that public opinion had a growing influence on Soviet policies. In a 1957 essay Harrison Salisbury, Soviet specialist of *The New York Times,* commented, "The Russian dictatorship, contrary to popular supposition, is not immune to the trends of public opinion. . . . Khrushchev himself . . . has tried to link his fortunes with all of the things which he thinks the Soviet people want" ("The Fatal Flaw in the Soviet System," p. 249).[2] Edward Crankshaw, London journalist, said in 1962 that the object of the visit was "to prove to the Soviet people . . . that he could bring them peace and an understanding in terms of equality with the greatest power in the world" (1962, p. 149).

Khrushchev's third motive undoubtedly was to speak frequently to the American people under conditions that would ensure maximum attention, to talk his way across the country and back. On a CBS newscast on September 15, 1959, Daniel Schorr conjectured that Khrushchev wanted to "put across the twin points of overwhelming Soviet power and overwhelming Soviet desire for peace. He's not sure he can sell our leaders; he does think he's enough of a salesman to make an effective pitch over their heads to the American people" (*Images of Peace,* p. 73; see also Frankland, p. 155).

Premier Khrushchev's tour is an unusually complex rhetorical transaction. Although ostensibly he spoke to a single audience, the American people, the people and governments of American allies, the Soviet Union, China, Soviet satellites, and uncommitted nations all responded to his message. The critic who looks at what Khrushchev said and did during the tour may focus on any of these audiences or on the way the responses of various audiences were interrelated. He may also wish to examine Khrushchev's rhetoric from the perspective of any of a number of rhetorical dimensions. Following are the dimensions we consider especially relevant:

1. Distance: How did Khrushchev try to decrease the interpersonal distance between himself and his hosts and the international distance between the Soviet Union and the United States?

---

[1] *See also Crankshaw, "The Men Behind Khrushchev," p. 29; Linden, p. 7; and Rush, pp. 111–113.*
[2] *See also Petrov, p. 290; Pietromarchi, p. 87; and Schapiro, pp. 398–399.*

2. Images: How did Khrushchev try to improve his own image and that of his country?

3. Power: How did Khrushchev try to improve his own power status and that of his country?

4. Maximizing agreement: How did Khrushchev employ the rhetorical strategy of de-emphasizing disagreement on specific controversies and emphasizing agreement that such disputes should not be allowed to result in a Soviet-American war?

5. Forcing a choice: How did Khrushchev employ the rhetorical strategy of the residues method of argument to force the United States to choose peaceful coexistence and nonmilitary competition as the only reasonable alternative to ideological conversion (dismissed as unrealistic) or to arms races and nuclear wars (dismissed as undesirable)?

6. Context: What is the function of the context in determining and evaluating the effect of a particular message on a specific occasion? What advantage has the critic in viewing the tour as a sequential campaign instead of as a disconnected series of speeches?

7. Channels: What were the roles of the interpreters and of the communication media in selecting (and sometimes in determining) what the public would see, hear, and read?

Each of these dimensions, as well as others that are not mentioned here, could function as a useful lens through which a critic can look at other dimensions in an attempt to frame a total picture of the rhetoric Premier Khrushchev employed from September 15 to September 27, 1959.

An Annotated Record of the Tour

At 12:24 P.M., September 15, the Soviet Premier and his party landed at Andrews Air Force Base in Maryland. After President Eisenhower led the way to a reception area and made a speech of welcome, Premier Khrushchev presented the first of twenty-four speeches he was to make in the United States.

The Speech At Andrews Field.[3] *Mr. President, ladies and gentlemen. Permit me at this moment, in first setting foot on American soil, to thank Mr. Eisenhower for the invitation to visit your country, and everyone present for the warm welcome accorded to us representatives of the Soviet Union.*[4]

[3] *The text is the interpreter's translation as transcribed and printed in* The New York Times, *September 16, 1959, p. 19.*

[4] *The opening paragraph serves the ceremonial function of satisfying audience expectations on such an occasion.*

Russians say every good job should be started in the morning. Our flight began in Moscow this morning and we now have the pleasure of first meeting you on American soil on the morning of the same day.[5]

As you see our countries are not so distant from each other.[6]

I accepted the invitation of the President of the United States to make an official visit to your country with great pleasure and gratitude and I will be glad to meet and talk with your statesmen, representatives of the business world, intellectuals, workers and farmers, and to learn about the life of the industrious and enterprising American people.

For our part we will be glad to receive Mr. Eisenhower, his family and those who will shortly accompany him to the Soviet Union. We will give the President a most cordial welcome and every opportunity to become familiar with the life of the Soviet people.[7]

We have always considered reciprocal visits and meetings of representatives of different countries as useful. Meetings and discussions between the statesmen of our two great countries, the Soviet Union and the United States of America, are especially important.

The people of all countries are profoundly interested in the maintenance and consolidation of peace and peaceful coexistence. War does not promise anyone any good, while peace is advantageous to all nations. This is the basic principle which we believe the statesmen of all countries should be guided by in order to realize the aspirations of the people.

We have come here with an open heart and good intentions. The Soviet people want to live in friendship with the American people. There are no obstacles to having relations between our countries develop as good neighborly relations.

The Soviet and the American people and the people of other countries fought well together in the Second World War against the common enemy and broke his backbone. In peaceful conditions we have even more reasons for friendship and cooperation between the people of our countries.[8]

---

[5] *Early in Mr. Khrushchev's first speech he seems to want to establish an informal relationship. One can almost imagine two gregarious Americans discussing the topic on a transcontinental flight.*

[6] *Khrushchev is doing more than merely passing the time of day. He has been using an informal social amenity to reduce distance and to argue by analogy his dominant theme: peaceful coexistence. In effect, he is saying that as our physical distance decreases our interpersonal and international distance should decrease.*

[7] *The fourth and fifth paragraphs are more formal; they include what might be expected in a speech of this sort. The theme and some of the language echo the announcement of the visits.*

[8] *After his attempt to establish a conversational tone with his audience, Khrushchev begins his first substantive argument: his theme of peaceful coexistence. The "open heart" and "good intentions" were phrases widely quoted.*

Shortly before this meeting with you, Mr. President, the Soviet scientists, engineers, technicians and workers filled our hearts with joy by launching a rocket to the moon.[9] A road has thus been blazed from the earth to the moon and the container of 390 kilograms with a pennant bearing the national emblem of the Soviet Union is now on the moon. Our earth has become somewhat lighter while the moon has gained several hundred pounds in weight.

I am sure that this historic achievement of peaceful science has brought joy not only to the Soviet people but to all who cherish peace and friendship among nations.

An atomic icebreaker has just been completed in the Soviet Union. This practical embodiment of the desire of all people to see nuclear energy put solely to peaceful uses is also a happy event.

We are aware, Mr. President, that the idea of the peaceful use of atomic energy is dear to you, and we note with gratification that your aims in this field coincide with ours.[10]

We have no doubt that the excellent scientists, engineers and workers of the United States of America who are engaged in the field of conquering the cosmos will also carry their pennant over to the moon. The Soviet pennant, as an old resident, will then welcome your pennant and they will live there together in peace and friendship, as we should live together on earth in peace and friendship and as all people should live who inhabit our common mother earth who is so generous to us with all her gifts.

In these first few minutes of our stay in the United States permit me to extend cordial greetings and best wishes to the American people on behalf of the Soviet Union, the Soviet Government and on my own behalf.[11]

Thank you.

In the Russian version of the speech the "live in friendship" slogan appears as "live in peace and friendship." The Soviet book in which these speeches are collected is entitled Live in Peace and Friendship.

[9] *Khrushchev's motivation for boasting of recent Soviet technological achievements could be twofold: (1) a feeling that such a statement would be expected of him by the Soviet people and government and (2) a desire to underscore Soviet technological might and hence to strike a note of urgency, even fear, which would favor accepting peaceful coexistence. Khrushchev's reference to lunar sputnik must have appeared to most Americans as an assertion of raw Soviet power. Furthermore, the condescension implied, later in the speech, by the image of the Soviet emblem patiently awaiting its delinquent American counterpart must have been abrasive to many Americans, who may have missed the speaker's attempt to relate the image to his theme of peaceful coexistence.*

[10] *The reference is to Eisenhower's "atoms for peace" proposal and represents the strategy of stressing agreement.*

[11] *The concluding paragraph, like the introductory one, is a rather perfunctory fulfillment of a ceremonial commitment. The relatively small amount of time Khrushchev characteristically spends on ritualistic rhetoric is striking.*

During Premier Khrushchev's first four days in this country, in Washington and in New York City, he made additional speeches at a White House dinner, at the National Press Club, at a meeting with congressional leaders and members of the Senate Foreign Relations Committee, at a dinner given for President Eisenhower at the Soviet Embassy, at a luncheon given by New York's Mayor Robert Wagner, at a dinner given by the Economics Club of New York, and at the U.N. at which, in a major address, he presented the Soviet proposal for "general and complete disarmament."

Premier Khrushchev's behavior during the first phase of the tour, covered extensively by the news media, was not especially dramatic. Large crowds lined up to see him in Washington and New York, but the people, though curious, were not demonstrative. A London reporter described the American response:

It is not easy to say what impact Mr. Khrushchev made on New York or it made on him. . . . The crowds lining the streets proved that the silence with which he was greeted in Washington was not simply a local phenomenon due to the restraining presence of President Eisenhower. The New Yorkers showed the same surprising, rather un-American reticence. Reporters, in their search for the right word to describe it, have run through a Roget's Thesaurus of adjectives: cool, chilly, restrained, reserved, aloof ("Communist's Progress," p. 1021; see also Shannon).

The rhetorical drama became more exciting on September 19, when Premier Khrushchev landed in Los Angeles. He was greeted so briefly by Mayor Norris Poulson that he discarded his prepared text and responded briefly in kind. Then at a luncheon at the studio of 20th-Century Fox, given by Eric Johnston, President of the Motion Pictures Association of America, and Sypros Skouras, President of 20th-Century Fox, Premier Khrushchev created the first major stir. After concluding his prepared text, he announced that, for security reasons, he would not be permitted to visit Disneyland:

But just now I was told that I could not go to Disneyland.[12] *I asked, "Why not?" What is it, do you have rocket-launching pads there? I do not know. And just listen—just listen to what I was told—to what reason*

___
[12] *The text was transcribed by a CBS affiliate, KNX-TV of Los Angeles, and appeared in* The New York Times, *September 20, 1959, p. 41. The reference to Disneyland is both ludicrous (a Soviet premier pouting over a denied pleasure) and appealing. Whatever else this passage may have done to modify American attitudes toward Khrushchev, it reduced distance by revealing something of the Premier's humanness.*

I was told. We, which means the American authorities, cannot guarantee your security if you go there.

What is it? Is there an epidemic of cholera there or something? Or have gangsters taken hold of the place that can destroy me? But your policemen are so tough they can lift a bull by the horns. And surely they can restore order if there are any gangsters around.

And I say, I would very much like to go and see Disneyland. But then, we cannot guarantee your security, they say. Then what must I do? Commit suicide?[13] *That's the situation I am in—your guest. For me, such a situation is inconceivable. I cannot find words to explain this to my people.*

The second explosion was more serious. It occurred that evening at a dinner sponsored by Los Angeles authorities and the Association of International Affairs. Mayor Poulson called attention to Mr. Khrushchev's celebrated "we will bury you" statement.[14] The Premier followed him to the podium. He waited until he had completed his prepared text before escalating tension to the peak of the tour.

The Threat.[15] *. . . Actually, that was the end of my prepared speech, but those—the speakers that preceded me raised a number of points which I cannot fail to answer.*[16] *I can put this text in my pocket now. I turn to you, Mr. Mayor, my dear host: in your speech you said that we wanted to bury you.*

You have shown us wonderful hospitality towards me and my comrades, and I thank you.

---

[13] *The Disneyland passage has a light and humorous touch likely to appeal to some Americans. Throughout his visit, Premier Khrushchev's attempts at humor probably had a good effect on his image.*

[14] *Khrushchev made the widely quoted statement on November 17, 1956, at a Kremlin reception. He had been irritated by an American refusal to respond reciprocally to a hint that Russia might withdraw from Hungary if the United States were to withdraw from some other part of Europe. The phrase "we will bury you" has been quoted out of context frequently. The entire passage is as follows: "If you don't like us, don't accept our invitations and don't invite us to come to see you! Whether you like it or not, history is on our side; we will bury you!!!" The time, the occasion, and the character of the speaker all suggest that these "flushed and impulsive words" are those "of a powerful but unsure man, shouting rather than whistling in the dark" (Lukacs, p. 151).*

[15] *The text of this extemporaneous explosion is taken from* The New York Times, *September 20, 1959, pp. 41–42.*

[16] *As in his earlier speech that day, Mr. Khrushchev drew a sharp line between the prepared text, which presumably represented carefully calculated rhetorical decisions, and his impromptu response to the occasion. One wonders if he welcomed the chance to take the hard line, to make explicit the alternative to peaceful co-existence. He may have felt that he should not complete the argument as a part of a prepared discourse.*

I want to say the truth. Can I do that here?[17] *I want to ask you why did you mention that fact? Already while I was here in the United States I have already had occasion to give clarification on that point. I trust that even mayors read the press. At least in our country the chairmen of the city councils read the press. If they don't, they risk not being elected next time.*[18]

Ladies and gentlemen, you want to get up on this favorite horse of yours and proceed in the same old direction. If you do get up on it and sit in the saddle, where can this horse lead you to? If you want a continuation of the arms race, you are doing right. You should then get up on this horse and go along in that old direction.

If you want to continue the arms race, if you want to have a war, then do get up on that horse. If you want to insist on this line, then there can be no talk of disarmament. There can only be talk of continuing the arms race.

If you are not ready for disarmament and you want to go on with the arms race, very well, we accept that challenge,[19] *for we now have the necessary strength and all the possibilities to create modern weapons, and as for the output of our rockets, those are on the assembly line.*[20]

I am talking seriously, because I have come here with serious intentions and you try to reduce the matter to simply a joke. It is a question of war or peace between our countries, a question of the life or death of the people.

---

[17] *On several occasions Khrushchev precedes hard talk with a justification for speaking plainly, even bluntly. He seems to be trying to show an awareness of the normal expectations of guest-host relationships even though he feels moved to violate one of them.*

[18] *Khrushchev's decision to ridicule Mayor Poulson was risky. No doubt Khrushchev would lose favor with some of his audience for being openly contemptuous of the Mayor in his own city. He may have reasoned that some would oppose the Mayor and that others might see the validity of the accusation that Poulson had not read Khrushchev's Washington speeches and should have done so. Although Khrushchev treats the situation humorously, the humor is heavy, if not brutal.*

[19] *Perhaps the principal logic of Khrushchev's rhetoric throughout the tour is the attempt to stress that the Soviet Union and the United States had two choices: cold war or peace and friendship. Khrushchev's strategy is to put the burden of choosing on the United States rather than on Soviet Russia. The rest of this speech places considerable emphasis on the "war or peace" strategy.*

[20] *Not only does Khrushchev emphasize the choice of war or peace; here more than in any other speech he tries to underscore the urgency of that choice by referring to the strength of the Soviet Union and by suggesting the consequences of nuclear war. Perhaps a principal motive for the trip was Khrushchev's hope of demonstrating to his own people, to his allies, to neutralist nations, and to the United States and its allies that the Soviet Union had reached a position equal to that of the United States. The implication of the undesirability of an American choice of war rather than peace dominates the rest of the speech.*

We are extending the hand of friendship, but if you don't want to—if you accept it, then you should manifest a reasonable approach to matters. One should not play upon words. We hold positions of too much responsibility and the consequences of a play upon words can be too sad for our peoples.

Ladies and gentlemen, I would like once again to clarify what I have already said once.[21] *When I spoke of the burial, that should not be understood literally, word for word, as if somebody was going to take a spade and start burying somebody. What I meant was the development of history, the evolution of human society and that is what we believe in, according to our philosophy.*

According to your philosophy, that is not so, but then let history be the judge of who is right. You live under capitalism and let us live under socialism. I have said that so many times that my tongue is tired of saying it. Let time show which social system is better. If the people see that your system is better, let that be proved.

If the people think that ours is better, let them take our system but let us not try to bury one another. If you prefer to live under your system, God be with you.

Ladies and gentlemen, your President Eisenhower invited me here as his guest, not just to have a cup of tea or perhaps a small glass of cognac. I have partners for that back home. I have not traveled thousands of miles for that. I am sure that your President also has enough partners at home without inviting me over.

The President offers me no hope of accepting our opinions, our philosophy regarding the development of human society, and I have no hope that the President will revert—will come over to the positions of communism. From that point of view, he is hopeless. And I have no such designs, just as I am sure that he has no designs of turning me into a capitalist.[22]

---

[21] *Although Mr. Khrushchev shows impatience at having to explain his famous statement one more time, he does not set aside this question as "provocative" and unworthy of an answer—as he did in response to several questions earlier in the tour. He may have answered the question whenever someone raised it because he could use it as another springboard for stating the peaceful competition argument of his peaceful coexistence theme. Questions about Hungary or about his own relations with Stalin had no such value and were rejected.*

[22] *This statement represents the change in communist ideology announced in Khrushchev's 1956 speech to the 20th Party Congress: the doctrine that war to the finish with capitalism is not inevitable. What he sees as inevitable is history's verdict that communism will ultimately triumph. Furthermore, Khrushchev is able to tell his own people (as he did on several other occasions) that he was in no danger whatsoever of being persuaded by his American hosts. Khrushchev recognizes, however, that a capitalist leader will not be persuaded on a short-term basis to accept communism.*

Then, why is it that—why is it that he invited me here? He showed, I think, state wisdom. He understood the duty to seek agreement with us, without feeling any esteem or respect for the teaching of communism. I assure you I am sure that you have no such esteem for that teaching, but we are neighbors, because the Pacific Ocean both divides us and unites us.

The question is one, ladies and gentlemen, of there being either peace or war between our two nations.

I am deeply concerned over these, I believe to be, conscious distortions of my thoughts which can lead to nothing but the aggravation of the "cold war." But choose for yourself the language you prefer to use.

I have not come here to appeal to you in any way. We are strong. We are no less strong than you are.

I have never in any of my addresses spoken or mentioned any rockets, but when I did so today, I had no other way out, because it would seem it could be made out from certain pronouncements that we have come here to beg something of you; that we have come here to beg you to eliminate the "cold war" because we are afraid of you.

If you think that the "cold war" is something which is profitable to you, then go ahead. Let us then compete in the "cold war."

The only thing is: that competition in the "cold war" means, with the modern means of—in the conditions of the existence of modern weapons.

The question as it stands now is one of whether this meeting of minds with President Eisenhower will lead to the elimination of the "cold war" or whether we will simply part.

After all, I am the first head of either Russia or the Soviet Union to have visited the United States in all your history, and yet we did live. If you do not accept these—all this, but I can go and I don't know when if ever another Russian Soviet Premier Minister will visit your country.

You may well say that without such a visit you too live in this world. That is true, certainly, but with equal certainty it is also true that it is much better to live in peace than to live in conditions—than to live with loaded pistols and guns trained at their objective.[23]

It is—[Applause].

It is better to have a friendly atmosphere—a friendly and a tranquil atmosphere so that people need not fear for their future, so they can

[23] *Khrushchev relieves a bit of the tension by shifting emphasis to the possibility and desirability of peace. The audience responded by applauding. The transcript that appeared in* The New York Times *indicates applause only at this point and after the next sentence, which underscores the advantage of peace.*

go to bed at night and be sure that war will not disturb their sleep neither today nor tomorrow nor the day after tomorrow; that they should be sure that peace will be eternal [Applause].

The though [sic] sometimes—the unpleasant thought sometimes creeps up on me here as to whether Khrushchev was not invited here to enable you to sort of rub him in your sauce and to show the might and the strength of the United States so as to make him—so as to make him shake at the knees. If that is so, then if it took me twelve hours to get here, I guess it will take no more than ten a [sic] half hours to fly back. . . .[24]

But I do believe that we will show more wisdom and find a common language and that we will all strive for this.

I am going to close. I have tired you out. I believe you suffered through my speech, but so was I made to suffer. I have such a nature that I do not want to remain in debt and I do not want to be misunderstood. . . .

The next day Premier Khrushchev traveled to San Francisco. Overnight, Khrushchev's mood and that of the Californians who went to see him had undergone a striking transformation. Security restrictions were relaxed; the Premier mingled more freely with people, and he received his first really warm welcome. A reporter from the London *Economist* described the change:

When the train stopped at Santa Barbara, . . . Mr. Khrushchev got off, breaking through the security that has thus far surrounded him, to shake hands and talk with the friendly throng waiting on the station platform to catch a glimpse of him.

These greetings, the first warm and spontaneous ones he had yet received in America, were followed by a hospitable welcome . . . from the Mayor of San Francisco and from a large cheering crowd that waited at the entrance to Mr. Khrushchev's hotel, high on Nob Hill ("Communist's Progress," pp. 1021–1022).

---

[24] *Khrushchev's threat to return to Russia without completing the tour, without talking to Eisenhower at Camp David, created a major stir in the press. John Osborne described the moment: "When he made the coldest and bluntest statement of the tour, . . . his audience kept a deathly silence. When he threatened to break off his tour and fly home, the fright in the hall was a tangible and present thing. When he relaxed into a lighter vein, the relief among his hearers was almost as frightening as their fright." During the remainder of the tour, Khrushchev was given more freedom of movement, more opportunity to mingle with people, more immunity from hecklers, and more solicitous concern by his official host, Henry Cabot Lodge. These effects would seem to be precisely what Premier Khrushchev wanted.*

Premier Khrushchev's interaction with San Franciscans was distinctly successful. Although his meeting with trade union leaders on September 20 was stormy, his speeches to the Longshoremen's Union and at the IBM Corporation Plant in San Jose were well received. Khrushchev's major address in the San Francisco area reflects his recognition that he is now getting the response he had been seeking. This speech was presented on September 21 at a joint dinner of the San Francisco Commonwealth Club and the World Affairs Council.

The San Francisco Address.[25] *Esteemed Mayor Christopher, esteemed Governor Brown, esteemed Chairman Rockwell, esteemed Chairman Johnson, ladies and gentlemen: I am very grateful to you for this invitation to address such a distinguished gathering.*

We came to San Francisco from Los Angeles. We traveled along a beautiful coast, enjoying the scenic beauties of California. We saw your wonderful land, and all along the route, the California sun shone as brightly as it did in the Crimea, where I rested before leaving for the United States.

But it is not sunlight alone that warms our hearts in this land so distant from our country. We have been cordially welcomed and received by the Californians, and I would like the friendship between our peoples to be as inextinguishable and bright as is your southern sun.
. . . [26] *[He discusses the history and resources of California and deplores the decrease in Soviet-American trade.]*

I have already said on more than one occasion that we have come to the United States with an open heart and the best of intentions. We want but one thing and that is to live in peace and friendship with you and with other peoples.[27]

It is my opinion that the distinguished Californians here tonight share these sentiments and aspirations with us.

[25] *The text is taken from* The New York Times, *September 22, 1959, p. 23.*

[26] *If one analyzes this speech without considering the context of the tour and of the explosions in Los Angeles, Premier Khrushchev might seem merely to be playing the flattering itinerant politician. Yet the difference in tone between the speeches in Los Angeles and in San Francisco is startling; newsmen were quick to see it. The audience was different. They gave Khrushchev what Harrison Salisbury of* The New York Times *the next day called "something like an ovation" before he spoke (p. 1). Whether the warm response represented a pervasive difference between the attitudes of people in the two California cities or whether San Franciscans wanted to avoid any behavior that might justify Khrushchev's termination of the trip is uncertain. Khrushchev is also different. Along the California coast and in San Francisco he had just received the first genuine hospitality in America. At any rate, the interaction between speaker and audience is friendly.*

[27] *Having dispensed with his introductory friendly remarks, Premier Khrushchev turns once again to the principal substantive theme of the tour and repeats the phrases "open heart" and "peace and friendship."*

Americans who have visited the Soviet Union returned with different opinions about our country and its life, but they will all confirm that the words "peace" and "friendship" are to be heard everywhere in our country.

They are to be seen in the white stone of the slopes of railway tracks. They are to be seen written in flowers in our parks and gardens. They are to be seen traced on house walls. They are in the heart of every Soviet citizen, and this is because all Soviet people are seeking by their peaceful labor to safeguard themselves and the entire world against the horrors of war.

We know well what war means, and though we are strong, we do not want war with its consequences and its destruction ever again to be visited upon mankind.[28]

It goes without saying that the best way to prevent war is to nip it in the bud, and that is to destroy the means of conducting war. A few days ago the Soviet Government submitted to the United Nations a proposal for general and complete disarmament, with the establishment of unlimited control.[29] *A little earlier, at the end of August, the Soviet Government decided not to resume nuclear tests in the Soviet Union unless such tests were resumed by the Western powers.*[30]

The Soviet Union will continue to struggle for a complete cessation of nuclear tests regarding this as an important step toward the termination of the nuclear armed race and elimination of the threat to the life and health of millions of people.

It is well understood everywhere that these are not the only problems that are of cardinal importance if peace is to be preserved. The existence of remnants of World War II is likewise fraught with the danger of a new war, and therefore this problem, too, must be solved.

We do not seek any unilateral advantages or benefits in proposing the conclusion of a peace treaty with Germany and proceeding from the existence of two German states. Who can think of advantages when it is a matter of putting out the still glowing embers of an old fire. The Soviet Government has often stated that it wants to normalize the situation in Germany, which would also eliminate the abnormal situation in Berlin. . . .[31] *[Khrushchev states the hope that his talks with the President will solve international problems.]*

---

[28] *Instead of using the open threat of assembly-line rockets, as in the Los Angeles speech, Khrushchev here says simply that Russia is strong.*

[29] *He is referring to his plan of "general and complete disarmament," which he had presented several days earlier in the U.N. He is careful to attribute the source of this proposal not to himself but to the Soviet government.*

[30] *This initiative taken by Khrushchev was probably timed to enhance his visit and message to the United States.*

[31] *The brevity of his reference to the principal trouble spot, Berlin, is consistent with Khrushchev's strategy of de-emphasizing disagreement.*

We want better to understand you and your motives, but there must be reciprocity. You also should better understand us and our motives. The Soviet Union does not seek any advantages. We want only one thing, that war should never again menace people anywhere on earth.

Well, that actually brings me to the close of my prepared speech to this responsible gathering, but if you have no objections I would like to share with you some of the impressions that I gained after this text was prepared. . . .[32] *[He describes the trip to San Francisco, his meeting with the Longshoremen's Union, and his visit to the IBM plant. He expresses gratification at his welcome and praises the city of San Francisco.]*

The main thing is not to touch upon the questions that divide us. We're all, I believe, sick and tired of discussions—of fruitless discussion on such issues, but the main thing is to speak of those points that unite us, that bring us together, to seek out those points where we can find agreement without touching upon the cardinal issues between us.[33]

After all, it is of course inconceivable that you could persuade me that the capitalist system was better, just as it is inconceivable that I could convince you that the Communist system was better.

We will evidently all remain with our own convictions, but that should in no way hinder us from going ahead, from living together in peace and caring for the welfare of our respective people.

I want to assure you, ladies and gentlemen, that I am not trying to entice you over into the Communist kingdom when I say this, but you will perhaps one day remember my words, and I want to say that when you get to know better us Communists, when you better get to know the thoughts and aspirations that guide us[34]*—this will not happen today, I realize—but you will see how noble are these aspirations of Communists when we seek to build a Communist society.*[35]

This is not a thing of today. It is a thing of tomorrow, but we conceive

[32] *Again, Khrushchev demarcates the carefully prepared portion of his speech from the impromptu part. The following day Salisbury wrote in* The New York Times *that Khrushchev had presented "one of the longest and most rambling extemporaneous talks of his tour" (p. 1). Presumably Salisbury refers to the final two-thirds of the speech, which begins at this point.*

[33] *Khrushchev here makes explicit his dominant strategy: maximizing agreement.*

[34] *Perhaps the main reason for Khrushchev's eagerness to make the trip was strong belief that relations could improve if the Americans understood the Russians better. He acts as though his primary interpersonal task is to reduce distance between the two groups. This passage is just one instance among many during the tour.*

[35] *The "live and let live" topic is another frequent one; it is part of the agreement for arriving at peaceful coexistence by discarding the competing ideas of conversion and war.*

this aspiration of ours as most sacred, as something that is most sacred for us. . . . [He compares the teachings of communism to the precepts of Christianity. He praises Mayor George Christopher, his dinner, and a supermarket he visited.]

I consider it also my duty here in San Francisco to say a few words about your neighbor city, the city of Los Angeles. I trust you will manifest patience and hear me out. I want to say some good things about the people of Los Angeles.[36]

Now if I were to use a somewhat poetic word, you have virtually charmed us here. You really are charmers, magicians, you have managed to charm me, a representative of a Socialist state.

You have charmed my heart, but in my head I still think that our system is a good system. You evidently think that your system is a good one, well, God be with you! Live under it. . . . [Khrushchev attributes the denial of permission to visit Disneyland to a tomato thrown at a car in which the Los Angeles chief of police was riding; he calls the change in schedule "superstitious." The Soviet Premier calls the altercation with Mayor Poulson an "unhappy incident," declares the question "closed," and extends again an invitation he had first made before the Los Angeles Civic Dinner for the Mayor to visit Russia. Khrushchev concludes his speech by inviting all present to make such a visit and by expressing once more the hope that his visit might bring the United States and the Soviet Union closer together.]

From San Francisco, Premier Khrushchev journeyed to Des Moines, Iowa, where he made a speech on agriculture at a reception sponsored by the Des Moines Chamber of Commerce, and to Coon Rapids, Iowa, where he inspected the hybrid-corn farm of Roswell Garst. Then the tour led to Pittsburgh. Khrushchev spoke at a luncheon at the University of Pittsburgh and visited a factory. The friendliness generated along the California coast increased during Khrushchev's stays in Iowa and Pittsburgh. On September 25 *The New York Times* headline read "PITTSBURGH STOP WARMEST OF TOUR."

On the afternoon of September 24, Premier Khrushchev returned to Washington for a weekend of private discussions with President Eisenhower. The rhetoric that for more than a week had been conducted on a public level with the American people through the mass media would now be carried on in private by the two leaders. One can only speculate about the rhetorical transaction between Eisenhower and Khru-

---

[36] *The audience doubtless hoped that Khrushchev would relieve the tension he had generated in Los Angeles. If San Francisco diners were thinking about Khrushchev's previous impromptu conclusions, they may well have been anxious and attentive when he talked of Los Angeles.*

shchev; transcriptions are not available, and their joint communique leaves much unsaid.

The Joint Communique.[37] *The Chairman of the Council of Ministers of the USSR, N. S. Khrushchev, and President Eisenhower have had a frank exchange of opinions at Camp David. In some of these conversations United States Secretary of State Herter and Soviet Foreign Minister Gromyko, as well as other officials from both countries, participated.*

Chairman Khrushchev and the President have agreed that these discussions have been useful in clarifying each other's position on a number of subjects. The talks were not undertaken to negotiate issues. It is hoped, however, that their exchanges of views will contribute to a better understanding of the motives and positions of each and thus to the achievement of a just and lasting peace.

The Chairman of the Council of Ministers of the USSR and the President of the United States agreed that the question of general disarmament is the most important one facing the world today. Both governments will make every effort to achieve a constructive solution of this problem.[38]

In the course of the conversations an exchange of views took place on the question of Germany including the question of a peace treaty with Germany, in which the positions of both sides were expounded.

With respect to the specific Berlin question, an understanding was reached, subject to the approval of the other parties directly concerned, that negotiations would be reopened with a view to achieving a solution which would be in accordance with the interests of all concerned and in the interest of the maintenance of peace.[39]

In addition to these matters useful conversations were held on a number of questions affecting the relations between the Union of Soviet Socialist Republics and the United States. These subjects included the question of trade between the two countries.[40] *With respect to an in-*

---

[37] *The text is taken from* The Department of State Bulletin, *41 (October 12, 1959), 499–500.*

[38] *This statement implies that the two governments were more interested in broadening agreement on the ground rules for their disputes so that war might be avoided than in settling substantive issues.*

[39] *On September 28* The New York Times *reported that the talks at Camp David on Berlin did not "go well." Mr. Khrushchev is said to have concluded "that his way of settling the problem was the only way he knew of reaching a settlement" (Reston, p. 1).*

[40] *The question of increased trade was probably included in the document at Premier Khrushchev's urging. The lack of any statement of consequence beyond the "conversations" probably represents President Eisenhower's realization that in 1959 Americans were not ready for "normal trade relations."*

crease in exchanges of persons and ideas, substantial progress was made in discussions between officials and it is expected that certain agreements will be reached in the near future.[41]

The Chairman of the Council of Ministers of the USSR and the President of the United States argreed that all outstanding international questions should be settled not by the application of force but by peaceful means through negotiation.[42]

Finally it was agreed that an exact date for the return visit of the President to the Soviet Union next spring would be arranged through diplomatic channels.

The private rhetorical exchange between Khrushchev and Eisenhower may have mirrored the public exchange between the Soviet Premier and the American people. No policy changes or ideological shifts resulted from either transaction. On the private level, perhaps the tacit understanding between the two men that international disputes must not lead to a Soviet-American war was strengthened; on the public level, the American people may have become conditioned to accept such a stipulation now—especially if publicly endorsed by Eisenhower —even if earlier in the decade they had been conditioned differently by the rhetoric of brinksmanship. Just as Khrushchev and the American people may have experienced publicly a reduction of interpersonal distance, so Khrushchev and Eisenhower privately may have come to understand one another better. The public statements of the two men after their talks support this supposition. In his press conference the day after Khrushchev's departure, Eisenhower characterized his Soviet visitor as "a dynamic and arresting personality" ("In Their Own Words," p. 104). In speaking in Moscow immediately upon his return, Khrushchev said that he "got the impression from the talks and discussions of concrete questions with the United States President that he sincerely wishes to end the state of cold war, to create normal relations between our two countries, to promote the improvement of relations among all states" ("In Their Own Words," p. 105).

Interpreting the Tour

In analyzing a campaign as complex as Khrushchev's 1959 tour of the United States, a critic must make choices. First, he must select an audience on which to focus. Although Khrushchev appeared before

[41] *The statement on cultural exchange programs is much more hopeful than the one on trade.*

[42] *The policy of refraining from hot war between the two nations had been manifest by the behavior of both governments throughout the 1950s. This sentence extends manifest policy to rhetorical commitment.*

different groups of Americans, he seemed always to be addressing an image of American public opinion. Certainly he was concerned about the leaders of his host government, and surely he knew that the response of his colleagues in the Kremlin was vital. But for the latter audiences, and perhaps for others, his ability to appeal to Americans generally would have great instrumental value. We choose, therefore, to focus on the general American audience.

Second, a critic may select a single dimension on which to focus his judgment. Our evaluation is that the visit was an important rhetorical *transaction that may have reduced the rhetorical distance between the* United States and the Soviet Union in the Cold War. The other dimensions . . . will be treated as subsidiary.

Viewing Khrushchev's rhetoric as reducing distance with the American audience, and looking at the relationships of six other dimensions of that function, constitutes one interpretation of the transaction. It does not, of course, exhaust the possibilities of criticism. Stressing a different dimension and considering other dimensions as secondary would create a new focus; focusing differently is not merely legitimate, it is essential. The total picture of any significant rhetorical transaction changes as a critic gains new perspective through his own efforts and through sharing the results of the efforts of others.

Distance Reduction. Our judgment is that this dimension is the single most important route to an understanding of the rhetoric of the tour. All the dimensions we treat as subsidiary seem relevant to an analysis of how Khrushchev reduced his distance from American audiences. He reduced distance by developing a strong, concrete, and human image; by insisting on parity between himself and Eisenhower and between the Soviet Union and the United States; by finding common ground in a desire to keep the peace; by forcing the United States to choose peaceful coexistence after rejecting other alternatives; and by skillfully using a campaign strategy and communication channels.

Premier Khrushchev reduced distance between himself and the American public, in part, by his vivid physical presence. Mary McGrory explains this factor:

Everybody is still reeling from the shock of that potent personality and from the endless incongruities that dogged him every step of the way. . . . No one could have predicted the force of his presence. . . . Mr. Khrushchev in person had the unarguable presence of a rock or tree.

Then, too, Khrushchev turned out to be far more "American" than anyone had expected. He seemed to be

the sort of person towards whom Americans instinctively warm: tough-spoken but probably good-hearted, a stranger to diplomatic niceties, a decisive leader who obviously springs from the people he leads. He possesses many of the qualities which the American voters thought they detected in Mr. Eisenhower in 1952 ("Without Horns or Tails," p. 43).[43]

Although Americans probably could not help feeling somewhat closer to the Soviet Premier after they had been exposed to his physical presence for nearly two weeks and had been saturated with the events of the tour through the mass media, the Soviet leader reinforced this tendency by some of the rhetorical decisions he made. In particular, Khrushchev's California speeches appeared to reduce interpersonal distance between himself and America. The reduced interpersonal distance may have lessened the chasm between the Soviet Union and the United States.[44]

Image Improvement. How was Khrushchev perceived in the United States before and after the tour? Did perceptions change? Many observers say, "Yes. He registered." Mark Frankland believes that Khrushchev's greatest achievement during the tour was "to leave the American people with a lasting impression of his vivid and at times prickly personality" (p. 163). A London reporter claimed that Premier Khrushchev "came to the United States as an abstract concept; he leaves as flesh and blood" ("Without Horns or Tails," p. 43).[45]

What were the primary features of the new image? Two seem repeated most often. First, many noted Khrushchev's determined, dynamic ability. What had been an unmixed hostility toward his hardness carried a new note of admiration. Senator Wayne Morse of Oregon remarked that the senators with whom he (Morse) had talked recognized they "were dealing with an exceedingly able man, a determined man" ("The Khrushchev Campaign," p. 104). A London reporter commented: "After his visit, there are a number of not entirely flattering adjectives they would happily apply to him—'pugnacious,' 'self-assured,' 'ruthless,'—but the number of those who think he is malevolent or

[43] *See also "The Great Encounter," Newsweek, 9-21-59, pp. 38–39; Schorr, "Traveling Salesmen," p. 22; Osborne; and "Dictator at Close Range," p. 75.*

[44] *Sources useful in further study of this dimension include Lukacs; Schorr, "Traveling Salesmen"; "Without Horns or Tails"; "Communist's Progress"; McGrory; Morris; and Seabury.*

[45] *See also Frankland, p. 55, and Gibney, p. 8.*

hypocritical has been sharply reduced" ("Without Horns or Tails," p. 43).[46]

A second characteristic of Khrushchev's new image was the recognition that he was less menacing—that he was a political, yet humane person with whom Americans could interact. A report prepared for the Senate Judiciary Committee by the Foreign Policy Research Institute of the University of Pennsylvania summarized this view: "The notion probably gained headway that somehow or other Khrushchev may indeed be the apostle of a new and less menacing kind of communism. . . . He has undeniably succeeded in imparting to the conduct of Soviet affairs a style . . . seemingly more humane and more acceptable than 'Stalinism' " (p. 1). Many writers noted the politician in the man and speculated about how the Russian would have fared in American politics. An editorial writer for *The Nation* represents this view: "What we actually saw was a Communist politician, as opportunistic and long-winded as any of his capitalist counterparts, but wittier than most, and a horse trader from head to toe. . . . He emerged as an antagonist who could be dealt with at the conference table" ("The Visit").[47]

If one accepts the judgment that Khrushchev changed the image Americans had of him in the directions suggested above, he may ponder several questions. How did Khrushchev do it? What kinds of rhetorical methods accounted for such changes? What, for example, accounted for the radical shift in American response as the Premier went from Los Angeles to San Francisco? How did he encourage a continuation of the San Francisco reaction in Coon Rapids and in Pittsburgh? Was he able to decrease the animosity toward the Soviet Union as he had decreased hostility toward himself? Did Americans feel closer to the new Khrushchev than to the old?[48]

Toward Power Parity. Many observers noted that Premier Khrushchev was able to get himself accepted as a powerful adversary after his visit to the United States. For example, Max Ascoli said:

Both fairness and the will to survive should compel us to pay tribute to a formidable enemy. During those 13 days he ran circles around the

---

[46] See also Sheerin, "What We Learned From Khrushchev," p. 80; Dodd, "If Coexistence Fails," pp. 409–410; Salisbury, "Khrushchev's Visit"; and "The Great Encounter," Newsweek, 10-5-59, p. 19.

[47] See also Whitney, p. 2; Sheerin, "What We Learned From Khrushchev," p. 80; Dodd, "If Coexistence Fails," pp. 409–410; "The Great Encounter," Newsweek, 10-5-59, pp. 19–24; and Halle, pp. 311, 390–391.

[48] Sources useful in further study of this dimension include Crankshaw, Khrushchev; "Without Horns or Tails"; Ascoli; Black; Bronfenbrenner; Dodd, "If Coexistence Fails"; Osborne; Sheerin, "Khrushchev Has Many Faces"; and "The Visit."

*American people and, it is to be feared, the high officials of the ad-
ministration. . . . We had never been exposed to the sight of a high-
powered live Communist. . . . We weren't immunized, and we were
upset (p. 21).*

Other observers commented on the Premier's attempt to communicate that he represented a powerful country. One writer put this idea
succinctly in *U.S. News and World Report:* "He is after respectability,
recognition as the legitimate ruler of Soviet Russia and its satellite
states. He wants the world to know that Russia can talk to America as
an equal" ("Questions of the Week," p. 39).[49] Khrushchev also wanted
this sort of recognition from the United States. As Fred W. Neal has
argued, the United States had "never really come psychologically to
acceptance of the Soviet Union as a force with which we must deal on
a basis of permanence and equality" (p. 53; see also *Current Digest of
the Soviet Press,* 11-4-59, p. 5). Khrushchev undoubtedly wanted this
distance in power reduced.

The critic who intends to pursue Khrushchev's drive for power parity
confronts several questions: How did Khrushchev's attempt to manifest
his personal authoritativeness complement his attempt to demonstrate
the power of the Soviet Union? How did both attempts contribute to a
reduction of distance? Is a person likely to identify with someone equal
in power or with someone significantly stronger or weaker? Is one nation apt to have more in common with another nation equal in power or
with one that is stronger or weaker? Can the speech at the Los Angeles
Civic Dinner be interpreted as Khrushchev's simultaneous effort to
stress his own power and that of the Soviet Union?[50]

Strategy of Maximizing Agreement. Throughout the tour Khrushchev
played down policy disputes that were impossible to settle in 1959 and
emphasized the need to handle the resulting conflict so that nuclear
war could not erupt.

The most threatening issue in 1959 was German reunification, especially the question of what to do about Berlin. The Premier refers to
that controversy in only five of his twenty-four speeches in the United
States; the references are usually brief, and he makes them without
truculence. In none of his angry outbursts does he refer to Berlin.
Nor does he raise the issue in his final press conference. When a
reporter raises it, Khrushchev's reply is brief and restrained; it avoids
controversy (*Khrushchev in America,* p. 193).

[49] *See also "Report on Washington," and Morgenthau, p. 386.*
[50] *Sources useful in further study of this dimension include Lukacs; Conquest; The Crimes of Khrushchev; Lowenthal; Morganthau; Neal; "Questions
of the Week"; and "Report on Washington."*

Aside from expressing his fury at questions concerning Hungary or his own activities during the Stalin era, Premier Khrushchev spent remarkably little time arguing about policy controversies. On the other hand, he stressed possible grounds of agreement. The principal common interest of the two countries, he argued, was the desire to avoid war. They had already arrived at a tacit understanding on this issue concerning policy. Lerche explains the agreement:

Lying beneath the surface indications of a total conceptual and operational confrontation is a substratum of agreement. . . . Probably the most fundamental manifestation of such agreement was . . . that the cold war could not be permitted to escalate into an armed conflict between the Soviet Union and the United States. . . . At the rhetorical level neither government pretends to take the other's word seriously, but operationally each counts upon at least this measure of restraint in estimating its opponent's intentions (p. 32).[51]

Premier Khrushchev seems to have adopted the strategy of extending the operational agreement to the rhetorical level. The need to avoid nuclear war is implicit in every speech, and arguments consonant with the need are made explicit in many. The final declaration by Eisenhower and Khrushchev in the joint communique amounts to a public commitment to avoid nuclear war and functions as a culmination of Khrushchev's strategy to maximize agreement.

Why did Khrushchev choose the strategy? How did he develop it? To what extent may his development of the strategy in speeches to the American people be viewed as a useful prelude to creating favorable conditions for the private discussions with Eisenhower? How did the emphasis on agreement reduce the distance between Khrushchev and his hosts?[52]

Strategy of Forcing a Choice. On several occasions Premier Khrushchev used a residues method of argument, presumably designed to induce Americans to accept the doctrine of peaceful coexistence because they had rejected the available alternatives. His fundamental argument is this: Because neither capitalism nor communism can convert the other side to its point of view, and because nuclear war is unthinkable, the only choice remaining is peaceful coexistence and nonmilitary competition.

When Khrushchev arrived in the United States, Schorr predicted on a CBS newscast, September 15, 1959, that the Premier wanted to "put

[51] *See also Seabury, p. 68, and "The Glacier Moves."*
[52] *Sources useful in further study of this dimension include Halle; Karol; Lerche; "The Glacier Moves"; and Seabury.*

across the twin points of overwhelming Soviet power and overwhelming Soviet desire for peace" (*Images of Peace,* p. 73). The "war or peace" strategy pervades all his speeches. At times Khrushchev recognizes that the ideological struggle between capitalism and communism cannot be settled instantly and declares the willingness of the Soviet Union to live and let live. At other times, as in Los Angeles, he stresses the military might of the Soviet Union and threatens either hot or cold war. But more frequently he is more optimistic and argues that peaceful coexistence is possible, indeed, that it is the only viable choice. A content analysis by the Foreign Policy Research Institute of the University of Pennsylvania reveals that the three most frequent themes of Khrushchev's speeches during the tour were improvement of Soviet-American relations; peaceful competition between the communist and the capitalist systems; and peaceful coexistence and the relaxation of international tensions (pp. 33–38).

If a critic wished to emphasize this dimension, he might investigate the forms in which Premier Khrushchev developed the argument. How does he argue that ideological conversion is unrealistic, that nuclear war is fearful, that peace is desirable? How does he vary his moods in creating and in relieving tensions as orchestration for the argument? How do the angry mood and warlike arguments of the speech at the Los Angeles Civic Dinner prepare the San Francisco audience for the friendly mood and conciliatory arguments? How does the "war or peace" strategy reduce distance?[53]

Context. Two contexts are especially important in a critical analysis of Khrushchev's tour. First, the tour took place within the context of the Cold War. A critic who is to understand the tour must understand the conflict itself. Second, each rhetorical action during the tour must be viewed within the context of the tour as a campaign.

The rhetoric of reducing distance did not develop as a result of a single remark or a single speech but as a result of the tour. The tour is a sequential campaign, not an independent series of speeches. Some of the themes and images recurred often enough to constitute a rhetorical strategy. A critic might investigate the timing of Khrushchev's various maneuvers (see Foreign Policy Research Institute, p. 9). For example, were the angry outbursts in Los Angeles well timed to create or promote a desirable campaign effect?[54]

---

[53] *Sources useful in further study of this dimension include Crankshaw,* Khrushchev's Russia; *Lerche; Schorr, "Khrushchev's 'Hard Sell' "; Kennan; Khrushchev; "On Peaceful Coexistence"; and Neal.*

[54] *Sources useful in further study of this dimension include the Foreign Policy Research Institute; Halle; Lerche; Lukacs; Whitney; and "Without Horns or Tails."*

Channels. Two channels are significant in this study: the interpreters and the mass media.

The two Soviet translators were Oleg Troyanovsky and Viktor Sukhodrev. Russian-speaking listeners claim that the American public did not receive the full force of Premier Khrushchev's language—that the translators, especially Troyanovsky, softened words in the speeches. Leon Volkov characterized Khrushchev's language as "colloquial, tough, and harsh. When angered, he threatens. One gets an almost frightening sense of ruthlessness on display. But Troyanovsky . . . dilutes the language so skillfully that the general purport comes through, but with most of the harshness extracted" (Volkov).[55] How did the interpreters influence the messages and images Premier Khrushchev tried to project? How did the interpreters vary in the decisions they made while translating the speeches?[56]

The various mass media—radio, television, newspapers, and news magazines—constitute a second influential channel. One effect was obvious: the intensive coverage of Khrushchev's behavior made them available to millions. Khrushchev capitalized on his opportunity in several ways. He was "accessible and responsive to newsmen," and played off "one reporter against another, handing out brief interviews, now to newspapermen, now to television reporters, 'mugging' for the nearest available cameraman, and hugely enjoying the entire process" (*Images of Peace,* p. 93).

The media may well have functions other than those of a passive channel through which messages and images flow. Did media specialists make rhetorical decisions of their own that may have either supplemented or contradicted those of Premier Khrushchev? To what extent did they create history as well as merely record it? Benjamin Bradlee argues persuasively that

the press did not cover the Khrushchev story. It smothered the Khrushchev story. In the process, it distorted almost beyond recognition the America Khrushchev saw, and by its very presence created other stories. . . . The truth is that in this Golden Age of Communications, whenever the press participates massively in history it changes history (p. 32).

One wonders to what extent reporters caused Premier Khrushchev to say and do things.

[55] *See also "Khrushchev's Outbursts" and the Foreign Policy Research Institute.*

[56] *Sources useful in further study of this dimension include* Images of Peace; *Foreign Policy Research Institute; Bradlee; "Khrushchev's Outbursts"; and Volkov.*

Each of these dimensions—and no doubt there are others—should be considered by the critic of rhetoric who analyzes Premier Khrushchev's 1959 visit to the United States. If a critic is imaginative and treats one dimension as primary and the others as subsidiary, he may be able to illuminate Khrushchev's exchange with the American public and with other audiences.

Our own conclusion is that Khrushchev's rhetorical decisions helped reduce distance between himself and the American public and, at least momentarily, between the Soviet Union and the United States. But that achievement was quickly undone by the U-2 incident.

Bibliography

Ascoli, Max. "Now That We've Seen Him," *The Reporter,* 21 (October 15, 1959), 18–22.

Black, Cyril E. "Soviet Political Life After Stalin," in Alex inkeles and Kent Geiger (eds.), *Soviet Society.* Boston: Houghton Mifflin, 1961. Pp. 182–189.

Bradlee, Benjamin. "Saturation Coverage," *The Reporter,* 21 (October 29, 1959), 32–34.

Bronfenbrenner, Urie. "The Mirror Image in Soviet-American Relations: A Social Psychologist's Report," *Journal of Social Issues,* Vol. 17, No. 3 (1961), pp. 45–56.

Caruthers, Osgood. "Nixon Wants Khrushchev to See U.S. at First Hand," *The New York Times,* August 3, 1959, pp. 1, 8.

"Communist's Progress," *The Economist,* September 26, 1959, pp. 1021–1022.

Conquest, Robert. *Russia After Khrushchev.* New York: Praeger, 1965.

Crankshaw, Edward. *Khrushchev: A Career.* New York: Viking, 1966.

———. *Khrushchev's Russia.* Rev. ed. Baltimore: Penguin, 1962.

———. "The Men Behind Khrushchev," *Atlantic Monthly,* 204 (July 1959), 27–32.

The Crimes of Khrushchev. Prepared for the use of the House Committee on Un-American Activities. Washington, D.C.: U.S. Government Printing Office, 1959.

Current Digest of the Soviet Press, October 6, 1959–December 2, 1959.

"Dictator at Close Range—End of a Mystery," *U.S. News and World Report,* 47 (October 5, 1959), 74–76.

Dodd, Thomas J. "If Coexistence Fails: The Khrushchev Visit Evaluated," *Orbis,* 3 (Winter 1960), 393–423.

———. "Khrushchev's Visit," *Vital Speeches of the Day,* 25 (September 15, 1959), 706–712.

Fainsod, Merle. "The Communist Party Since Stalin," in "Russia Since Stalin," *Annals of the American Academy of Political and Social Sciences,* 303 (January 1956), 23–36.

Foreign Policy Research Institute, University of Pennsylvania. *Khrushchev's Strategy and Its Meaning for America.* Washington, D.C.: U.S. Government Printing Office, 1960.

Frankland, Mark. *Khrushchev.* New York: Stein & Day, 1967.

Gibney, Frank. *The Khrushchev Pattern.* New York: Duell, Sloan & Pearce, 1960.

"The Glacier Moves," *The New Statesman,* 58 (October 3, 1959), 413.

"The Great Encounter," *Newsweek,* 54 (September 21, 1959), 37–47; (September 28, 1959), 33–38; (October 5, 1959), 19–24.

Halle, Louis J. *The Cold War as History.* New York: Harper & Row, 1967.

Hearst, William Randolph, Frank Coniff, and Bob Considine. *Ask Me Anything.* New York: McGraw-Hill, 1960. Pp. 232–252.

"How to Handle Khrushchev," *Newsweek,* 54 (August 17, 1959), 22–23.

Images of Peace. CBS booklet, 1960.

"In the Home Stretch," *U.S. News and World Report,* 47 (October 5, 1959), 43–48.

"In Their Own Words," *U.S. News and World Report,* 47 (October 12, 1959), 103–105.

Karol, K. S. "Khrushchev's View of the World," *The New Statesman,* 58 (October 24, 1959), 532–534.

Kennan, George F. "Peaceful Coexistence: A Western View," *Foreign Affairs,* 38 (January 1960), 171–190.

Khrushchev, Nikita S. "On Peaceful Coexistence," *Foreign Affairs,* 38 (October 1959), 1–18.

————. Speech at Andrews Field, Maryland, September 15, 1959. *The New York Times,* September 16, 1959, p. 19.

————. Speech at Dinner sponsored by the City of Los Angeles and the Association of International Affairs, Los Angeles, September 19, 1959. *The New York Times,* September 20, 1959, pp. 41–42.

————. Speech at Dinner sponsored by the San Francisco Commonwealth Club and the World Affairs Council, San Francisco, September 21, 1959. *The New York Times,* September 22, 1959, p. 23.

————. Speech at Luncheon at the 20th-Century Fox Studio, Los Angeles, September 19, 1959. *The New York Times,* September 20, 1959, p. 41.

————, and Dwight D. Eisenhower. "President Eisenhower and Chairman Khrushchev Issue Communique at Conclusion of Talks at Camp David." *The Department of State Bulletin,* 41 (October 12, 1959), 499–500.

"The Khrushchev Campaign in U.S.—What His Speeches Show," *U.S. News and World Report,* 47 (September 28, 1959), 96–109.

Khrushchev in America. New York: Crosscurrents Press, 1960.

"Khrushchev's Outbursts—and the Language Barrier," *U.S. News and World Report,* 47 (October 5, 1959), 71–72.

Lerche, Charles O. *The Cold War and After.* Englewood Cliffs, N.J.: Prentice-Hall, 1965.

Linden, Carl A. *Khrushchev and the Soviet Leadership.* Baltimore: Johns Hopkins Press, 1966.

Live in Peace and Friendship. New York: Crosscurrents Press, 1960.

Lowenthal, Richard. "The Nature of Khrushchev's Power," in Abraham Brumberg (ed.), *Russia Under Khrushchev.* New York: Praeger, 1962. Pp. 114–126.

Lukacs, John. *A New History of the Cold War.* 3rd ed. Garden City, N.Y.: Doubleday, 1966.

McGrory, Mary. "Gone But Not Forgotten," *America,* 102 (October 17, 1959), 63.

Morgenthau, Hans J. "Khrushchev's New Cold War Strategy: Prestige Diplomacy," *Commentary,* 28 (November 1959), 381–388.

Morris, Bernard. *International Communism and American Policy.* New York: Atherton Press, 1961.

Neal, Fred W. *U.S. Foreign Policy and the Soviet Union.* Santa Barbara, Calif.: Center for the Study of Democratic Institutions, 1961.

Osborne, John. "Final Image: A Man With Ironclad Views Who Left No Doubt About What He's After," *Life,* 47 (October 5, 1959), 42.

Osgood, Charles E. "An Analysis of the Cold War Mentality," *Journal of Social Issues,* Vol. 17, No. 3 (1961), pp. 12–19.

Petrov, Vladimir. "Whither Soviet Evolution," *Orbis,* 3 (Fall 1959), 282–296.

Pietromarchi, Luca. *The Soviet World.* Lovett F. Edwards (tr.). London: Allen & Unwin, 1965.

"Questions of the Week," *U.S. News and World Report,* 47 (September 21, 1959), 39–41.

"The Range of Reaction in Congress," *U.S. News and World Report,* (September 7, 1959), 69–72.

"Report on Washington," *Atlantic Monthly,* 204 (November 1959), 8, 11.

Reston, James. "Views Unchanged," *The New York Times,* September 28, 1959, pp. 1, 20.

Rush, Myron. *Political Succession in the USSR.* New York: Columbia University Press, 1965.

Salisbury, Harrison E. "Fatal Flaw in the Soviet System," in Samuel Hendel (ed.), *The Soviet Crucible: The Soviet Government in Theory and Practice.* Princeton, N.J.: D. Van Nostrand, 1959. Pp. 246–251.

———. "Khrushchev, in a Warm Speech, Renews Appeal for Friendship; President Again Asks Courtesy," *The New York Times,* September 22, 1959, pp. 1, 21.

————. "Khrushchev Visit: Impact in U.S.," *The New York Times,* September 20, 1959, p. E-5.

Schapiro, Leonard. "Has Russia Changed?" *Foreign Affairs,* 38 (April 1960), 391–401.

Schorr, Daniel. "Khrushchev's 'Hard Sell,' " *The New Leader,* 42 (October 19, 1959), 6–8.

————. "Traveling Salesmen for Two Ways of Life," *The New York Times Magazine,* March 13, 1960, pp. 22, 88–92.

Seabury, Paul. *The Rise and Decline of the Cold War.* New York: Basic Books, 1967.

Shannon, William V. "The Last Ten Days," *The New Statesman,* 58 (September 26, 1959), 379.

Sheerin, John B. "Khrushchev Has Many Faces," *The Catholic World,* 191 (August 1960), 264–268.

————. "What We Learned From Khrushchev," *The Catholic World,* 190 (November 1959), 79–80.

Slusser, Robert M. "America, China, and the Hydra-Headed Opposition: The Dynamics of Soviet Foreign Policy," in Peter H. Juviler and Henry W. Morton (eds.), *Soviet Policy-Making: Studies of Communism in Transition.* New York: Praeger, 1967. Pp. 183–269.

Stevenson, Adlai E. "Tour for Khrushchev—The Real America," *The New York Times Magazine,* July 5, 1959, pp. 5–7.

"The Visit," *The Nation,* 189 (October 3, 1959), 181.

Volkov, Leon. "The Tough and the Gentle," *Newsweek,* 54 (September 28, 1959), 37.

"What Americans Think," *Newsweek,* 54 (September 28, 1959), 39–40.

Whitney, Thomas P. "Introduction: The Tireless Voice of the Kremlin," in Thomas P. Whitney (ed.), *Khrushchev Speaks.* Ann Arbor: University of Michigan Press, 1963.

"Without Horns or Tails," *The Economist,* October 3, 1959, pp. 43–44.

The Sociocultural-Psychological Approach

MIND, Body, and the Unconscious
by Kenneth Burke

I

The issue: If man is the symbol-using animal, some motives must derive from his animality, some from his symbolicity, and some from mixtures of the two. The computer can't serve as our model (or "terministic screen"). For it is not an animal, but an artifact. And it can't truly be said to "act." Its operations are but a complex set of sheerly physical *motions*. Thus, we must if possible distinguish between the symbolic action of a *person* and the behavior of such a mere *thing*.

On the other hand, psychoanalysis has a concept of "symbolic action" that does distinctly apply to *persons*. But it is not identical with such eventfulness in the sheerly "Dramatistic" sense. By "symbolic action" in the Dramatistic sense is meant any use of symbol systems in general; I am acting symbolically, in the Dramatistic sense, when I speak these sentences to you, and you are acting symbolically insofar as you "follow" them, and thus size up their "drift" or "meaning." True, there are some "Unconscious" processes involved in my speaking and your interpreting what I say. But as we shall see, this is not what Freud had in mind with *his* concept of the "Unconscious" and its relation to what *he* calls "symbolic action." For he specifically says that the "concept of unconscious psychic activity which is peculiar to psychoanalysis" is to be sharply distinguished "from philosophical speculations about the unconscious." (The point is made near the beginning of his essay "History of the Psychoanalytic Movement.")

In the discussion of "terministic screens" we offered reasons why a definition of man must be a general "philosophic" problem rather than a specifically "scientific" one. Each specific science could not be its characteristic self except insofar as it abided by its particular terminology. And each such terminology is designed for a specific set of observations rather than for mediations on the nature of man in general.

A Dramatistic terminology (built around a definition of man as the symbol-using, symbol-misusing, symbol-making, and symbol-made animal) must steer midway between the computer on one side (when taken as a model of the mind) and the neurotic on the other. For instance, while greatly admiring and subscribing to much that Freud discussed so ingeniously and imaginatively in his *Psychopathology of Everyday Life,* Dramatism cannot reduce symbolic action in *general* to the *specific* sense of symbolic action that Freud is dealing with in his studies of neuroses and the unconscious.

As regards our basic Dramatistic distinction, "Things move, persons act," the person who designs a computing device would be *acting,* whereas the device itself would but be going through whatever sheer *motions* its design makes possible. These motions could also be so utilized as to function like a voice in a dialogue. For instance, when you weigh something, it is as though you asked the scales, "How much does this weigh?" and they "answered," though they would have given the same "answer" if something of the same weight had happened to fall upon the scales, and no one happened to be "asking" any question at all. The fact that a machine can be made to function *like* a partici- pant in a human dialogue does not require us to treat the two kinds of behavior as identical. And in one notable respect a *conditioned animal* would be a better model than a computer for the reductive interpreta- tion of man, since it suffers the pains and pleasures of hunger and satiety, along with other manifest forms of distress and gratification, though it's weak in the ways of smiling and laughing.

In brief, man differs qualitatively from other animals since they are too poor in symbolicity, just as man differs qualitatively from his ma- chines, since these man-made caricatures of man are too poor in ani- mality. So our main concern in this talk will be not with the Charybdis of the computer but with the Scylla of "symbolic action" in the specifi- cally psychoanalytic sense of the term. In Freud's sense an action is "symbolic" when, as interpreted in terms of his particular "terministic screen," it reveals the presence of a neurotic motive involving "repres- sions" due to the particular kind of "Unconscious" which he postulates as a locus of motives. Freud also offers as a synonym for "symbolic action" in this specific psychoanalytic sense the term "symptomatic action." For instance, if a person found it almost impossible to cross streets even when there was no apparent objective danger (as from traffic), the situation might be neurotically symbolic or symptomatic of an inability to arrive at a decision in some other matter that was of great importance to the sufferer, but was not consciously or rationally asso- ciated with the crossing of streets.

So this chapter will be concerned primarily with thoughts on the nature of the "Unconscious," in both Freudian and other senses. But first, we must consider some vexing matters having to do with the nega- tive. The question is vexing because, just as the negative has a major place in the Dramatistic view of symbolicity, it is likewise of great moment with regard to the two realms that Dramatism must somehow steer between.

Some years ago, a bit uneasily, I proposed this notion:[1]

The binary system in mathematics may be no more nor less negatively infused than, say, the decimal system. But this much seems clear: In the application of the binary system to the "electronic brains" of the new calculating devices, the genius of the negative is uppermost, as it is in the stop-go signals of traffic regulation. For the binary system lends itself well to technological devices whereby every number is stated as a succession of choices between the closing of an electrical current and the leaving of the contact open. In effect, then, the number is expressed by a series of yeses and noes, given in one particular order.

I am always uneasy when venturing into such areas. But now I can quote for authority from an interesting, and at times even charming little book, by D. S. Halacy, Jr., *Computers, the Machines We Think With,* which on several occasions refers to the "on-off, yes-no nature" of the digital computer. The author thus views the brain as being constructed like a digital computer, "composed of billions of neurons, each capable of being on or off," though he concedes that "many philosophers build a strong case for the yes-no-maybe approach with its large areas of gray." Neurons or no neurons, I have myself subscribed to the yes-no-maybe approach, where human symbolicity is concerned. See, for instance, in the symposium, *Freedom and Authority in Our Time* (pp. 371–372) my discussion of the problem that arises when the public demands "simple yes-no solutions for yes-no-maybe situations." At least language certainly has plenty of *words* (for ideas or images) that, like "maybe" itself, fall under the heading of attitudes midway between yes and no, whether or not the sheer motions of the brain operate on a flat yes-no basis (like traffic signals that would not allow for right, left, or U turns). And one possible lure of imagery resides in the fact that it so readily transcends strict logical distinctions or clear-cut decisions. The main thing for our purposes is to note Mr. Halacy's point about the "power of the digital, yes-no approach," due to the fact that, in such computers, "a single switch can only be on or off," the amazing results being obtained by the complex interconnections among such switches (plus the speed of the operations).

Freud's concept of "repression" in the "Unconscious" is on its face

---

[1] *From "Postscripts on the Negative,"* Quarterly Journal of Speech, *April, 1953.*

doubly saturated with the negative. Thus we might sum up by saying: According to the Freudian nomenclature, the "unconscious" process of "repression" involves the fact that the thou-shalt-not's of the "super-ego" would negate the desires of the "id," that portion of the "uncon-scious" which knows no Negation (or, more resonantly, "knows no No"). And "symbolic" or "symptomatic" kinds of action are said to result from unconscious attempts to elude the repressions imposed by the tyranny of the "superego."

Though the role of the negative in the Dramatistic concept of "sym-bolic action" covers a wider area than Freud's usage, the two realms are by no means mutually exclusive. Each in its way stresses the im-portance of the moralistic negative. But whereas the Freudian negative is identified solely with the process of *repression* in the *Unconscious,* the Dramatistic negative must focus attention upon the negative as a peculiar resource of *symbol systems.* Simplest example: If A explicitly says to B, "Don't do that," the message could hardly be reduced sim-ply to terms of "unconscious repression." The order is clear enough on its face. And far from being "repressive," the remark may even be quite helpful advice, as when an expert is telling a learner how to avoid a mistake. Or when a mathematician's equations introduce a minus sign, we could hardly put such operations in the same class with the "negativism" of a disobedient child.

Or consider the two closely related terms in the Freudian nomencla-ture, "condensation" and "displacement." In Freudian usage, they refer specifically to an aspect of symbolism characteristic of dreams and neuroses. And Freud has done well by them in that connection. For instance, an "unconscious" resentment against A might be so dis-placed that it reveals itself as a resentment against B. And "condensa-tion" can take place when, if A is associated in your Unconscious with B, you might have a dream in which various traits of both A and B are combined in a single image. Here would be instances of "symbolic action" in the specifically psychoanalytic sense.

Yet as regards "symbolic action" in general, there are such "dis-placements" as when a mathematician substitutes a symbol for an equation, or when a translator substitutes terms in one language for terms in another. And a kind of "condensation" results in every case where one moves to a higher order of generalization, as when one goes from "mother and father" to "parents," or from "brothers and sis-ters" to "siblings." Or, if we may revert to the discussion of poetics in particular and language in general, whereas the logic of symbolism in general might induce a poet to use imagery of death as a surrogate for "perfection" (or "finishedness"), or as a way of dignifying his theme, the implications of a specifically psychoanalytic terminology might sug-gest rather that a "death wish" was involved. Such instances, I hope, will serve as first rough approximate to indicate the difference between "symbolic action" in the specifically psychoanalytic sense and its more general Dramatistic meaning.

But another problem arises:

Since we began this talk by a reference to Freud's explicit admonition that psychoanalysis applies the concept of the "Unconscious" in a way to be differentiated from the "philosophic" uses of the term, just how might the two realms of meaning diverge, as regards the requirements of Dramatism in general?

Otherwise put: If man is the symbol-using animal, and if his animality is by definition categorically distinguishable from symbolicity (as our bodies differ in essence from the words we utter, or as nobody can live by the sheer *words* for "bread" alone), and as we build around the distinction between "motion" and "action" (which is motion-plus), then how about this realm of the "Unconscious"? How many categories might we need, when discussing the problem of the relation between our bodies, as sheer physical objects, and their emergence into articulacy (that is, symbolicity)? All that has been said up to now has been but a necessary introduction to the list I shall tentatively propose (under the sign of yes-no-maybe).

II
Varieties of "Unconscious"

1) There is the unconscious aspect of sheerly bodily processes (growth, metabolism, digestion, peristaltic "action," respiration, functions of the various organs, secretions of the endocrine glands, ways in which elements in the bloodstream reinforce or check one another, and so on). One may observe the healing of a wound: but there is a sense in which, even under strict observation, the processes of healing proceed *outside* one's consciousness. Possibly we have "repressed" our awareness of all such processes. At least, it is certain that, if we were specifically aware of them all (as some neurotics are sometimes aware of some visceral processes), we'd be in a condition that, as judged by our present norms, would be little short of horrible. Maybe our transcending of all such happenings (except for the "feeling tone" that may strike our "consciousness" as an overall "attitude" or "state of mind"), is to be treated as a kind of "repression." But it seems to differ from the *moralistic* kind of repression with which Freud was concerned. When we read a sentence, we are wholly "unconscious" of all the neural processes involved in our hearing and understanding of that sentence. Indeed, we must even find it hard to understand how the simplest sentence "makes sense." Here also might be included processes of training, or habit, whereby conscious effort becomes spontaneous (as with learning to walk or talk).

2) Freudian nomenclature is partial to what we might call an "archaizing principle," an explanation in terms of the *temporally* prior. Thus, adult disturbances are analyzed as vestiges of experiences undergone in childhood, infancy, and even farther back, in conditions that might possibly have prevailed during "prehistory." Similarly, even "normal" dreams are considered from this "vestigial" point of view. And the thinking of "primitive" peoples is studied in the same light. Hence, many aspects of expression that once might have been studied in terms of *rhetorical* resources *natural* to language at *all* stages of history are treated rather as *survivals* from eras of primitive magic, ritual, and myth. There is a sense in which this "archaizing principle" can be given a more general, "philosophic" application. I have in mind the thought that *any* present moment is the "Unconscious" repository of the past, not just as regards some possible "primal" scene or "Oedipal" crime, but in terms of *all* the evolutionary unfoldings that are somehow summed up in each of us, at his given moment in history. Viewed thus, even our most mature and conscious functions are but "survivals" from conditions in the remote past. And though one may by a methodic analysis of "free associations" restore the "repressed" memory of a few supposedly "forgotten" details in a particular patient's past, all such conscious recoveries are but *infinitesimal,* as compared with the totality of the past that is somehow unconsciously implicit in us. We shall consider this matter from another standpoint in a later category.

2a) As a kind of "aside" here, we might note that even the specifically Freudian concept of unconscious repression implies at least two kinds of unconsciousness. For instance, in his essay "On the Transformation of Instincts with Special Reference to Anal Eroticism," besides noting that certain symbols "are seldom distinguished and are easily interchangeable," Freud admonishes that he is speaking "figuratively," since some of the terms to which he is referring do not properly belong to the realm of the Unconscious. He then charts some "processes of development" involving different ways in which sheer *equivalence* among terms is replaced by different *sequences* (with corresponding differences in the formation of character). That is, an unconscious *equating* of terms A and B would allow for another kind of unconscious process, the step *from A to B* in *contrast with* the step *from B to A.*

2b) A further "aside" is in order here. The Freudian concept of the "id" envisions an inborn cauldron of desires that "know no No," so that each desire is experienced without regard to the claims of any other desire ("repressions" being presumably due to the unconscious workings of the "superego"). Extending such a concept Dramatistically, one discovers that the same terministic design is involved in the Constitution of the United States. The various "principles" embodied in our

Constitution are, in effect, a set of *wishes,* each proclaimed in its own right, without regard to the others. Thus, there are the principles, or "wishes," proclaiming the rights of the individual, of the States, of police powers, of national emergency, of public welfare, and so on. Each is there as a Constitutionally asserted wish, without explicit reference to the other wishes. But legal conflicts arise because, in particular cases, this "id"-like wishing on the part of the Constitution confronts problems of *denial.* In gratifying one Constitutional wish, the courts must frustrate or "repress" another. At such times, the Supreme Court is called upon to decide which wish shall be deemed *primus inter pares* in the given situation. And, necessarily, the history of the Supreme Court has been a history of changing choices as regards the *hierarchy* of such wishes (decisions as to which of the wishes should be given preferential rating), since for better or worse there is nothing in our egalitarian Constitution itself that establishes such a scale once and for all.

In my *Grammar of Motives* I had treated the Constitution's principles thus, as a set of "sovereign wishes" confronting one another like sovereign states, but I had not explicitly noted their analogy to the Freudian "id."

3) There are many kinds of unconscious memories which, though not explicitly recalled, are recallable on demand. Many of the "facts" we learn are of this sort. Thus there are variations in our ability to recall, as some trains of thought contain associations that help us recall certain otherwise "forgotten" bits of knowledge, while other trains of thought throw us off the track, by directing our attention into other associative channels. For instance, if one forgot a language that one had not spoken since childhood, surely this would not be a prime example of repression in Freud's moralistic sense. However, Freud might offer invaluable cues as to why, of a sudden, the "lost" words began turning up again.

4) The above category suggests the possibility of different sub-personalities variously at odds with one another, and to that extent in a corresponding Unconscious relationship. Thus, while writing, an author might embody a different order of motives from those he responds to, in his life outside his study. Or there can be a discontinuity between one's character under alcohol and one's character when sober, with each of them, over the years, coming to have its own character, or order of associations (so that things remembered or given primary importance under one of these dispensations are neglected in the other). Owing to the great dissociation between sleeping and waking, this thought of an Unconscious relation, or disrelation, between sub-personalities brings up another likelihood: That the symbolic consummations in forgotten or vaguely remembered dreams might serve as moti-

vational incentives (as sources of guilt, and the like). The dreams might secretly have the effect of profoundly experienced actualities (as children who watch the brutalities on television may, as it were, "actually" participate in such behavior). But for more on this point, we must consider the next category.

5) Freud's overwhelmingly tendency to treat of motives in terms of the *temporally* prior (as per Rule Two, the "archaizing" principle) might deflect our attention from the possibility of refurbishing the Aristotelian concept of the "entelechy" for use in naming a species of Unconscious. By the Unconscious in this sense, I have in mind the implications of a symbol system, its *"future* possibilities" in a purely *formal* sense. Surely, in this sense, the relation between Conscious and Unconscious is not to be considered as a matter of "repression" in the specifically Freudian sense of the term. For instance, one can hardly be said to have "repressed" one's understanding of the propositions that Euclid deduced from the definitions and axioms of his geometry. Rather, we must look upon Euclid as having *developed with thoroughness* the implications of his position. If I discover a body wandering in outer space, and if by my computations I conclude that it will strike the earth at a certain time, thereby destroying all life on this planet, I might well argue for the justice of my computations even though I didn't want the calamity to take place. True, my prophecy might happen to be reinforced by a neurotic yearning for absolute suicide. Or I may even prophesy (out of my hat) a similar calamity. But there is also the sheerly technical fact, as regards the nature of symbolism in general, that the thoroughness of my devotion to my work with a given symbol system may lead me to this "perfect" conclusion. This I call the "entelechial" motive, a motive intrinsic sheerly to symbol systems. And in this connection, the "Unconscious" implications may not be "made conscious" until one has *methodically* devoted oneself to the task of inquiring into the *fulfillment* of a given symbol system as such.

When emerging from infancy into linguistic articulacy, a child "unconsciously learns the rules" of his language's particular grammar and syntax, though these "rules" may never have been systematically formulated. If the rules were never formulated, when speaking his language he will necessarily exemplify these rules while being "unconscious" of them, as regards the *grammarian's* particular kind of explicit consciousness. Plato was much exercised about our unconscious knowledge in this sense (a kind of sheerly formal awareness that is not reducible to terms of the "repressed" in the specifically Freudian sense). Similarly, as was considered in an earlier chapter, a poet may make revisions simply because they "feel right." But *implicit* in such revisions there is a set of judgments, or aesthetic norms, which some critic might translate into an explicit set of poetic principles.

6) Quite closely related to our sixth category there is the sheerly

terministic situation whereby *any* "conscious" nomenclature gives rise to a corresponding realm of the "unconscious." This kind of consideration turns up in an interesting way with regard to Marx's adaptation of Hegel's views on "consciousness" and "false consciousness." In Marx's scheme, "class consciousness" greatly overlaps upon what we might well call "class unconsciousness." For instance: By Marx's scheme, if the bourgeois conceives of all mankind in terms of the bourgeois, said bourgeois has *unconsciously* represented (or revealed) his bourgeois *consciousness.* And any concept of "development" or "progress" gives rise to corresponding concepts of "regression" (though we resist the thought that, when breathing naturally, the body is "regressing" to processes that evolved millions of years ago; and we reserve the term for the partial regression that occurs in psychogenic asthma).

So, necessarily, we must here concern ourselves with many aspects of the Unconscious that are not wholly understandable in Freudian terms of repression. We here confront kinds of *attention* that often are not reducible to terms of *repression.* But any terminology for *directing the attention* is ultimately reducible to terms of a *principle.* That is, in its hypothetical *perfection* it can be called a kind of "Ism." Yet, any examples of the given motive that occurred prior to the formula or without knowledge of it may be said to exemplify that motive "unconsciously." In this sense, there is a kind of "unconsciousness" that is sheerly a reflection of whatever terminology one happens to be using.

7) By the Unconscious we often mean the "intuitive" or "instinctive," the weather eye of the weather prophet, the ability to be a "good judge of character," the mathematical physicist's ability to "idealize" a problem in a way that affords a solution, the expert player's ability to make exactly the right adjustments needed for his play, the ability to so "size up a situation" that one knows *uno intuitu* whether a certain thing should or should not be done, the wit to see a joke, the area of "taste," "tact," "propriety," what the Greeks called *to prepon* and the Latins *decorum,* and the eighteenth century *je ne sais quoi*—in sum, the recognition that something is as it is, without pausing to ask exactly how one arrived at precisely that decision.

If B is greater than A, and C is greater than B, then "obviously" C is greater than A—but who can say how he "consciously" arrived at this result?! The process involved in such a judgment is as far beyond our "consciousness" as the operation of a miracle. It "just is." Yet surely our bepuzzlements here are not instances of "repression" in the strictly Freudian sense. Someday we might have some more terms for "consciously" charting this process; but we don't have them now. And even if we do, such consciousness is most likely to be "from without," as with our possibly "conscious" ways of describing how a wound heals. One may be wholly conscious of the "feeling tone" that sums up, in a kind of attitude, the diseased or healthy condition of his body. But even if the medical study of symptoms were advanced vastly beyond its present state of knowledge, such conscious "feeling tone" would but correspond to a practically infinite number of relationships about which one is almost as "unconscious" as a book's title is "unconscious" of the book's specific contents.

8) We might add a catchall category, labeled "Error, Ignorance, Uncertainty." One may eat a certain contaminated food through sheer ignorance, not owing to any psychological "repression" of such knowledge. One just happens to be "unconscious" of its true nature. And this category shades off into many kinds of inadequately criticized responsiveness. Thus, we might make this decision rather than that, not because we have "repressed" a knowledge of the results, but because such adequate knowledge is not available to us. (For instance, what voter can possibly have adequate foreknowledge of exactly how his candidate will behave under conditions that the candidate himself has not yet confronted?)

All told, then, we have tentatively listed these kinds of "unconscious" (many of which are obviously not reducible to the specifically Freudian concept of repression), our idea being that the very genius of the Freudian terminology leads beyond the specifically psychiatric analysis of symbolic action (the symptoms of sick souls) to thoughts on symbolic action in general.

To sum up, as possible kinds of Unconscious we have listed:

1) The sheerly physiological processes of the body.

2) The universal incorporation of the past within the present.

2a) A possible distinction between the mere unconscious equivalence of terms and unconscious ways of proceeding from one to another.

2b) Comments on the respects in which the Constitution's set of sovereign wishes (each propounded in its own right) is analogous to the Freudian concept of the "Id."

3) The recallable but not explicitly recalled. Here also might be included knowledge which one has, but which does not happen to be associated with the given topic under discussion. My concept of "perspective by incongruity" (as discussed especially in *Permanence and Change*) is concerned with the way in which poets enliven language by metaphors that leap like lightning across such gaps, and thereby bring together terms which we had unconsciously classed as mutually exclusive.

4) The closely related category of dissociation among "sub-personalities."

5) The "entelechial" kind of "futurity" (as certain kinds of observations or conclusions may be *implicit* in a given terminology, quite in the sense that a grammar and syntax are implicit in a given language). One

can be moved by a "terministic compulsion" to track down such possibilities.

6) The "Ismic" paradox whereby any terminology that systematically calls attention to a hitherto unnoticed area of speculation by the same token creates a corresponding kind of "unconscious."

7) The "intuitive" recognition that something is as it is.

8) A catchall category. Error, confusion, or uncertainty, due simply to the fact that the conditions for making an accurate judgment are not present (as when trying to identify an object too far off to be seen clearly, or when voting for a candidate when nobody in the world, including the candidate himself, knows how he will act if the unforeseen pressures of history build up this way rather than that).

III
The Five Dogs

So much for our tentative categories of the Unconscious. But where problems of terminology are concerned, we must always keep on the move. So, for a windup, let's try a different slant, having in mind both the psychoanalytic and the Dramatistic concepts of "symbolic action."

Animalistically, there are many species of dogs. But Dramatistically, these reduce to five (not a single one of which might meet the requirements of a dog-fancier—or should we say, a dog-man?).

For a finish, I would propose this other cut across our subject:

First, along psychoanalytic lines, there is the "primal" dog, the first dog you knew, or loved, or were frightened by, or lost. It secretly ties in with what the anthropologist Malinowski would call "context of situation." For though many or all of the details that are associated with that dog may have been forgotten (and thus become "unconscious"), we now know that they are still there within you somehow (and can be disclosed by drugs, hypnosis or psychoanalysis).

Next, there's the "jingle" dog. It concerns the sheerly accidental nature of the *word* "dog," what it rhymes with in English as distinct from what the corresponding word rhymes with in other languages, and above all, in English, we might well keep in mind Cummings' undeniable observation that the jingle dog is "God spelled backwards." (Or did he say it the other way round?)

Third comes the "lexical" dog. This is the one defined in the dictionary, "by genus and differentia." It is the most public, normal, and rational of all dogs—and the emptiest of all, as regards the attitude of either poets or neurotics. If that great, good, sound, healthy, public meaning for "dog" were all we had, I can confidently assure you that the world would be completely clear of poetry. This is the only definition that wholly makes sense, if the world is to be kept going. But along with the fact that this definition of "dog" is tremendously necessary, there's also the fact that "dog" as so conceived is totally inane. You know what I mean. But if you want documentation besides, just track down all the references to dogs in Aeschylus' *Oresteia* (or see the pages on "dog" in William Empson's *The Structure of Complex Words*).

Fourth, there's an "entelechial dog." This is the "perfect" dog *towards which* one might aspire. I might give a roundabout example of this sort: Beginning with the material substance, *bread*, let us next move to the *word* "bread." Once we have that *word*, through sheerly verbal manipulations we can arrive at a term for "perfect bread." Having got to that point, we find two quite different kinds of resources open to us. (1) We may feel disillusioned about "reality" because the *thing* bread falls so tragically short of the ideal that flits about our *word* for "perfect" bread. Or (2) we might be graced with the opportunity to discern, all around us, evidences of ways whereby even the worst of bread embodies, however finitely, the *principle* of an infinitely and absolutely "perfect" bread. Dogs endowed with "personalities" in animal stories would be a fictional variant of such an "entelechial" motive. In their way, they are "perfect" embodiments of certain traits. Lassie has been the Machinery's prime exhibit, as regards the entelechial dog.

Finally, there is the "tautological" dog. We here have in mind the fact that a dog involves a particular set of associations which, in a sense, reproduce his "spirit." For instance: kennel, dog food, master, the hunt, cat, protection, loyalty, slavishness, the place where the dog was killed, and so on. When I was young, I always had a dog, and I always thought of lions as big dogs. It was quite a blow to me when I first learned that lions are really big cats. Looking back, I incline to believe that I had a "cycle" or "ladder" of terms, running from dog, to boy, to father, to lion, to king (or generally, ruler or authority), to God. Here would be a "tautological" terminology in the sense I now have in mind.

Our five dogs overlap considerably, I concede. But there are terministic situations when each is most directly to be considered in its own right, though we should always keep the whole lot in mind, when inquiring into the relations between the overt symbol and its possible dissolvings into the "Where is it?" of the Unconscious.

Eds. note: In the book from which we have taken the "Mind, Body, and the Unconscious," Burke appends a lengthy set of "comments" developing some of his thought further. Some readers will be interested in these notes. (*Language as Symbolic Action*, pp. 74–80.)

The Rhetoric of Hitler's "Battle"
by Kenneth Burke

The appearance of *Mein Kampf* in unexpurgated translation has called forth far too many vandalistic comments. There are other ways of burning books than on the pyre—and the favorite method of the hasty reviewer is to deprive himself and his readers by inattention. I maintain that it is thoroughly vandalistic for the reviewer to content himself with the mere inflicting of a few symbolic wounds upon this book and its author, of an intensity varying with the resources of the reviewer and the time at his disposal. Hitler's "Battle" is exasperating, even nauseating; yet the fact remains: If the reviewer but knocks off a few adverse attitudinizings and calls it a day, with a guaranty in advance that his article will have a favorable reception among the decent members of our population, he is contributing more to our gratification than to our enlightenment.

Here is the testament of a man who swung a great people into his wake. Let us watch it carefully; and let us watch it, not merely to discover some grounds for prophesying what political move is to follow Munich, and what move to follow that move, etc.; let us try also to discover what kind of "medicine" this medicine-man has concocted, that we may know, with greater accuracy, exactly what to guard against, if we are to forestall the concocting of similar medicine in America.

Already, in many quarters of our country, we are "beyond" the stage where we are being saved from Nazism by our *virtues*. And fascist integration is being staved off, rather, by the *conflicts among our vices*. Our vices cannot get together in a grand united front of prejudices; and the result of this frustration, if or until they succeed in surmounting it, speaks, as the Bible might say, "in the name of" democracy. Hitler found a panacea, a "cure for what ails you," a "snakeoil," that made such sinister unifying possible within his own nation. And he was helpful enough to put his cards face up on the table, that we might examine his hands. Let us, then, for God's sake, examine them. This book is the well of Nazi magic; crude magic, but effective. A people trained in pragmatism should want to inspect this magic.

1.

Every movement that would recruit its followers from among many discordant and divergent bands, must have some spot towards which all roads lead. Each man may get there in his own way, but it must be the one unifying center of reference for all. Hitler considered this mat-

This essay is reprinted with the permission of Kenneth Burke from *The Philosophy of Literary Form,* Louisiana State University Press, second edition, 1967; first edition, 1941. The book is also available in a Vintage paperback edition, 1957.

ter carefully, and decided that this center must be not merely a centralizing hub of *ideas,* but a mecca geographically located, towards which all eyes could turn at the appointed hours of prayer (or, in this case, the appointed hours of prayer-in-reverse, the hours of vituperation). So he selected Munich, as the *materialization* of his unifying panacea. As he puts it:

The geo-political importance of a center of a movement cannot be overrated. Only the presence of such a center and of a place, bathed in the magic of a Mecca or a Rome, can at length give a movement that force which is rooted in the inner unity and in the recognition of a hand that represents this unity.

If a movement must have its Rome, it must also have its devil. For as Russell pointed out years ago, an important ingredient of unity in the Middle Ages (an ingredient that long did its unifying work despite the many factors driving towards disunity) was the symbol of a *common enemy,* the Prince of Evil himself. Men who can unite on nothing else can unite on the basis of a foe shared by all. Hitler himself states the case very succinctly:

As a whole, and at all times, the efficiency of the truly national leader consists primarily in preventing the division of the attention of a people, and always in concentrating it on a single enemy. The more uniformly the fighting will of a people is put into action, the greater will be the magnetic force of the movement and the more powerful the impetus of the blow. It is part of the genius of a great leader to make adversaries of different fields appear as always belonging to one category only, because to weak and unstable characters the knowledge that there are various enemies will lead only too easily to incipient doubts as to their own cause.

As soon as the wavering masses find themselves confronted with too many enemies, objectivity at once steps in, and the question is raised whether actually all the others are wrong and their own nation or their own movement alone is right.

Also with this comes the first paralysis of their own strength. Therefore, a number of essentially different enemies must always be regarded as one in such a way that in the opinion of the mass of one's own adherents the war is being waged against one enemy alone. This strengthens the belief in one's own cause and increases one's bitterness against the attacker.

As everyone knows, this policy was exemplified in his selection of an "international" devil, the "international Jew" (the Prince was international, universal, "catholic"). This *materialization* of a religious pattern is, I think, one terrifically effective weapon of propaganda in a period where religion has been progressively weakened by many centuries of capitalist materialism. You need but go back to the sermonizing of centuries to be reminded that religion had a powerful enemy long before organized atheism came upon the scene. Religion is based upon the "prosperity of poverty," upon the use of ways for converting our sufferings and handicaps into a good—but capitalism is based upon the prosperity of acquisitions, the only scheme of value, in fact, by which its proliferating store of gadgets could be sold, insofar as capitalism does not get so drastically in its own way that it can't sell its gadgets even after it has trained people to feel that human dignity, the "higher standard of living," could be attained only by such vast private accumulation.

So, we have, as unifying step No. 1, the international devil materialized, in the visible, point-to-able form of people with a certain kind of "blood," a burlesque of contemporary neo-positivism's ideal of meaning, which insists upon a *material* reference.

Once Hitler has thus essentialized his enemy, all "proof" henceforth is automatic. If you point out the enormous amount of evidence to show that the Jewish worker is at odds with the "international Jew stock exchange capitalist," Hitler replies with one hundred per cent regularity: That is one more indication of the cunning with which the "Jewish plot" is being engineered. Or would you point to "Aryans" who do the same as his conspiratorial Jews? Very well; that is proof that the "Aryan" has been "seduced" by the Jew.

The sexual symbolism that runs through Hitler's book, lying in wait to draw upon the responses of contemporary sexual values, is easily characterized: Germany in dispersion is the "dehorned Siegfried." The masses are "feminine." As such, they desire to be led by a dominating male. This male, as orator, woos them—and, when he has won them, he commands them. The rival male, the villainous Jew, would on the contrary "seduce" them. If he succeeds, he poisons their blood by intermingling with them. Whereupon, by purely associative connections of ideas, we are moved into attacks upon syphilis, prostitution, incest, and other similar misfortunes, which are introduced as a kind of "musical" argument when he is on the subject of "blood-poisoning" by intermarriage or, in its "spiritual" equivalent, by the infection of "Jewish" ideas, such as democracy.[1]

The "medicinal" appeal of the Jew as scapegoat operates from another angle. The middle class contains, within the mind of each member, a duality: its members simultaneously have a cult of money and a

---

[1] *Hitler also strongly insists upon the total identification between leader and people. Thus, in wooing the people, he would in a roundabout way be wooing himself. The thought might suggest how the Führer, dominating the feminine masses by his diction, would have an incentive to remain unmarried.*

detestation of this cult. When capitalism is going well, this conflict is left more or less in abeyance. But when capitalism is balked, it comes to the fore. Hence, there is "medicine" for the "Aryan" members of the middle class in the projective device of the scapegoat, whereby the "bad" features can be allocated to the "devil," and one can "respect himself" by a distinction between "good" capitalism and "bad" capitalism, with those of a different lodge being the vessels of the "bad" capitalism. It is doubtless the "relief" of this solution that spared Hitler the necessity of explaining just how the "Jewish plot" was to work out. Nowhere does this book, which is so full of war plans, make the slightest attempt to explain the steps whereby the triumph of "Jewish Bolshevism," which destroys *all* finance, will be the triumph of *"Jewish"* finance. Hitler well knows the point at which his "elucidations" should rely upon the lurid alone.

The question arises, in those trying to gauge Hitler: Was his selection of the Jew, as his unifying devil-function, a purely calculating act? Despite the quotation I have already given, I believe that it was *not*. The vigor with which he utilized it, I think, derives from a much more complex state of affairs. It seems that, when Hitler went to Vienna, in a state close to total poverty, he genuinely suffered. He lived among the impoverished; and he describes his misery at the spectacle. He was *sensitive* to it; and his way of manifesting this sensitiveness impresses me that he is, at this point, wholly genuine, as with his wincing at the broken family relationships caused by alcoholism, which he in turn relates to impoverishment. During this time he began his attempts at political theorizing; and his disturbance was considerably increased by the skill with which Marxists tied him into knots. One passage in particular gives you reason, reading between the lines, to believe that the dialecticians of the class struggle, in their skill at blasting his muddled speculations, put him into a state of uncertainty that was finally "solved" by rage:

The more I argued with them, the more I got to know their dialectics. First, they counted on the ignorance of their adversary; then, when there was no way out, they themselves pretended stupidity. If all this was of no avail, they refused to understand or they changed the subject when driven into a corner; they brought up truisms, but they immediately transferred their acceptance to quite different subjects, and, if attacked again, they gave way and pretended to know nothing exactly. Wherever one attacked one of these prophets, one's hands seized slimy jelly; it slipped through one's fingers only to collect again in the next moment. If one smote one of them so thoroughly that, with the bystanders watching, he could but agree, and if one thus thought he had advanced at least one step, one was greatly astonished the following day. The Jew did not in the least remember the day before, he continued to

*talk in the same old strain as if nothing had happened, and if indig-
nantly confronted, he pretended to be astonished and could not remember anything except that his assertions had already been proved true
the day before.*

Often I was stunned.

*One did not know what to admire more: their glibness of tongue or
their skill in lying.*

I gradually began to hate them.

At this point, I think, he is tracing the *spontaneous* rise of his anti-
Semitism. He tells how, once he had discovered the "cause" of the
misery about him, he could *confront it*. Where he had had to avert his
eyes, he could now *positively welcome* the scene. Here his drastic
structure of *acceptance* was being formed. He tells of the "internal happiness" that descended upon him.

*This was the time in which the greatest change I was ever to experi-
ence took place in me.*

From a feeble cosmopolite I turned into a fanatical anti-Semite,

and thence we move, by one of those associational tricks which he
brings forth at all strategic moments, into a vision of the end of the
world—out of which in turn he emerges with his slogan: "I am acting
in the sense of the Almighty Creator: *By warding off Jews I am fighting
for the Lord's work*" (italics his).

He talks of this transition as a period of "double life," a struggle of
"reason" and "reality" against his "heart."[2] It was as "bitter" as it was

---

[2] *Other aspects of the career symbolism: Hitler's book begins: "Today I
consider it my good fortune that Fate designated Braunau on the Inn as the
place of my birth. For this small town is situated on the border between those
two German States, the reunion of which seems, at least to us of the younger
generation, a task to be furthered with every means our lives long," an indication of his "transitional" mind, what Wordsworth might have called the
"borderer." He neglects to give the date of his birth, 1889, which is supplied
by the editors. Again there is a certain "correctness" here, as Hitler was not
"born" until many years later—but he does give the exact date of his war
wounds, which were indeed formative. During his early years in Vienna and
Munich, he foregoes protest, on the grounds that he is "nameless." And when
his party is finally organized and effective, he stresses the fact that his "nameless" period is over (i.e., he has shaped himself an identity). When reading
in an earlier passage of his book some generalizations to the effect that one
should not crystallize his political views until he is thirty, I made a note: "See
what Hitler does at thirty." I felt sure that, though such generalizations may be
dubious as applied to people as a whole, they must, given the Hitler type of
mind (with his complete identification between himself and his followers), be
valid statements about himself. One should do what he did. The hunch was
verified: about the age of thirty Hitler, in a group of seven, began working with
the party that was to conquer Germany. I trace these steps particularly because*

"blissful." And finally, it was "reason" that won! Which prompts us to note that those who attack Hitlerism as a cult of the irrational should emend their statements to this extent: irrational it is, but it is carried on under the *slogan* of "Reason." Similarly, his cult of war is developed "in the name of" humility, love, and peace. Judged on a quantitative basis, Hitler's book certainly falls under the classification of hate. Its venom is everywhere, its charity is sparse. But the rationalized family tree for this hate situates it in "Aryan love." Some deep-probing German poets, whose work adumbrated the Nazi movement, did gravitate towards thinking *in the name of* war, irrationality, and hate. But Hitler was not among them. After all, when it is so easy to draw a doctrine of war out of a doctrine of peace, why should the astute politician do otherwise, particularly when Hitler has slung together his doctrines, without the slightest effort at logical symmetry? Furthermore, Church thinking always got to its wars in Hitler's "sounder" manner; and the patterns of Hitler's thought are a bastardized or caricatured version of religious thought.

I spoke of Hitler's fury at the dialectics of those who opposed him when his structure was in the stage of scaffolding. From this we may move to another tremendously important aspect of his theory: his attack upon the *parliamentary*. For it is again, I submit, an important aspect of his medicine, in its function as medicine for him personally and as medicine for those who were later to identify themselves with him.

There is a "problem" in the parliament—and nowhere was this problem more acutely in evidence than in the pre-war Vienna that was to serve as Hitler's political schooling. For the parliament, at its best, is a "babel" of voices. There is the wrangle of men representing interests lying awkwardly on the bias across one another, sometimes opposing, sometimes vaguely divergent. Morton Prince's psychiatric study of "Miss Beauchamp," the case of a woman split into several subpersonalities at odds with one another, variously combining under hypnosis, and frequently in turmoil, is the allegory of a democracy fallen upon evil days. The parliament of the Habsburg Empire just prior to its collapse was an especially drastic instance of such disruption, such vocal diaspora, with movements that would reduce one to a disinte-

---

I believe that the orator who has a strong sense of his own "rebirth" has this to draw upon when persuading his audiences that he is offering them the way to a "new life." However, I see no categorical objection to this attitude; its menace derives solely from the values in which it is exemplified. They may be wholesome or unwholesome. If they are unwholesome, but backed by conviction, the basic sincerity of the conviction acts as a sound virtue to reinforce a vice— and this combination is the most disastrous one that a people can encounter in a demagogue.

grated mass of fragments if he attempted to encompass the totality of its discordancies. So Hitler, suffering under the alienation of poverty and confusion, yearning for some integrative core, came to take this parliament as the basic symbol of all that he would move away from. He damned the tottering Habsburg Empire as a "State of Nationalities." The many conflicting voices of the spokesmen of the many political blocs arose from the fact that various separationist movements of a nationalistic sort had arisen within a Catholic imperial structure formed prior to the nationalistic emphasis and slowly breaking apart under its development. So, you had this babel of voices; and, by the method of associative mergers, *using ideas as imagery,* it became tied up, in the Hitler rhetoric, with "Babylon," Vienna as the city of poverty, prostitution, immorality, coalitions, half-measures, incest, democracy (i.e., majority rule leading to "lack of personal responsibility"), death, internationalism, seduction, and anything else of thumbsdown sort the associative enterprise cared to add on this side of the balance.

Hitler's way of treating the parliamentary babel, I am sorry to say, was at one important point not much different from that of the customary editorial in our own newspapers. Every conflict among the parliamentary spokesmen represents a corresponding conflict among the material interests of the groups for whom they are speaking. But Hitler did not discuss the babel from this angle. He discussed it on a purely *symptomatic* basis. The strategy of our orthodox press, in thus ridiculing the cacaphonous verbal output of Congress, is obvious: by thus centering attack upon the *symptoms* of business conflict, as they reveal themselves on the dial of political wrangling, and leaving the underlying cause, the business conflicts themselves, out of the case, they can gratify the very public they would otherwise alienate: namely, the businessmen who are the activating members of their reading public. Hitler, however, went them one better. For not only did he stress the purely *symptomatic* attack here. He proceeded to search for the "cause." And this "cause," of course, he derived from his medicine, his racial theory by which he could give a noneconomic interpretation of a phenomenon economically engendered.

Here again is where Hitler's corrupt use of religious patterns comes to the fore. Church thought, being primarily concerned with matters of the "personality," with problems of moral betterment, naturally, and I think rightly, stresses as a necessary feature, the act of will upon the part of the individual. Hence its resistance to a purely "environmental" account of human ills. Hence its emphasis upon the "person." Hence its proneness to seek a noneconomic explanation of economic phenomena. Hitler's proposal of a noneconomic "cause" for the disturbances thus had much to recommend it from this angle. And, as a matter of fact, it was Lueger's Christian-Social Party in Vienna that taught Hitler the tactics of tying up a program of social betterment with an anti-Semitic "unifier." The two parties that he carefully studied at that time were this Catholic faction and Schoenerer's Pan-German group. And his analysis of their attainments and shortcomings, from the standpoint of demagogic efficacy, is an extremely astute piece of work, revealing how carefully this man used the current situation in Vienna as an experimental laboratory for the maturing of his plans.

His unification device, we may summarize, had the following important features:

(1) Inborn dignity. In both religious and humanistic patterns of thought, a "natural born" dignity of man is stressed. And this categorical dignity is considered to be an attribute of *all* men, if they will but avail themselves of it, by right thinking and right living. But Hitler gives this ennobling attitude an ominous twist by his theories of race and nation, whereby the "Aryan" is elevated above all others by the innate endowment of his blood, while other "races," in particular Jews and Negroes, are innately inferior. This sinister secularized revision of Christian theology thus puts the sense of dignity upon a fighting basis, requiring the conquest of "inferior races." After the defeat of Germany in the World War, there were especially strong emotional needs that this compensatory doctrine of an *inborn* superiority could gratify.

(2) *Projection* device. The "curative" process that comes with the ability to hand over one's ills to a scapegoat, thereby getting purification by dissociation. This was especially medicinal, since the sense of frustration leads to a self-questioning. Hence if one can hand over his infirmities to a vessel, or "cause," outside the self, one can battle an external enemy instead of battling an enemy within. And the greater one's internal inadequacies, the greater amount of evils one can load upon the back of "the enemy." This device is furthermore given a semblance of reason because the individual properly realizes that he is not alone responsible for his condition. There *are* inimical factors in the scene itself. And he wants to have them "placed," preferably in a way that would require a minimum change in the ways of thinking to which he had been accustomed. This was especially appealing to the middle class, who were encouraged to feel that they could conduct their businesses without any basic change whatever, once the businessmen of a different "race" were eliminated.

(3) Symbolic rebirth. Another aspect of the two features already noted. The projective device of the scapegoat, coupled with the Hitlerite doctrine of inborn racial superiority, provides its followers with a "positive" view of life. They can again get the feel of *moving forward,* towards a *goal* (a promissory feature of which Hitler makes much). In Hitler, as the group's prophet, such rebirth involved a symbolic change of lineage. Here, above all, we see Hitler giving a malign twist to a be-

nign aspect of Christian thought. For whereas the Pope, in the familistic pattern of thought basic to the Church, stated that the Hebrew prophets were the *spiritual ancestors* of Christianity, Hitler uses this same mode of thinking in reverse. He renounces this "ancestry" in a "materialistic" way by voting himself and the members of his lodge a different "blood stream" from that of the Jews.

(4) Commercial use. Hitler obviously here had something to sell—and it was but a question of time until he sold it (i.e., got financial backers for his movement). For it provided a *noneconomic interpretation of economic ills.* As such, it served with maximum efficiency in deflecting the attention from the economic factors involved in modern conflict; hence by attacking "Jew finance" instead of *finance,* it could stimulate an enthusiastic movement that left "Aryan" finance in control.

Never once, throughout his book, does Hitler deviate from such a formula. Invariably, he ends his diatribes against contemporary economic ills by a shift into an insistence that we must get to the "true" cause, which is centered in "race." The "Aryan" is "constructive"; the Jew is "destructive"; and the "Aryan," to continue his *construction,* must *destroy* the Jewish *destruction.* The Aryan, as the vessel of *love,* must *hate* the Jewish *hate.*

Perhaps the most enterprising use of his method is in his chapter, "The Causes of the Collapse," where he refuses to consider Germany's plight as in any basic way connected with the consequences of war. Economic factors, he insists, are "only of second or even third importance," but "political, ethical-moral, as well as factors of blood and race, are of the first importance." His rhetorical steps are especially interesting here, in that he begins by seeming to flout the national susceptibilities: "The military defeat of the German people is not an undeserved catastrophe, but rather a deserved punishment by eternal retribution." He then proceeds to present the military collapse as but a "consequence of moral poisoning, visible to all, the consequence of a decrease in the instinct of self-preservation . . . which had already begun to undermine the foundations of the people and the Reich many years before." This moral decay derived from "a sin against the blood and the degradation of the race," so its innerness was an outerness after all: the Jew, who thereupon gets saddled with a vast amalgamation of evils, among them being capitalism, democracy, pacifism, journalism, poor housing, modernism, big cities, loss of religion, half measures, ill health, and weakness of the monarch.

2.

Hitler had here another important psychological ingredient to play upon. If a State is in economic collapse (and his theories, tentatively taking shape in the pre-war Vienna, were but developed with greater efficiency in post-war Munich), you cannot possibly derive dignity from economic stability. Dignity must come first—and if you possess it, and implement it, from it may follow its economic counterpart. There is much justice to this line of reasoning, so far as it goes. A people in collapse, suffering under economic frustration and the defeat of nationalistic aspirations, with the very midrib of their integrative efforts (the army) in a state of dispersion, have little other than some "spiritual" basis to which they could refer their nationalistic dignity. Hence, the categorical dignity of superior race was a perfect recipe for the situation. It was "spiritual" in so far as it was "above" crude economic "interests," but it was "materialized" at the psychologically "right" spot in that "the enemy" was something you could *see.*

Furthermore, you had the desire for unity, such as a discussion of class conflict, on the basis of conflicting interests, could not satisfy. The yearning for unity is so great that people are always willing to meet you halfway if you will give it to them by fiat, by flat statement, regardless of the facts. Hence, Hitler consistently refused to consider internal political conflict on the basis of conflicting interests. Here again, he could draw upon a religious pattern, by insisting upon a *personal* statement of the relation between classes, the relation between leaders and followers, each group in its way fulfilling the same commonality of interests, as the soldiers and captains of an army share a common interest in victory. People so dislike the idea of internal division that, where there is a real internal division, their dislike can easily be turned against the man or group who would so much as *name* it, let alone proposing to act upon it. Their natural and justified resentment against internal division itself, is turned against the diagnostician who states it as a *fact.* This diagnostician, it is felt, is the *cause* of the disunity he named.

Cutting in from another angle, therefore, we note how two sets of equations were built up, with Hitler combining or coalescing *ideas* the way a poet combines or coalesces *images.* On the one side, were the ideas, or images, of disunity, centering in the parliamentary wrangle of the Habsburg "State of Nationalities." This was offered as the antithesis of German nationality, which was presented in the curative imagery of unity, focused upon the glories of the Prussian Reich, with its mecca now moved to "folkish" Vienna. For though Hitler at first attacked the many "folkish" movements, with their hankerings after a kind of Wagnerian mythology of Germanic origins, he subsequently took "folkish" as a basic word by which to conjure. It was, after all, another noneconomic basis of reference. At first we find him objecting to "those who drift about with the word 'folkish' on their caps," and asserting that "such a Babel of opinions cannot serve as the basis of a political fighting movement." But later he seems to have realized, as he well should, that its vagueness was a major point in its favor. So it was incorporated in the grand coalition of his ideational imagery, or imagistic ideation; and Chapter XI ends with the vision of "a State which represents not a mechanism of economic considerations and interests, alien to the people, but a folkish organism."

So, as against the disunity equations, already listed briefly in our discussion of his attacks upon the parliamentary, we get a contrary purifying set; the wrangle of the parliamentary is to be stilled by the giving of *one* voice to the whole people, this to be the "inner voice" of Hitler, made uniform throughout the German boundaries, as leader and people were completely identified with each other. In sum: Hitler's inner voice, equals leader-people identification, equals unity, equals Reich, equals the mecca of Munich, equals plow, equals sword, equals work, equals war, equals army as midrib, equals responsibility (the personal responsibility of the absolute ruler), equals sacrifice, equals the theory of "German democracy" (the free popular choice of the leader, who then accepts the responsibility, and demands absolute obedience in exchange for his sacrifice), equals love (with the masses as feminine), equals idealism, equals obedience to nature, equals race, nation.[3]

And, of course, the two keystones of these opposite equations were Aryan "heroism" and "sacrifice" vs. Jewish "cunning" and "arrogance." Here again we get an astounding caricature of religious thought. For Hitler presents the concept of "Aryan" superiority in terms of nothing less than "Aryan humility." This "humility" is extracted by a very delicate process that requires, I am afraid, considerable "good will" on the part of the reader who would follow it:

The Church, we may recall, had proclaimed an integral relationship between Divine Law and Natural Law. Natural Law was the expression of the Will of God. Thus, in the Middle Ages, it was a result of natural law, working through tradition, that some people were serfs and other

---

[3] *One could carry out the equations further, on both the disunity and unity side. In the aesthetic field, for instance, we have expressionism on the thumbs-down side, as against aesthetic hygiene on the thumbs-up side. This again is a particularly ironic moment in Hitler's strategy. For the expressionist movement was unquestionably a symptom of unhealthiness. It reflected the increasing alienation that went with the movement towards world war and the disorganization after the world war. It was "lost," vague in identity, a drastically accurate reflection of the response to material confusion, a pathetic attempt by sincere artists to make their wretchedness bearable at least to the extent that comes of giving it expression. And it attained its height during the period of wild inflation, when the capitalist world, which bases its morality of work and savings upon the soundness of its money structure, had this last prop of stability removed. The anguish, in short, reflected precisely the kind of disruption that made people ripe for a Hitler. It was the antecedent in a phrase of which Hitlerism was the consequent. But by thundering against this symptom he could gain persuasiveness, though attacking the very foreshadowings of himself.*

people nobles. And every good member of the Church was "obedient" to this law. Everybody resigned himself to it. Hence, the serf resigned himself to his poverty, and the noble resigned himself to his riches. The monarch resigned himself to his position as representative of the people. And at times the Churchmen resigned themselves to the need of trying to represent the people instead. And the pattern was made symmetrical by the consideration that each traditional "right" had its corresponding "obligations." Similarly, the Aryan doctrine is a doctrine of resignation, hence of humility. It is in accordance with the laws of nature that the "Aryan blood" is superior to all other bloods. Also, the "law of the survival of the fittest" is God's law, working through natural law. Hence, if the Aryan blood has been vested with the awful responsibility of its inborn superiority, the bearers of this "culture-creating" blood must resign themselves to struggle in behalf of its triumph. Otherwise, the laws of God have been disobeyed, with human decadence as a result. We must fight, he says, in order to "deserve to be alive." The Aryan "obeys" nature. It is only "Jewish arrogance" that thinks of "conquering" nature by democratic ideals of equality.

This picture has some nice distinctions worth following. The major virtue of the Aryan race was its instinct for self-preservation (in obedience to natural law). But the major vice of the Jew was his instinct for self-preservation; for, if he did not have this instinct to a maximum degree, he would not be the "perfect" enemy—that is, he wouldn't be strong enough to account for the ubiquitousness and omnipotence of his conspiracy in destroying the world to become its master.

How, then, are we to distinguish between the benign instinct of self-preservation at the roots of Aryanism, and the malign instinct of self-preservation at the roots of Semitism? We shall distinguish thus: The Aryan self-preservation is based upon *sacrifice,* the sacrifice of the individual to the group, hence, militarism, army discipline, and one big company union. But Jewish self-preservation is based upon individualism, which attains its cunning ends by the exploitation of peace. How, then, can such arrant individualists concoct the world-wide plot? By the help of their "herd instinct." By their sheer "herd instinct" individualists can band together for a common end. They have no real solidarity, but unite opportunistically to seduce the Aryan. Still, that brings up another technical problem. For we have been hearing much about the importance of the *person.* We have been told how, by the "law of the survival of the fittest," there is a sifting of people on the basis of their individual capacities. We even have a special chapter of pure Aryanism: "The Strong Man is Mightiest Alone." Hence, another distinction is necessary: The Jew represents individualism; the Aryan represents "super-individualism."

I had thought, when coming upon the "Strong Man is Mightiest

Alone" chapter, that I was going to find Hitler at his weakest. Instead, I found him at his strongest. (I am not referring to *quality,* but to *demagogic effectiveness.*) For the chapter is not at all, as you might infer from the title, done in a "rise of Adolph Hitler" manner. Instead, it deals with the Nazis' gradual absorption of the many disrelated "folkish" groups. And it is managed throughout by means of a spontaneous identification between leader and people. Hence, the Strong Man's "aloneness" is presented as a *public* attribute, in terms of tactics for the struggle against the *Party's* dismemberment under the pressure of rival saviors. There is no explicit talk of Hitler at all. And it is simply *taken for granted* that *his* leadership is the norm, and all other leaderships the abnorm. There is no "philosophy of the superman," in Nietzschean cast. Instead, Hitler's blandishments so integrate leader and people, commingling them so inextricably, that the politician does not even present himself as candidate. Somehow, the battle is over already, the decision has been made. "German democracy" has chosen. And the deployments of politics are, you might say, the chartings of Hitler's private mind translated into the vocabulary of nationalistic events. He says *what he thought* in terms of *what parties did.*

Here, I think, we see the distinguishing quality of Hitler's method as an instrument of persuasion, with reference to the question whether Hitler is sincere or deliberate, whether his vision of the omnipotent conspirator has the drastic honesty of paranoia or the sheer shrewdness of a demagogue trained in *Realpolitik* of the Machiavellian sort.[4] Must we choose? Or may we not, rather, replace the "either—or" with a "both —and"? Have we not by now offered grounds enough for our contention that Hitler's sinister powers of persuasion derive from the fact that he spontaneously evolved his "cure-all" in response to inner necessities?

---

[4] *I should not want to use the word "Machiavellian," however, without offering a kind of apology to Machiavelli. It seems to me that Machiavelli's Prince has more to be said in extenuation than is usually said of it. Machiavelli's strategy, as I see it, was something like this: He accepted the values of the Renaissance rule as a fact. That is: whether you like these values or not, they were there and operating, and it was useless to try persuading the ambitious ruler to adopt other values, such as those of the Church. These men believed in the cult of material power, and they had the power to implement their beliefs. With so much as "the given," could anything in the way of benefits for the people be salvaged? Machiavelli evolved a typical "Machiavellian" argument in favor of popular benefits, on the basis of the prince's own scheme of values. That is: the ruler, to attain the maximum strength, requires the backing of the populace. That this backing be as effective as possible, the populace should be made as strong as possible. And that the populace be as strong as possible, they should be well treated. Their gratitude would further repay itself in the form of increased loyalty.*

It was Machiavelli's hope that, for this roundabout project, he would be rewarded with a well-paying office in the prince's administrative bureaucracy.

3.

So much, then, was "spontaneous." It was further channelized into the anti-Semitic pattern by the incentives he derived from the Catholic Christian-Social Party in Vienna itself. Add, now, the step into *criticism*. Not criticism in the "parliamentary" sense of doubt, of hearkening to the opposition and attempting to mature a policy in the light of counter-policies; but the "unified" kind of criticism that simply seeks for conscious ways of making one's position more "efficient," more thoroughly itself. This is the kind of criticism at which Hitler was an adept. As a result, he could *spontaneously* turn to a scapegoat mechanism, and he could, by conscious planning, perfect the symmetry of the solution towards which he had spontaneously turned.

This is the meaning of Hitler's diatribes against "objectivity." "Objectivity" is interference-criticism. What Hitler wanted was the kind of criticism that would be a pure and simple coefficient of power, enabling him to go most effectively in the direction he had chosen. And the "inner voice" of which he speaks would henceforth dictate to him the greatest amount of realism, as regards the tactics of efficiency. For instance, having decided that the masses required certainty, and simple certainty, quite as he did himself, he later worked out a 25-point program as the platform of his National Socialist German Workers Party. And he resolutely refused to change one single item in this program, even for purposes of "improvement." He felt that the *fixity* of the platform was more important for propagandistic purposes than any revision of his slogans could be, even though the revisions in themselves had much to be said in their favor. The astounding thing is that, although such an attitude gave good cause to doubt the Hitlerite promises, he could explicitly explain his tactics in his book and still employ them without loss of effectiveness.[5]

Hitler also tells of his technique in speaking, once the Nazi party had become effectively organized, and had its army of guards, or bouncers, to maltreat hecklers and throw them from the hall. He would, he recounts, fill his speech with *provocative* remarks, whereat his bouncers would promptly swoop down in flying formation, with swing-

---

[5] *On this point Hitler reasons as follows: "Here, too, one can learn from the Catholic Church. Although its structure of doctrines in many instances collides, quite unnecessarily, with exact science and research, yet it is unwilling to sacrifice even one little syllable of its dogmas. It has rightly recognized that its resistibility does not lie in a more or less great adjustment to the scientific results of the moment, which in reality are always changing, but rather in a strict adherence to dogmas, once laid down, which alone give the entire structure the character of creed. Today, therefore, the Catholic Church stands firmer than ever. One can prophesy that in the same measure in which the appearances flee, the Church itself, as the resting pole in the flight of appearances, will gain more and more blind adherence."*

ing fists, upon anyone whom these provocative remarks provoked to answer. The efficiency of Hitlerism is the efficiency of the one voice, implemented throughout a total organization. The trinity of government which he finally offers is: *popularity* of the leader, *force* to back the popularity, and popularity and force maintained together long enough to become backed by a *tradition*. Is such thinking spontaneous or deliberate—or is it not rather both?[6]

Freud has given us a succinct paragraph that bears upon the spontaneous aspect of Hitler's persecution mania. (A persecution mania, I should add, different from the pure product in that it was constructed of *public* materials; all the ingredients Hitler stirred into his brew were already rife, with spokesmen and bands of followers, before Hitler "took them over." Both the pre-war and post-war periods were dotted with saviors, of nationalistic and "folkish" cast. This proliferation was analogous to the swarm of barter schemes and currency-tinkering that burst loose upon the United States after the crash of 1929. Also, the commercial availability of Hitler's politics was, in a low sense of the term, a *public* qualification, removing it from the realm of "pure" paranoia, where the sufferer develops a wholly *private* structure of interpretations.)

I cite from *Totem and Taboo:*

Another trait in the attitude of primitive races towards their rulers recalls a mechanism which is universally present in mental disturbances, and is openly revealed in the so-called delusions of persecution. Here the importance of a particular person is extraordinarily heightened and his omnipotence is raised to the improbable in order to make it easier to attribute to him responsibility for everything painful which happens to the patient. Savages really do not act differently towards their

---

[6] *Hitler also paid great attention to the conditions under which political oratory is most effective. He sums up thus:*

"All these cases involve encroachments upon man's freedom of will. This applies, of course, most of all to meetings to which people with a contrary orientation of will are coming, and who now have to be won for new intentions. It seems that in the morning and even during the day men's will power revolts with highest energy against an attempt at being forced under another's will and another's opinion. In the evening, however, they succumb more easily to the dominating force of a stronger will. For truly every such meeting presents a wrestling match between two opposed forces. The superior oratorical talent of a domineering apostolic nature will now succeed more easily in winning for the new will people who themselves have in turn experienced a weakening of their force of resistance in the most natural way, than people who still have full command of the energies of their minds and their will power.

"The same purpose serves also the ·artificially created and yet mysterious dusk of the Catholic churches, the burning candles, incense, censers, etc."

THE EXPERIENTIAL PERSPECTIVE 254

rulers when they ascribe to them power over rain and shine, wind and weather, and then dethrone them or kill them because nature has disappointed their expectation of a good hunt or a ripe harvest. The prototype which the paranoiac reconstructs in his persecution mania is found in the relation of the child to its father. Such omnipotence is regularly attributed to the father in the imagination of the son, and distrust of the father has been shown to be intimately connected with the heightened esteem for him. When a paranoiac names a person of his acquaintance as his "persecutor," he thereby elevates him to the paternal succession and brings him under conditions which enable him to make him responsible for all the misfortune which he experiences.

I have already proposed my modifications of this account when discussing the symbolic change of lineage connected with Hitler's project of a "new way of life." Hitler is symbolically changing from the "spiritual ancestry" of the Hebrew prophets to the "superior" ancestry of "Aryanism," and has given his story a kind of bastardized modernization, along the lines of naturalistic, materialistic "science," by his fiction of the special "blood-stream." He is voting himself a new identity (something contrary to the wrangles of the Habsburg Babylon, a soothing national unity); whereupon the vessels of the old identity become a "bad" father, i.e., the persecutor. It is not hard to see how, as his enmity becomes implemented by the backing of an organization, the rôle of "persecutor" is transformed into the rôle of persecuted, as he sets out with his like-minded band to "destroy the destroyer."

Were Hitler simply a poet, he might have written a work with an anti-Semitic turn, and let it go at that. But Hitler, who began as a student of painting, and later shifted to architecture, himself treats his political activities as an extension of his artistic ambitions. He remained, in his own eyes, an "architect," building a "folkish" State that was to match, in political materials, the "folkish" architecture of Munich.

We might consider the matter this way (still trying, that is, to make precise the relationship between the drastically sincere and the deliberately scheming): Do we not know of many authors who seem, as they turn from the rôle of citizen to the rôle of spokesman, to leave one room and enter another? Or who has not, on occasion, talked with a man in private conversation, and then been almost startled at the transformation this man undergoes when addressing a public audience? And I know persons today, who shift between the writing of items in the class of academic, philosophic speculation to items of political pamphleteering, and whose entire style and method changes with this change of rôle. In their academic manner, they are cautious, painstaking, eager to present all significant aspects of the case they are considering; but when they turn to political pamphleteering, they hammer forth with

vituperation, they systematically misrepresent the position of their opponent, they go into a kind of political trance, in which, during its
throes, they throb like a locomotive; and behold, a moment later, the
mediumistic state is abandoned, and they are the most moderate of
men.

Now, one will find few pages in Hitler that one could call "moderate." But there are many pages in which he gauges resistances and
opportunities with the "rationality" of a skilled advertising man planning a new sales campaign. Politics, he says, must be sold like soap—
and soap is not sold in a trance. But he did have the experience of his
trance, in the "exaltation" of his anti-Semitism. And later, as he became
a successful orator (he insists that revolutions are made solely by the
power of the spoken word), he had this "poetic" rôle to draw upon,
plus the great relief it provided as a way of slipping from the burden of
logical analysis into the pure "spirituality" of vituperative prophecy.
What more natural, therefore, than that a man so insistent upon unification would integrate this mood with less ecstatic moments, particularly when he had found the followers and the backers that put a price,
both spiritual and material, upon such unification?

Once this happy "unity" is under way, one has a "logic" for the development of a method. One knows when to "spiritualize" a material
issue, and when to "materialize" a spiritual one. Thus, when it is a
matter of materialistic interests that cause a conflict between employer
and employee, Hitler here disdainfully shifts to a high moral plane. He
is "above" such low concerns. Everything becomes a matter of "sacri-
fices" and "personality." It becomes crass to treat employers and em-
ployees as different *classes* with a corresponding difference in the
classification of their interests. Instead, relations between employer
and employee must be on the "personal" basis of leader and follower,
and "whatever may have a divisive effect in national life should be
given a unifying effect through the army." When talking of national ri-
valries, however, he makes a very shrewd materialistic gauging of
Britain and France with relation to Germany. France, he says, desires
the "Balkanization of Germany" (i.e., its breakup into separationist
movements—the "disunity" theme again) in order to maintain commercial hegemony on the continent. But Britain desires the "Balkanization
of *Europe*," hence would favor a fairly strong and unified Germany, to
use as a counter-weight against French hegemony. *German* nationality,
however, is unified by the *spiritual* quality of Aryanism (that would produce the national organization via the Party) while this in turn is
materialized in the myth of the blood-stream.

What are we to learn from Hitler's book? For one thing, I believe that
he has shown, to a very disturbing degree, the power of endless repetition. Every circular advertising a Nazi meeting had, at the bottom, two

slogans: "Jews are not admitted" and "War victims free." And the substance of Nazi propaganda was built about these two "complementary" themes. He describes the power of spectacle; insists that mass meetings are a fundamental way of giving the individual the sense of being protectively surrounded by a movement, the sense of "community." He also drops one wise hint that I wish the American authorities would take in treating Nazi gatherings. He says that the presence of a special Nazi guard, in Nazi uniforms, was of great importance in building up, among the followers, a tendency to place the center of authority in the Nazi party. I believe that we should take him at his word here, but use the advice in reverse, by insisting that, where Nazi meetings are to be permitted, they be policed by the authorities alone, and that uniformed Nazi guards to enforce the law be prohibited.

And is it possible that an equally important feature of appeal was not so much in the repetitiousness per se, but in the fact that, by means of it, Hitler provided a "world view" for people who had previously seen the world but piecemeal? Did not much of his lure derive, once more, from the *bad* filling of a *good* need? Are not those who insist upon a purely *planless* working of the market asking people to accept far too slovenly a scheme of human purpose, a slovenly scheme that can be accepted so long as it operates with a fair degree of satisfaction, but becomes abhorrent to the victims of its disarray? Are they not then psychologically ready for a rationale, *any* rationale, if it but offer them some specious "universal" explanation? Hence, I doubt whether the appeal was in the sloganizing element alone (particularly as even slogans can only be hammered home, in speech after speech, and two or three hours at a stretch, by endless variations on the themes). And Hitler himself somewhat justifies my interpretation by laying so much stress upon the *half-measures* of the middle-class politicians, and the contrasting *certainty* of his own methods. He was not offering people a *rival* world view; rather, he was offering a world view to people who had no other to pit against it.

As for the basic Nazi trick: the "curative" unification by a fictitious devil-function, gradually made convincing by the sloganizing repetitiousness of standard advertising technique—the opposition must be as unwearying in the attack upon it. It may well be that people, in their human frailty, require an enemy as well as a goal. Very well: Hitlerism itself has provided us with such an enemy—and the clear example of its operation is guaranty that we have, in Hitler and all he stands for, no purely fictitious "devil-function" made to look like a world menace by rhetorical blandishments, but a reality whose ominousness is clarified by the record of its conduct to date. In selecting his brand of doctrine as our "scapegoat," and in tracking down its equivalents in America, we shall be at the very center of accuracy. The Nazis themselves have made the task of clarification easier. Add to them Japan and Italy, and you have *case histories* of fascism for those who might find it more difficult to approach an understanding of its imperialistic drives by a vigorously economic explanation.

But above all, I believe, we must make it apparent that Hitler appeals by relying upon a bastardization of fundamentally religious patterns of thought. In this, if properly presented, there is no slight to religion. There is nothing in religion proper that requires a fascist state. There is much in religion, when misused, that does lead to a fascist state. There is a Latin proverb, *Corruptio optimi pessima,* "the corruption of the best is the worst." And it is the corruptors of religion who are a major menace to the world today, in giving the profound patterns of religious thought a crude and sinister distortion.

Our job, then, our anti-Hitler Battle, is to find all available ways of making the Hitlerite distortions of religion apparent, in order that politicians of his kind in America be unable to perform a similar swindle. The desire for unity is genuine and admirable. The desire for national unity, in the present state of the world, is genuine and admirable. But this unity, if attained on a deceptive basis, by emotional trickeries that shift our criticism from the accurate locus of our trouble, is no unity at all. For, even if we are among those who happen to be "Aryans," we solve no problems even for ourselves by such solutions, since the factors pressing towards calamity remain. Thus, in Germany, after all the upheaval, we see nothing beyond a drive for ever more and more upheaval, precisely because the "new way of life" was no new way, but the dismally oldest way of sheer deception—hence, after all the "change," the factors driving towards unrest are left intact, and even strengthened. True, the Germans had the resentment of a lost war to increase their susceptibility to Hitler's rhetoric. But in a wider sense, it has repeatedly been observed, the whole world lost the war—and the accumulating ills of the capitalist order were but accelerated in their movements towards confusion. Hence, here too there are the resentments that go with frustration of men's ability to work and earn. At that point a certain kind of industrial or financial monopolist may, annoyed by the contrary voices of our parliament, wish for the momentary peace of one voice, amplified by social organizations, with all the others not merely quieted but given the quietus. So he might, under Nazi promptings, be tempted to back a group of gangsters who, on becoming the political rulers of the state, would protect him against the necessary demands of the workers. His gangsters, then, would be his insurance against his workers. But who would be his insurance against his gangsters?

The Critical Perspective of the "New Rhetorics"

RECENTLY the academic fields of speech and English, and even sociology, political science, and history, have been astir with talk of a "new rhetoric." In writing about the increasing tempo of activity, Martin Steinmann, Jr., remarks, "I say 'new rhetorics' rather than 'a new rhetoric' because modern concepts of rhetoric are so diverse that a family of new disciplines rather than a single one seems to be evolving."[1] We would join Steinmann and others in stressing the plural. But we believe that within the diversity there is a family resemblance—especially when the new rhetorics are applied to criticism—that helps us discern a second direction, different from the experiential, in the breakdown of faith in the traditional perspective.

Both of these directions share a rejection of the speaker orientation of the traditional perspective, but the perspective of the new rhetorics also rejects the experiential centering on the critic. The new rhetorician, like the traditional, looks toward a unified theory to inform his criticism, but his faith tends to be in a non-Aristotelian system. Some of these critics seem to harbor the hope that their particular embryonic theory will grow to be a new paradigm for criticism, but at this point there is little evidence to suggest that any single theory will gain a position equal to that of Aristotelianism in the traditional rhetorical criticism.

As we have indicated, prior to the rather clear breakdown of the paradigm in the 1960s, some spokesmen not only registered their dissatisfaction with traditional theory and criticism but attempted to establish new systems that would be more compatible with contemporary views of man and reality. Alfred Korzybski, author of *Science and Sanity,* provided one source of impetus.[2] A few critics drew from Korzybski for their critical method; they were also influenced by Korzybski's disciples in the general semantics movement—such men as Irving Lee, Wendell Johnson, S. I. Hayakawa, Anatole Rapoport, and Stuart Chase. The General Semanticists shared the belief that traditional rhetoric was prescientific and elementistic and, as a result, was the source of many of man's problems, including mental ills.

Another writer who rejected the traditional perspective prior to the 1960s was Kenneth Burke. Burke's rhetorical philosophy evolved through literary criticism into social criticism, with the result that his dramatistic approach has a markedly sociopsychological tone. His rejection of the Aristotelian rhetoric differs from the General Semanti-

---

[1] *Martin Steinmann, Jr.,* New Rhetorics, *New York, Scribner's, 1967, p. iii.*
[2] *Alfred Korzybski,* Science and Sanity. *Lakewood, Conn., Institute of General Semantics, 1933.*

cists' in that his builds on the Aristotelian philosophy and extends its range. Burke's rhetoric was introduced into the field of speech in 1952 by an essay in *The Quarterly Journal of Speech* written by Marie Hochmuth Nichols.[3] Her essay was immediately followed in the same journal by two articles by Burke himself, "A Dramatistic View of the Origins of Language" and "Postscripts on the Negative."[4] With these examples before them, critics in the field of speech began to use a Burkeian vocabulary, although in a manner reminiscent of neo-Aristotelianism, that is, mechanically, aiming at description by affixing a series of labels. If we are correct in our judgment, then the situation was ironic, for much of Burke's writing in the late 1930s and 1940s was motivated by what he considered to be the mechanical and inadequate explanations of human behavior that were then current in the social sciences.

A sign of the break from traditional rhetoric was the publication in 1959 of Daniel Fogarty's *Roots for a New Rhetoric.*[5] He saw an amalgam of three theories, those of I. A. Richards, Kenneth Burke, and the General Semanticists, as providing the basis for a unified system. Fogarty seemed hopeful that the new rhetoric would be paradigmatic, but the decade of the 1960s has scarcely fulfilled his hope.

Characteristics of the Critical Perspective of the "New Rhetorics"

Although it is quite premature to say that there is a new rhetoric, we do believe that a rough consensus can be discerned, and several assumptions differentiate this critical perspective from the traditional and the experiential.

First, like the experiential, the perspective of the new rhetorics stresses society as being in a continual state of process. Thus, critics working from this perspective will stress interaction and change. However, unlike the experiential, the new rhetoricians seem to believe that stable relationships can be discovered within the complex interactions of man and his social and physical context. From these stable relationships, they believe that it should be possible to construct a unified rhetorical theory.

Second, the belief in stable relationships is an assumption much like that of the traditional perspective. At the moment, a number of

[3] *Marie Hochmuth Nichols, "Kenneth Burke and the 'New Rhetoric,' "* The Quarterly Journal of Speech, *XXXVIII, 2 (April 1952), 133–144.*

[4] *Kenneth Burke, "A Dramatistic View of the Origins of Language,"* The Quarterly Journal of Speech; *"Part One," XXXVIII, 3 (October 1952), 251–264; "Part Two," XXXVIII, 4 (December 1952), 446–460; and "Part Three," XXXIX, 1 (February 1953), 79–92.*

——— *"Postscripts on the Negative,"* The Quarterly Journal of Speech, *XXXIX, 2 (April 1953), 209–216.*

[5] *Daniel Fogarty,* Roots for a New Rhetoric, *New York, Teachers College Press, 1959.*

competing systems, or at least moves toward competing systems, mark the new rhetorical criticism. If the assumption concerning the degree of social stability is correct, continued work ought to lead toward a critical consensus on a method flexible enough to enable the critic to analyze rhetorical patterns typical of the social process.

A third assumption flows from the word-thought-thing relationship. Again, this perspective is like that of the experiential critics. The word-thought-thing relationship is reciprocal, that is, not only does the nature of the object (or relationship) affect the selection of words but the use of a symbol system affects a person's perception of reality. The presumed interactions of language and reality create a focal point for criticism.

After studying the current theory and application, we have concluded that it may be useful to differentiate two basic approaches within the general perspective of the new rhetorics. One of these we call the "semantical-grammatical" and the other, the "dramatistic."

Within the semantical-grammatical approach we not only bring together such theorists as I. A. Richards and the General Semanticists but also classify much of the work being done by our colleagues in English departments on style and stylistics. Representative of such an approach is the work of Richard Ohmann, Martin Steinmann, Jr., and W. Ross Winterowd.

The semantical-grammatical approach is based on the assumption that the rhetorical critic should begin his analysis with the speaker's or writer's use of language. Typically these critics make either qualitative or quantitative textual analyses in an effort to establish language patterns that will increase the understanding of the rhetorical act. For example, Richard Ohmann in *Shaw, the Style and the Man* uses Roman Jakobson's theory of arrangement to analyze Shaw's "modes of expression," "habitual patterns of thought," and "lines of connection between rhetoric and conceptual schemes."[6] Quite different from Ohmann's adaptation of a linguistic frame of analysis,[7] John Sommerville's "Language and the Cold War" adapts a general semantics approach to argue for a cross-cultural semantic analysis to end the cold war.[8] We classify both works as falling in the broad range of the semantical-grammatical. As our examples indicate, many competing theories under

---

[6] *Richard Ohmann,* Shaw, the Style and the Man, *Middlebury, Conn., Wesleyan University Press, 1962.*

[7] *We considered using the term "linguistic" for this approach rather than "semantical-grammatical," but decided that, since contemporary linguists often limit their analysis to the syntactic relationships, the former label might be misleading and the admittedly clumsy but broader label was perhaps more apt.*

[8] *John Sommerville, "Language and the Cold War,"* Etc., A Review of General Semantics, *XXIII, 4 (December 1966), 425–434.*

different labels are current; we would classify any critical application as semantical-grammatical if the stress falls on the language itself as the starting point of analysis.

We have chosen Richard Weaver's essay, "Some Rhetorical Aspects of Grammatical Categories," to illustrate how a critic can construct a theory within the semantical-grammatical frame. In his *Ethics of Rhetoric,*[9] Weaver covers a number of rhetorical topics in broad strokes—he discusses the relationship between ideology and strategy in "Edmund Burke and the Argument from Circumstance" and "Abraham Lincoln and the Argument from Definition"; he considers the substantive value of rhetoric in "The Rhetoric of the Social Sciences"; and he contrasts the conflict of assumptions in "Dialectic and Rhetoric at Dayton, Tennessee." Initially these essays seem quite diverse, but they all have a common methodological characteristic: The conclusions are based upon a careful analysis of the language. In "Some Rhetorical Aspects of Grammatical Categories" Weaver makes explicit some aspects of grammatical analysis.

To illustrate the application of the semantical-grammatical approach we have chosen Hermann Stelzner's analysis of Franklin Roosevelt's "War Message" speech. Stelzner makes a close textual analysis by focusing on Roosevelt's stylistic choices as strategies to assure the acceptance of his proposed action. The essay represents a qualitative rather than a quantitative semantical-grammatical approach to rhetorical criticism.

To label another approach within the perspective of the new rhetorics, we have chosen one of Kenneth Burke's key terms, "dramatistic." In transcending the traditional speaker orientation, Burke shifts the focus of rhetoric from persuasion (the speaker's purpose) to identification (the result of all the components in the rhetorical act). He highlights the psychological constituent of rhetoric by concentrating on the analysis of motive. Burke's books that pertain most directly to rhetoric are *A Rhetoric of Motives*[10] and *The Rhetoric of Religion.*[11] So successful is Burke in weaving all his concepts into a pattern and creating a feeling of Gestalt, that one cannot fully understand the dramatistic without familiarity with all his work.

Because of the enormous effort necessary to grasp his system, Burke has gained a number of interpreters and translators. An early attempt at describing Burke's rhetoric and evaluating his influence was made by Stanley E. Hyman in his essay, "Kenneth Burke and the Criti-

[9] *Richard M. Weaver,* The Ethics of Rhetoric, *Chicago, Henry Regnery, 1953.*
[10] *Kenneth Burke,* A Rhetoric of Motives, *Englewood Cliffs, N.J., Prentice-Hall, 1950.*
[11] *Kenneth Burke,* The Rhetoric of Religion, *Boston, Beacon Press, 1961.*

cism of Symbolic Action."[12] This essay was followed by that of Marie Hochmuth Nicholas, mentioned before, and by such books as George Knox's *Critical Moments: Kenneth Burke's Categories and Critiques,*[13] and L. Virginia Holland's *Counterpoint: Kenneth Burke and Aristotle's Theories of Rhetoric.*[14] But probably the most understandable and useful interpretation is supplied by William Rueckert in his book *Kenneth Burke and the Drama of Human Relations.*[15]

To illustrate dramatistic theory, we have chosen an essay written specifically for this book by Bernard L. Brock, "Rhetorical Criticism: A Burkeian Approach." Brock has found Burke's concepts especially useful in the rhetorical criticism of contemporary political persuasion, as can be seen in his essay, "Political Speaking: A Burkeian Approach."[16]

Illustrating the application of dramatistic criticism, we have included David Ling's article "A Pentadic Analysis of Senator Edward Kennedy's Address to the People of Massachusetts." In addition to utilizing effectively Burke's pentad, Ling shows how the critic can discover and communicate an insight that would likely remain hidden except for the application of the dramatistic method.

As one considers the works that demonstrate a concern with the new rhetorics, one inevitably is struck by the rich variety of theorizing and the comparative absence of critical application. Again, we must say that this situation is consistent with Thomas Kuhn's contention that the normal business of science, and we would extend the generalization to criticism, is to apply theory to as many different circumstances as possible *once a paradigm is agreed upon.* In looking at both the experiential perspective and the perspective of the new rhetorics, we would conclude that, currently, rhetoric and rhetorical criticism are preparadigmatic.

[12] *Stanley E. Hyman,* The Armed Vision: A Study in the Methods of Modern Literary Criticism, *New York, Knopf, 1948, pp. 347–394.*

[13] *George Knox,* Critical Moments: Kenneth Burke's Categories and Critiques, *Seattle, University of Washington Press, 1957.*

[14] *L. Virginia Holland,* Counterpoint: Kenneth Burke and Aristotle's Theories of Rhetoric, *New York, Philosophical Library, 1959.*

[15] *William H. Rueckert,* Kenneth Burke and the Drama of Human Relations, *Minneapolis, University of Minnesota Press, 1963.*

[16] *Bernard L. Brock, in William H. Rueckert (ed.),* Critical Responses to Kenneth Burke, *Minneapolis, University of Minnesota Press, 1969, pp. 444–455.*

The Grammatical-Semantical Approach

SOME Rhetorical Aspects of Grammatical Categories
by Richard M. Weaver

In an earlier part of this work we defined rhetoric as something which creates an informed appetition for the good. Such definition must recognize the rhetorical force of things existing outside the realm of speech; but since our concern is primarily with spoken rhetoric, which cannot be disengaged from certain patterns or regularities of language, we now turn our attention to the pressure of these formal patterns.

All students of language concede to it a certain public character. Insofar as it serves in communication, it is a publicly-agreed-upon thing; and when one passes the outer limits of the agreement, one abandons comprehensibility. Now rhetoric affects us primarily by setting forth images which inform and attract. Yet because this setting forth is accomplished through a public instrumentality, it is not free; it is tied more or less closely to the formalizations of usage. The more general and rigid of these formalizations we recognize as grammar, and we shall here speak of grammar as a system of forms of public speech. In the larger aspect, discourse is at once bound and free, and we are here interested to discover how the bound character affects our ability to teach and to persuade.

We soon realize that different ways of saying a thing denote different interests in saying it, or to take this in reverse as we do when we become conscious users of language, different interests in a matter will dictate different patterns of expression. Rhetoric in its practice is a matter of selection and arrangement, but conventional grammar imposes restraints upon both of these. All this amounts to saying what every sensitive user of language has sometimes felt; namely, that language is not a purely passive instrument, but that, owing to this public acceptance, while you are doing something with it, it is doing something with you, or with your intention.[1] It does not exactly fight back; rather it has a set of postures and balances which somehow modify your thrusts and holds. The sentence form is certainly one of these. You pour into it your meaning, and it deflects, and molds into certain shapes. The user of language must know how this counterpressure can

[1] *To mention a simple example, the sarcasm uttered as a pleasantry sometimes leaves a wound because its formal signification is not entirely removed by the intonation of the user or by the speech situation.*

be turned to the advantage of his general purpose. The failure of those who are careless, or insensitive, to the rhetoric of grammar is that they allow the counter force to impede their design, whereas a perspicacious use of it will forward the design. One cannot, for example, employ just any modifier to stand for a substantive or just any substantive to express a quality, or change a stabilized pattern of arrangement without a change in net effect, although some of these changes register but faintly. But style shows through an accumulation of small particulars, and the artist in language may ponder a long while, as Conrad is said to have done, over whether to describe a character as "penniless" or "without a penny."

In this approach, then, we are regarding language as a standard objective reality, analyzable into categories which have inherent potentialities. A knowledge of these objective potentialities can prevent a loss of force through friction. The friction we refer to occurs whenever a given unit of the system of grammar is tending to say one thing while the semantic meaning and the general organization are tending to say another. A language has certain abilities or even inclinations which the wise user can draw into the service of his own rhetorical effort. Using a language may be compared to riding a horse; much of one's success depends upon an understanding of what it *can* and *will* do. Or to employ a different figure in illustration, there is a kind of use of language which goes against the grain as that grain is constituted by the categories, and there is a kind which facilitates the speaker's projection by going with it. Our task is an exploration of the congruence between well understood rhetorical objectives and the inherent character of major elements in modern English.

The problem of which category to begin with raises some questions. It is arguable that the rhetoric of any piece is dependent upon its total intention, and that consequently no single sentence can be appraised apart from the tendency of the whole discourse. Our position does not deny that, since we are assuming merely that within the greater effect there are lesser effects, cooperating well or ill. Having accepted that limitation, it seems permissible for us to begin with the largest unit of grammar, which is the sentence. We shall take up first the sentence as such and then discriminate between formal types of sentences.

Because a sentence form exists in most if not all languages, there is some ground to suppose that it reflects a necessary operation of the mind, and this means not simply of the mind as psychologically constituted but also as logically constrained.

It is evident that when the mind frames a sentence, it performs the basic intellectual operation of analysis and re-synthesis. In this complete operation the mind is taking two or more classes and uniting them at least to the extent at which they share in a formal unity. The unity

itself, built up through many such associations, comes to have an existence all its own, as we shall see. It is the repeated congruence in
experience or in the imagination of such classes as "sun-heat," "snow-
cold," which establishes the pattern, but our point is that the pattern
once established can become disciplinary in itself and compel us to
look for meaning within the formal unity it imposes. So it is natural for
us to perceive through a primitive analysis the compresence of sun
and hot weather, and to combine these into the unity "the sun is hot";
but the articulation represented by this joining now becomes a thing
in itself, which can be grasped before the meaning of its component
parts is evident. Accordingly, although sentences are supposed to
grow out of meanings, we can have sentences before meanings are
apparent, and this is indeed the central point of our rhetoric of grammar. When we thus grasp the scope of the pattern before we interpret
the meaning of the components, we are being affected by grammatical
system.

I should like to put this principle to a supreme sort of test by using a
few lines of highly modern verse. In Allen Tate's poem "The Subway"
we find the following:

> *I am become geometries, and glut*
> *Expansions like a blind astronomer*
> *Dazed, while the wordless heavens bulge and reel*
> *In the cold reverie of an idiot.*

I do not propose to interpret this further than to say that the features
present of word classification and word position cause us to look for
meaning along certain lines. It seems highly probable that we shall have
to exercise much imagination to fit our classes together with meaning
as they are fitted by formal classification and sentence order ("I am
become geometries"); yet it remains true that we take in the first line
as a formal predication; and I do not think that this formal character
could ever be separated entirely from the substance in an interpretation. Once we gain admission of that point with regard to a sentence,
some rhetorical status for grammar has been definitely secured.

In total rhetorical effect the sentence seems to be peculiarly "the
thing said," whereas all other elements are "the things named." And
accordingly the right to utter a sentence is one of the very greatest
liberties; and we are entitled to little wonder that freedom of utterance
should be, in every society, one of the most contentious and ill-defined
rights. The liberty to impose this formal unity is a liberty to handle the
world, to remake it, if only a little, and to hand it to others in a shape
which may influence their actions. It is interesting to speculate whether
the Greeks did not, for this very reason, describe the man clever at

speech as δεινός, an epithet meaning, in addition to "clever," "fearful" and "terrible." The sentence through its office of assertion is a force adding itself to the forces of the world, and therefore the man clever with his sentences—which is to say with his combinations—was regarded with that uneasiness which we feel in the presence of power. The changes wrought by sentences are changes in the world rather than in the physical earth, but it is to be remembered that changes in the world bring about changes in the earth. Thus this practice of yoking together classes of the world, of saying "Charles is King" or "My country is God's country" is a unique rhetorical fact which we have to take into account, although it stands somewhat prior to our main discussion.

As we turn now to the different formal types of sentences, we shall follow the traditional grammatical classification and discuss the rhetorical inclination of each in turn.

Through its form, the simple sentence tends to emphasize the discreteness of phenomena within the structural unity. To be more specific, its pattern of subject-verb-object or complement, without major competing elements, leaves our attention fixed upon the classes involved: "Charles is King." The effect remains when the simple sentence compounds its subject and predicate: "Peaches and cantaloupes grew in abundance"; "Men and boys hunted and fished." The single subject-predicate frame has the broad sense of listing or itemizing, and the list becomes what the sentence is about semantically.

Sentences of this kind are often the unconscious style of one who sees the world as a conglomerate of things, like the child; sometimes they are the conscious style of one who seeks to present certain things as eminent against a background of matter uniform or flat. One can imagine, for example, the simple sentence "He never worked" coming after a long and tedious recital which it is supposed to highlight. Or one can imagine the sentence "The world is round" leaping out of a context with which it contrasts in meaning, in brevity, or in sententiousness.

There is some descriptive value in saying that the simple sentence is the most "logical" type of sentence because, like the simple categorical proposition, it has this function of relating two classes. This fact, combined with its usual brevity and its structural simplicity, makes it a useful sentence for beginnings and endings (of important meaning-groups, not so much of formal introductions and conclusions). It is a sentence of unclouded perspective, so to speak. Nothing could be more beautifully anticipatory than Burke's "The proposition is peace."

At the very minimum, we can affirm that the simple sentence tends to throw subject and predicate classes into relief by the structure it presents them in; that the two-part categorical form of its copulation indicates a positive mood on the part of the user, and that its brevity often induces a generality of approach, which is an aid to perspicuous style. These opportunities are found out by the speaker or writer who senses the need for some synoptic or dramatic spot in his discourse. Thus when he selects the simple sentence, he is going "with the grain"; he is putting the objective form to work for him.

The complex sentence has a different potentiality. Whereas the simple sentence emphasizes through its form the co-existence of classes (and it must be already apparent that we regard "things existing or occurring" as a class where the predicate consists only of a verb), the complex sentence emphasizes a more complex relationship; that is to say, it reflects another kind of discriminating activity, which does not stop with seeing discrete classes as co-existing, but distinguishes them according to rank or value, or places them in an order of cause and effect. "Rome fell because valor declined" is the utterance of a reflective mind because the conjunction of parts depends on something ascertainable by the intellect but not by simple perception. This is evidence that the complex sentence does not appear until experience has undergone some refinement by the mind. Then, because it goes beyond simple observation and begins to perceive things like causal principle, or begins to grade things according to a standard of interest, it brings in the notion of dependence to supplement that of simple togetherness. And consequently the complex sentence will be found nearly always to express some sort of hierarchy, whether spatial, moral, or causal, with its subordinate members describing the lower orders. In simple-sentence style we would write: "Tragedy began in Greece. It is the highest form of literary art." There is no disputing that these sentences, in this sequence, could have a place in mature expression. But they do not have the same effect as "Tragedy, which is the highest form of literary art, began in Greece" or "Tragedy, which began in Greece, is the highest form of literary art." What has occurred is the critical process of subordination. The two ideas have been transferred from a conglomerate to an articulated unity, and the very fact of subordination makes inevitable the emergence of a focus of interest. Is our passage about the highest form of literary art or about the cultural history of Greece? The form of the complex sentence makes it unnecessary to waste any words in explicit assertion of that. Here it is plain that grammatical form is capital upon which we can draw, provided that other necessities have been taken care of.

To see how a writer of consummate sensibility toward expression-forms proceeded, let us take a fairly typical sentence from Henry James:

Merton Densher, who passed the best hours of each night at the office of his newspaper, had at times, during the day, a sense, or at least an appearance, of leisure, in accordance with which he was not infrequently to be met, in different parts of the town, at moments when men of business were hidden from the public eye.[2]

Leaving aside the phrases, which are employed by James in extension and refinement of the same effect, we see here three dependent clauses used to explain the contingencies of "Merton Densher had an appearance of leisure." These clauses have the function of surrounding the central statement in such a fashion that we have an intricate design of thought characterized by involution, or the emergence of one detail out of another. James' famous practice of using the dependent clause not only for qualification, but for the qualification of qualification, and in some cases for the qualification of qualification of qualification, indicates a persistent sorting out of experience expressive of the highly civilized mind. Perhaps the leading quality of the civilized mind is that it is sophisticated as to causes and effects (also as to other contiguities); and the complex sentence, required to give these a scrupulous ordering, is its natural vehicle.

At the same time the spatial form of ordering to which the complex sentence lends itself makes it a useful tool in scientific analysis, and one can find brilliant examples of it in the work of scientists who have been skillful in communication. When T. H. Huxley, for instance, explains a piece of anatomy, the complex sentence is the frame of explanation. In almost every sentence it will be observed that he is focussing interest upon one part while keeping its relationship—spatial or causal—clear with reference to surrounding parts. In Huxley's expository prose, therefore, one finds the dominant sentence type to consist of a main clause at the beginning followed by a series of dependent clauses which fill in these facts of relationship. We may follow the pattern of the sentences in his account of the protoplasm of the common nettle:

Each stinging-needle tapers from a broad base to a slender summit, which, though rounded at the end, is of such microscopic fineness that it readily penetrates, and breaks off in, the skin. The whole hair consists of a very delicate outer case of wood, closely applied to the inner surface of which is a layer of semi-fluid matter full of innumerable granules of extreme minuteness. This semi-fluid lining is protoplasm, which thus constitutes a kind of bag, full of limpid liquid, and roughly corresponding in form with the interior of the hair which it fills.[3]

[2] The Wings of the Dove (*Modern Library ed., New York, 1937*), p. 53.
[3] *"On the Physical Basis of Life,"* Lay Sermons, Addresses and Reviews (*New York, 1883*), pp. 123–24.

This is, of course, the "loose" sentence of traditional rhetorical analysis, and it has no dramatic force; yet it is for this very reason adapted to the scientist's purpose.[4] The rhetorical adaptation shows in the accommodation of a little hierarchy of details.

This appears to be the sentence of a developed mentality also, because it is created through a patient, disciplined observation, and not through impression, as the simple sentence can be. To the infant's mind, as William James observed in a now famous passage, the world is a "buzzing, blooming confusion," and to the immature mind much older it often appears something done in broad, uniform strokes. But to the mind of a trained scientist it has to appear a cosmos—else, no science. So in Huxley the objective world is presented as a series of details, each of which has its own cluster of satellites in the form of minor clauses. This is the way the world has to be reported when our objective is maximum perception and minimum desire to obtrude or influence.

Henry James was explaining with a somewhat comparable interest a different kind of world, in which all sorts of human and non-material forces are at work, and he tried with extreme conscientiousness to measure them. In that process of quantification and qualification the complex sentence was often brought by him to an extraordinary height of ramification.

In summation, then, the complex sentence is the branching sentence, or the sentence with parts growing off other parts. Those who have used it most properly have performed a second act of analysis, in which the objects of perception, after being seen discretely, are put into a ranked structure. This type of sentence imposes the greatest demand upon the reader because it carries him farthest into the reality existing outside self. This point will take on importance as we turn to the compound sentence.

The structure of the compound sentence often reflects a simple artlessness—the uncritical pouring together of simple sentences, as in the speech of Huckleberry Finn. The child who is relating an adventure is likely to make it a flat recital of conjoined simple predications, because to him the important fact is that the things were, not that they can be read to signify this or that. His even juxtapositions are therefore sometimes amusing, for now and then he will produce a coordination that unintentionally illuminates. This would, of course, be a result of lack of control over the rhetoric of grammar.

On the other hand, the compound sentence can be a very "mature"

---

[4] *On this point it is pertinent to cite Huxley's remark in another lay sermon, "On the Study of Zoology" (ibid., p. 110): "I have a strong impression that the better a discourse is, as an oration, the worse it is as a lecture."*

sentence when its structure conforms with a settled view of the world. The latter possibility will be seen as we think of the balance it presents. When a sentence consists of two main clauses we have two predications of similar structure bidding for our attention. Our first supposal is that this produces a sentence of unusual tension, with two equal parts (and of course sometimes more than two equal parts) in a sort of competition. Yet it appears on fuller acquaintance that this tension is a tension of stasis, and that the compound sentence has, in practice, been markedly favored by periods of repose like that of the eighteenth century. There is congeniality between its internal balance and a concept of the world as an equilibrium of forces. As a general rule, it appears that whereas the complex sentence favors the presentation of the world as a system of facts or as a dynamism, the compound sentence favors the presentation of it in a more or less philosophical picture. This world as a philosophical cosmos will have to be a sort of compensatory system. We know from other evidences that the eighteenth century loved to see things in balance; in fact, it required the idea of balance as a foundation for its institutions. Quite naturally then, since motives of this kind reach into expression-forms, this was the age of masters of the balanced sentence—Dryden, Johnson, Gibbon, and others, the *genre* of whose style derives largely from this practice of compounding. Often the balance which they achieved was more intricate than simple conjunction of main clauses because they balanced lesser elements too, but the informing impulse was the same. That impulse was the desire for counterpoise, which was one of the powerful motives of their culture.

In this pattern of balance, various elements are used in the off-settings. Thus when one attends closely to the meanings of the balanced parts, one finds these compounds recurring: an abstract statement is balanced (in a second independent clause) by a more concrete expression of the same thing; a fact is balanced by its causal explanation; a statement of positive mode is balanced by one of negative mode; a clause of praise is balanced by a clause of qualified censure; a description of one part is balanced by a description of a contrasting part, and so on through a good many conventional pairings. Now in these collocations cause and effect and other relationships are presented, yet the attempt seems not so much to explore reality as to clothe it in decent form. Culture is a delicate reconciliation of opposites, and consequently a man who sees the world through the eyes of a culture makes effort in this direction. We know that the world of eighteenth century culture was a rationalist world, and in a rationalist world everything must be "accounted for." The virtue of the compound sentence is that its second part gives "the other half," so to speak. As the pattern works out, every fact has its cause; every virtue is compensated for by a vice;

every excursion into generality must be made up for by attention to concrete circumstances and vice versa. The perfection of this art form is found in Johnson and Gibbon, where such pairings occur with a frequency which has given rise to the phrase "the balanced style." When Gibbon, for example, writes of religion in the Age of Antonines: "The superstition of the people was not embittered by any mixture of theological rancour; nor was it confined by the chains of any speculative system,"[5] we have almost the feeling that the case of religion has been settled by this neat artifice of expression. This is a "just" view of affairs, which sees both sides and leaves a kind of balanced account. It looks somewhat subjective, or at least humanized; it gives us the gross world a little tidied up by thought. Often, moreover, this balance of structure together with the act of saying a thing equivocally—in the narrower etymological sense of that word—suggests the finality of art. This will be found true of many of the poetical passages of the King James Bible, although these come from an earlier date. "The heavens declare the glory of God; and the firmament sheweth his handiwork"; "Man cometh forth as a flower and is cut down; he fleeth also as a shadow and continueth not." By thus stating the matter in two ways, through balanced clauses, the sentence achieves a degree of formal completeness missing in sentences where the interest is in mere assertion. Generally speaking the balanced compound sentence, by the very contrivedness of its structure, suggests something formed above the welter of experience, and this form, as we have by now substantially said, transfers something of itself to the meaning. In declaring that the compound sentence may seem subjective, we are not saying that it is arbitrary, its correspondence being with the philosophical interpretation rather than with the factual reality. Thus if the complex sentence is about the world, the compound sentence is about our idea about the world, into which some notion of compensation forces itself. One notices that even Huxley, when he draws away from his simple expositions of fact and seeks play for his great powers of persuasion, begins to compound his sentences. On the whole, the compound sentence conveys that completeness and symmetry which the world *ought* to have, and which we manage to get, in some measure, into our most satisfactory explanations of it. It is most agreeable to those ages and those individuals who feel that they have come to terms with the world, and are masters in a domain. But understandably enough, in a world which has come to be centrifugal and infinite, as ours has become since the great revolutions, it tends to seem artificial and mechanical in its containment.

Since the difference between sentence and clause is negligible as

[5] Decline and Fall of the Roman Empire (*Bury's ed., London, 1900*), I, 28.

far as the issues of this subject are concerned, we shall next look at the word, and conclude with a few remarks on some lesser combinations. This brings up at once the convention of parts of speech. Here again I shall follow the traditional classification, on the supposition that categories to which usage is referred for correction have accumulated some rhetorical force, whatever may be said for the merits of some other and more scientific classification.

The Noun

It is difficult not to feel that both usage and speculation agree on the rhetorical quality of nouns. The noun derives its special dignity from being a *name* word, and names persist, in spite of all the cautions of modern semanticists, in being thought of as words for substances. We apprehend the significance of that when we realize that in the ancient philosophical regimen to which the West is heir, and which influences our thought far more than we are aware at any one moment, substances are assigned a higher degree of being than actions or qualities. Substance is that which primordially *is,* and one may doubt whether recent attempts to revolutionize both ontology and grammar have made any impression at all against this feeling. For that reason a substantive comes to us as something that is peculiarly fulfilled;[6] or it is like a piece in a game which has superior powers of movement and capture. The fact that a substantive is the word in a sentence which the other words are "about" in various relationships gives it a superior status.[7]

Nouns then express things whose being is completed, not whose being is in process, or whose being depends upon some other being. And that no doubt accounts for the feeling that when one is using nouns, one is manipulating the symbols of a self-subsistent reality.[8] There seems little doubt that an ancient metaphysical system, grown to be an *habitus* of the mind through long acceptance, gives the substantive word a prime status, and this fact has importance when we come to compare the noun with the adjective in power to convince by

---

[6] Cf. Kenneth Burke, Attitudes Toward History (New York, 1937), I, 82–83: "Looking over the titles of books written by Huysmans, who went from naturalism, through Satanism, to Catholicism, we find that his titles of the naturalistic period are with one exception nouns, all those of the transitional period are prepositions actually or in quality ("A-Vau-l'Eau," "En Rade," "A Rebours," "La Bas," "En Route") and all in his period of Catholic realism are nouns."

[7] In German all nouns are regularly capitalized, and the German word for noun substantive is Hauptwort or "head word." In this grammatical vision the noun becomes a sort of "captain" in the sentence.

[8] Cf. Aristotle, Rhetoric, 1410 b: "And let this be our fundamental principle: for the receiving of information with ease, is naturally pleasing to all; and nouns are significant of something; so that all those nouns whatsoever which produce knowledge in the mind, are most pleasing."

making real. Suffice it to say here that the noun, whether it be a pointer to things that one can touch and see, as *apple, bird, sky,* or to the more or less hypothetical substances such as *fairness, spook, nothingness,* by rule stands at the head of things and is ministered to by the other parts of speech and by combinations.

The Adjective

The adjective is, by the principle of determination just reviewed, a word of secondary status and force. Its burden is an attribute, or something added. In the order of being to which reference has been made, the noun can exist without the adjective, but not the adjective without the noun. Thus we can have "men" without having "excellent men"; but we cannot have "excellent" without having something (if only something understood) to receive the attribution. There are very practical rhetorical lessons to be drawn from this truth. Since adjectives express attributes which are conceptually dispensable to the substances wherein they are present, the adjective tends to be a supernumerary. Long before we are aware of this fact through analysis, we sense it through our resentment of any attempt to gain maximum effect through the adjective. Our intuition of speech seems to tell us that the adjective is question-begging; that is to say, if the thing to be expressed is real, it will be expressed through a substantive; if it is expressed mainly through adjectives, there is something defective in its reality, since it has gone for secondary support.[9] If someone should say to us, "Have some white milk," we must suppose either that the situation is curious, other kinds of milk being available, or that the speaker is trying to impose upon us by a piece of persiflage. Again, a mountain is a mountain without being called "huge"; if we have to call it huge, there is some defect in the original image which is being made up. Of course there are speech situations in which such modifiers do make a useful contribution, but as a general rule, to be applied with discretion, a style is stronger when it depends mainly upon substantives sharp enough to convey their own attributes.

Furthermore, because the class of the adjective contains so many terms of dialectical import, such as *good, evil, noble, base, useful, useless,* there is bound to exist an initial suspicion of all adjectives. (Even when they are the positive kind, as is true with most limiting adjectives, there lurk the questions "Who made up the statistics?" and "How were they gathered?") The dialectical adjective is too often a "fighting word" to be used casually. Because in its very origin it is the product of dis-

---

[9] *Compare the following passage by Carl Sandburg in "Trying to Write,"* Atlantic Monthly, *Vol. 186, No. 3 (September, 1950), p. 33: "I am still studying verbs and the mystery of how they connect nouns. I am more suspicious of adjectives than at any other time in all my born days."*

putation, one is far from being certain in advance of assent to it. How would you wish to characterize the world? If you wish to characterize it as "round," you will win a very general assent, although not a universal one. But if you wish, with the poet, to characterize it as "sorry," you take a position in respect to which there are all sorts of contrary positions. In strictest thought one might say that every noun contains its own analysis, but an adjective applied to a noun is apparatus brought in from the outside; and the result is the object slightly "fictionized." Since adjectives thus initiate changes in the more widely received substantive words, one has to have permission of his audience to talk in adjectives. Karl Shapiro seems to have had something like this in mind in the following passage from his *Essay on Rime:*

> *for the tyrannical epithet*
> *Relies upon the adjective to produce*
> *The image; and no serious construction*
> *In rime can build upon the modifier.*[10]

One of the common mistakes of the inexperienced writer, in prose as well as poetry, is to suppose that the adjective can set the key of a discourse. Later he learns what Shapiro indicates, that nearly always the adjective has to have the way prepared for it. Otherwise, the adjective introduced before its noun collapses for want of support. There is a perceptible difference between "the irresponsible conduct of the opposition with regard to the Smith bill" and "the conduct of the opposition with regard to the Smith bill has been irresponsible," which is accounted for in part by the fact that the adjective comes after the substantive has made its firm impression. In like manner we are prepared to receive Henley's

> *Out of the night that covers me,*
> *Black as the Pit from pole to pole*

because "night" has preceded "black." I submit that if the poem had begun "Black as . . ." it would have lost a great deal of its rhetorical force because of the inherent character of the opening word. The adjective would have been felt presumptuous, as it were, and probably no amount of supplementation could have overcome this unfortunate effect.

I shall offer one more example to show that costly mistakes in emphasis may result from supposing that the adjective can compete with the noun. This one came under my observation, and has remained with

[10] Essay on Rime *(New York, 1945), p. 43, ll. 1224–1227.*

me as a classical instance of rhetorical ineptitude. On a certain university campus "Peace Week" was being observed, and a prominent part of the program was a series of talks. The object of these talks was to draw attention to those forces which seemed to be leading mankind toward a third world war. One of the speakers undertook to point out the extent to which the Western nations, and especially the United States, were at fault. He declared that a chief source of the bellicose tendency of the United States was its "proud rectitude," and it is this expression which I wish to examine critically. The fault of the phrase is that it makes "rectitude" the villain of the peace, whereas sense calls for making "pride." If we are correct in assigning the substantive a greater intrinsic weight, then it follows that "rectitude" exerts the greater force here. But rectitude is not an inciter of wars; it is rather that rectitude which is made rigid or unreasonable by pride which may be a factor in the starting of wars, and pride is really the provoking agent. For the most fortunate effect, then, the grammatical relationship should be reversed, and we should have "rectitude" modifying "pride." But since the accident of linguistic development has not provided it with an adjective form of equivalent meaning, let us try "pride of rectitude." This is not the best expression imaginable, but it is somewhat better since it turns "proud" into a substantive and demotes "rectitude" to a place in a prepositional phrase. The weightings are now more in accordance with meaning: what grammar had anomalously made the chief word is now properly tributary, and we have a closer delineation of reality. As it was, the audience went away confused and uninspired, and I have thought of this ever since as a situation in which a little awareness of the rhetoric of grammar—there were other instances of imperceptive usage—could have turned a merely well-intentioned speech into an effective one.

Having laid down this relationship between adjective and substantive as a principle, we must not ignore the real or seeming exceptions. For the alert reader will likely ask, what about such combinations as "new potatoes," "drunk men," "a warlike nation"? Are we prepared to say that in each of these the substantive gets the major attention, that we are more interested in "potatoes" than in their being "new," in "men" than their being "drunk," and so forth? Is that not too complacent a rule about the priority of the substantive over the adjective?

We have to admit that there are certain examples in which the adjective may eclipse the substantive. This may occur (1) when one's intonation (or italics) directs attention to the modifier: *"white* horses"; *"five* dollars, not four." (2) when there is a striking clash of meaning between the adjective and the substantive, such that one gives a second thought to the modifier: "a murderous smile"; "a gentleman gambler." (3) when the adjective is naturally of such exciting associations

THE CRITICAL PERSPECTIVE OF THE "NEW RHETORICS" **282**

that it has become a sort of traditional introduction to matter of moment: "a warlike nation"; "a desperate deed"; etc. Having admitted these possibilities of departure from the rule, we still feel right in saying that the rule has some force. It will be found useful in cases which are doubtful, which are the cases where no strong semantic or phonetic considerations override the grammatical pattern. In brief, when the immediate act of our mind does not tell us whether an expression should be in this form or the other, the principle of the relationship of adjective and substantive may settle the matter with an insight which the particular instance has not called forth.

The Adverb

The adverb is distinguished from the other parts of speech by its superior mobility; roughly speaking, it can locate itself anywhere in the sentence, and this affords a clue to its character. "Certainly the day is warm"; "The day certainly is warm"; "The day is certainly warm"; "The day is warm certainly" are all "normal" utterances. This superior mobility, amounting to a kind of detachment, makes the adverb peculiarly a word of judgment. Here the distinction between the adverb and the adjective seems to be that the latter depends more upon public agreement and less upon private intention in its applications. It is a matter of common observation that the adverb is used frequently to express an attitude which is the speaker's projection of himself. "Surely the war will end soon" is not, for example, a piece of objective reporting but an expression of subjective feeling. We of course recognize degrees of difference in the personal or subjective element. Thomas Carlyle is much given to the use of the adverb, and when we study his adverbs in context, we discover that they are often little more than explosions of feeling. They are employed to make more positive, abrupt, sensational, or intense whatever his sentence is otherwise saying. Indeed, take from Carlyle his adverbs and one robs him of that great hortatory sweep which makes him one of the great preachers in English literature. On the other hand Henry James, although given to this use to comparable extent, gets a different effect from his adverbs. With him they are the exponents of scrupulous or meticulous feeling; they are often in fact words of definite measure. When James says "fully" or "quickly" or "bravely" he is usually expressing a definite perception, and sometimes the adverb will have its own phrasal modifier to give it the proper direction or limitation of sense. Therefore James' adverbs, instead of having a merely expletive force, as do many of Carlyle's, tend to integrate themselves with his more objective description. All this amounts to saying that adverbial "judgments" can be differently based; and the use of the adverb will affect a style accordingly.

The caution against presumptuous use of the adjective can be repeated with somewhat greater force for the adverb. It is the most tempting of all the parts of speech to question-beg with. It costs little, for instance, to say "certainly," "surely," or even "terribly," "awfully," "undoubtedly"; but it often costs a great deal to create the picture upon which these words are a justifiable verdict. Asking the reader to accept them upon the strength of simple assertion is obviously a form of taking without earning. We realize that a significant part of every speech situation is the character of the speaker; and there are characters who can risk an unproved "certainly" or "undoubtedly." They bring to the speech situation a kind of ethical proof which accentuates their language. Carlyle's reflective life was so intense, as we know from *Sartor Resartus* and other sources, that it wins for him a certain right to this asseverative style. As a general rule, though, it will be found that those who are most entitled to this credit use it least, which is to say, they prefer to make their demonstrations. We point out in summary that the adverb is frequently dependent upon the character of its user, and that, since it is often the qualifier of a qualifier, it may stand at one more remove from what we have defined as the primary symbol. This is why beginners should use it least—should use it only after they have demonstrated that they can get their results by other means.

The Verb

The verb is regularly ranked with the noun in force, and it seems that these two parts of speech express the two aspects under which we habitually see phenomena, that of determinate things and that of actions or states of being. Between them the two divide up the world at a pretty fundamental depth; and it is a commonplace of rhetorical instruction that a style made up predominantly of nouns and verbs will be a vigorous style. These are the symbols of the prime entities, words of stasis and words of movement (even when the verb is said to express a "state of being," we accept that as a kind of modal action, a process of going on, or having existential quality), which set forth the broad circumstances of any subject of discussion. This truth is supported by the facts that the substantive is the heart of a grammatical subject and the verb of a grammatical predicate.

When we pass beyond the matter of broad categorization to look at the verb's possibilities, we find the greatest need of instruction to lie in the verb epithet. It may be needless to impress any literate person with the verb's relative importance, but it is necessary to point out, even to some practiced writers, that the verb itself can modify the action it asserts, or, so to put it, can carry its own epithet. Looking at the copious supply of verbs in English, we often find it possible to choose one so selective in meaning that no adverb is needed to accompany it. If we wish to assert that "the man moves *quickly*," we can say, depending on the tone of our passage and the general signification, that he *hastens, rushes, flies, scrambles, speeds, tears, races, bolts,* to name only a few. If we wish to assert that a man is not telling the truth, we have the choice of *lies, prevaricates, falsifies, distorts, exaggerates,* and some others. As this may seem to treat the matter at too didactic a level, let us generalize by saying that there is such a thing as the characterizing verb, and that there is no telling how many words could have been saved, how many passages could have dispensed with a lumbering and perhaps inaccurate adverb, if this simple truth about the verb were better appreciated. The best writers of description and narration know it. Mark Twain's most vivid passages are created largely through a frequent and perceptive use of the verb epithet. Turn to almost any page of *Life on the Mississippi:*

> *Ship channels are buoyed and lighted, and therefore it is a comparatively easy undertaking to learn to run them; clear-water rivers, with gravel bottoms, change their channels very gradually, and therefore one needs to learn them but once; but piloting becomes another matter when you apply it to vast streams like the Mississippi and the Missouri, whose alluvial banks cave and change constantly, whose snags are always hunting up new quarters, whose sand-bars are never at rest, whose channels are forever dodging and shirking, and whose obstructions must be confronted in all nights and all weathers without the aid of a single lighthouse or a single buoy, for there is neither light nor buoy to be found anywhere in all this three or four thousand miles of villainous river.* [11]

Here there occurs not just action, but expressive action, to which something is contributed by Twain's subtle appreciation of modal variations in the verb.

There is a rough parallelism between the use of the complex sentence, with its detail put away in subordinate constructions, and the use of the verb epithet. In both instances the user has learned to dispense with a second member of equal or nearly equal weight in order to get an effect. As the adverbial qualification is fused with the verb, so in lesser degree, of course, is the detail of the complex sentence fused with its principal assertion. These devices of economy and compression, although they may be carried to a point at which the style seems forced and unnatural, are among the most important means of rhetoric.

The Conjunction

The conjunction, in its simple role as joiner, seems not to have much character, yet its use expresses of relatedness of things, which is

---

[11] Life on the Mississippi (*New York, 1903*), *p. 73.*

bound to have signification. As either coordinator or subordinator of entities, it puts the world into a condition of mutual relationship through which a large variety of ideas may be suggested. From the different ways in which this relationship is expressed, the reader will consciously and even unconsciously infer different things. Sometimes the simple "and . . . and" coordination is the expression of childlike mentality, as we saw in our discussion of the compound sentence. On the other hand, in a different speech situation it can produce a quite different effect: readers of the King James version of the Bible are aware of how the "and" which joins long sequences of verses sets up a kind of expectancy which is peculiarly in keeping with sacred text. One gets the feeling from the reiteration of "and" that the story is confirmed and inevitable; there are no contingencies, and everything happens with the double assurance of something foretold. When this pattern is dropped, as it is in a recent "American" version of the Bible, the text collapses into a kind of news story.

The frequent use of "but" to join the parts of a compound sentence seems to indicate a habit of mind. It is found congenial by those who take a "balanced view," or who are uneasy over an assertion until it has been qualified or until some recognition has been made of its negative. Its influence is in the direction of the cautious or pedantic style because it makes this sort of disjunction, whereas "and" generously joins everything up.

Since conjunctions are usually interpreted as giving the plot of one's thought, it is essential to realize that they have implicit meanings. They usually come at points where a pause is natural, and there is a temptation, if one may judge by indulgence in the habit, to lean upon the first one that comes to mind without reflecting critically upon its significance, so that although the conjunction may formally connect at this point, its semantic meaning does not aid in making the connection precise. A common instance of this fault is the casual interchange of "therefore" and "thus." "Therefore" means "in consequence of," but "thus" means "in this manner" and so indicates that some manner has already been described. "Hence" may take the place of "therefore" but "thus" may not. "Also" is a connective used with unimaginative regularity by poor speakers and writers, for whom it seems to signalize the next thought coming. Yet in precise meaning "also" signifies only a mechanical sort of addition such as we have in listing one item after another. To signalize the extension of an idea, "moreover" is usually more appropriate than "also." Although "while" is often used in place of "whereas" to mean "on the other hand," it has its other duty of signifying "at the same time." "Whereas," despite its pedantic or legalistic overtone, will be preferred in passages where precise relationship is the governing consideration. On the whole it would seem that the average writer suffers, in the department, from nothing more than poverty of vocabulary. What he does (what every writer does to some extent) is to keep on hand a small set of conjunctions and to use them in a sort of rotation without giving attention to how their distinctive meanings could further his purpose.

The Preposition

The preposition too is a word expressing relationships, but this definition gives only a faint idea of its great resources. When the false rules about the preposition have been set aside, it is seen that this is a tremendously inventive word. Like the adverb, it is a free rover, standing almost anywhere; it is constantly entering into combinations with verbs and nouns, in which it may direct, qualify, intensify, or even add something quite new to the meaning; at other times it combines with some other preposition to produce an indispensable idiom. It has given us "get out," "put over," "come across," "eat up," "butt in," "off of," "in between," and many other expressions without which English, especially on the vital colloquial level, would be poorer indeed. Thornton Wilder maintains that it is in this extremely free use of the preposition that modern American English shows its superiority over British English. Such bold use of prepositional combinations gives to American English a certain flavor of the grand style, which British English has not had since the seventeenth century. Melville, an author working peculiarly on his own, is characterized in style by this imaginative use of the preposition.

Considered with reference to principle, the preposition seems to do what the adverb does, but to do it with a kind of substantive force. "Groundward," for example, seems weak beside "toward the ground," "lengthwise" beside "along the length of," or "centrally" beside "in the center of." The explanation may well lie in the preposition's characteristic position; as a regular orderer of nouns and of verbs, it takes upon itself something of their solidity of meaning. "What is that for?" and "Where did you send it to?" lose none of their force through being terminated by these brief words of relationship.

The Phrase

It will not be necessary to say much about the phrase because its possibilities have been fairly well covered by our discussion of the noun and adjective. One qualifying remark about the force of the prepositional phrase, however, deserves making. The strength normally found in the preposition can be greatly diminished by connection with an abstract noun. That is to say, when the terminus of the preposition is lacking in vigor or concreteness, the whole expression may succumb to vagueness, in which cases the single adjective or adverb will be stronger by comparison. Thus the idea conveyed by "lazy" is largely frustrated by "of a lazy disposition"; that of "mercenary" by "of a mercenary character"; that of "deep" by "of depth," and so on.

After the prepositional phrase, the most important phrasal combination to examine, from the standpoint of rhetorical usages, is the participial phrase. We could infer this truth from the fact alone that the Greeks made a very extensive use of the participle, as every student of that marvellous language knows. Greek will frequently use a participle where English employs a dependent clause or even a full sentence, so that the English expression "the man who is carrying a spear" would be in Greek "the spear carrying man"; "the one who spoke" would be "the one having spoken" and further accordingly, with even more economy of language than these examples indicate. I am disposed to think that the Greeks developed this habit because they were very quick to see opportunities of subordination. The clarity and subtlety of the Greek language derives in no small part from this highly "organized" character, in which auxiliary thoughts are compactly placed in auxiliary structures, where they permit the central thought to emerge more readily. In English the auxiliary status of the participle (recognized formally through its classification as an adjective) is not always used to like advantage.

One consequence of this is that although English intonation and normal word order tend to make the last part of a sentence the most emphatic, unskillful writers sometimes lose this emphasis by concluding a sentence with a participial phrase. We may take as examples "He returned home in September, having been gone for a year"; and "Having been gone for a year, he returned home in September." The second of these puts the weightier construction in the emphatic position. Of course the matter of their relative merit cannot be separated from their purpose; there are sentences whose total meanings are best served by a *retardo* or *diminuendo* effect at the end, and for such closes the participial phrase is well suited for reasons already given. But in the majority of utterances it contributes best by modifying at some internal position, or by expressing some detail or some condition at the beginning of the sentence. The latter use may be quite effective in climactic orderings, and it will be found that journalists have virtually stereotyped this opening for their "lead" sentences: "Threatened with an exhausted food supply by the strike, hospitals today made special arrangements for the delivery of essentials"; "Reaching a new high for seven weeks, the stock market yesterday pushed into new territory." This form is a successful if often crude result of effort toward compact and dramatic presentation.

But to summarize our observations on the participial phrase in English: It is formally a weak member of the grammatical family; but it is useful for economy, for shaded effects, and sometimes the phrase will contain words whose semantic force makes us forget that they are in a secondary construction. Perhaps it is enough to say that the mature writer has learned more things that can be done with the participle, but has also learned to respect its limitations.

In Conclusion

I can imagine being told that this chapter is nothing more than an exposition of prejudices, and that every principle discussed here can be defied. I would not be surprised if that were proved through single examples, or small sets of examples. But I would still hazard that if these show certain tendencies, my examples show stronger ones, and we have to remember that there is such a thing as a vector of forces in language too. Even though an effect may sometimes be obtained by crowding or even breaking a rule, the lines of force are still there, to be used by the skillful writer scientifically, and grammar is a kind of scientific nomenclature. Beyond this, of course, he will use them according to art, where he will be guided by his artistic intuition, and by the residual cautions of his experience.

In the long view a due respect for the canons of grammar seems a part of one's citizenship. One does not remain uncritical; but one does "go along." It has proved impossible to show that grammar is determined by the "best people," or by the pedants, or by any other presumptive authority, and this is more reason for saying that it incorporates the people as a whole. Therefore the attitude of unthinking adoption and the attitude of personal defiance are both dubious, because they look away from the point where issues, whenever they appear, will be decided. That point seems to be some communal sense about the fitness of a word or a construction for what has communal importance, and this indicates at least some suprapersonal basis. Much evidence could be offered to show that language is something which is born psychological but is ever striving to become logical. At this task of making it more logical everybody works more or less. Like the political citizenship defined by Aristotle, language citizenship makes one a potential magistrate, or one empowered to decide. The work is best carried on, however, by those who are aware that language must have some connection with the intelligential world, and that is why one must think about the rhetorical nature even of grammatical categories.

"War Message," December 8, 1941:
An Approach to Language
by Hermann G. Stelzner

I

Two recent books[1] are responses to an uneasiness with much rhetorical criticism which has appeared in print. In raising questions the authors hope to stimulate more meaningful and insightful analyses of rhetorical activities and processes. They goad critics to experiment, to describe and to evaluate in ways heretofore little practiced. Both authors ask that "beginnings" be made.

Reviewers have pointed to difficulties. Arnold's review of Nichols' work asks for a sample of the criticism "I am exhorted to produce. . . . " He feels that Nichols "does not illustrate in pointed ways how criticism may, in practice, resolve the . . . issues raised. . . ."[2] Responding to Black's work, Ehninger agrees with Black's assessment of much criticism but believes Black's alternatives "are not worked out in enough detail to be viable." The "ingredients . . . are not developed into anything approaching a critical method" nor are "characteristics and possibilities . . . systematized into a program of attack and procedure which the critic . . . may apply."[3] Yet neither Black nor Nichols sets out to develop systems. Black observes:

We have not evolved any system of rhetorical criticism, but only, at best, an orientation to it. An orientation, together with taste and intelligence, is all that a critic needs. If his criticism is fruitful, he may end with a system, but he should not, in our present state of knowledge, begin with one. We simply do not know enough yet about rhetorical discourse to place our faith in systems, and it is only through imaginative criticism that we are likely to learn more.[4]

Concluding her remarks on I. A. Richards, Nichols states:

One of the most useful things about I. A. Richards . . . is his demonstration of the possibility of finding an orderly methodology. . . . I do

From *Speech Monographs*, XXXIII, 4 (November 1966), 419–437. Used by permission of the author and the Speech Communication Association. Mr. Stelzner is Associate Professor of Speech at the University of Massachusetts.

[1] *Marie Hochmuth Nichols*, Rhetoric and Criticism (*Baton Rouge, La., 1963*); *Edwin Black*, Rhetorical Criticism (*New York, 1965*).

[2] *Carroll C. Arnold, review of* Rhetoric and Criticism *in* Southern Speech Journal, *XXX (Fall 1964), 62.*

[3] *Douglas Ehninger, "Rhetoric and the Critic," Western Speech, XXIX (Fall 1965), 231.*

[4] *Black, p. 177.*

not mean that Richards' method should be adopted. . . . What I do
mean is that we also should be looking for an orderly methodology.[5]

The thrust of Nichols' and Black's analyses is macrocosmic. Most
criticism, Black states, is limited to "an estimate of the historically factual effects of the discourse on its relatively immediate audience."[6] He
argues for enlargement, for an "interpretation of the discourse that
realizes all that is in it and that aims 'to see the object as it really
is.' . . ."[7]

A rhetorical act is both rich and complex. To probe it fully requires
all the critical postures, approaches, and talents described by Stanley
Hyman in his portrait of an "ideal" critic.[8] Full disclosure is the ideal.

The posture of this study is microcosmic. We center on the language
of Franklin D. Roosevelt's "War Message" to Congress, December 8,
1941. The analysis is motivated by the treatment of language found in
much traditional criticism. Often critics fragment discourse, investigate
chosen samples of language as independent variables and draw conclusions. One analyst, after studying Stevenson's 1952 campaign addresses, reported that Stevenson had a "middle" style, "neither plain
nor grand."[9] To the traditional procedures, Nichols has responded:
"Hoary with age. . . ."[10] She believes that the usual approaches have
failed to treat language adequately: "Year after year, language, if it
is handled at all, gets a few words about rhetorical questions, antithesis,
and metaphors. . . ."[11] Ehninger's description of existing criticism
includes like comments:

Instead of describing what is going on in a discourse as it works to
achieve its ends, they [critics] focus on how the discourse came into
being, on the circumstances under which it was delivered, and on the
reactions or results it produced. Analysis of the speech itself not only
is slanted, but to the extent that it is present it tends to consist of a
classification of certain grosser properties, cast under the heads of the
traditional modes and canons—to be a mechanical accounting or sum-
ming up of how well the speech fits an a priori mold.[12]

The present approach to Franklin D. Roosevelt's "War Message" is
"topographical." The speech is the "particular place" and, to assess

[5] *Nichols, pp. 106–107.*
[6] *Black, p. 48.*
[7] Ibid.
[8] *Stanley Edgar Hyman,* The Armed Vision *(New York, 1955), pp. 386–391.*
[9] *Nichols, p. 107.*
[10] Ibid.
[11] Ibid.
[12] *Ehninger, p. 230.*

the configurations of its language, its "roads," "rivers," "cities," "lakes," and "relief" are examined. To shift the figure, fragments of language are not selected from the speech and regarded as the dominant lights, independent and autonomous. The concern is with the constellation, not the major stars alone. Interest centers on the order, movement, meanings, and interrelations of the language; the object is to discover not only what goes on, but how it goes on. The aim is full disclosure.

We explicate. We try, inductively, a kind of "statistical inspection"[13] to find out what goes on and how the "on-going" is generated. We note development *"from what through what to what,"*[14] shifting from grammar to syntax to diction to logic to rhythm to figure or whatever, when the speech itself demands a shift to account for the totality of tensions in the language. Speeches, including those of the expository genre, are more than collections of statements. Explicating is more than paraphrasing. It is "the ex*plicit*ation of the implicit."[15] We explore the lexical possibilities of words and word combinations. As a way of demonstrating what is going on in a speech, explication is analogous to Hyman's description of Burke's mode: "Use All There Is to Use," which means "the rather disorganized organizing principle of investigating every possible line of significance."[16]

The speech provides the clues. The available drafts of Roosevelt's address have been examined and, when variations in the drafts bear on the analysis, we cite them.[17] However, the primary purpose is not to trace the *development* of the "War Message" of December 8, 1941. How the speech *is,* not how it came to be, is the concern.

We do not suggest that Roosevelt himself consciously structured the relationships we explore and evaluate. It "cannot be said too often that a poet does not fully know what is the poem he is writing until he has written it"[18] applies to all composition. Burke argues it is not until *"after the completion* of the work"[19] that interrelationships in it can be

---

[13] *Kenneth Burke,* The Philosophy of Literary Form *(New York, 1957), p. 59; on p. 75 Burke refers to the examination as an "inductive inspection."*

[14] *Ibid., p. 60; italics his.*

[15] *W. K. Wimsatt, Jr.,* The Verbal Icon *(Lexington, Ky., 1954), p. 249; italics his.*

[16] *Hyman, p. 390.*

[17] *The Franklin D. Roosevelt Library, Hyde Park, New York, has four drafts of this message. They were examined and are referred to by number. Changes from draft to draft are not extensive. Grace Tully, Roosevelt's secretary, indicates that the address was delivered in almost the identical form in which it was originally dictated to her by the President. See Grace Tully,* F. D. R., My Boss *(New York, 1949), p. 256.*

[18] *C. Day Lewis,* The Poetic Image *(London, 1947), p. 71.*

[19] *Burke, p. 18; italics his.*

analyzed; analysis of these involves both "quantitative and qualitative considerations":[20]

Now, the work of every writer contains a set of implicit equations. . . . And though he be perfectly conscious of the act of writing, . . . he cannot possibly be conscious of the interrelationships among all these equations. . . . The motivation out of which he writes is synonymous with the structural way in which he puts events and values together when he writes; and however consciously he may go about such work, there is a kind of generalization about these interrelations that he could not have been conscious of, since the generalization could be made by the kind of inspection that is possible only after the completion of the work.[21]

Because this analysis is limited to the language of a single speech, we cannot generalize from it to "style." The inability to generalize from a single example presents the reverse of a difficulty which reviewers saw in Nichols' and Black's macrocosmic postures: the difficulty of implementation. And microscopic analysis, no matter how successful, does not shed much light on discourse in general. Yet William E. Leuchtenburg's insightful essay, "The New Deal and the Analogue of War,"[22] offers possibilities for extending the analysis undertaken in these pages. He points out that much New Deal policy was accomplished through the figure of war. Roosevelt himself often applied the topic, "war," to social and economic problems. In a sense his December 8, 1941 "War Message" was but another treatment of that topic. Scrutiny of a number of his addresses might provide insights into his use of language, his "style," on the topic "war"; generalization would then be possible. Speaking to the point of generalization, Burke states that it is first necessary to trace down the "interrelationships as revealed by the objective structure of the book itself":

The first step . . . requires us to get our equations inductively, by tracing down the interrelationships as revealed by the objective structure of the book itself. [Eventually one may] . . . offer 'generalizations atop generalizations' whereby different modes of concrete imagery may be classed together. That is, one book may give us 'into the night' imagery; another 'to the bottom of the sea' imagery; another the 'apo-

[20] Ibid., *p. 59.*
[21] Ibid., *p. 18; italics his.*
[22] *William E. Leuchtenburg, "The New Deal and the Analogue of War," in* Change and Continuity in Twentieth-Century America, *ed. John Braeman* (Columbus, Ohio, 1964), pp. 81–143.

plectic' imagery . . . and we may propose some over-all category . . . that would justify us in classing all these works together on the basis of a common strategy despite differences in concrete imagery.[23]

The objective structure of a speech, as well as of a book, is a composite of subtly balanced meanings; all language is weighted toward something, hence away from something; for something, hence opposed to something. A "statistical inspection" of a speech reveals what the speaker talked about, and from that knowledge the balance of his meanings can be established. For example, in the "War Message" of December 8, 1941 "time" is central to Roosevelt's discussion. He uses the future and the past, even as he speaks in, about, and to the present. Future is balanced against Past; these are poles of a continuum along which "goods" and their opposites balance antithetically. The past is given negative valence in Roosevelt's address; and in like manner other concepts, entities, and conditions are antithetically balanced. The balanced meanings are listed below. Those on the left have "positive" quality; those on the right are "negative." *Successive* balances emerge as the speech advances and they, hence, constitute a structural pattern according to which analysis of the address may proceed.

An arrangement of the balanced meanings of an address, such as the arrangement just set forth, describes the relationships of the topics discussed by the speaker; the arrangement does not, however, explicate these relationships. There remains the task of revealing not only the weight of each pole in a particular balance of meaning but how the weighting, hence relationship, was rhetorically achieved.

Future time	*Past time*
God	*"Devil"*
United States	*Japan*
government	*government*
military	*military*
people	*people*
Absence of Danger (presence	*Presence of Danger (absence*
of peace)	*of peace)*
International involvement	*Isolationistic non-involvement*
"I" of address	*Non-"I"*[24]

---

[23] *Burke, p. 59.*

[24] *In a speech situation, the speaker, the "I," is never wholly absent. Listeners may respond to his voice and/or his physical presence even when he handles materials largely denotative and expository in character. The continuum of "presence-absence" is one of convenience, establishing poles and making possible relative weighting.*

We may turn now to the text of Roosevelt's address:

War Message[25]

II

The man who writes or speaks of an "anticipated war . . . must select his material out of the past and the present."[26] He is committed to speak in some fashion about history. On December 7, 1941, history was made suddenly and directly. The equally direct, initial, verbal response (1–3) parallels the historical facts which made statement necessary. Moreover, the mass media had described fully the international activities of December 7, 1941, and listeners could easily fit the speaker's initial statement into a larger and ordered background.

"Yesterday" quickly anchors the address to the immediate historical

---

[25] *This text is the transcript of the message as delivered. Text from Franklin D. Roosevelt Library, Hyde Park, New York.*

1 *Yesterday, December 7, 1941—a date which will live in infamy—the United*
2 *States of America was suddenly and deliberately attacked by naval and air forces of*
3 *the Empire of Japan.*
4 *The United States was at peace with that nation and, at the solicitation of*
5 *Japan, was still in conversation with its Government and its Emperor looking toward*
6 *the maintenance of peace in the Pacific.*
7 *Indeed, one hour after Japanese air squadrons had commenced bombing in the*
8 *American island of Oahu, the Japanese Ambassador to the United States and his colleague*
9 *delivered to our Secretary of State a formal reply to a recent American message. And*
10 *while this reply stated that it seemed useless to continue the existing diplomatic*
11 *negotiations, it contained no threat or hint of war or of armed attack.*
12 *It will be recorded that the distance of Hawaii from Japan makes it obvious that*
13 *the attack was deliberately planned many days or even weeks ago. During the inter-*
14 *vening time the Japanese Government has deliberately sought to deceive the United*
15 *States by false statements and expressions of hope for continued peace.*
16 *The attack yesterday on the Hawaiian Islands has caused severe damage to American*
17 *naval and military forces. I regret to tell you that very many American lives have*
18 *been lost. In addition American ships have been reported torpedoed on the high seas*
19 *between San Francisco and Honolulu.*
20 *Yesterday the Japanese Government also launched an attack against Malaya.*
21 *Last night Japanese forces attacked Hong Kong.*
22 *Last night Japanese forces attacked Guam.*
23 *Last night Japanese forces attacked the Philippine Islands.*
24 *Last night the Japanese attacked Wake Island.*
25 *And this morning the Japanese attacked Midway Island.*
26 *Japan has, therefore, undertaken a surprise offensive extending throughout the*
27 *Pacific area. The facts of yesterday and today speak for themselves. The people of*
28 *the United States have already formed their opinions and well understand the impli-*
29 *cations to the very life and safety of our nation.*
30 *As Commander-in-Chief of the Army and Navy I have directed that all measures*
31 *be taken for our defense. But always will our whole nation remember the character*
32 *of the onslaught against us.*
33 *No matter how long it may take us to overcome this premeditated invasion, the*
34 *American people in their righteous might will win through to absolute victory.*
35 *I believe that I interpret the will of the Congress and of the people when I*
36 *assert that we will not only defend ourselves to the uttermost but will make it*
37 *very certain that this form of treachery shall never again endanger us.*
38 *Hostilities exist. There is no blinking at the fact that our people, our*
39 *territory and our interests are in grave danger.*
40 *With confidence in our armed forces, with the unbounding determination of our*
41 *people, we will gain the inevitable triumph—so help us God.*
42 *I ask that the Congress declare that since the unprovoked and dastardly*
43 *attack by Japan on Sunday, December 7, 1941, a state of war has existed between the*
44 *United States and the Japanese Empire.*

[26] *Burke, p. 203.*

past, to the events of December seventh. It suggests that the speaker does not intend to go deeply into the past or to discuss it as part of the recommendations he will ultimately make.[27] The meaning of the immediate past was clearly less important than the present and the future. This placement of yesterday contributes to the overall past-present-future structure of the address and to the connotative values of "time" in it. The direct announcement (1–3) ruptures "yesterday," a time of reasonable stability and peace. That mind which wished to wander even fleetingly back over time, is restrained and controlled by the appositive, December 7, 1941. The speaker acknowledges that his listeners understood (27–29) the "leisure," the peaceful "timelessness" of yesterday had gone; but he impresses the point upon them.

The appositive, December 7, 1941, not only defines the specific yesterday among the potentially many. It establishes the date, which for historical purposes is more important than the day, Sunday, here omitted. The personal value judgment—"a date which will live in infamy"—colors the appositive and introduces the future into the discussion. Introduced as an "aside," the future already acts, offering judgments about the present. The matter is carefully handled. The speaker did not say: the date will live in infamy. A shift from the indefinite to the definite article and the excision of the relative pronoun *which* makes the speaker's personal judgment categorical, forcing on the historical future a value judgment which only the historical future can rightfully make.

That a sense of and a sensitivity to history operates[28] can be seen by testing alternatives: *Yesterday, a day which will live in infamy. . . .* Here the appositive is omitted, a possibility because it was unlikely that any member of the immediate audience would have been unaware of the date. History, however, catalogues dates, not yesterdays or days; the date is supplied. Omitting the appositive also makes necessary the revision of "a date which" to "a day which"; the former is somewhat more precise and sustains better the historical overtones of the initial announcement (1–3). Thus, the first twelve words of Roosevelt's ad-

[27] *Tully, p. 256, reports that when the message was being prepared Roosevelt called Secretary of State Cordell Hull to the White House to examine a draft. "The Secretary brought with him an alternative message drafted by Sumner Welles, longer and more comprehensive in its review of the circumstances leading to the state of war. It was rejected by the Boss. . . ."*

[28] *Roosevelt "regarded history as an imposing drama and himself as a conspicuous actor. Again and again he carefully staged a historic scene: as when, going before Congress on December 8, 1941 to call for a recognition of war with Japan, he took pains to see that Mrs. Woodrow Wilson accompanied Mrs. Roosevelt to the Capitol, thus linking the First and Second World Wars." Allan Nevins, "The Place of Franklin D. Roosevelt in History," American Heritage, XVII (June 1966), 12.*

dress join past and future; the present is represented by speaker and audience. And the immediate present—unsettled, disrupted, and anxiety-provoking—is somewhat stabilized by the past-future continuum which provides a sense of continuity. In the speaker's judgmental aside, the future renders a verdict on present activities which favors us; implicatively the future is on "our side."

The passive voice of the initial announcement makes possible some specific relationships between time, the actors in time, and the judgmental aside about the time. Though the statement's subject is the naval and air forces of the Empire of Japan, in the passive voice the subject becomes a marginal, omissible part of the sentence and its sense. The speaker could have said: . . . *the United States of America was suddenly and deliberately attacked.* But as delivered, the first statement treats the Japanese Empire as "marginal," subordinate. The passive emphasizes the United States as receiver of the action on a specific date, a day of peace until the attack which was infamous in character. The interrelationship of the three allows the immediate audience and history to record these facts. The initial statement might have been active: *Yesterday, December 7, 1941, a date which will live in infamy, naval and air forces of the Empire of Japan suddenly and deliberately attacked the United States.* Not only would the Japanese Empire have become central and active, but the United States would have been removed from its relationship to time. Yet time is essential to the well-being of the country. Past time treated her badly; future time (33–34, 40–41) will heal her wounds.

Even as yesterday was ruptured, the formal, settled, and trusted diplomatic conventions (4–6) were in process. These, too, will be broken (9–15) as the speaker particularizes some of the specific details in the deliberations. The formal and elevated diplomatic language describes. "Nation" (4) is more formal and concrete than a possible alternative, *country.* "Solicitation" (4) is more formal than *request,* and "conversation" (5) is more formal than *discussion* or *conference.* Consistent with the formality of the language is its loose, alliterative quality, more pronounced here than in any section of the address. "Peace" (4, 6) opens and closes the section, its sound sense somewhat reinforced by a weak alliterative echo: "Pacific." Between these points, "nation," "solicitation," "conversation" occur in rapid order; "maintenance," modifies the pattern by introducing a different, though not wholly dissimilar, sound tension.

Time remains central to the development. "The United States was at peace"[29]—past, "still in conversation"—present, "looking toward the

[29] *In drafts I, II, and III the line reads: "The United States was at the moment at peace. . . ." The "at the moment" phrase emphasizes time unnecessarily;*

maintenance"—future. The actors in the drama are polarized. Responding to a Japanese "solicitation," we were still concerned with tomorrow, even as they were not. The formal, diplomatic language (4–6) symbolizes a mask behind which duplicity is hidden. The duplicity, one dimension of a key term, "infamous" (1), is woven into the texture of the address. For example, the close relationship of "yesterday" (1, 16, 20) to the repeated "deliberately" (2, 13, 14) intensifies and supports the duplicity or infamy. The formal language (4–6) foreshadows the recital of specific events (7–11).

"Indeed," injecting emphasis and force, begins the recitation and colors the neutrality of formal, diplomatic language. Not *yet, still, but,* nor *however* would have functioned as well to introduce the formal, but false, overtures of the Japanese. "Indeed" imprints a reaction of the individual "I" on the yet-to-be-stated particulars. Moreover, "indeed" gains force and support from the earlier "yesterday," "infamy," "deliberately," "at peace," "still in conversation," and "maintenance of peace." Following the expletive, the speaker says "one hour after" (7), not merely *after.* "One hour after" makes time concrete, supports the emotional dimensions of "indeed," and forecasts the brazen, formal action of the Japanese Ambassador and the duplicity behind his formality. Also supporting duplicity is a subdued temporal pattern (7–11): after Japanese air squadrons attacked—past, the Ambassador delivers his reply—present, concerning *future* relationships.

"Japanese air squadrons" (7) were the instruments of attack. The phrase might have been rendered: *after the Japanese air force* or *after Japanese air forces.* These alternatives parallel better the first reference to the Japanese military (1); but therein lies a weakness. The modified repetition provides some variety. More important is the matter of image. *Air force* and *air forces* denote and connote mass, a large quantity which blankets a sky. Such a mass moves, but in droning and lumbering fashion. "Air squadrons" is a sharper, definable form of the force, as an image in the mind's eye. The image is of small groups, of well-defined patterns in the total mass, of tightly knit units sweeping in and out over the target.

"Air squadrons" is quantitative, definitive, and repetitive. To the extent that squadrons are patterns, the image presents formal patterns inflicting damage. Formal patterns are the enemy: of the past—"one hour

---

it contributes little to clarity or sense, and its excision is merited. Further, its excision diminishes the possibility of the immediate listeners' setting up the balance: was at the moment—is at this moment. "At this moment" (i.e., the moment of the address) the United States was in practical terms at war. Yet the President was speaking formally to the Congress to whom the legal right formally to declare war belonged. "At this moment" we were "legally" still at peace. Excision of "at the moment" diminished the possibility of a mistaken response by either the Congressional or the general audience.

after" (7), as well as the near present—"the Japanese Ambassador . . . delivered" (8–9). The formality of pattern connoted by "Japanese air squadrons" is also explicitly denoted of the Ambassador's act; he delivers a "formal reply" (9), which is contrasted to a slightly less formal "American message" (9). Had the description been of an *American note,* it would have been overly informal. Slightly more formal and rigid than "our Secretary of State" (9) is "the Japanese Ambassador" (8). If there is in these lines a heightened sense of the "formal" and if formality marks the enemy, all formality becomes symbolic—a mask—for duplicity and infamy. The closed, distant, difficult-to-read "formal" opposes the somewhat easier-to-read, open "informality." Such suggestion is consistent with the Western, especially American, stereotype of the Orient and Oriental, *circa* 1941. Duplicity masked by formality is thus further intensified. On first glance the construction of line 11[30] appears anticlimactic. "War" (11) is more encompassing and potentially more dangerous than "armed attack." However, "war" connotes a formal, open declaration of conflict. The Japanese dispensed with that formality, favoring "armed attack," an action outside the conventions of diplomacy.

Thus far no objective evidence has been offered to support the charge of duplicity. The speaker has been reporting diplomatic relationships (4–6) which the listeners themselves cannot verify; they are dependent upon him. But the shift is now to a geographical relationship (12) which supports the charge. "It will be recorded. . . ." By whom? The immediate audience certainly, but the historical audience as well. The verb "record" alters the speaker's stance and the passive "will be recorded" his perspective. The speaker's verb refers to, points to, the intellectual activity of man. Together, in concert, the speaker and the listeners function as detached observers—they measure mileage—and as commentators. "Makes it obvious" (12) is a phrase which befits such activity—of seeing, of reasoning, of understanding. The passive allows the evidence to be offered in dependent clauses, which contain the signs upon which the conclusion depends; it provides the "distance" necessary to detached, intellectual analysis. All the signs, and especially the final, objective, mileage sign, which is positioned nearest the conclusion which all signs support, contribute to one judgment: infamous duplicity. Finally, "the distance of Hawaii from Japan"

---

[30] *In draft II lines 10–11 read: "This reply contained a statement that it seemed useless to continue the diplomatic negotiations, but it contained no threat nor hint of war or of armed attack." Drafts III and IV are consistent with the final text (pp. 422–423). The draft II version is a compound sentence and fails to stress the "no threat nor hint of war. . . ." The revision, a dependent-independent arrangement, emphasizes the "no threat nor hint of war. . . ." It emphasizes duplicity.*

(12), a particular sign, is embedded in a sentence which itself spans syntactical distance.

The passive construction makes possible analysis of events which are outside the direct experience of the speaker. Events of the more immediate past (14–15) are handled differently; they are not in dependent clauses and the subject of detached, intellectual analysis. Of these events, the speaker has direct knowledge, and he shifts to the active voice. Japan acts. The language which responds is categorical and conclusive: "deliberately sought to deceive the United States by false statements and expressions of hope . . ." (14–15). Was the deception successful? The ambiguous "sought" leaves the question open, even as the speaker's emphasis on Japan's deliberateness and falsity tend to forestall the asking of it.

As further details are enumerated, time shifts slightly in importance. In "the attack yesterday" (16), the act is more important than the time. The emphasis on time could have been maintained: *yesterday's attack*. The new arrangement is less emphatic. The shift in emphasis does not however alter the basic time-act or act-time relationship. A legitimate alternative would have considerably weakened, if not broken, it: *the attack on the Hawaiian Islands yesterday. . . .*

From the description the personal "I" (17) emerges to link the speaker with the "blackest" event yet—the specific human tragedy. Both the "I" and the tragedy gain stature from the relationship. Had the "I" chosen a compound sentence, he could have avoided announcing the loss of life: the attack . . . *caused* . . . *damage to* . . . *forces and very many American lives have been lost.* Or he might have said simply: *Very many American lives have been lost.* These choices diminish both the ethical posture of the "I" and the dignity of the men who lost their lives. The "I" reveals (17–18), explicitly and implicitly, something of his regard for life—he separates it from the materials of war—and of his concept of duty, as a human being and as President and Commander-in-Chief. He demonstrates his understanding of and his respect for the conventions of tragic announcement. Moreover, he emerges "to tell" (17) his listeners. The direct, common verb suggests closeness—he to them and they to him. A close relationship must exist between the bearer and the receivers of tragic tidings for the verb "tell" to operate. When there is distance the tendency is toward formality, neutrality, and elevation: to *inform,* to *report,* or to *announce.*

"In addition" (18) adds still another detail. Is it of equal, more, or less importance than others? That depends upon the reaction of the listener to the total configuration. But the speaker by his placement of it reveals his assessment of its importance. Japanese submarines have approached the United States; they act not at far-off Hawaii, but nearer home. For an already upset nation the news is serious and distressing. The distress is minimized somewhat by placing it following the announcement of the loss of life, which absorbed most, if not all, emotional energies. The statement which follows the news helps to minimize the danger from the submarines. Attention and concern are diverted by the quick, crisp movement to Malaya (20)—about as far as danger could be removed.

Additional forces further diminish the submarine threat; distance is achieved by having the ships torpedoed on the high seas between San Francisco and Honolulu. The language moves danger "away from" the shores of the United States. The proper nouns, San Francisco and Honolulu (19), are necessary to the overall effect. Let the speaker say: *In addition, American ships have been reported torpedoed on the high seas.* Responses become: Where? Everywhere? Close to the United States? How close? Distant? How distant? The proper nouns meet some of the questions. Where? On a direct path between San Francisco and Honolulu. One can almost see it on the wall map of the mind—the narrow, well-defined shipping route. Close? How close? Ambiguously the image suggests movement *away from.* One may speculate on the range of possible responses had the speaker said, *on the high seas between Honolulu and San Francisco,* or merely *on the high seas.*

The choice and arrangement of the proper nouns diminish danger; a vague term in the same sentence (18–19) functions similarly. "Have been reported torpedoed . . .," said the speaker. "Reported" has truth-value, but relative to source and circumstance. Reports of that time were somewhat chaotic and unreliable. The speaker hints at doubt and uncertainty. The weight of the office of President and Commander-in-Chief does not support the reports. An alternative could diminish doubt: *American ships have been torpedoed.* The specific and the concrete joined in the same sentence to the vague and ambiguous moderate danger.

The announcement of the attack against Malaya (20), which partially relieved concern for the movement of Japanese submarines, has another function. It quietly extends the conflict, joining the United States as partner and ally of the British. The United States' involvement is not to be limited; it will become global. "Also" (20) signals this extension, though "Malaya" and "Hong Kong" must be heard to make the idea meaningful. The concluding generalization, "a surprise offensive extending throughout the Pacific area" (26–27), also quietly involves the country with allies and quietly prepares it for total involvement without the speaker's need to expend ethos to stress the necessity of an international commitment.[31]

---

[31] *James Reston,* New York Times, *December 9, 1941, p. 5, wrote: "Two facts seemed to impress this gathering* [Congress] *more perhaps than the*

The announcement of the attack against Malaya (20) also introduces a shift in the movement and tone of the address. The former will be quickened, the latter be made emphatic. The statement of the attack against Malaya parallels in substance lines 1–3; it begins "yesterday"; its subject is Japanese activity. However, its voice is active; it has neither qualifiers nor dependent clauses; its verb is simple, past tense. No other statement in the address thus far is as compressed or moves as quickly.

The "yesterday" which introduces the attack against Malaya concludes a compression among the yesterdays; note only the distance between them (1, 16, 20). This compression occurring over time and distance foreshadows, even as it is counterbalanced by, the tightly compressed "last night" series (21–24), including as well the modified restatement of time: "this morning" (25). These compressions of time herald the end of discussion about events in the immediate past. Attention will soon be directed (27–29) to what must be done today and tomorrow.

The tonalities of the "last night" series (21–25) are controlled by line 20 which begins formally: "the Japanese Government." The verb, "launched," quickly tarnishes the formal recognition. Rather than "launched," why not *began, commenced,* or the still simpler *attacked?* None of these verbs reinforces or sustains as well the connotations of "suddenly and deliberately attacked" (2) and "deliberately planned" (13), which emphasize that Japanese activities were outside the conventions of diplomacy. Had they been within those conventions, "launch" might have been an inappropriate description. A verb of strong thrust and impulse, "launch" has sufficient energy to encompass all remaining action (21–25).

Formal agents and agencies, "Japanese forces" (21–23), advance the action. Soon the less formal and somewhat ambiguous "the Japanese" (24–25) forward it. Is the referent only the Japanese Government and/or its agents? Or has there been a subtle expansion to include the citizens of Japan, as well? The choice of "Japan" (26) suggests the latter explanation. "Japan"—not the Empire of Japan, nor the Emperor, nor the Ambassador, nor the Government—merely Japan; the common term describes the nation. The Government and its agents are the explicit enemy; by implication the people are also numbered among the enemy. Nowhere before has the term, Japan, been used in this naked fashion. The "Japan" of line 5 occurs within the context of elevated, diplomatic language; in line 12 the reference is a straightforward, geographical one. The common term is later repeated (43) and tarnished completely

---

simple words of the speech. By not the slightest inflection did he suggest that the facts of the world situation had finally justified his policy, as even his opponents were admitting today he might very well have done."

by "unprovoked and dastardly" (42). The national name is finally too good to serve to describe the country. Reduction of Japan is effected by carefully controlled and disciplined language. Men in the street could and did say "Japs." The speaker could not. To have done so would have diminished not only the stature of the office of President but also the occasion and the place, the formal chambers in which affairs of state were conducted. Equally important, to have said "Japs" would have reduced the leader to the level of the led; distance, however defined, is necessary to effective leadership.

The "last night" series (21–24) supports the pace and quality of the attacks. Logically, last night, a part of yesterday, is illogical. The compressed "last nights," figuratively ticking off the clock, bring yesterday to a climactic end. The three "yesterdays" (1, 16, 20) spanned time and space; the night and the events in the night move faster. Simple declarative sentences present facts—actor, action, acted upon. The lengthy iteration is necessary to establish the magnitude of the Japanese thrust. However, had it been extended by the addition of only a few details, it would have been compromised, having its force, pace, and energy enervated. Finally, the verb "launched" more than attacks; it launched a series of sentences which structurally (i.e., in form) harmonize with the acts embedded in them. The actions (i.e., their substance) and the manner of describing them (form) are one. The syntax is itself symbolic of the fast moving military operations.

The connotations from the cluster of "last nights" do more than support the emotional responses rising from "in the quiet of the night when all were abed and defenseless." The cluster is the turning point in a chain of emotive phrases. Prior to the "last night" series, descriptions are relatively mild and basically denotative: "suddenly and deliberately" (2), "deliberately planned" (13), "deliberately sought to deceive" (14), and "false statements" (15). Following the cluster and supported by it is a chain of increasingly stronger phrases: a mild "surprise offensive" (26), a slightly stronger "premeditated invasion" (33), the strong "this form of treachery" (37), and the vehement "unprovoked and dastardly" (42). As the descriptions of the Japanese actions become stronger, so also does the language which responds. Later shifts in verb and voice which describe the response of the United States will be noted.

Finally, the stress which the language contributes, sustains and intensifies the general emphasis of the "last night" passage (20–25). "Yesterday" has three syllables, the first being accented. The phrase "last night" has two accented syllables, relatively equal in stress. Each "last night" is encircled by "attack" or "attacked." The stress pattern of the language is a bombardment. The final line (25) begins with a conjunction which readies the listener for the final "to top it all off." Thus "and," too, is a term of some stress and strength. "And this morning," a phrase of four syllables, the first three accented, concludes the bombardment.

How well this discourse is managed is seen best by examining some alternatives. Compare "Last night Japanese forces attacked Hong Kong" (21) with: (a) *Japanese forces attacked Hong Kong last night,* or (b) *last night Hong Kong was attacked by Japanese forces.* Alternative (a) maintains the active voice, emphasizing Japanese forces. But the immediacy of "last night" is lost when the phrase concludes the thought. The arrangement also negates the effect produced by accent and stress. "Japanese" contains three syllables, relative stress being unaccented, unaccented, accented. Bombardment by stress is weaker. Further, alternative (a) significantly changes the range of the connotative values of "last night," which now modifies Hong Kong and which divides the emotional response. Sympathy goes out to the people of Hong Kong who experienced catastrophy during the night, yet this relieves somewhat the intensity of the negative emotional response centered on the Japanese, the central actors in the night. Alternative (b) is also unable to capitalize fully on the connotative values of "last night." The passive construction of (b) slows the pace; it also makes the subject, "Japanese forces," a marginal part of the sense. Yet the "last night" series (20–25) is the speaker's final statement about yesterday's activities. He soon directs his listeners (27–29) to respond positively. Their active responses are directed to and focused on something central, not marginal.

Finally, the passive construction of alternative (b) puts the places attacked prior to the act of attack and the attacking forces. Place names, Malaya, Hong Kong, Guam, are presented to the listener first, and though the places are scattered over geography, mentioning them first tends to fix them within a general geographical framework. Anchoring the place names makes the image somewhat static. In the active construction (20–25), the image has more movement. The attacks push on places which are in turn pushed over geographical distance enlarging the area of the conflict. The image thus better foreshadows the concluding, explicit reference to a surprise offensive "extending throughout the Pacific area" (26–27).

Roosevelt's conclusion is introduced by the formal, logical sign, "therefore" (26). His demonstration concluded, the speaker again shifts posture, removing himself altogether from the discussion. He chooses to let a transcendental power suggest action. He personifies: "The facts . . . speak for themselves" (27). The information could have been conveyed in other ways: *the facts . . . are clear; the facts . . . are obvious; the facts . . . are self-evident; the facts . . . are self-explanatory.* But, "facts . . . speak. . . ." To whom? Directly, which none of the alternatives above manages quite as well, to "the people of the United States," the subject of the following sentence. How do the people respond? What do they do? Verbs (28) indicate that they use their intellects and power to reason. They have "formed their opinions and well understand." So powerful were the facts that they spoke; so reasoned were the people that they needed no guidance to arrive at a conclusion. No intermediary stands between the facts and the people of intellect. What conclusion had the people "already" (28) reached? To support the action which the speaker announces he has "already" taken (30–32).

The people of the United States are presented as acting on the danger before their Government. Though the danger is not well defined, they understand the "implications" and react positively. When the speaker first mentions the danger he embeds it in his statement about the people (27–29). Their positive response envelops danger, thereby minimizing it.

The speaker's treatment of the situation and the course of action asserts a commonplace of democratic decision making: the people (27–29), the president (30), the troops (30–31) act jointly. Though they act jointly, the people are presented as having the power to effect decisions.[32] The point is demonstrated by rearranging the speaker's language so that it violates the commonplace:

The facts of yesterday and today speak for themselves. As Commander-in-Chief of the Army and Navy, I have directed that all measures be taken for our defense. The people of the United States, understanding well the implications to the very life and safety of our nation, have already formed their opinions as to the necessity of this action.

---

[32] *The power structure upon which the democracy rests compares favorably with that of the enemy: the Emperor, the troops, the people, the latter recognized by their omission. Two reasons partially explain the absence of any formal recognition of the Japanese people, thereby implicatively numbering them among the enemy. First, the conflict does not become one between people; the enemy scapegoat is clearly displayed and well-defined to allow reactions to center on it. Second, the people have to be handled as a totality, as an entity. Even were it possible to define some as "enemy" and others as "friend" the difficulties would have been great. Fine distinctions would have necessitated logical and legalistic development which would have slowed and weakened the movement of the address. The problem would have been only slightly less difficult had the speaker said categorically: The United States has no quarrel with the Japanese people. (Substitute the word German for Japanese in this sentence and it becomes Woodrow Wilson's position in his "War Message" on April 2, 1917. Roosevelt's treatment of the Japanese people is quite different from Wilson's treatment of the German people.) Quite apart from the fact that the Japanese had made American citizens part of the conflict, the speaker, perhaps ahead of the mass of men, realized that such a statement, with its overtone of righteousness, had no place in the mid-twentieth century. War was total. To have said publicly that the people of Japan were not a part of the conflict would have involved the speaker in an untruth, at worst, or in "mere rhetoric," at best. These charges he had earlier levied against Japan.*

To take the action which the logic of the people demanded, man must act. The speaker shifts stance to act in their behalf: "directed" (30) and "taken" (31) indicate reinvolvement with immediate circumstances. He has been reporting. Now he leads: "I direct" (31), "I believe" (35), "I interpret" (35), "I assert" (36), "I ask" (42). Henceforth energies are marshalled and thrust upon the circumstances which face the country. In the prepositional phrase of interrelation and interaction, "between the United States and the Japanese Empire" (43–44), the United States is mentioned first, giving an additional sense of thrust to our energies. After the speaker announces that the "facts of yesterday . . . speak for themselves," the United States becomes active and positive in its response to those facts. The shift in movement is marked when compared to earlier activity, lines 1–3 being but one example.

The turning point in this address having been reached, the events of yesterday now sustain and support the energy of the country. "That always will our whole nation remember the character of the onslaught against us" (31–32)[33] is in a syntactically dependent position. Though the clause is somewhat awkward and forced, it does foreshadow the first comment about the ultimate outcome (33–34): "no matter how long it may take" (33) which tempers hopes of a quick conclusion. The introductory qualification needs its present emphasis so that listeners' hopes may not be falsely supported. Had the speaker said: *the American people . . . will win through to absolute victory, no matter how long it may take,* listeners might have missed the qualification. Patience, determination, and fortitude are connoted to counterbalance the zeal with which the people, who had "already" (28) reached a judgment, meet the challenge. The zeal is not destroyed, but protected: zeal often becomes impatient when detours or setbacks delay progress. The "righteous might" (34) not only provides alliteration and balance for "premeditated invasion" (33), but also triggers a new chain of images: from "righteous might" (34) to "God" (41) to "Sunday" (43). "God" in medial position reflects backward and forward.

Though the specific "I" has emerged to act, his actions vary. What he is and what he does are partially revealed by the choice of verbs. Three verbs (35–37) point to intellectual activity: "I believe," "I interpret," "I assert." Having earlier "directed" and "taken" (30–31), he now becomes an observer of evidence and a commentator thereon. A

---

[33] *In drafts I, II, and III this line reads: "Long will we remember the character of the onslaught against us." In draft III "long" is struck and "always" substituted. "Always," positive and categorical, is stronger than "long," a relative term. "Always" also better suits the historical overtones in the address and the emphasis on future time. "Long" appears again in line 33, but the repetition serves no rhetorical purpose.*

slow reading of lines 35–37 reveals the tentative, cautious, distant quality of the prose. These lines contain three dependent clauses; no other lines in the address contain as many. Moving through the clauses, the speaker searches for and examines present signs as a basis for his "assertion" (36): "that this form of treachery shall never again endanger us."[34]

Following this intellectual-activity statement, long in the sense of distance and tone and by word count the longest in the address, Roosevelt shifts posture again, jolting listeners to a blunt recognition of present difficulty. "Hostilities exist" (38) is his shortest and most direct statement. Yet so mild, so objective, and so matter-of-fact is it that it functions as understatement. Responses spill out and over it; reactions are some variant of "that puts it mildly." Emotional responses to the events are stronger than this statement about the events. Thus, some response spills into lines 38–39 finding resolution in, and providing support for, the judgment, "grave danger" (39).

"Hostilities exist" has another function. Though the future is of concern, listeners could not long tolerate intellectual analysis of the present and future. They might allow the speaker to speculate, but their impulses were for direct action, having "already" (28) reached a judgment. Yet the distant quality of understated assessment dulls somewhat the listener's emotional edge, taking his mind momentarily off the present; it rests the mind before that mind has to accept the judgment of "grave danger" (39). When the speaker turns from intellectual analysis to the present, he indicates that he has not forgotten immediate concerns. He meets the present head-on.

Earlier the facts spoke to the people. They must now look directly at the facts: "There is no blinking at the fact that our people, our territory and our interests are in grave danger" (38–39). In the first three drafts, this line read: "There is no mincing the fact. . . ." The revision is clearer and stronger. To give "no mincing" meaning, an auditor might have to find a context which helped explain it; for example, I'll not mince words. "Blinking at" is clearer; its meaning is rooted in a com-

---

[34] In drafts I, II, and III line 35 begins: "I speak the will of the Congress and of the people. . . ." This construction is much more emphatic and direct than what the speaker actually said, and he would not have been inaccurate had he said it. Yet his actual statement better suits the commonplace of democracy which holds that the President speaks as a result of what the people and their representatives will. He does not say: I speak your will; but rather, "as a result of your will, I speak." And he gives the appearance of "sounding out" the will and responding to it, even as he knows what that will is. Also in drafts I, II, and III lines 36–37, "but will make it very certain" read "but will see to it." The latter expresses the tone of determination but not the finality of the result. The actual statement is categorical in a way which "see to it" is not; moreover "see to it" is somewhat more colloquial than "make it very certain."

mon physiological process and in common usage. Moreover, a sound-sense equivalent to "blinking at" is "winking at"; and if sense were a problem the latter would easily furnish it. A sound-sense equivalent to "mincing" is "wincing"; the listener who sought meaning analogically would be misled.

The degree of danger is finally stated explicitly. Though "grave" (39) is judgmental, it stands as "fact" (38). Heretofore "grave danger" has been suggested in various ways: "character of the onslaught against us," "premeditated invasion." The statement, "There is no blinking at the fact that our people, our territory and our interests are in grave danger," is a modified repetition and an extension of "The people of the United States have already formed their opinions and well understand the implications to the very life and safety of our nation." New meaning is given to "implications." They are "grave."

However, the gravity (38–39) is tempered by its position in the general pattern. It is preceded by the statement which indicates that we shall respond so that this "form of treachery shall never again endanger us" (35–37) and followed by a statement prophesying "inevitable triumph" (40–41). The tensions created by gravity are counterbalanced by terms of positive outlook and mounting force: "confidence," "unbounding determination," "inevitable triumph," "God." The danger, though grave, is relative and does not connote absolute destruction; "unbounding," "inevitable," and "God" are positive, categorical, and absolute. The swing of the pendulum of construction is longer, stronger, and more forceful than the swing of destruction. Contributing to the strength of the categorical language of lines 40–41 is the loose, but recognizable and felt, iambic meter, which moves firmly to the inevitable triumph, "so help us God."

"With confidence in our armed forces, with the unbounding determination of our people, we will gain the inevitable triumph, so help us God" is the leader-speaker's oath, publicly taken.[35] So commonplace is its structure, diction, and rhythm that once underway the line cannot be turned nor resisted. Its sweep catches all. The well-being of the country is set in the timeless future. Rearranging the structure, diction,

[35] *Lines 40–41 do not appear in drafts I, II, and III. Harry Hopkins suggested the addition, though his second phrase read: "with faith in our people," Roosevelt altered this to "with the unbounding determination of our people." Since Roosevelt's entire statement (40–41) is a confession of faith, the excision of "faith" in Hopkins' second phrase is appropriate. Too, "faith" has but one syllable, making Hopkins' second phrase shorter than his first and third and restricting somewhat the "swelling" movement of the entire confession. Roosevelt's "the unbounding determination of" is not only phonetically more expansive, but the additional syllables support better the rhythmical movement to the climactic "so help us God."*

and rhythm upsets the sweep of the statement and weakens it as an article of faith: *We have confidence in our armed forces; our people have unbounding determination; we will gain the inevitable triumph, so help us God.*

The oath taken, no further thematic development is necessary. Only the formal declaration of war (42–44) remains.[36] However, additional modified repetitions woven into the formal declaration enlarge and emphasize thoughts, values, and feelings in the address. "Unprovoked and dastardly" (42) not only balances but also intensifies and enlarges "suddenly and deliberately" (1). The common "Japan" (43) is elevated to the "Japanese Empire" (44) which parallels the formality of "Empire of Japan" (3). The final elevation is one of form only; "dastardly Japan" is the subject. The day, as well as the date, has value. "Sunday" (43) extends and reinforces the connotations of "last night"; its proximity to "dastardly" (43) intensifies the connotations of that term, even as "Sunday" itself gains value and support from its relationship to "God" (41).

The generic negation, the Devil term, is "dastardly" (42).[37] Its appearance is surprising; its choice, apt. Though not a term of the vernacular, it is clear, conveying a dimension of the speaker's moral indignation. As the Devil term, it stands in antithesis to "righteous might" (34), "Sunday" (43), and "God" (41). It has another function. It is as close as the President, speaking to the country in a public chamber, could come to profanity. The movement from "dastardly" to "bastardly" is slight and swift; the latter epitomizes one dimension of the public mood on December 8, 1941. Infamous duplicity has become bastardly duplicity. The leader-speaker controls his emotions before his public and again maintains his distance from his public. Yet the adroit and adept rhetorical choice effects a public catharsis.

The dependent clauses in the final statement (42–44) allow the speaker his judgment of "unprovoked and dastardly" and permit a return to the past: "a state of war has existed." Though the safe and settled formal language of diplomacy and the settled and safe historical past are upset and sundered by the declaration, its formality suggests that the United States respects the conventions of diplomacy even when confronted by dastardly actions outside the accepted conven-

---

[36] *In drafts I, II, and III line 42 begins: "I, therefore, ask that . . ." The formal, logical sign is unnecessary; Roosevelt's logical and rhetorical conclusion was lines 40–41; lines 42–44 are a formal, ceremonial statement dictated by the nature of the occasion and the place.*

[37] *For an interesting observation on the word "dastardly," which bears on the discussion here, see Barbara W. Tuchman, "History by the Ounce," Harper's, CCXXXI (July 1965), 74.*

tions. Formality marks the conclusion as well as the beginning. The address has come full circle.

III

Elements of the "War Message," which sets forth Roosevelt's doctrine of demonology, need to be placed in the larger context of culture. We do not suggest that a direct, causal relationship exists between the speech and events in the culture. Cultural conditions have multiple causes; only rarely have they single causes. We do maintain that an address helps to create and sustain a "climate" which justifies activities, even though the speech itself is not *the* cause of any activity. The language of an address by the President of the United States in a time of crisis helps to create and sustain a "climate." It also begins to pattern the perceptions and the behaviors of those who hear it. Optimum language bears on perceptions and behaviors in a cohesive way.

The emphasis which Roosevelt gave to topics in his address provided his listeners an orientation to the Japanese and to the nature of the conflict; these had immediate and long-range consequences. He emphasized the infamous duplicity behind the Japanese attacks; they carefully and deliberately prepared their military onslaught, masking their preparations behind neutral and formal diplomatic negotiations. American political folklore and the folklore of the people generally hold such behavior in low esteem; the regard is revealed by popular maxims: the man who wears two hats; the man who works both sides of the street; the man who talks out of both sides of his mouth. Roosevelt's portrayal of the Japanese and their activities fits the sense of such widely known and well-understood commonplaces.

Too, the people of the United States generally knew little about the Orient, and stereotypes were associated with it and the Oriental long before December 7, 1941. Even in California, Washington, Oregon, and Arizona, where most of the Japanese in the United States lived, they were little known. The "War Message" enlarged and intensified the stereotypes. These long-standing cultural raw data were supported. On December 7–8, 1941, additional raw data came to the country from the news reports of the conflict. The latter data especially were confusing and anxiety-provoking. To them, Roosevelt gave meaning as he structured a climate of opinion and orientation.

The President's description of the Japanese Government as marginal, fraudulent, dangerous, and capable of dastardly-bastardly behavior has its parallels in the treatment of the Japanese people in the United States. For example, the Commanding General of the Western Defense Command, John L. DeWitt, agreed, as did others, that the Japanese on the West Coast had not engaged in any sabotage after Pearl Harbor. Yet on February 14, 1942, General DeWitt publicly cited the absence of sabotage as "a disturbing and confirming indication that such action will be taken."[38]

On February 6, 1942 in Los Angeles, Mayor Fletcher Brown, "an able and honest public official,"[39] said in a radio broadcast: "If there is intrigue going on, and it is reasonably certain that there is, right here is the hot bed, the nerve center of the spy system, of planning for sabotage." The Mayor recommended "removal of the entire Japanese population—alien and native born—inland for several hundred miles."[40] Ultimately Japanese were removed to relocation centers, but those details lie outside the present concern.

United States military policy toward Nisei, American citizens of Japanese-American ancestry, reflected Roosevelt's portrayal of the Japanese in his "War Message." Nisei inducted into military service before Pearl Harbor were, shortly after December 7, 1941, given honorable discharges, with no specification of cause of dismissal. In March, 1942, potential Nisei inductees were arbitrarily assigned IV-F, ineligible for service because of physical defects; on September 1, 1942, this classification was changed to IV-C, the category ordinarily used for enemy aliens.[41]

Not until January 28, 1943 were Japanese-American citizens eligible for military service on the same basis as other citizens. President Roosevelt publicly approved, saying "no . . . citizen of the United States should be denied the democratic right to exercise the responsibilities of his citizenship, regardless of his ancestry."[42]

Of course the general anxiety of the civilian population immediately after December 7, 1941 contributed to development of hostility toward Japanese-Americans. It also made the civilian population susceptible to the rantings of professional patriots, witch hunters, alien haters, and others with private aims, who used the cover of wartime patriotism to achieve what they wanted to do in peace time—rid the West Coast of the Japanese.

Numerous private citizens and officials of Government sought to redress such attacks upon the Japanese-Americans. For example, the San Francisco *Chronicle*, December 9, 1941, said editorially: "The roundup of Japanese citizens in various parts of the country . . . is not

---

[38] *Carey McWilliams*, Prejudice: Japanese-Americans, Symbol of Racial Intolerence (*Boston, 1945*), *p. 110; Dorothy S. Thomas and Richard S. Nishimoto,* The Spoilage (*Berkeley, Calif., 1946*), *p. 6.*
[39] *McWilliams, p. 252.*
[40] *Alexander H. Leighton,* The Governing of Men (*New York, 1964*), *p. 20.*
[41] *Thomas and Nishimoto, p. 56.*
[42] Ibid.

a call for volunteer spy hunters to go into action. Neither is it a reason to lift an eyebrow at a Japanese, whether American-born or not. . . ."[43] On balance, the voices of tolerance and fair play were the weaker.

President Roosevelt's "War Message" prepared the United States for a long military operation against the Japanese Empire. The nature of the political and military enemy abroad was clear. Indirectly, he supported a civilian army, equally anxious to do its duty, in its march against the civilian "enemy" at home. The "War Message" offered no protection to Japanese-Americans. In the terms of the analysis here presented these people were given "no weight." Two phrases, "the people of the United States" (27–28) and "the American people" (33–34), only implicitly recognize this group, and as a group they were a minority and a marginal part of the culture. Moreover, the two phrases do not contain positive terms; they contain dialectical terms, which reflect value judgments.[44] In this connection, note that Roosevelt's public statement in support of the induction of Nisei into the military service (p. 435) did contain the positive term, "citizen," which transcends even as it anchors such dialectical phrases as "the American people."

We do not suggest that had the "War Message" contained and emphasized the term, citizen, the address itself would have diminished attacks upon Japanese-Americans in the United States. We note only the absence of any protection, a matter of weighting, and thus conclude that the address contributed to the development of a climate for the attacks by strengthening the attitudes of those who, for whatever reasons, wished to attack. Equally important, those wishing to counter such attacks could find in the "War Message" of the President little to support them and the Japanese-Americans.

Though the primary concern of this analysis has been the language of the "War Message," we have in the paragraphs above extended the analysis and speculated upon possible cultural effects. We have done so because the major elements of any speech work on listeners' perceptions and when other factors, rhetorical and non-rhetorical, are present, perceptions become translated into behavior.

IV

We have centered on the language of an address because in much published criticism language has been neglected in favor of analysis of other factors in the rhetorical environment. What goes on in a speech? has been the question. To say that the "last night" series (20–25) is parallel and repetitive, thus contributing force and energy, is

---

[43] Ibid., *pp. 17–18. Also see, McWilliams, pp. 271–273.*
[44] *Richard M. Weaver,* The Ethics of Rhetoric (*Chicago, 1953*), *pp. 16; 187–188.*

to say too little. We have tried to link the section with preceding and following configurations of language and to analyze closely the section itself. The "last night" series is not in the active voice merely because the active voice is clear, direct, and emphatic, among other things. Had the series been structured differently (see p. 429) the image would have become static and less able to sustain the speaker's conclusion about the magnitude of Japanese activity: "a surprise offensive extending throughout the Pacific area" (26–27). The "last night" series is the turning point in the address; following it the United States becomes active, reacting to the events of yesterday. Had the series been structured differently, the Japanese actors would have become less central and the reaction of the United States more difficult to direct and focus. Though it makes sense for the speaker to choose to handle the Japanese Empire as "marginal" in his first recognition of the enemy (1–3), it makes equal sense for him to place the Japanese in a central position in the "last night" series. To expose linguistic strategies of rhetoric one needs thus to see language as "moving," as "linking," and as "ordering a hierarchy."

The critical posture here has been microcosmic; the analysis, microscopic. Such analysis does not reveal much about discourse in general. Yet it may be helpful to those who search for orderly methodologies for dealing with all rhetorical activities and processes. The interplay of the microcosmic and the macrocosmic may yield insights which will lead to more fruitful and productive rhetorical criticism.

The Dramatistic Approach

RHETORICAL Criticism: A Burkeian Approach
by Bernard L. Brock

Rhetorical criticism requires that a critic make a descriptive, interpretative judgment regarding the effectiveness of rhetoric. In this process the critic not only needs a language to describe man as he responds to his world but also a theoretical framework for understanding man's basic rhetorical tendencies. Kenneth Burke's dramatistic approach to rhetoric provides the critic with such a language and theoretical structure; thus many critics have turned from Aristotle to Kenneth Burke for a rhetorical theory to guide them in making critical judgments.

Kenneth Burke's rhetorical philosophy evolves from the view that language is a strategic response to a situation.[1] This view underlies all his major works: *Counter-Statement,* 1931; *Permanence and Change,* 1935; *Attitudes Toward History,* 1937; *The Philosophy of Literary Form,* 1941; *A Grammar of Motive,* 1945; *A Rhetoric of Motives,* 1950; *Rhetoric of Religion,* 1961; and *Language as Symbolic Action,* 1966. His writing, though unified, is quite complex, and thus has been difficult to apply as a system of rhetorical criticism.

Structuring Burke's rhetorical theories into a system of rhetorical criticism necessitates (1) identifying his philosophy of rhetoric, (2) framing a structure that reflects his philosophy, and (3) showing how the dramatistic approach unites substance and rhetorical devices. Then, one can suggest specifically how the rhetorical critic might use Kenneth Burke's dramatistic approach.

Burke's Philosophy of Rhetoric

The foundation of Burke's rhetorical philosophy can be found in *Attitudes Toward History.* He indicates that one assesses the "human situation" and shapes appropriate attitudes by constructing his conception of the world around him. In the process he perceives "certain functions or relationships as either friendly or unfriendly," and then, weighing his own potential against probable opposition, he selects his strategies for coping with the "human situation."[2] These strategies or stylized answers are symbols that reflect attitudes.[3]

By starting with man as he reacts symbolically to his environment, Kenneth Burke arrives at the function of rhetoric—"the use of words

---

[1] *Kenneth Burke,* The Philosophy of Literary Form, *New York, Random House, 1957, p. 3.*

[2] *Kenneth Burke,* Attitudes Toward History, *Boston, Beacon Press, 1961, pp. 3 and 4.*

[3] *Burke,* The Philosophy of Literary Form, op. cit., p. 3.

by human agents to form attitudes or to induce actions in other human agents."[4] Rhetoric originates not from "any past condition of human society," but from "an essential function of language itself." The act of using language to induce cooperation among people automatically focuses one's attention upon the language or the symbols employed.[5] From roots within its function two major concepts of Burke's philosophy of rhetoric evolve: Verbal symbols are meaningful acts in response to situations from which motives can be derived and society is dramatistic in nature.

Burke clearly demonstrates his view that verbal symbols are meaningful acts from which motives can be derived when he discusses the relationship betwen symbols and action. He points out that in acting wisely "we must name the friendly or unfriendly functions and relationships in such a way that we are able to do something about them."[6] The words that one assigns to these functions and relationships not only reveal the process of sorting out the world but also communicate an attitude that is a cue for the behavior of others. Burke clearly indicates that the act of selecting one symbol over another locks the speaker's attitude into the language. For this reason verbal symbols are meaningful acts from which human motives can be derived. These motives constitute the foundation or the substance of the speech, and through the ability to identify them by the cues in verbal symbols, Burke constructs a philosophy of rhetoric.

In considering the nature of society as fundamental to Burke's philosophy of rhetoric, one can turn to *Permanence and Change.* Burke explains that "action and end" as opposed to "motion and position" and "dramatistic terms" rather than "theories of knowledge" are appropriate in discussing human conduct.[7] The human tendency toward action makes a dramatistic vocabulary appropriate to the study of man. Burke describes man's society as a dramatistic process, which includes the elements of hierarchy, acceptance and rejection, and guilt, purification, and redemption.

Hierarchy generates the structure of our dramatistic society. In society the social, economic, and political powers are unevenly divided. Power endows individuals with authority. Authority, in turn, establishes definite relationships among people, reflecting the degree to which they possess power. These relationships can be viewed as a ladder of authority or the hierarchy of society.[8] As people accept their positions

[4] *Kenneth Burke,* A Rhetoric of Motives, *New York, Prentice-Hall, 1950, p. 41.*
[5] Ibid., *p. 43.*
[6] *Burke,* Attitudes Toward History, op. cit., *p. 4.*
[7] *Kenneth Burke,* Permanence and Change, *Los Altos, Calif. Hermes, 1954, p. 274.*
[8] Ibid., *p. 276.*

and work within a hierarchical structure, the structure is "bureaucratized" or given a definite organization. With the bureaucratization of the hierarchy comes order in society. This process makes hierarchy the structural principle of a dramatistic society.[9]

Another element of the dramatistic society is the concept of acceptance and rejection. Burke's philosophy of rhetoric is based upon man's propensity to accept or reject the "human situation" and his attempts to symbolize his reaction. The concept of acceptance follows from a positive reaction to the human situation and rejection from a negative reaction. Burke explains, however, that language allows the negative or rejection: "The essential distinction between the verbal and the non-verbal is in the fact that language adds the peculiar possibility of the Negative."[10] In nature everything is positive: What exists, simply exists. The negative or nonexistence results from language or the separation of a symbol from the thing that it represents. Burke further points out that historically, since there is no negative in nature, the negative in language has probably developed through the negative command, "Do not do that."[11] Language enables man to accept or reject his hierarchical position or even the hierarchy itself. Acceptance results in satisfaction and order, whereas rejection results in alienation and disorder.

To complete the dramatistic process, guilt, purification, and redemption must be understood. These terms represent the effects of acceptance and rejection of the hierarchy. Whenever man rejects the traditional hierarchy, he "falls," and thereby acquires a feeling of guilt. Burke feels that guilt is inherent in society because man cannot accept all the impositions of his traditional hierarchy. Conditions change, resulting in the rejection of some of the traditional modes. Also, each social institution—the family, school, church, clubs, and other "bureaucracies"—has its own hierarchy, and when any one of these hierarchies is in conflict with another, rejection of one will inevitably occur.[12] Since man cannot satisfy all the requirements of his traditional hierarchies, he is saddled with eternal guilt.[13]

The nature of hierarchy itself is another source of eternal guilt. Hierarchy, representing differences in authority between superiors and inferiors in society, always creates mystery. Moreover, inferiors always want to move up within the hierarchy or to change its nature. The

[9] Ibid., *pp. 282 and 283.*
[10] *Kenneth Burke, "A Dramatistic View of the Origins of Language: Part One,"* The Quarterly Journal of Speech, *XXXVIII (October 1952), p. 252.*
[11] Ibid., *p. 253.*
[12] *Burke,* Permanence and Change, *op: cit., p. 283.*
[13] Ibid., *p. 284.*

sense of mystery that one class holds for another class and the upward tendencies of the lower classes create a guilt that is inherent in the hierarchy itself.[14]

Burke compares the eternal secular guilt with original sin. However, neither secular guilt nor original sin result from man's "personal transgression, but by reason of a tribal or dynastic inheritance."[15] In spite of this fact, guilt still sets off a psychological reaction in man. Guilt reduces social cohesion and gives man the feeling of being less than whole, so that he strives to have his guilt canceled or to receive redemption. The act of purification may be either mortification or victimage. Mortification is an act of self-sacrifice that relieves man of his guilt, whereas victimage is the purging of guilt through a scapegoat that symbolizes society's guilt. To be effective, the process of purification and redemption must be balanced: The act of purification must be equivalent to the degree of guilt if one is to receive redemption. Psychological guilt, purification, and redemption result from the rejection of hierarchy.

Burke believes that the dramatistic nature of society may be explained by considering the interrelationships among the (1) concepts of the hierarchy, (2) acceptance and rejection, and (3) guilt, purification, and redemption. This assumption together with the belief that verbal symbols are meaningful acts in response to situations from which motives can be derived, is the philosophic foundation of Kenneth Burke's system of rhetoric.

Structure in Burke's Rhetoric

Burke's dramatistic approach to rhetoric supplies a language that describes man as he responds to his world, but to be useful to the critic, this language must be transformed into a more definite structure. Two concepts are basic to such a structure: identification and the pentad. These concepts can be used as rhetorical tools to discover the attitudes expressed within a speech and to describe its dramatistic process. Identification is the major tool used to discover the attitudes and the dramatistic process: The pentad provides a model for their description.

In Burke's philosophy of rhetoric the verbal symbol carries within it the attitude of the speaker. Burke states that the basic function of rhetoric is "the use of words by human agents to form attitudes or to induce actions in other human agents."[16] In connection with this function Burke introduces identification, which is defined in *A Rhetoric of*

[14] Ibid., *p. 287.*
[15] Ibid.
[16] *Burke,* A Rhetoric of Motives, op. cit., *p. 41.*

Motives: "A is not identical with his colleague, B. But insofar as their interests are joined, A is *identified* with B. Or he may *identify himself* with B even when their interests are not joined, if he assumes that they are, or is persuaded to believe so."[17]

Burke sees identification as an "acting together" that grows out of the ambiguities of substance. Both division and unity exist simultaneously, division because each person remains unique and unity or "consubstantiality" to the extent that the actors share a locus of motives.[18] The speaker, whose attitudes are reflected in his language, will accept some ideas, people, and institutions, and reject others; his audience will to some extent both agree and disagree with him. To the extent that the audience accepts and rejects the same ideas, people, and institutions that the speaker does, identification occurs. The speaker's language will reveal the substance out of which he expects to identify with his listeners. Consciously or unconsciously his words will reveal his attitudes or stylized answers to the obvious divisions. The concept of identification will help the critic structure his insight into a speaker's sense of unity by grouping strategies into "clusters" until relationships indicate the speaker's concept of hierarchy and reflect the process of guilt, purification, and redemption. Identification, the tool that is applied directly to verbal symbols for the purpose of uncovering relationships among these symbols, is the critic's key to the speaker's attitudes and the dramatistic process.

Kenneth Burke labels one of his procedures as "statistical." He advises gathering lists of recurrent terms until the critic begins to sense those that are essential—which terms cluster and where. Beginnings and endings, he argues, are particularly likely to reveal key terms. The critic may verify the hypotheses he constructs by making a reasoned case for the consistencies of the parts and the whole, that is, for the manner in which the terms fit the apparent situation. In his work there is no substitute for intelligence and effort, both made sensitive by wide experience. But Kenneth Burke does suggest one more aid to finding and proving rhetorical structure.

Kenneth Burke's well-known pentad is this aid. He uses the device as a model to describe the dramatistic nature of society. In *A Grammar of Motives* Burke attempts to answer the question, What is involved when we say what people are doing and why they are doing it? As an explanation he introduces and defines the pentad:

We shall use five terms as generating principle of our investigation. They are: Act, Scene, Agent, Agency, and Purpose. In a rounded state-

---

[17] Ibid., *p. 20. Emphasis Burke's.*
[18] Ibid., *p. 21.*

ment about motives, you must have some word that names the act *(names what took place, in thought or deed), and another that names the* scene *(the background of the act, the situation in which it occurred); also, you must indicate what person or kind of person* (agent) *performed the act, what means or instruments he used* (agency), *and the* purpose.[19]

Men will disagree about the nature of these terms or what they represent, but they necessarily must provide some answer to these five questions: "what was done (act), when or where it was done (scene), who did it (agent), how he did it (agency), and why (purpose)."[20] Thus, these terms are the key to human motives, because statements assigning motives "arise out of them and terminate in them."

Any man, Kenneth Burke argues, will tend to feature in his thought one of these terms—although, of course, each may have his own vocabulary that reveals the set that dominates his thinking and speaking. Some men, for example, will ask "What?" and then "Who?" Others "Who?" and then "What?" In Burke's language an "act-agent" ratio properly labels the first sequence of questions, and an "agent-act" the second. Given his starting place (and starting places tend to be ending places), we can trace a constellation of ratios in a coherent, well-formed piece of rhetorical discourse. Domination by agent may reveal agent-act concern, then agent-purpose, then agent-scene. Given a man's dominant set or his term, a critic may trace the complete pentad in a discourse; but probably a few ratios, and especially one term, will typify that discourse.

The pentad, together with a knowledge of identification and the innately dramatistic nature of human society, provides the critic with a vocabulary and way of proceeding. To understand the process, however, the critic must understand each term of the pentad with its corresponding philosophy and terminology.

Following from the belief that society is dramatistic in nature, the *act* for Burke is the central term in the pentad. The act answers the question, What is done? Burke explains that when the act is *featured* in discourse, the philosophy that dominates within the speech is realism.[21] In defining realism Burke cites Aristotle: "Things are more or less real according as they are more or less *energeia* (*actu,* from which our 'actuality' is derived)."[22] The act or realism is not just existence, it is "taking form." The realist grammar begins with a tribal concept and

---

[19] *Kenneth Burke,* A Grammar of Motives, *Englewood Cliffs, N.J., Prentice-Hall, 1945, p. x. Italics Burke's.*
[20] Ibid. *parentheses Burke's.*
[21] Ibid., *p. 128.*
[22] Ibid., *p. 227.*

treats the individual as a participant in substance. The terminology that is associated with the act would suggest an emphasis upon verbs.[23]

The term scene corresponds with a philosophy of materialism. Burke cites Baldwin's *Dictionary of Philosophy and Psychology* to define materialism, "that metaphysical theory which regards all the facts of the universe as sufficiently explained by the assumption of body and matter, conceived as extended, impenetrable, eternally existent, and susceptible of movement or change of relative position."[24] Darwin's *The Origin of the Species* illustrates some of the terminology that accompanies the domination of the scene: "accidental variation," "conditions of existence," "adjustment," "natural selection," and "survival of the fittest."[25]

The scene, which is the background or setting for the drama, is generally revealed in secular or material terms. Since it is the background, the emphasis can easily shift from the scene to the act, agent, agency, or purpose. But these shifts, which will be slight if the rhetoric is consistent, will continue to reveal the determinism of the material situation characteristic with the domination of a mind by the scene.

The philosophy corresponding to *agent* is idealism. Burke again turns to Baldwin's dictionary in defining idealism: "In metaphysics, any theory which maintains the universe to be throughout the work of reason and mind."[26] Burke points to terms such as "ego," "self," "superego," "mind," "spirit," and "oversoul" as a sign of a stress on agent. He also suggests that treating ideas—church, race, nation, historical periods, cultural movements—as "personalities" usually indicates idealism. Furthermore, the dominance of agent grows out of the spiritualization of the family. Whenever important human economic relations have become idealized or spiritualized, the agent is featured.

We have considered three terms from the pentad—act, scene, and agent. For convenience of explanation, we may draw together agency and purpose in a means-ends relationship. Burke points out that "means are considered in terms of ends." But as "you play down the concept of final cause (as modern science does), . . . there is a reversal of causal ancestry—and whereas means were treated in terms of ends, ends become treated in terms of means."[27] To illustrate this shift between means and ends Burke shows that money, which is the means (agency) of obtaining goods and services, simultaneously is the end (purpose) of work.[28]

[23] Ibid., *p. 228.*
[24] Ibid., *p. 131.*
[25] Ibid., *p. 153.*
[26] Ibid., *p. 171.*
[27] Ibid., *p. 276.*
[28] Ibid., *pp. 108 and 276.*

In featuring the means, or agency, the pragmatic philosophy is dominant. Pragmatism is defined by Kant as "the means necessary to the attainment of happiness."[29] John Dewey refers to his pragmatist doctrine as Instrumentalism. In modern science, method or agency dominates all other terms of the human drama. Along with modern science and pragmatism, the technologically oriented line of action has appeared and is identified with terms such as "useful," "practical," and "serviceable."[30] William James not only asserts that Pragmatism is "a method only," but he goes on to indicate that "consequence," "function," "what it is 'good for,'" and "the difference it will make to you and me" are pragmatic evaluations. However, pure pragmatism goes beyond James to transcend purpose, as in the applied sciences, when the method is built into the instrument itself. At this point agency becomes the focus of the entire means-ends relationship.

The process may be reversed, featuring *purpose* rather than agency. The philosophy corresponding to purpose is mysticism.

The Baldwin dictionary describes the philosophy of mysticism:

. . . those forms of speculative and religious thought which profess to attain an immediate apprehension of the divine essence or essence or the ultimate ground of existence. . . . Penetrated by the thought of the ultimate of all experience, and impatient of even a seeming separation from the creative source of things, mysticism succumbs to a species of meta-physical fascination.[31]

Mysticism equals purpose because of such references as "the divine essence" and "the creative source." In mysticism the element of unity is emphasized to the point that individuality disappears. Identification often becomes so strong as to indicate the "unity of the individual with some cosmic or universal purpose."[32] The universal purpose becomes a compulsive force against which everything else is judged.

Aristotle and Plato reflect elements of mysticism. Aristotle's mystic absolutism can be seen in his purpose for society—happiness. Plato's mysticism goes well beyond that of Aristotle and completely equates "good" and "purpose." His concept of reality is drawn from his idea of the "good," and the rest of the world is arranged in accordance with this ideal.[33]

---

[29] Ibid., p. 275.
[30] C. Wright Mills, Power, Politics and People, New York, Ballantine, 1963, p. 441.
[31] Burke, A Grammar of Motives, op. cit., p. 287.
[32] Ibid., p. 288.
[33] Ibid., pp. 292–294.

In any discussion of human motivation all five terms of the pentad are necessary. To the extent that these terms are represented as separate elements there is division; however, to the extent that one term is featured and the other terms seem to grow out of this term, there is unity. As a model, the pentad can express both possibilities, unity and division.

To illustrate the operation of the pentad Kenneth Burke compares it to the human hand. He likens the five terms to the fingers, which are distinct from each other and possess their own individuality; yet, at the same time, they merge into a unity at the palm of the hand. With this simultaneous division and unity (identification) one can leap from one term to another or one can move slowly from one to another through the palm.[34] The analogy illustrates both aspects of the operation of the pentad—flexibility of movement and unity and division. The analogy also brings out another aspect of Burke's rhetorical philosophy and structure (which will be discussed later), whereby the palm represents the unity of the terms or substance of the speech that is discovered by determining which of the terms is featured in the discourse.

At this point identification and the pentad merge as tools in Burke's rhetorical structure. The speaker may use the strategy of featuring the agent, then, in proving a point, proceed to an agent-scene or agent-act ratio. Then he may move to purpose and finally to agency. Each step represents an act that symbolizes an attitude, and the total series represents the dramatistic process in action as the speaker sees it. Using identification one can discover each step that reflects the speaker's stylized answers to situation or strategies, and with the pentad as a model the steps can be plotted so as to describe the dramatistic process operating in the speech.

Unity of Substance and Rhetorical Devices

The structural tools of identification and the pentad bring about a unity of strategies or rhetorical devices and substance. This unity aids the critic in understanding and explaining man's basic rhetorical tendencies.

Substance, according to Burke, is the philosophical foundation of the message in the speech. In the analogy with the hand, substance represents the palm—the place where all other elements are unified. To define substance Burke starts with Webster's dictionary, "the most important element in any existence; the characteristic and essential import, purpose."[35] He concludes, literally, that substance is that which stands beneath something. The principle of substance is important in

---

[34] Ibid., *p. xxiv.*
[35] Ibid., *p. 21.*

Burke's rhetorical criticism because all speeches must establish a substance that is the context for the speech or the key to the speaker's attitudes. Burke defines four types of substance: familial, directional, geometric, and dialectic. Each type of substance is established when a given term from the pentad is featured to the point that it dominates the speech.

Geometric substance places an object in its setting as "existing both in itself and as part of its background."[36] This featuring leads to a materialistic notion of determinism, which is most consistent with the term scene from the pentad.

When agent is featured, a familial substance evolves. "It stresses common ancestry in the strictly biological sense, as literal descent from material or paternal sources."[37] However, the concept of family is often spiritualized so as to include social and national groups and beliefs.

Directional substance is also biologically derived; however, it comes "from a sense of free motion."[38] The feeling of movement provides a sense of motivation from within. All generalizations such as "the reasonable man" or "the economic man" fall in this category. Also, "terminologies that situate the driving force of human action in human passion"[39] and treat emotion as motive are classified as directional substance. Finally, "doctrines that reduce mental states to materialistic terms treat motion as motive," and encourage "sociological speculation in terms of 'tendencies' or 'trends.'"[40] The term agency follows from this context.

The last type of substance, dialectic, reflects "the ambiguities of substance, since symbolic communication is not a merely external instrument, but also intrinsic to men as agents. The motivational properties of dialectic substance characterize both the 'human situation' and what men are 'in themselves.'" The ambiguity of external and internal motivation creates dialectic substance. "The most thoroughgoing dialectic opposition, however, centers in that key pair: Being and Not-Being."[41] For example, Burke shows how dialectic substance can transcend to the "ultimate abstract Oneness." "The human person, for instance, may be derived from God as a 'super-person.' Or human purpose may be derived from an All-Purpose, or Cosmic Purpose, or Universal Purpose, or Absolute Purpose, or Pure Purpose, or Inner Purpose, etc."[42] The term central to dialectic substance is *purpose*.

---

36 Ibid., *p. 29.*
37 Ibid.
38 Ibid., *p. 31.*
39 Ibid., *p. 32.*
40 Ibid.
41 Ibid., *p. 34.*
42 Ibid., *p. 35.*

Substance as the context of the speech is the source of the subject matter for the speech, of the motives and attitudes of the speaker, and of the strategies or rhetorical devices used by the speaker. The structural tools—identification and pentad—are useful in determining and describing both the substance of the speech and the speaker's rhetorical strategies. The critic is able to uncover the substance of the speech and the rhetorical strategies used by the speaker for three reasons: (1) because verbal symbols are meaningful acts that are strategies reflecting the attitudes of the speaker, (2) because these attitudes represent the speaker's acceptance and rejection of the present hierarchy of society, and (3) because acceptance and rejection results in the eternal process of guilt, purification, and redemption for society. The total interrelationship of terms and processes represents Kenneth Burke's dramatistic approach to rhetoric.

In addition to the basic dramatistic structure of his rhetorical system, Burke discusses various special rhetorical elements. The two most significant ones for rhetorical criticism are the forms of style and the levels of symbolic action. These special devices aid in describing the dramatistic process but are subordinate to the process. In *Counter-Statement* Burke indicates that form "is an arousing and fulfillment of desires."[43] Form provides sequence—one portion of the speech prepares the audience for another part. The kinds of form that Burke discusses are syllogistic and qualitative progression, repetitive form, conventional form, and minor or incidental form.[44] Because each speaker will structure his speech differently, various kinds of form aid the critic in establishing patterns for the development of the dramatistic process that takes place. Syllogistic progression is a step-by-step method of presenting an argument: "To go from A to E through stages B, C, and D is to obtain such form."[45] Qualitative progression is more subtle in its development. The speaker's ideas progress through the construction of a mood or a quality rather than in a step-by-step manner. Repetitive form is the process of restating a principle in a slightly different manner. The speaker may vary the details of the support with each restatement but the principle is consistent. Conventional form is the persuasive appeal resulting from "form as form." A syllogism or analogy has appeal simply as form, independent of the argument constructed. Any work also has minor or incidental forms "such as metaphor, paradox, disclosure, reversal, contraction, expansion, bathos, apostrophe, series, chiasmus—which can be discussed as formal events in themselves."[46]

[43] *Kenneth Burke,* Counter-Statement, *Chicago, University of Chicago Press, 1957, p. 124.*
[44] Ibid., *pp. 124–126.*
[45] Ibid., *p. 124.*
[46] Ibid., *p. 127.*

After describing the types of form, Burke indicates that there is both interrelation and conflict of forms. "Progressive, repetitive, and conventional and minor forms necessarily overlap."[47] However, the important thing is not that they overlap but that their use should be identified. The critic should discover the circumstances under which various forms are used. Not only do formal principles intermingle, they also conflict. Burke suggests that a writer may create a character who, according to the plot or the logic of fiction, "should be destroyed." But if this character is completely accepted by the audience, it may desire "the character's salvation." "Here would be a conflict between syllogistic and qualitative progression."[48] Burke also indicates that syllogistic and repetitive forms, as well as repetitive and conventional forms, may conflict. The form that the dramatistic process takes is another tool available to the rhetorical critic.

In describing the dramatistic process, the levels of symbolic action can also be of value to the critic. The speaker strategically selects verbal symbols that represent his attitudes and which he feels will be effective in inducing "identification" with his audience. One method of describing these symbols is to categorize them according to their level of symbolic action or level of abstraction. In *The Philosophy of Literary Form* Burke considers three levels of symbolic action: the bodily or biological level, the personal or familistic level, and the abstract level.[49] In *Rhetoric of Religion* he discusses "four realms to which words may refer. . . . First, there are words for the natural. . . . Second, there are words for the socio-political realm. . . . Third, there are words about words,"[50] and fourth, there are "words for the 'supernatural.' "[51] Again, these levels of symbolic action and realms for words will overlap in discourse, but the critic should identify their occurrence along with the circumstances in which they occur.

Burke's special devices of form, levels of symbolic action, and realms to which words may refer represent tools for rhetorical criticism that can be used in conjunction with his basic dramatistic structure of rhetoric. These techniques, taken together, constitute a definite system in which the substance of the speech and the rhetorical tools used by the speaker interlock.

Suggestions for the Rhetorical Critic

In executing rhetorical criticism the critic not only describes man's rhetorical efforts but also makes interpretative judgments based upon

---

[47] Ibid., *p. 128.*
[48] Ibid., *p. 129.*
[49] *Burke,* The Philosophy of Literary Form, op. cit., *pp. 31–33.*
[50] *Kenneth Burke,* The Rhetoric of Religion, *Boston, Beacon Press, 1961, p. 14.*
[51] Ibid., *p. 15.*

rhetorical norms or principles. Burke's dramatism gives the critic a method of analysis capable of establishing, at least tentatively, rhetorical norms through repeated application. Only through such application, sufficiently wide and varied to give a thorough test to the principles that arise, can critics be certain that they have a firm basis for judgment. But the long-range task necessitates consistent use of a critical vocabulary. The point of this essay has been to outline such a vocabulary and to suggest how the terms that compose it work together and aid the critic in making rhetorical judgments.

The following are some specific ways that a critic can use Burke's dramatistic rhetoric in establishing norms or principles for judgment:

1. Each of the Burkeian rhetorical concepts can be used to discover stylistic characteristics of a given speech or speaker.
2. The critic can observe the conditions under which various strategies are employed, thereby inductively constructing a theory about their use.
3. He can identify correlations in the use of various strategies to learn more about man's basic rhetorical tendencies and patterns. The relationship between substance and other strategies could be especially interesting.
4. The critic should study the stages in the dramatistic process— acceptance and rejection, and guilt, purification, and redemption— and determine how each stage is developed and stressed.
5. He should also discover the circumstances in which incompatible strategies are used—for example, when two terms from the pentad receive equal stress so that no discernible substance evolves.

Kenneth Burke's dramatistic approach to rhetoric provides the critic with a language and theoretical structure that allows him to describe man as he responds to his world and to understand man's basic rhetorical tendencies. With such a system the critic is able to make descriptive, interpretative judgments regarding the effectiveness of rhetoric.

A Pentadic Analysis of Senator Edward Kennedy's Address to the People of Massachusetts, July 25, 1969
by David A. Ling

On July 25, 1969 Senator Edward Kennedy addressed the people of the state of Massachusetts for the purpose of describing the events surrounding the death of Miss Mary Jo Kopechne. The broadcasting net-

From *The Central States Speech Journal*, XXI, 2 (Summer 1970), 81–86. Used by permission of the author and the Central States Speech Association. Mr. Ling is an instructor in speech at Wayne State University.

works provided prime time coverage of Senator Kennedy's address, and a national audience listened as Kennedy recounted the events of the previous week. The impact of that incident and Kennedy's subsequent explanation have been a subject of continuing comment ever since.

This paper will examine some of the rhetorical choices Kennedy made either consciously or unconsciously in his address of July 25th. It will then speculate on the possible impact that those choices may have on audience response to the speech. The principle tool used for this investigation will be the "Dramatistic Pentad" found in the writings of Kenneth Burke.

The Pentad and Human Motivation

The pentad evolved out of Burke's attempts to understand the bases of human conduct and motivation. Burke argues that "human conduct being in the realm of action and end . . . is most directly discussible in dramatistic terms."[1] He maintains that, in a broad sense, history can be viewed as a play, and, just as there are a limited number of basic plots available to the author, so also there are a limited number of situations that occur to man. It, therefore, seems appropriate to talk about situations that occur to man in the language of the stage. As man sees these similar situations (or dramas) occurring, he develops strategies to explain what is happening. When man uses language, according to Burke, he indicates his strategies for dealing with these situations. That is, as man speaks he indicates how he perceives the world around him.

Burke argues that whenever a man describes a situation he provides answers to five questions: "What was done (act), when or where it was done (scene), who did it (agent), how he did it (agency), and why (purpose)."[2] Act, scene, agent, agency, and purpose are the five terms that constitute the "Dramatistic Pentad." As man describes the situation around him, he orders these five elements to reflect his view of that situation.

Perhaps the clearest way to explain how the pentad functions is to examine Burke's own use of the concept in *The Grammar of Motives*.[3] In that work, Burke argues that various philosophical schools feature different elements of the human situation. For example, the materialist school adopts a vocabulary that focuses on the scene as the central element in any situation. The agent, act, agency and purpose are

[1] *Kenneth Burke*, Permanence and Change (*Los Altos, California: Hermes Publications, 1954*), p. 274.
[2] *Kenneth Burke*, A Grammar of Motives and a Rhetoric of Motives (*Cleveland: The World Publishing Company, 1962*), p. xvii.
[3] Ibid., *pp. 127–320.*

viewed as functions of the scene. On the other hand, the idealist school views the agent (or individual) as central and subordinates the other elements to the agent. Thus, both the materialist and the idealist, looking at the same situation, would describe the same five elements as existing in that situation. However, each views a different element as central and controlling. In Burke's own analysis he further suggests philosophical schools that relate to the other three elements of the pentad: the act, agency and purpose. What is important in this analysis is not which philosophical schools are related to the featuring of each element. What is important is that as one describes a situation his ordering of the five elements will suggest which of the several different views of that situation he has, depending on which element he describes as controlling.

This use of the pentad suggests two conclusions. First, the pentad functions as a tool for content analysis. The five terms provide a method of determining how a speaker views the world. Indeed, this is what Burke means when he says that the pentad provides "a synoptic way to talk about their [man's] talk-about [his world]."[4]

A second conclusion that results from this analysis is that man's description of a situation reveals what he regards as the appropriate response to various human situations. For example, the speaker who views the agent as the cause of a problem, will reflect by his language not only what Burke would call an idealist philosophy, but he will be limited to proposing solutions that attempt to limit the actions of the agent or to remove the agent completely. The speaker who finds the agent to be the victim of the scene not only reflects a materialist philosophy but will propose solutions that attempt to limit the actions of the agent or to remove the agent completely. The speaker who finds the agent to be the victim of the scene not only reflects a materialistic philosophy but will propose solutions that would change the scene. Thus, an individual who describes the problem of slums as largely a matter of man's unwillingness to change his environment will propose self-help as the answer to the problem. The person who, looking at the same situation, describes man as a victim of his environment will propose that the slums be razed and its inhabitants be relocated into a more conducive environment. The way in which a speaker describes a situation reflects his perception of reality and indicates what choices of action are available to him.

The Pentad and Rhetorical Criticism

But what has all this to do with rhetoric? If persuasion is viewed as the attempt of one man to get another to accept his view of reality as

4 Ibid., *p. 56.*

the correct one, then the pentad can be used as a means of examining how the persuader has attempted to achieve the restructuring of the audience's view of reality. Burke suggests how such an analysis might take place when he says in *The Grammar:* "Indeed, though our concern here is with the Grammar of Motives, we may note a related resource of Rhetoric: one may deflect attention from scenic matters by situating the motives of an act in the agent (as were one to account for wars purely on the basis of a 'warlike instinct' in people): or conversely, one may deflect attention from criticism of personal motives by deriving an act or attitude not from traits of the agent but from the nature of the situation."[5]

Thus, beginning with the language of the stage, the Pentad, it is possible to examine a speaker's discourse to determine what view of the world he would have an audience accept. One may then make a judgment as to both the appropriateness and adequacy of the description the speaker has presented.

Edward Kennedy's July 25th Address

Having suggested the methodology we now turn to a consideration of Senator Edward Kennedy's address of July 25th to the people of Massachusetts. The analysis will attempt to establish two conclusions. First, the speech functioned to minimize Kennedy's responsibility for his actions after the death of Miss Kopechne. Second, the speech was also intended to place responsibility for Kennedy's future on the shoulders of the people of Massachusetts. These conclusions are the direct antithesis of statements made by Kennedy during the speech. Halfway through the presentation, Kennedy commented: "I do not seek to escape responsibility for my actions by placing blame either on the physical, emotional trauma brought on by the accident or on anyone else. I regard as indefensible the fact that I did not report the accident to the police immediately."[6] Late in the speech, in discussing the decision on whether or not to remain in the Senate, Kennedy stated that, "this is a decision that I will have finally to make on my own." These statements indicated that Kennedy accepted both the blame for the events of that evening and the responsibility for the decision regarding his future. However, the description of reality presented by Kennedy in this speech forced the audience to reject these two conclusions.

Edward Kennedy—Victim of the Scene. The speech can best be examined in two parts. The first is the narrative in which Kennedy explained

---

[5] Ibid., *p. 17.*

[6] *This and all subsequent references to the text of Senator Edward Kennedy's speech of July 25, 1969 are taken from* The New York Times, *CXVII (July 26, 1969), p. 10.*

what occurred on the evening of July 18th. The second part of the speech involved Kennedy's concern over remaining in the U.S. Senate.

In Kennedy's statement concerning the events of July 18th we can identify these elements:

The scene (the events surrounding the death of Miss Kopechne)
The agent (Kennedy)
The act (Kennedy's failure to report immediately the accident)
The agency (whatever methods were available to make such a report)
The purpose (to fulfill his legal and moral responsibilities)

In describing this situation Kennedy ordered the elements of the situation in such a way that the scene became controlling. In Kennedy's description of the events of that evening, he began with statements that were, in essence, simple denials of any illicit relationship between Miss Kopechne and himself. "There is no truth, no truth whatever to the widely circulated suspicions of immoral conduct that have been leveled at my behavior and hers regarding that night. There has never been a private relationship between us of any kind." Kennedy further denied that he was "driving under the influence of liquor." These statements function rhetorically to minimize his role as agent in this situation. That is, the statements suggest an agent whose actions were both moral and rational prior to the accident. Kennedy then turned to a description of the accident itself: "Little over a mile away the car that I was driving on an *unlit* road went off a *narrow bridge* which had *no guard rails* and was built on a *left angle* to the road. The car overturned into a *deep pond* and immediately filled with water" (emphasis mine). Such a statement placed Kennedy in the position of an agent caught in a situation not of his own making. It suggests the scene as the controlling element.

Even in Kennedy's description of his escape from the car, there is the implicit assumption that his survival was more a result of chance or fate than of his own actions. He commented: "I remember thinking as the cold water rushed in around my head that I was for certain drowning. Then water entered my lungs and I actually felt the sensation of drowning. But somehow I struggled to the surface alive." The suggestion in Kennedy's statement was that he was in fact at the mercy of the situation, and that his survival was not the result of his own calculated actions. As an agent he was not in control of the scene, but rather its helpless victim.

After reaching the surface of the pond, Kennedy said that he "made repeated efforts to save Mary Jo." However, the "strong" and "murky" tide not only prevented him from accomplishing the rescue, but only succeeded in "increasing [his] state of utter exhaustion and alarm."

The situation described is, then, one of an agent totally at the mercy of a scene that he cannot control. Added to this was Kennedy's statement that his physicians verified a cerebral concussion. If the audience accepted this entire description, it cannot conclude that Kennedy's actions during the next few hours were "indefensible." The audience rather must conclude that Kennedy was the victim of a tragic set of circumstances.

At this point in the speech Senator Kennedy commented on the confused and irrational nature of his thoughts, thoughts which he "would not have seriously entertained under normal circumstances." But, as Kennedy described them, these were not normal circumstances, and this was *not* a situation over which he had control.

Kennedy provided an even broader context for viewing him as the victim when he expressed the concern that "some awful curse did actually hang over the Kennedys." What greater justification could be provided for concluding that an agent is not responsible for his acts than to suggest that the agent is, in fact, the victim of some tragic fate.

Thus, in spite of his conclusion that his actions were "indefensible," the description of reality presented by Kennedy suggested that he, as agent, was the victim of a situation (the scene) over which he had no control.

Kennedy's Senate Seat: In the Hands of the People. In the second part and much shorter development of the speech, the situation changes. Here we can identify the following elements:

The scene (current reaction to the events of July 18th)
The agent (the people of Massachusetts)
The act (Kennedy's decision on whether to resign)
The agency (statement of resignation)
The purpose (to remove Kennedy from office)

Here, again, Kennedy described himself as having little control over the situation. However, it was not the scene that was controlling, but rather it was agents other than Kennedy. That is, Kennedy's decision on whether or not he will continue in the Senate was not to be based on the "whispers" and "innuendo" that constitute the scene. Rather his decision would be based on whether or not the people of Massachusetts believed those whispers.

Kennedy commented: "If at any time the citizens of Massachusetts should lack confidence in their senator's character or his ability, with or without justification, he could not, in my opinion, adequately perform his duties and should not continue in office." Thus, were Kennedy to decide not to remain in the Senate it would be because the people of

Massachusetts had lost confidence in him; responsibility in the situation rests with agents other than Kennedy.

This analysis suggests that Kennedy presented descriptions of reality which, if accepted, would lead the audience to two conclusions:

1. Kennedy was a tragic victim of a scene he could not control.
2. His future depended, not on his own decision, but on whether or not the people of Massachusetts accepted the whispers and innuendo that constituted the immediate scene.

Acceptance of the first conclusion would, in essence, constitute a rejection of any real guilt on the part of Kennedy. Acceptance of the second conclusion meant that responsibility for Kennedy's future was dependent on whether or not the people of Massachusetts believed Kennedy's description of what happened on the evening of July 18th, or if they would believe "whispers and innuendo."

Rhetorical Choice and Audience Response

If this analysis is correct, then it suggests some tentative implications concerning the effect of the speech. First, the positive response of the people of Massachusetts was virtually assured. During the next few days thousands of letters of support poured into Kennedy's office. The overwhelming endorsement was as much an act of purification for the people of that state as it was of Kennedy. That is, the citizenry was saying "We choose not to believe whispers and innuendo. Therefore, there is no reason for Ted Kennedy to resign." Support also indicated that the audience accepted his description of reality rather than his conclusion that he was responsible for his actions. Guilt has, therefore, shifted from Kennedy to the people of Massachusetts. Having presented a description of the events of July 18th which restricts his responsibility for those events, Kennedy suggested that the real "sin" would be for the people to believe that the "whispers and innuendoes" were true. As James Reston has commented, "What he [Kennedy] has really asked the people of Massachusetts is whether they want to kick a man when he is down, and clearly they are not going to do that to this doom-ridden and battered family."[7] The act of writing a letter of support becomes the means by which the people "absolve" themselves of guilt. The speech functioned to place responsibility for Kennedy's future as a Senator in the hands of the people and then provided a description that limited them to only one realistic alternative.

While the speech seemed to secure, at least temporarily, Kennedy's

[7] *James Reston, "Senator Kennedy's Impossible Question," The New York Times, CXVII (July 27, 1969), section 4, p. 24.*

Senate seat, its effect on his national future appeared negligible, if not detrimental. There are three reasons for this conclusion. First, Kennedy's description of the events of July 18th presented him as a normal agent who was overcome by an extraordinary scene. However, the myth that has always surrounded the office of the President is that it must be held by an agent who can make clear, rational decisions in an extraordinary scene. Kennedy, in this speech was, at least in part, conceding that he may not be able to handle such situations. This may explain why 57 per cent of those who responded to a CBS poll were still favorably impressed by Kennedy after his speech, but 87 per cent thought his chances of becoming President had been hurt by the incident.[8]

A second reason why the speech may not have had a positive influence on Kennedy's national future was the way in which the speech was prepared. Prior to the presentation of Kennedy's speech important Kennedy advisers were summoned to Hyannis Port, among them Robert McNamara and Theodore Sorensen. It was common knowledge that these advisers played an important role in the preparation of that presentation. Such an approach to the formulation was rhetorically inconsistent with the description of reality Kennedy presented. If Kennedy was the simple victim of the scene he could not control, then, in the minds of the audience that should be a simple matter to convey. However, the vision of professionals "manipulating" the speech, suggested in the minds of his audience that Kennedy may have been hiding his true role as agent. Here was an instance of an agent trying to control the scene. But given Kennedy's description of what occurred on July 18th such "manipulation" appeared unnecessary and inappropriate. The result was a credibility gap between Kennedy and his audience.

A third factor that may have mitigated against the success of this speech was the lack of detail in Kennedy's description. A number of questions relating to the incident were left unanswered: Why the wrong turn? What was the purpose of the trip, etc.? These were questions that had been voiced in the media and by the general public during the week preceding Senator Kennedy's address. Kennedy's failure to mention these details raised the speculation in the minds of some columnists and citizens that Kennedy may, in fact, have been responsible for the situation having occurred: the agent may have determined the scene. If this was not the case, then Kennedy's lack of important detail may have been a mistake rhetorically. Thus, while Kennedy's speech resulted in the kind of immediate and overt response necessary to secure his seat in the Senate, the speech and the conditions under

---

[8] "C.B.S. Evening News," C.B.S. Telecast, July 31, 1969.

which it was prepared appear to have done little to enhance Kennedy's chances for the Presidency.

Conclusion

Much of the analysis of the effect of this speech has been speculative. Judging the response of an audience to a speech is a difficult matter; judging the reasons for that response is even more precarious. The methodology employed here has suggested two conclusions. First, in spite of his statements to the contrary, Kennedy's presentation portrayed him, in the first instance, as a victim of the scene and in the second, the possible victim of other agents. Second, the pentad, in suggesting that only five elements exist in the description of a situation, indicated what alternative descriptions were available to Kennedy. Given those choices, an attempt was made to suggest some of the possible implications of the choices Kennedy made.

Writing Rhetorical Criticism

FUNDAMENTALLY, each critic must decide what he is trying to do when dealing with material that interests him; in making this decision he assumes a perspective toward his work. The consciousness of a perspective, like the consciousness of anything else, may wax and wane. Since the critic works from assumptions that affect the shape of his final materials, he must be aware of his point of view.

This book is premised on the contentions that various perspectives can be differentiated from one another and that distinguishing them will aid those interested in criticism to see its potentialities more clearly.

The Characteristics of the Perspectives

We would like to reiterate the characteristics of the various perspectives in outline form. We do so to enable one to compare and contrast them quickly. Furthermore, we hope that presenting them in this form will stress a general truth, that is, that generalizations are possible only at the expense of omitting detail. The characteristics we attribute are abstracted from a large collection of unique writing about rhetoric and rhetorical criticism. Therefore, like any set of labels, ours will have considerable variety, and some theoretical and critical works will be difficult to classify, given our headings.

The Traditional Perspective

1. *Orientation.* The critic concentrates on the speaker (or the apparent source of discourse). His purpose is to consider the speaker's response to the rhetorical problems that the speaking situation poses.
2. *Assumptions.*
   a. Society is stable; people, circumstances, and rhetorical principles are fundamentally the same throughout history.
   b. Rhetoricians have discovered the essential principles of public discourse.
   c. Rhetorical concepts are reasonably discrete and can be studied apart from one another in the process of analyzing rhetorical discourse.
   d. A reasonably close word-thought-thing relationship exists. Rhetorical concepts accurately describe an assumed reality.
3. *Consensus.* Rhetoricians generally agree on what the ideal rhetorical process is.

The Experiential Perspective

1. *Orientation.* No single element or rhetorical principle can be assumed as the starting point for criticism. Thus, the critic, depending

on his sensitivity and knowledge, must make the fundamental choice of emphasis.

2. *Assumptions.*
   a. Society is in a continual state of process.
   b. An infinite combination of concepts, strategies, and principles are available for the study of public discourse.
   c. Any system of categorizing is arbitrary and does not accurately reflect an assumed external reality for extended periods of time.
3. *Consensus.* No special pattern exists for the study of public discourse. Therefore, discourse must continually be studied afresh.

The Perspective of the "New Rhetorics"

1. *Orientation.* Rhetoric and criticism must find a starting point in the interaction of man and his social environment.
2. *Assumptions.*
   a. Society is in process, but fairly stable relationships can be found that govern man's interactions with his environment.
   b. A flexible framework may be constructed for the study of public discourse.
   c. Man's symbol system influences his perception of reality.
3. *Consensus.* A unified rhetorical framework is necessary for the productive study of rhetoric and criticism.

Making Basic Choices in Writing Criticism

Some writers believe that criticism is an intuitive process for which one has or has not the necessary instinct and experience. Although they recognize that the critic implicitly makes numerous choices as he engages in the act of criticism, these writers are apt to assert that making these choices explicit tears the process of criticism apart and destroys it. There is certainly an element of truth to their position; but if we are to think about and teach criticism, we must attempt to delineate at least in general terms some of the decisions the rhetorical critic makes implicitly or explicitly each time he attempts to write. We suggest five centers of interest. We do *not* suggest the order given as an ideal sequence through which the critic should move, nor do we imply that these centers of interest will always be distinct or that they exhaust the possibilities.

1. *Focus.* The critic should struggle to find a focus for his work. His interest will probably be aroused by some specific public discourse, but he should keep his interest general for a time, asking: "Just what is it that attracts me? What is it that puzzles me?" Obviously, the *it* is vague. Probably the critic's focal point will gradually take the form

of a thesis statement. At any rate, the focus should be capable of unifying all the necessary elements of the critical act.

2. *Vocabulary.* In describing, interpreting, and evaluating a speech, a career, a movement, a dominant strategy, and so forth, a writer needs a critical vocabulary that is instrumental to the sort of interest he is trying to develop. He may look toward established theories for his terms; he may select among them or he may develop them for his particular task. Two important influences on his choice of vocabulary will be his past experience and the necessities imposed by the nature of the material with which he is dealing.

3. *Perspective.* Any criticism will automatically have a starting point even though the critic does not consciously make such a decision. However, if the decision is consciously made (which in some cases will mean that the critic seeks to uncover his perspective), he can be more certain that it is consistent with his material, his purpose, and the sort of judgments he intends to make. Consciously selecting a perspective from which to approach his work will probably enable the critic to make his writing more consistent internally.

4. *Judgment.* The critic should determine the sort of judgment he wishes to make. We have already indicated that a given criticism may be descriptive, interpretive, or evaluative. Traditional criticism tends to be primarily descriptive, and the criticism typifying the new rhetorics tends to be primarily interpretive. In general, rhetorical critics have backed away from the evaluative. Too often, however, we believe that critics have failed to think through the implications of their choice of purpose. The critic must be certain that his purpose is consistent with the focus of his thesis and the end he wishes to achieve through his work.

5. *End.* The critic must conceive carefully the end he wishes to achieve through his work. Does he wish to provide insight into a given body of public discourse? And, if so, what sort of insight will suffice? Or is he primarily interested in building rhetorical theory or in influencing society? The broad end he wishes to achieve is the underlying motive that influences all his decisions. If the critic is concerned with applying or building theory, his critical vocabulary and probably his perspective will have been determined for him. If he is interested in influencing society, he will almost certainly be required to make explicitly or to suggest strongly an evaluative judgment. On the other hand, so intimately related are his basic choices in writing criticism that selecting a critical vocabulary, perspective, and type of judgment may determine the ultimate end the critique can serve.

Whether criticism is an intuitive process or whether choices such as these briefly outlined are made explicitly, they must be made because they are inherent in the critical act. In our opinion, the critic will profit in terms of the clarity and insight of his work by striving to become aware of the basic choices he makes and of the implications of these choices.

A fully formed, coherent piece of criticism is an ideal that may always be just beyond the grasp of the critic. But the impulse to criticize is a human one. Developing the capacity to strive carefully and conscientiously toward the ideal is humanizing.

On the Distinctness of the Perspectives:
Some Further Examples of Criticism

WE have taken the position that the critic must inevitably make a number of choices relevant to his procedures. However, at a time when rhetorical criticism is pre-paradigmatic and many theories are competing for acceptance, we discover that critics frequently make choices that seem to combine elements of what we have purported to be distinct perspectives. For example, an essay may exhibit a critical orientation that is typical of an experiential perspective, but the vocabulary employed may be neo-Aristotelian or dramatistic. It is not difficult to imagine that a critic might use a basically semantical-grammatical approach but take a speaker orientation, or a critical orientation with descriptive-historical development of the subject matter, or a number of other possible combinations.

We believe that in most cases of mixed forms the assumptions made by the critic will line up substantially with one perspective or another. However, what seems to us to be a hybrid form may prove to be one of a number of instances that demonstrate a fresh perspective. Regardless of the classificatory system, a crossing and overlapping will always reflect a process reality and the arbitrary and ambiguous nature of language.

The student of criticism will be interested in studying a variety of cases and will soon learn not to expect all of them to be "pure." In seeing what others have done, he will discover possibilities for his own work.

One interest, which seems to be gaining strength and is especially likely to result in fresh combinations of approaches, is called the "movement study." The difficulty of defining what is meant by a rhetorical movement and some suggestions for dealing with them are concerns of Leland M. Griffin's ground-breaking article, "The Rhetoric of Historical Movements." Griffin's case study, "The Rhetorical Structure of the 'New Left' Movement," is a particularly striking example drawn upon a plethora of current materials and, in method, exhibits a shift toward a dramatistic vocabulary.[1] We shall include both of these essays in this section.[2]

[1] *A later work of this writer that demonstrates a completely dramatistic critical vocabulary is "A Dramatistic Theory of the Rhetoric of Movements," in William H. Rueckert (ed.),* Critical Responses to Kenneth Burke, *Minneapolis, University of Minnesota Press, 1969, pp. 456–478.*

[2] *Another highly stimulating treatment of theory for dealing with movements is Herbert W. Simons's "Requirements, Problems, and Strategies: A Theory of Persuasion of Social Movements,"* The Quarterly Journal of Speech, *LVI, 1 (February 1970), 1–11.*

The final essay included here is Michael Osborn's "Archetypal Meta-phor in Rhetoric: The Light-Dark Family," an example of the use of critical comment for illustration. But the illustration, if it is to be effec-tive, must be insightful criticism. Osborn's concern is to show the im-portance of what he calls "archetypal metaphor." We would classify the work roughly as grammatical-semantical, but perhaps work like Os-born's will contribute to insights that will structure a new rhetoric.

The Rhetoric of Historical Movements
by Leland M. Griffin

When the student undertakes the rhetorical pursuit of an individual orator, he enters a scholarly bailiwick whose boundaries are clearly demarked. Convenient temporal limits for the study are set by the ora-tor's vital dates; the speaker himself supplies the point of focus, the thread of his life a motif, and his career, analyzed and evaluated in all its ramifications from "early speech training" to climactic utterances, provides the matter of the study. Techniques of analysis and appraisal in the biographical approach have become conventionalized, and the central problem for those concerned with research in this area, for the moment at least, would appear to be one of objective rather than of method. Many useful biographical studies have been produced, many more will be, and a fund of information about orators will eventually be accumulated.

Nevertheless, the belief has taken increasing hold that approaches to the study of public address other than the biographical ought to be encouraged. The recommendation has been made,[1] for example, that we pay somewhat less attention to the single speaker and more to speakers—that we turn our attention from the individual "great orator" and undertake research into such selected acts and atmospheres of public address as would permit the study of a multiplicity of speakers, speeches, audiences, and occasions. For the student who would move in this direction, at least four approaches would seem to be available: the period study; the regional, or regional-period study; the case study, or more properly, the collection of case studies confined to a specific theme and time; and the movement study, concerned with the survey of public address, in historical movements. Of the four approaches listed, the one last mentioned has received perhaps the least attention. As with the other approaches, various questions concerning critical method and objective will confront the student who undertakes the

From *The Quarterly Journal of Speech*, XXXVIII, 2 (April 1952), 184–188. Used by permission of the author and the Speech Communication Association. Mr. Griffin is Professor of Public Address at Northwestern University.

[1] *Specifically, by Herbert A. Wichelns in "The Study of Public Address," a paper read at the 1946 conference of the Speech Association of America.*

rhetorical study of a movement. This paper undertakes to set forth some questions and suggest some answers.

I

A first question which may confront the student: *what should be the point of focus in the movement study?*

Let us say that an historical movement has occurred when, at some time in the past: 1. men have become dissatisfied with some aspect of their environment; 2. they desire change—social, economic, political, religious, intellectual, or otherwise—and desiring change, they make efforts to alter their environment; 3. eventually, their efforts result in some degree of success or failure; the desired change is, or is not, effected; and we may say that the historical movement has come to its termination.

As students of rhetoric our concern is obviously with those efforts which attempt to effectuate change, not through the forces of wealth or arms, but through the force of persuasion. In the term *historical movement,* then, *movement* is for us the significant word; and in particular, that part of the connotative baggage of the word which implies change, conveys the quality of dynamism. For as the historical movement, looked upon as a sustained process of social inference, is dynamic, and has its beginning, its progression, and its termination, so the rhetorical component of the movement is dynamic, and has its inception, its development, and its consummation. The student's task is to isolate the rhetorical movement within the matrix of the historical movement: the rhetorical movement is the focus of his study. It is to be isolated, analyzed, evaluated, and described, so that he can say, for the particular historical movement which he investigates: this was the pattern of public discussion, the configuration of discourse, the physiognomy of persuasion, peculiar to the movement.

II

A second question relates to scope: *what kind of movement should the student select for study, and how much of the movement should he study?*

The qualitative answer may be given briefly: 1. any movement, whether predominantly social, political, economic, religious, or intellectual; 2. any movement, whether present opinion considers it to have been successful or not. As students of persuasion, interested not so much in the accomplished change of opinion as in the attempt to effectuate change, we should find the rhetorical structure of the lost cause as meaningful as that of the cause victorious.

As for the quantitative answer, although movement studies are in their rudimentary stage, the practice followed in the biographical studies might well be reversed. That is, let the student take not the "biggest," but the briefest historical movement he can find. Let him take a brief movement, as long as it is a movement with adequate rhetorical remains such as he, a single investigator, can encompass with scholarly accuracy and completeness. The first movements surveyed should above all be brief, in order that the survey may be undertaken by the single scholar. For the single scholar is more likely to achieve the synoptic view essential to the effective isolation, analysis, and evaluation of the rhetorical pattern of the movement.

When studies of a number of briefer movements have been completed, when the rhetorical structures peculiar to them have been identified, researchers may then be in a better position to cope with the methodological problems involved in the segmental study, the type of study which must of necessity prevail in the survey of massive movements, such as the antislavery and the temperance movements, which might defy the labors of the single scholar.

III

A third question: *how should the student go about the business of isolating and analyzing the rhetorical movement?*

Let us say that two broad classes of rhetorical movements may be distinguished: 1. *pro* movements, in which the rhetorical attempt is to arouse public opinion to the creation or acceptance of an institution or idea; and, 2. *anti* movements, in which the rhetorical attempt is to arouse public opinion to the destruction or rejection of an existing institution or idea.

Let us say that within each movement two classes of rhetoricians may be distinguished: 1. aggressor orators and journalists who attempt, in the *pro* movement, to establish, and in the *anti* movement, to destroy; and, 2. defendant rhetoricians who attempt, in the *pro* movement, to resist reform, and in the *anti* movement, to defend institutions.

Let us say, further, that within each movement, three phases of development may be noted: 1. *a period of inception,* a time when the roots of a pre-existing sentiment, nourished by interested rhetoricians, begin to flower into public notice, or when some striking event occurs which immediately creates a host of aggressor rhetoricians and is itself sufficient to initiate the movement; 2. *a period of rhetorical crisis,* a time when one of the opposing groups of rhetoricians (perhaps through the forsaking of trite or ineffective appeals, the initiation of new arguments, the employment of additional channels of propagation, or merely through the flooding of existing channels with a moving tide of discourse) succeeds in irrevocably disturbing that balance between the groups which had existed in the mind of the collective audience; and 3. *a period of consummation,* a time when the great proportion of aggressor rhetoricians abandon their efforts, either because they are convinced that opinion has been satisfactorily developed and the cause won, or because they are convinced that perseverance is useless, or merely because they meet the press of new interests.

The foregoing assumptions may serve to establish a working hypothesis, an hypothesis, to be sure, which future studies will undoubtedly serve to emend. Such studies may indicate, for example, that during the course of most historical movements, aggressor and defendant rhetoricians are likely to be presented with the problem of establishing the credibility of "seceders"—recusants who, deserting the opposition, stand as potentially invaluable sources of testimony. Again, such studies may demonstrate that the group which would assure itself of victory must necessarily generate a flood of persuasive argument and appeal, and employ all, or nearly all, of the available channels of propagation; that, paradoxically, this necessary multiplicity of discourse, amplified beyond a perhaps indefinable optimum, will inevitably exasperate the public, lead to a loss of favorable opinion and, possibly, to ultimate defeat; and that the central problem of the rhetoricians of any cause, therefore, is to move the public to the desired action before the point of alienation is reached and reaction develops.

Some such generalized pattern as the one suggested, at any rate, may prove useful to the student when (his reading in the appropriate historical background completed, his reading in secondary works devoted to the movement itself concluded) he begins to read in the mass of discourse, and so to cope with the problem of isolating the rhetorical movement. The reading in the discourse should be chronological, proceeding from the period of inception to the period of consummation; and the reading should also be analytical. Thus, as he reads, the student will note the crystallization of fundamental issues, the successive emergence of argument, appeal, counter-argument and counter-appeal, and the sanctions invoked by rhetoricians of both sides; he will note, by a process of imaginative re-living in the age, by an analysis of consequences, the persuasive techniques which were effective and those which were ineffective; and he will note a time, very likely, when invention runs dry, when both aggressor and defendant rhetoricians tend to repeat their stock of argument and appeal. He will naturally note, during the period of inception, the emergence of a group of aggressor rhetoricians and a group of defendant rhetoricians; and he will note, as the movement progresses, the gradual swelling of their ranks. He will be concerned with the discourse of both writers and speakers; with those who invented and those who echoed; with lecturers, pulpit, political, legislative, academic, and forensic orators, with editors, journalists, novelists, dramatists, and poets. He will also note the development and employment of media of discourse. Assuming the movement selected occurred during the first half of the nineteenth century, for example, he will find the opposing groups using some or all of such channels of propagation as books, pamphlets, broadsides, tracts, almanacs, newspapers, and periodicals, the pulpit, the lecture platform, the political rostrum, the stump, and the stage. He may note the development of organizations designed to facilitate the dissemination of argument, such as the lecture bureau, the committee of correspondence, and the political party. Finally, as he reads, the student will note the increasing circulation and the ultimate extent of the appeal; the development of audiences; and as the movement spreads, the geographical and social stratification of these audiences.

IV

A fourth question: *what rhetorical criteria should the student use in evaluating the public address of the movement?*

A first and obvious principle is that the critic must judge the effectiveness of the discourse, individual as well as collective acts of utterance, in terms of the ends projected by the speakers and writers. He will not need to be cautioned against the error of assuming a necessary identity between ends publicly announced and those privately maintained.

A second, and derivative, principle is that the critic must judge the discourse in terms of the theories of rhetoric and public opinion indigenous to the times. This principle means that the critic will operate within the climate of theory of rhetoric and public opinion in which the speakers and writers he judges were reared, and in which they practiced; in other words, that he will measure practice in terms of the theories available, not to himself, but to the speakers and writers whom he judges. The principle means that the student of an early nineteenth-century movement will ground his judgments in the theories of Blair and Campbell; that the critic of a movement occurring within the last thirty years, on the other hand, will operate within the theoretical atmosphere created by latter-day rhetoricians, that he will acknowledge the presence of the propagandist, and the various devices of propaganda, in the theoretical atmosphere of the times. The principle demonstrates, one might add, that a need exists for further background studies in the development of theories of rhetoric and public opinion, and in the history of the teaching of rhetoric as well—studies such as those completed by Guthrie, Utterback, and Perrin; and a need for a body of period and regional-period studies which will give us specific demonstrations of the integration of theory and practice.

V

A fifth question: *how should the student go about the process of synthesis involved in reporting the movement?*

The general method of presenting the material, I believe, should be that of the literary historian rather than that of the statistician. That is, we should strive for movement studies which will preserve the idiom in which the movement was actually expressed. The movement, then, will not be completely atomized; rather it will be so presented as to convey the quality of dynamism, the sense of action, chronologically; and even chapters essentially topical will be chronological in development.

The inherent difficulty arising from the necessity for the researcher to treat speakers, speeches, and audiences analytically, while at the same time he endeavors to present the movement synthetically, in a broad, chronological manner, may be resolved by a method of turning the movement on a spit, as it were, by piercing it now from one angle, now from another, as the movement spirals to its consummation. Thus, by centering on a significant series of debates, or a convention, or a political rally, of 1830; by centering on an important editorial, pamphlet, or book of 1831; by centering on an effective drama, satire, or sermon of 1832, he may accomplish the business of pushing the movement forward, and of piercing it from many angles. By threading the careers of selected speakers through the course of his study, the writer will achieve a sense of unity. In short, he will make use of the techniques of the case study and of the biographical study.

Obviously the writer will reinforce and enliven the study with ample quotation from the discourse; he will make full use of memoirs, letters, and other contemporary documents to give the study flesh and blood.

It is equally obvious that the introductory chapters of the study will be devoted to backgrounds—to the historical background and the rhetorical background of the movement; that the body of the study will be devoted to description, analysis, and criticism of the inception, development, and consummation phases of the rhetorical movement; that the final chapters will serve to reset the rhetorical movement in the matrix of the historical movement, the historical movement itself in the times; and that it will summarize the rhetorical pattern peculiar to the movement and present other pertinent conclusions.

VI

The reply to questions concerning primary objective in any particular movement study should now be apparent: essentially, the student's goal is to *discover*, in a wide sense of the term, the rhetorical pattern inherent in the movement selected for investigation.

But as the historical movement becomes a discrete field for research in public address, as studies employing the movement approach accumulate, certain broader results may become manifest. From the identification of a number of rhetorical patterns, we may discover the various configurations of public discussion, whether rhetorical patterns repeat themselves when like movements occur in the intervals of time, whether a consistent set of forms may be said to exist. We may learn something more about orators—even about the great orators—whom we may come to see from a new perspective, since they rarely speak except within the framework of a movement; and we may come to a more acute appreciation of the significance of the historically insignificant speaker, the minor orator who, we may find, is often the true fountainhead of the moving flood of ideas and words. By seeing numbers of men in an act and atmosphere of discourse, we may indeed produce fresh transcripts of particular moments of the past. We may come closer to discovering the degree of validity in our fundamental assumption: that rhetoric has had and does have a vital function as a shaping agent in human affairs. And finally, we may arrive at generalizations useful to those anticipated writers of the comprehensive histories of public address—histories that might well be conceived in terms of movements rather than of individuals.

The Rhetorical Structure of the "New Left" Movement: Part I
by Leland M. Griffin

> *Politics above all is drama.*
> —Kenneth Burke

Kenneth Burke has made a distinction between positive, dialectical, and ultimate terms. "Left" would seem to be a dialectical term—one that requires an opposite for its definition. With the development of a "New American Right" during the fifties, out of opposition to the "Old Left," it became reasonable to anticipate that a "New Left" movement would eventually make its appearance. It is the suggestion of this paper that such a movement is now in its period of inception; and that the structure of its rhetoric, both *in esse* and *in posse,* merits attention in any survey of the spectrum of contemporary political discourse.

1.

As a "watershed moment," one containing shadows and foreshadows of both the Old and the "New Left," one might take the final sentence of Howard K. Smith's *The State of Europe* (1949):

The American liberals of both parties—in alliance with the Socialists of Europe and their allies among the liberal-minded Europeans—have

From *The Quarterly Journal of Speech,* L, 2 (April 1964), 113–135. Used by permission of the author and the Speech Communication Association. Mr. Griffin is Professor of Public Address at Northwestern University.

their job cut out for them: to apply every means of pressure to confound the backers both of the Communist Century and of the American Century, to restore American foreign policy to its people and thereby force the same restoration at last in the East—to resume the creation, interrupted these four years, of the Century of One World.[1]

The "four years" interruption refers, of course, to the advent of the Cold War. It need not be said, perhaps, that the Cold War itself is the overarching scene within which all acts of political utterance in our time must be understood; that it is a scene, moreover, in its very substance rhetorical—a logomachy, a waging of war not only through the use of persuasive words, but also by means of rhetorical deeds of deterrence and ingratiation. At any rate, in his call for a united effort of American liberals and European socialists to end the Cold War, it is not surprising that Smith made no mention of American socialists.

For by 1949 the strength of the non-Communists left in America had sharply declined. The following year, at its 1950 convention in Detroit, the Socialist party debated whether or not to withdraw from politics. Norman Thomas "announced that he would not run again and urged the convention not to run a national ticket in 1952."[2] The socialists did elect to run a candidate in that year; and he received a total of 20,189 votes—fewer votes than the candidate for the Prohibition party.[3] It was the poorest showing that a socialist candidate for president had ever made; and for socialists and the left generally, the time was clearly one for peripety—a time for reversal, for a "dramatic change of identity"— if the spirit of radicalism was to survive in American life.

As the specific moment of reversal, the initiating terminus of the "New Left" movement, one might point to the inauguration of the "*Dissent* project" in the fall of 1953. The editors of *Dissent*

. . . had diverse backgrounds and interests: some had been committed intellectually to the idea of socialism for a long time, others were veterans of American radicalism who had come to feel that the few remaining leftist groups were sterile and that a new start was necessary, and still others were young writers and teachers—radical though not always socialist—who wished to attack the spirit of conformity that had descended on the nation during the post-war years. . . .[4]

[1] *Howard K. Smith,* The State of Europe *(New York, 1949), p. 408.*
[2] *David A. Shannon,* The Socialist Party in America *(New York, 1955), p. 256.*
[3] Ibid.
[4] *Irving Howe, "A Few Words About Dissent,"* Voices of Dissent *(New York, 1959), p. 11.*

The editors—among them Lewis Coser, Irving Howe, Erich Fromm, Norman Mailer, and A. J. Muste—felt that "the socialist movement in America [had] reached its nadir and could rarely intervene as a political force in our political or trade union life."[5] They felt that their "main task was to deal with socialism in the realm of ideas, to make democratic-radicalism seem relevant to at least part of the American intellectual community."[6] They felt it "essential to project an image of a fraternal society in which men planned and controlled their political and economic affairs in terms of democratic participation and in which no small group of owners or party bosses could dominate society."[7] They were interested in providing a "sustained radical criticism" of the "claims and pretensions" of American society; and they felt that

> . . . for a radical criticism of American society to acquire depth and coherence, it needed as an ideal norm some vision of the good—or at least of a better—society. This vision was what we meant by socialism.[8]

On the one hand, they set themselves off from the "authoritarians of the Left"—from "Communism in all its manifestations"; on the other, from "liberalism" and the "liberals"—whom they tended to personify in the form of Hubert Humphrey, Arthur Schlesinger, Jr., and the ADA. In the judgment of C. Wright Mills, who pressed the point in the first issue of *Dissent,* and often thereafter, the "conservative mood" of America had captured the rhetoric of liberalism. Liberalism, he felt, while once a "fighting creed," had "come to a dead end and now serves as a rationale and rhetoric for upholding the irresponsible rule of the Power Elite."[9]

In sum, taking the *"Dissent* project" as an initiating terminus, one may view the peripety as composed of the following elements: (1) an attempt by agents, viewing themselves in the main as "radical intellectuals," to make a "new start"; (2) a decision to set their course in the direction of a democratic, "socialist humanism,"[10] steering between

---

[5] Ibid.
[6] Ibid.
[7] Ibid., *p. 13.*
[8] Ibid.
[9] *William F. Warde, "The Marxists,"* International Socialist Review (*Summer 1962*), *p. 67. See also C. Wright Mills, "The Conservative Mood,"* Dissent, *I* (*Winter 1954*), *22–31. Also Mills,* The Power Elite (*New York, 1956*), *Ch. 14, "The Conservative Mood," pp. 325–342.*

See also Harvey Swados, "Does America Deserve the New Frontier?" New Politics (*Summer 1963*), *pp. 33–51, a recent "New Left" response to Arthur M. Schlesinger, Jr., "The Administration and the Left,"* New Statesman (*February 8, 1963*).

[10] *Daniel Bell,* The End of Ideology (*Glencoe, III., 1960*), *p. 295.*

the Scylla of Communism and the Charybdis of "liberalism" (i.e., "conservative mood," status quo "capitalism"); and (3) an inclination to
direct their address primarily to intellectuals; to see the intellectual,
rather than the worker, as the essential maker of history, the agent of
change. And viewing the early issues of *Dissent* as a set of "representative anecdotes," a source for the discovery of "key terms," one may
chart the "clusters" that have continued to prevail in the vocabulary
of the "New Left": "devil terms"—such as *competition, alienation, conformity, absurdity (the irrational), loneliness, passivity, fear, bondage
(authoritarianism), hate, anxiety, the "warfare state," the Holocaust;* and
"god terms"—such as *coöperation, identification, commitment, sanity
(the rational), community, action, hope, freedom (autonomy), love,
peace, transcendence, the "good society," utopia.*[11] It is, in general,
the vocabulary of existentialist humanism—whether the frame be political, religious, psychological, sociological, or philosophical. And it is
also, to a suggestive extent, the vocabulary of the "comic frame"—
another name for which, as Burke notes, might be "humanism." It is
for this reason that the critic of contemporary left rhetoric, in his search
for compatible instruments of analysis and speculation, may well look
to Burke for models and modes of "humanistic contemplation."[12]

[11] *As will be apparent, the terms have been selected and ordered in rough
"equations" designed to illustrate "progressive forms" ("syllogistic progres-
sions") that seem to be implicit in "New Left" frames of rejection and acceptance. One term in the "vocabulary," not included in the equations above, might
serve to epitomize the lot—crisis.*
[12] *Particularly the first editions of* Permanence and Change, Attitudes Toward
History, *and* The Philosophy of Literary Form, *books written out of a period
when Burke had "plumped grandly" for a word "now locally in great disgrace"
and both the* Grammar *and* Rhetoric of Motives, *two books in his current project
"directed 'towards the purification of war.' " The essay in which Burke attempts
to "codify" his ideas on "the relation between Freudian psychology and
Marxism" ("Twelve Propositions by Kenneth Burke on the Relation between
Economics and Psychology,"* Science & Society: A Marxian Quarterly *[Spring
1938], pp. 242–249; also* Philosophy of Literary Form *[New York, 1957], pp.
263–270) is helpful; so also is the 1935 address on "Revolutionary Symbolism
in America" (see* American Writers' Congress, *ed. Henry Hart [New York,
1935], pp. 87–93, 167–171). Attention should also be given to references to
Burke in the section on "Marxian Socialism" in* Socialism and American Life,
*eds. Donald Egbert and Stow Persons (Princeton, N.J., 1952), I, 189; and in
Daniel Aaron,* Writers on the Left *(New York, 1961), pp. 288–291.*
*The filters of Burke's "humanism" have, of course, changed through the
years; and the critic will also give attention to the Prologue of the emended
edition of* Permanence and Change, *to both the Introduction and the After-Word
to the second edition of* Attitudes Toward History, *to the "Curriculum Criticum"
which appears at the end of the second edition of* Counter-Statement, *and to
the final section of the* Grammar *("A Neo-Liberal Ideal"). Note should be taken
of Burke's resolve (in the 1954 Prologue of* Permanence and Change) *not to
attempt "to present his brand of Crisis-thinking in current Existentialist terms."*
*The rhetorical analysis of a movement in its unfolding is a difficult, and per-
haps quixotic, undertaking. The present paper has been attempted, nevertheless,*

Other points in the curve of development may be charted. Nineteen fifty-three, the year of the *Dissent* project, was also the year of the death of Stalin. Nineteen fifty-four was the year of the fall of McCarthy: with his censure the grues [*sic*] of the "liberals" lessened, but the long night of the "hysteria"—the ordeal of the "crucible"—had fatally transformed them in the eyes of the radicals. In the scornful phrase of C. Wright Mills, many of the "liberals" had been "so busy celebrating the civil liberties that they . . . had less time to defend them," while others had been "so busy defending them that they had neither the time nor the inclination to *use* them."[13]

Nineteen fifty-six was the year that signaled the essential ambiguity of Khrushchev as a Cold War figure: whispers of hope in the "secret speech"—thunderous denial in the smashing of the Hungarian Revolution. Nineteen fifty-six was also the year in which Mills put his finger on the "power elite"—the morally-irresponsible symbols of authority (the "political directorate, the corporate rich, and the ascendant military") that controlled the history-making process in America, and that must be rejected. And 1956, finally, was the year of the founding of *Liberation* magazine. Like the founders of *Dissent,* the editors of *Liberation*—among them Dave Dellinger, Roy Finch, A. J. Muste, Bayard Rustin, Sidney Lens, Robert Pickus, and Mulford Sibley—were concerned at the "decline of independent radicalism and the gradual falling into silence of prophetic and rebellious voices. . . ." In an initial "Tract for the Times" they offered critiques of both "Liberalism" and "Marxism," and set out guide lines for a "Politics of the Future." They found it an "illuminating insight of pragmatism that means and ends condition each other reciprocally and that the ends must be built into the means"; and they declared that any "truly radical movement today . . . must commit itself to an essentially democratic and non-violent strategy." They announced that they did "not conceive the problem of revolution or the building of a better society as one of accumulating power"; it was rather "the transformation of society by human decision and action" that they sought. Toward this end, *Liberation* would endeavor

. . . to inspire its readers not only to fresh thinking but to action now —refusal to run away or to conform, concrete resistance in the com-

---

as an exploration of possibilities for the application of Burkeian procedures within a framework of movement analysis which I have previously suggested (see Leland M. Griffin, "The Rhetoric of Historical Movements," QJS, XXXVIII [April 1952], 184–188; and "The Rhetorical Structure of the Antimasonic Movement," in The Rhetorical Idiom, *ed. Donald C. Bryant [Ithaca, N.Y., 1958], pp. 145–159).*

[13] *Mills,* The Power Elite, *p. 334.*

munities in which we live to all the ways in which human beings are regimented and corrupted, dehumanized and deprived of their freedom; experimentation in creative living by individuals, families, and groups; day to day support of movements to abolish colonialism and racism, or for the freedom of all individuals from domination, whether military, economic, political, or cultural.[14]

In 1958, in *The Causes of World War III,* Mills continued his attack on the "power elite." In the "crack pot realism" of their Cold War policies lay the causes of World War III; in the continuance of their policies lay the inevitable Holocaust. But "to reflect upon war is to reflect upon the human condition," he wrote; and war, in becoming total, had become "absurd."[15] "What the United States ought to do," he declared

. . . is to abandon the military metaphysics and the doctrinaire idea of capitalism, and, in the reasonableness thus gained, reconsider the terms of the world encounter. We must subvert the monolithic American dogma that now constitutes the one line of elite assumption. . . .

The only realistic military view is the view that war, and not Russia, is now the enemy. The only realistic political view is the view that the cold warrior, on either side, not just the Russian, is the enemy.[16]

In line with his view that the intellectual, not the worker, had become the historic agent of social change, Mills sounded his call to "intellectuals, preachers, scientists": they must "drop the liberal rhetoric and the conservative default . . . now parts of one and the same line." They must "transcend that line."[17] In this "disgraceful cold war," the intellectuals should at once become "conscientious objectors." They must become political; they must "set forth alternatives"; they must wage the politics of peace.[18] The "conditions of the struggle" were such that

. . . an attack on war-making is also an attack on the U.S. power elite. An attack on this power elite is also a fight for the democratic means of history-making. A fight for such means is necessary to any serious fight for peace; it is part of that fight.[19]

[14] *"Tract for the Times,"* eds. Dave Dellinger et al., Liberation, I (March 1956), 3–6.
[15] *C. Wright Mills,* The Causes of World War III (*New York, 1958*), p. 16.
[16] Ibid., *p. 19.*
[17] Ibid., *p. 16.*
[18] Ibid., *p. 157.*
[19] Ibid., *p. 140.*

Nineteen fifty-eight was significant for other signs of the rise of a "New Left" spirit. The elections of that year were interpreted, at least by the socialist Michael Harrington, as marking a "turn to the Left"; and the welcome extended to former members of the Independent Socialist League by the newly-established SP-SDF (Socialist Party-Social Democratic Federation) was hailed as "a further step in making the SP-SDF the all-inclusive party of democratic socialism in the United States."[20] Harrington was also cheered by the progress the "Yipsels" were making: he saw this youth affiliate of the SP-SDF as playing "an extremely important role in organizing socialist and political clubs on campuses throughout the nation."[21]

Nineteen fifty-eight was significant, finally, as the year which saw the founding of the "Liberal Project"—an association of political intellectuals and intellectual politicians who were, as David Riesman and Michael Maccoby have written, "in general outlook far to the left of . . . [Hubert] Humphrey," although "the tag 'left' is one of those dated legacies they hope to surmount."[22] It was the hope of the members of the Liberal Project, apparently, that they might serve the national government as a kind of "unofficial Fabian Society."[23]

In March, 1960, the Committee of Correspondence, now known as the Council for Correspondence, was formed. Its general position and purpose was set forth in the so-called "Bear Mountain Statement." In this statement members of the Committee observed that "purely national loyalties have become an anachronism," and that "we must create a deep loyalty to all men, a loyalty capable of supporting international institutions, and the reign of law in international life." They recognized "the many obstacles to peace in the world today and the radical changes peace would require in our society." They asked people "to consciously reject the idea that democratic values can be defended or international problems solved by military means in the world today"; and they asked people to join with them

---

[20] *Michael Harrington, "New Hope for Socialism: The American Left Unites,"* Anvil and Student Partisan (*Winter 1959), p. 4.*

[21] Ibid.

[22] *David Riesman and Michael Maccoby, "The American Crisis,"* New Left Review (*September-October 1960), p. 25.*

[23] Ibid., *p. 24. And see Harris Dienstfrey, " 'Fabianism' in Washington,"* Commentary (*July 1960), pp. 22–28. For a recent attempt to establish a "Neo-Fabian Society" in New York City, see Daniel M. Friedenberg, "A Fabian Program for America,"* Dissent, X (*Summer 1963), 232–248.

While members of the "Liberal Project" might be considered a "pivotal group," it is more likely that the significant pivotal groups of the movement in its present period are those associated with the "Dissent project," Liberation magazine, the Council for Correspondence, and Turn Toward Peace. For the place of the "pivotal group" in the development of a movement, see Burke,* Counter-Statement (*Chicago, 1957), p. 71; and the discussion of "Sect" in* Attitudes Toward History (*Boston, 1959), pp. 320–321.*

. . . in a continuing attempt to construct alternatives to organized violence; to see that these alternatives receive a hearing by our government and our fellow citizens in the press, in correspondence, and by
the spoken word; to direct their attention steadfastly to the problem
of finding other solutions in an unremitting struggle for life.[24]

In its search for alternatives, for means of ending the Cold War, the
Committee hoped to establish "a very loose affiliation of groups in
different university communities," and to "enlist intellectuals in realizing
an inventive and radical response to the problem of war and its implications for American culture."[25] As a kind of "discussion network," it
aimed to provide "national and regional forums for the presentation and
discussion of ideas intended to help find alternatives to armed violence," and to encourage the formation of local groups devoted to the
same end.[26] As an historical note, the Committee pointed out that after
the founding of the first Committee of Correspondence by Samuel
Adams, committees

. . . arose in Virginia and in other colonies. Through their exchange a
widespread area of popular discontent was discovered and a number
of mutually accepted beliefs crystallized. Out of this came the idea of
holding a Continental Congress, and from this in turn came the concerted movement for independence that led to the revolution and the
birth of the United States.[27]

The original membership of the Committee (made up of "leading pacificists," "one or two labor intellectuals," "several socialists" and a
"growing group of academicians")[28] included, among others, David

---

[24] Bear Mountain Statement (March 1960), pp. 2, 5, 6. See also Barbara
Deming, "Courage for the New Age: The Committee of Correspondence,"
Liberation, VII (November 1962), 13–16; and A. J. Muste, "Let's Radicalize the
Peace Movement," Liberation, VIII (June 1963), 28.

[25] Riesman and Maccoby, op. cit., p. 25. The "American Crisis" essay originally appeared in Commentary (June 1960), pp. 461–472, and was reprinted
in The Liberal Papers, ed. James Roosevelt (New York, 1962), pp. 13–47. The
paragraph mentioning the Committee of Correspondence appears only in the
New Left Review version of the essay.

[26] Bear Mountain Statement, back cover. In the first weeks of its operation,
the Committee "held seminars in Cambridge, Massachusetts, to discuss the
consequences of disarmament; and American policy vis-à-vis Cuba at the University of Illinois. . . ." Riesman and Maccoby, op. cit., p. 25. However, the
writer has been informed by Theodore Olson, administrative secretary of the
Council for Correspondence, that "We have not sponsored as a national group
any seminars, etc., though the New York committee does this regularly. . . .
Other CFC people help to further the process through their own faculties, professional societies, etc." Letter dated October 30, 1962.

[27] Bear Mountain Statement, p. 1.

[28] Riesman and Maccoby, op. cit., p. 25.

Riesman, Michael Maccoby, William Davidon, Erich Fromm, Robert Gilmore, H. Stuart Hughes, Sidney Lens, Stewart Meacham, A. J. Muste, Clarence Pickett, Robert Pickus, Mark Raskin, Mulford Sibley, and Harold Taylor.[29]

In October, 1960, the SP-SDF launched its official newspaper, *New America,* under the editorship of Michael Harrington. In the same month, the British publication, *New Left Review,* published C. Wright Mills' "Letter to the New Left." In that "Letter" Mills once again affirmed his belief in the "intellectual" class as a "possible, immediate, radical agency of change." He called for "ideological analysis" of the "historical agencies of structural change," and for the "rhetoric with which to carry it out."[30] In addition to Mills' "Letter," the same issue of the *New Left Review* published Riesman and Maccoby's "American Crisis" paper. This essay is important not only for its discussion of the Liberal Project and for its announcement of the formation of the Committee of Correspondence, but also for its analysis of the "trail blazer" attitude that the authors saw as motivating our current Cold War rhetoric ("talking tough"), and for its discussion of means by which that attitude might be altered ("lobbying 'upward' is necessary"). They suggested that

. . . *we need energetically to influence the military, industrial, political, and educational elites into letting go of their investments in the cold war and into working not only for a safer but for a better world.*

The need of America in its time of crisis, they concluded, is for "political programs which transcend the details of the present."[31]

---

[29] *Bear Mountain Statement, back cover. Subscribers to the statement, forty-seven in number, included Kenneth Boulding, Lewis Coser, W. H. Ferry, Paul Goodman, Michael Harrington, Mark Harris, S. I. Hayakawa, Robert Heilbroner, Hallock Hoffman, Robert Maynard Hutchins, Alexander Meiklejohn, Seymour Melman, Walter Millis, Herbert Muller, Lewis Mumford, Charles Osgood, Kenneth Rexroth, I. A. Richards, and other distinguished intellectuals.*

[30] C. Wright Mills, "Letter to the New Left," New Left Review (*September-October 1960), p. 20.

[31] *Riesman and Maccoby, op. cit., p. 35. For an earlier discussion of possibilities for effecting change "from below" (i.e., "lobbying upward") see David Riesman, "The College Student in an Age of Organization," Chicago Review* (Autumn 1958), pp. 63–64. Cf. Burke on *"pivotal groups" and the belief that political movements "must arise 'from the grass roots,'"* Counter-Statement (Chicago, 1957), pp. 71–72.

For discussion of Mills' thesis that the radical intellectual should direct his persuasion to the "power elite," see Eugene V. Schneider, "C. Wright Mills and the American Left," Monthly Review (February 1963), *pp. 561–562. Cf. David Riesman,* The Lonely Crowd, rev. ed. (New Haven, Conn., 1961), *pp. xxxix: ". . . political activation of new ways of thought can no longer depend on capturing the leadership of an unorganized non-elite group as the basis for a political movement; with the growth of affluence, it is the malaise of the*

In the summer of 1960, the *Socialist Call* published Fromm's "socialist manifesto and program," *Let Man Prevail*. Socialism, Fromm affirmed, "differs from other party programs in that it has a vision . . . it aims at a goal which transcends the given empirical social reality." In outlining the principles of his "democratic, humanist socialism," Fromm indicated what he thought should be both the short-range and the long-range goals of the SP-SDF. He was aware that "it will take considerable time until the majority of the people of the United States will be convinced of the validity of socialist principles and goals."[32] Until that time, it must be the task of the SP-SDF to "become the moral and intellectual conscience of the United States, and divulge its analyses and judgments in the widest possible manner."[33] It must "develop an extensive educational campaign among workers, students, professionals, and members of all social classes who can be expected to have a potential understanding for socialist criticism and socialist ideals."[34]

2.

By the fall of 1961, if it was apparent that a new spirit of radicalism had been gradually emerging during the preceding half-dozen years, it was equally clear that two other movements—both more highly publicized—had been developing simultaneously and at a rapid rate: the movement for "civil rights" and the movement for "peace." During the half-dozen years preceding the fall of 1961, older groups like the "legalistic" NAACP and the Congress of Racial Equality had become more active in behalf of the "civil rights" of Negroes. In 1956, CORE (since its founding in 1942 devoted to Muste's [and Gandhi's] method of *satyagraha*—that is, to a non-violent, direct-action "rhetoric" of resistance—had "hired its first field secretary, and soon thereafter began its Southern work in earnest. . . ."[35] In 1956 Martin Luther King brought the Montgomery bus boycott to a successful conclusion; and in the following year he organized his Southern Christian Leadership Conference (SCLC). In 1960, the Student Nonviolent Coordinating Committee (SNCC), and the Negro American Labor Council (designed to

---

privileged . . . that becomes increasingly relevant." And see Norman Birnbaum, "David Riesman's Image of Political Process," Culture and Social Character, eds. Seymour Martin Lipset and Leo Loewenthal (New York, 1961), pp. 224–225.

[32] Erich Fromm, "Let Man Prevail: A Socialist Manifesto and Program," Socialist Call (Summer 1960), p. 21.

[33] Ibid., p. 22.

[34] Ibid.

[35] August Meier, "New Currents in the Civil Rights Movement," New Politics (Summer 1963), p. 11.

combat discriminatory trade-union practices within the AFL-CIO) were established. And in 1960 the college student "sit-ins" began at Greensboro—an act which constituted, in the opinion of one student of the civil rights movement, the "truly decisive break with the past":

These sit-ins involved, for the first time, the employment of nonviolent direct action on a massive South-wide scale that led to thousands of arrests and elicited the participation of tens of thousands of people. Moreover, a period was inaugurated in which youth were to become the spearhead of the civil-rights struggle. And this is still the case—for it has been the youth who have been the chief dynamic force in compelling the established civil-rights organizations to revamp their strategy [i.e., to become "committed to direct action"], which they found it imperative to do to retain their leadership in the movement.[36]

As for the peace movement, during the period under consideration, groups of long lineage had grown more active in the name of "peace" —the American Friends Service Committee, the Fellowship of Reconciliation, the Brotherhood of Sleeping Car Porters, Students for a Democratic Society, the War Resisters League, and the Women's International League for Peace and Freedom. New groups had sprung up—the Committee for Non-Violent Action, the Committee for World Development and Disarmament, SANE, the Council for Correspondence; and various "peace research" institutes had been established, often on university campuses.[37]

Meanwhile, other "New Left" journals had been appearing. By the fall of 1961, *Studies on the Left* (sponsored by James Baldwin, Erich Fromm, Murray Kempton, Sidney Lens, A. J. Muste, Kenneth Rexroth, Bayard Rustin, Mulford Sibley, Norman Thomas, and others) had been devoting itself to "a revival of radical thought among American intellectuals" for more than a year.[38] In the fall of 1961, *New Politics: A Journal of Socialist Thought* began publication. Its sponsors included James Baldwin, Erich Fromm, Michael Harrington, Murray Kempton,

---

[36] Ibid., p. 13.

[37] *For recent discussions of the peace movement, see Michael Harrington, "The New Peace Movement," The New Leader (August 20, 1962), pp. 6–8; Roy Finch, "The New Peace Movement—I," Dissent, IX (Winter 1962), 86–95; "The New Peace Movement—II," Dissent, X (Spring 1963), 133–148; Norman Thomas et al., "American Socialism and Thermonuclear War," New Politics (Spring 1962); Norman Thomas et al., "Politics and Peace Symposium," New America (March 12, 1963), pp. 4–5, and (April 25, 1963), pp. 4–5; and relevant articles in the May and June, 1963, issues of Liberation.*

[38] Studies on the Left, II, No. 2 (1961), p. 94. Cf. Andrew Hacker, "The Rebelling Young Scholars," Commentary (November 1961), pp. 404–412; and Richard Chase, "The New Campus Magazines," Harper's (October 1961), pp. 168–172.

Sidney Lens, A. J. Muste, Robert Pickus, Kenneth Rexroth, Bayard Rustin, Mulford Sibley, Harvey Swados, Norman Thomas, and others.[39] And in the fall of 1961, perhaps moved by their belief in the need for a "new politics," Norman Thomas and Robert Pickus combined the peace groups that have been mentioned in the preceding paragraph— along with some twenty other groups representing labor, religious, veterans' and public affairs interests—into a centralized framework that they called "Turn Toward Peace."[40]

The member organizations of the TTP were in general agreement as to their ultimate goal—"a disarmed world under law, safe for free societies and democratic values"; and, with various exceptions, in agreement on steps that must be taken in their progress toward that goal: the "reduction of international tensions"; "disarmament"; the "development of non-violent forces to defend freedom and democratic values"; "support of just demands for revolutionary change among the oppressed peoples of the world"; the development of "economic planning for a peaceful world"; the development of "a sense of world community"; and the "growth toward world law."[41] And it may be suggested that there was also agreement, if implicit and unconscious, on a general rhetorical program. It was a program that involved two phases: *Phase one*—the substitution in the public mind of "peace consciousness" for "war consciousness" (i.e., the overcoming of the "trail-blazer" attitude) by the creation of a climate of opinion that would be receptive to the *idea* of "alternatives" to prevailing Cold War policy; and *Phase two*— the undertaking of a series of unilateral *acts* (i.e., "American initiatives") that would compel the Cold War opponent to move with America, gradually, into a permanent world of peace (i.e., a "disarmed world under law, safe for free societies and democratic values").[42] It was a

---

[39] *Advertisement,* Studies on the Left, *Vol. II, No. 2 (1961), p. 58; see also title page,* New Politics, *Vol. I, No. 1 (1962).*

[40] Harrington, *"The New Peace Movement,"* op. cit. (*above, note 37*), p. 8.

[41] *Brochure,* Turn Toward Peace, *included in the 1962 "American Initiatives Kit." Compare this program with the one advanced in the 1962 platform of the Socialist party, "To Build a Better World."*

[42] *Cf. the two-phase program ("Turns Toward Peace," "Turns Toward Life") discussed by Hallock Hoffman in* The Control of National Policy (*Council for Correspondence pamphlet, June, 1962); and the two-phase program ("I—reversal of the tensions/arms-race spiral," "II—maintaining the peace") discussed by Charles E. Osgood in "How We Might Win the Hot War and Lose the Cold,"* Midway, *No. 4 (1960). Osgood notes (p. 88): "It is apparent that many of the conditions supporting the Communist way of life cannot be manipulated directly in our present world situation. They all require penetration of the 'iron curtains' in one way or another, and, therefore, strategies pertaining to them belong in Phase II. On the other hand, we can manipulate the condition of external threat directly. This variable is at least partly under our control—because we ourselves, in our words and actions, contribute to the level of threat which the Russians perceive. We can behave so as to raise this threat or lower it. . . ."*

rhetorical program, in short, which assumed the validity of the theory that by an act which alters the quality of a scene, one moves (or persuades) one's opponent into a new act in keeping with the new scene; whereupon one initiates a new act which creates a new scene, which requires a new act from one's opponent—and so on, until the ultimate rhetorical objective has been achieved.

That those concerned with the establishment of a "New Left" in American politics should be interested in movements for "peace" and "civil rights," in a time of Cold War, is not surprising. In Riesman's view, as Birnbaum interprets it, Cold War "political conditions preclude the development of human autonomy." The nation "suffers from a psychological *immobilisme*"—the result "not alone of demoniacal images of Communism, but of the lack of alternatives to America's present extremely limited, internal political goals." Those who "should be formulating these alternatives . . . are in fact mobilized for the Cold War." Thus the "current political motivation" (*act*) "is a result of the current political situation [*scene*] and not vice versa."[43] In such a *scene,* how is one who would be truly *human* (i.e., "individual," "sane," "autonomous") to *act?* Following Emerson ("whoso would be a man must be a nonconformist"), one must choose (*act*) to "transcend" the Cold War *scene* through "rejection" of it ("nonconformity," "dissociation," "civil disobedience"), through "commitment" of oneself to *mobility*—though the movements one "accepts" must be directed, of course, toward "peace," "equality," and other virtues of the "better world" of the "good society." At any rate, it seems plain that the "good society"—or at least that utopian society envisioned by democratic, socialist humanists—cannot be achieved except in a world at peace. For as Kenneth Burke has noted, "you can't get a fully socialist *act* unless you have a fully socialist *scene*";[44] and such a scene requires peace—for "the standards of peace" are the "proper tests for judging a socialist economy."[45]

Cf. the "GRIT" program discussed by Osgood in his chapter on "Reciprocal Initiatives," in The Liberal Papers, ed. James Roosevelt, pp. 155–228.

For a recent critique of the unilateral initiatives idea within the context of prevailing "Confederate" and "Federal styles of rhetoric," with comment on the "American forensic climate" in general, see David Riesman, "Reflections on Containment and Initiatives," Council for Correspondence Newsletter (February 1963), pp. 21–30.

[43] Birnbaum, "David Riesman's Image of Political Process," op. cit. (above, note 31), pp. 225–226.

[44] Grammar of Motives (New York, 1945), p. 14. Burke makes this observation within the context of a discussion of "instances of the scene-act ratio in dialectical materialism."

[45] Attitudes Toward History (Boston, 1961), p. 272.

None of which is to suggest that all "New Leftists" have been active in movements for "peace" and "civil rights"; nor, obviously, that all supporters of these movements are "New Leftists." It is not to suggest, again, that "peace" constitutes the primary strategic concern in the rhetoric of those committed to "a fundamental restructuring of society, a redistribution of property and power, along democratic lines."[46] As the scene requires, other strategies will share place with "peace" in the rhetorical corpus of the "New Left." And as may be inevitable in what is *in esse* an *anti* movement (i.e., since the "New Leftist's" "alienation" is synonymous with his need to reject the "reigning symbols of authority," the basic "attitude" from which his "strategies" arise is necessarily one of "rejection"),[47] many of the strategies most aggressively asserted must be essentially negativistic—e.g., *against* "conformity," *against* the "uncommitted," *against* the "American Celebration," *against* the concept of the "nation state," *against* "civil defense," *against* "mass culture," *against* "HUAC," *against* the "Connolly Reservation," *against* the "Liberal Establishment," the "New Conservatives," the "Ultra Right," and *against* "the political directorate, the corporate rich, the ascendant military," et cetera. The employment of negativistic (uncoöperative) strategies in a movement toward the "good society" (of democratic, socialist humanism) is perhaps anomalous, since the controlling attitude of the "good society," when realized *in posse,* is to be one of affirmation (coöperation). Yet a *pro* movement (with its rhetoric of acceptance) is not likely to replace the present *anti* movement as long as "Socialism" remains "a word on the Devil's tongue,"[48] and proponents of the movement must accordingly persuade "covertly." Meanwhile, assuagement for the "discomfitures of rejection," opportunities for the employment of positive strategies, may

[46] *Irving Howe's recent definition of "Socialism" in "A Revival of Radicalism?" Dissent, X (Spring 1963), 114.*

[47] *Burke, Philosophy of Literary Form (New York, 1957), p. 264. On the inevitability of negativistic rhetoric when a potentially pro movement is in its incipient, anti stage, Will Herberg says: "Bourgeois politics, even when radical, is essentially affirmative: its aim is to reform, improve, and consolidate the existing order. Socialist politics, however, even at its most 'moderate,' is essentially negative and oppositional; its true constructive role socialism reserves for the upbuilding of the new social order that is to supersede capitalism. Both work for tomorrow, but in a very different sense: for the one, tomorrow is but today perfected through progress; for the other it is today negated and transcended in a future that marks the consummation of history." See "American Marxist Political Theory," in Socialism and American Life, eds. Donald Egbert and Stow Persons, I, 489.*

[48] *Erich Fromm, Marx's Concept of Man (New York, 1961), p. vii. For similar recognition of "socialism" as a "bad word," see Norman Thomas's University of Colorado speech, "The Need for Socialism," New America (May 12, 1963), p. 3; and Staughton Lynd, "Socialism, the Forbidden Word," Studies on the Left, Vol. III, No. 3 (1963), pp. 14–20.*

be found through participation in movements for "peace," "equality," "civil rights," et cetera.

3.

The death of C. Wright Mills in the spring of 1962 deprived the "New Left" of one of its most forceful voices, and certainly one of its most sophisticated rhetorical theorists.[49] What specific measures Mills might have advocated had he lived to complete his projected book, a "program" for the "New Left," cannot be asserted.[50] But he surely would have continued to insist on the duty of the radical, whether socialist or not, to take an activist role in the "peace race."

At the time of Mills' death, when "Phase one" of the TTP program was in the midst of its first year, the "peace race" was in active progress. Mothers were marching, women striking, Dr. Spock speaking, professors petitioning, students demonstrating—all in the name of peace; "peace centers" were springing up in the cities and suburbs; peace "workshops," seminars, symposia, posters, vigils, walks—all abounded in the land; and it was no fault of peace advocates if "peace consciousness" was not beginning to make its way into the public mind.

But the events of October and November, 1962, dealt a heavy blow to the peace movement. It was not merely the decisive defeat of almost all of the thirty-two "peace candidates," including Sidney Lens and H. Stuart Hughes, that discouraged; it was the whole reversal of hopes represented by the President's aggressive response in the Cuban crisis. In moments of reversal, according to Burke, some "ritual of rebirth" is required; and for such a ritual, a "scapegoat" is needed. Perhaps this was a significance, for the Left, that a Burkeian critic might attach to Howard K. Smith's broadcast on "The Political Obituary of Richard Nixon."[51]

For months, throughout the fall and winter of 1962, the peace movement remained in what Professor Hughes, in a speech before the New York local of the Socialist party, called the "post-Cuba trough."[52] At length, in the spring of 1963, *New America* invited a number of "leaders and activists in the peace, civil rights and labor" movements to partici-

[49] *For a suggestion of the influence of Burke on the rhetorical theories of Mills, see the 1940 essay "Situated Actions and Vocabularies of Motive," reprinted in I. L. Horowitz, Power, Politics and People (New York, 1963), pp. 439–452; and the section on "Vocabularies of Motive," in Hans Gerth and C. Wright Mills, Character and Social Structure (New York, 1953), pp. 114 ff.*
[50] *Warde, "The Marxists," op. cit. (above, note 9), p. 69.*
[51] *That is, "symbolic slaying," in the presence of Hiss, of Nixon as "consubstantial representative" (with Kennedy) of the Cold War "power elite." It is necessary to recall the tendency of the Left to equate Nixon and Kennedy ("Tweedle-dee and Tweedle-dum") during the 1960 campaign.*
[52] *See* New America *(May 31, 1963), p. 6.*

pate in a symposium on "Political Directions for the Peace Movement." The assessment of the movement offered by Norman Thomas was gloomy:

It is a bitter fact that at this moment there is small chance of the building of a vigorous democratic left into a political party or movement. We Socialists exist in large part to bring such a movement into being. In the meantime we cannot act as if we had it. The peace movement is badly divided, and the best we can do at present to pull it together is along the lines of Turn Toward Peace. It cannot function as a strong, politically organized left under present conditions.

All these important problems of organization, strategy and tactics in the last analysis depend on our ability to do a much better job than we have yet done in persuading people of the position in regard to peace which I think is best expressed in our own platform.[53]

"Our present question," he remarked, "is a tactical one: how best to advance this program under our crazy political system in which there is no clear-cut alignment of the major parties on either domestic or foreign issues." On the question of tactics, other members of the symposium offered various opinions. David McReynolds, of the War Resisters League, felt that "the job of the peace movement now is to join forces with Dagmar Wilson and others in fighting the Dodd subcommittee and HUAC."[54] Sanford Gottlieb, of SANE, held that "the major emphasis of the peace movement should be directed toward work within the political parties, especially in primaries where there is a chance of winning party nomination."[55] Stewart Meacham, of the American Friends Service Committee, held that "peace will become politically potent not because the choice has been made between emphasis on a third party or on independent candidates on the one hand and infiltrating the major parties on the other, but rather by both things happening at once."[56] Sidney Lens disagreed "firmly with those in the peace movement who propose that we burrow into the major political parties." He argued:

Electoral activity, though important in enlarging the peace constituency and gaining a voice within the establishment, is only part of political activity. Direct action, such as peace walks, demonstrations, non-violent sit-ins, are also politics, and politics of the highest order.[57]

[53] *"Symposium on Politics and Peace,"* New America (*April 25, 1963*), *p. 4.*
[54] Ibid.
[55] New America (*March 12, 1963*), *p. 4.*
[56] Ibid., *p. 5.*
[57] Ibid., *p. 4.*

Bayard Rustin, executive secretary of the War Resisters League and "Former Advisor to Martin Luther King," declared that "the main problem is to get other social forces that are in movement to see that the struggle for survival is a part of their struggles." He suggested that "the dynamic and method of the civil rights movement offers great hope":

In the civil rights movement, people are in motion and are at this moment affecting the social and political climate of the country, and, with a little more success, may open the way for a realignment of the Democratic Party in the South.

Obviously, if this energy could be brought into a broader movement for social change, including the struggle for peace, the movement for a "new America" would take on profound political significance. I point out here merely that there is infinitely more of an immediate response possible from the civil rights movement than from labor or any other of the elements that are required for social change in the U.S.[58]

Rustin's position on the question of tactics received further support in the June issue of *Liberation*. In that issue, which carried Martin Luther King's "Letter from Birmingham Jail" and Rustin's "The Meaning of Birmingham," A. J. Muste suggested that the time had come to "radicalize the peace movement." Drawing a "lesson from the integration movement," Muste pointed out that what "is plain for everyone to see now is that there was no 'communication' . . . between Negroes and whites, even liberal whites, under the old pattern":

Communication began when the "powers that be" had to listen, i.e., when real and hence controversial issues were talked about. In the same way, whether nationally or locally, as peace advocates we have a chance actually to communicate if we are known as dissenters, not if the fact is hidden.[59]

C. V. Parkinson, in another article, scored the philosophy of "conservative, restrained communication" that had been followed by Turn Toward Peace, SANE, and the community peace groups. He saw in this "lukewarm approach, this nibbling away at the concern of the uncommitted, the dead hand of Madison Avenue"; and he felt that all concerned with peace must now face the questions: *"Should the proper attempt of the peace movement as presently constituted be to communicate with the*

[58] Ibid., *p. 5.*
[59] *Muste, "Let's Radicalize the Peace Movement," op. cit. (above, note 24), VIII, 29.*

public at the public's level, or *Should the attempt be to create a move-ment that the public can reach?"* He saw a "profound difference. It is the difference between an evolving image and a firm image . . . be-tween persuasion and conviction."[60] And Dave Dellinger, in a lead editorial denouncing "Uncle Tom-ism in the Peace Movement," con-cluded with the question:

Whatever the material costs may be, can we evade the "unrespectable" direct-action tactics of economic boycott, massive social disruption, and civil disobedience which have made the nonviolent movement for integration a powerful force for revolutionary change?[61]

Two thousand extra copies of the June *Liberation* were printed "in order to get copies in the hands of key field workers and demonstrators throughout the country." But even as the magazine was being prepared for the mails, significant changes in the "objective environment" (in Muste's phrase) began to occur.

On June 11, President Kennedy spoke to the nation, in an address entitled "A Moral Imperative: Equality of Treatment," on the question of civil rights; and the preceding day, at the commencement exercises of American University, he had delivered an address on "The Strategy of Peace." In that speech, the President had identified "peace . . . as the necessary rational end of rational men"; had suggested that Amer-icans "re-examine" their "attitude toward the Soviet Union"; had confided that American diplomats had been "instructed to avoid un-necessary irritants and purely rhetorical hostility"; had stressed the necessity for a "new effort to achieve world law—a new context for world discussion"; had affirmed that "our primary long-range interest . . . is general and complete disarmament—designed to take place by stages, permitting parallel political developments to build the new institutions of peace which would take the place of arms"; and had announced, in climax, that "high level discussions" would "shortly begin in Moscow towards early agreement on a comprehensive test ban treaty."[62]

The negotiation of the partial "Nuclear Test Ban Treaty" began in Moscow in mid-July; and on August 6 the treaty was formally signed. Described by the President as "a step toward peace—a step toward reason—a step away from war," the treaty was hailed by a heartened

---

[60] C. V. Parkinson, *"Levelling with the Public,"* Liberation, *VIII (June 1963),* 25.

[61] *[Dave Dellinger], "Uncle Tom-ism in the Peace Movement,"* Liberation, *VIII (June 1963), 3.*

[62] *For texts of the Kennedy addresses, see* Vital Speeches of the Day *(July 1, 1963), pp. 546–547, 558–561.*

New America as "a step toward peace," a "small step toward sanity," and "a step away from war." The socialist publication went on to advise the "democratic left" to

. . . use the opening provided by the test ban agreement to demand a Nuclear-free zone in central Europe. Demilitarization of central Europe must be begun by the disengagement of American and Russian troops from the continent.

It warned the "left" to "continue to oppose any deals between the US and Russia to maintain the status quo and their spheres of influence"; to continue to support "self-determination for the people of Eastern Europe under Communist domination as well as for the people in the world oppressed by Western colonialism"; and to continue to work for an end to "all military and economic support to the reactionary regimes in Portugal and Viet Nam." In conclusion, *New America* declared:

The political forces which are capable of creating this new foreign policy are marching on Washington for equal rights. All those who want further steps toward peace should join with the labor, liberal and civil rights movements in this direct assault on the Republican-Dixiecrat Coalition—the bastion of domestic and foreign reaction.[63]

In the same issue of *New America,* the official call to the "March on Washington for Jobs and Freedom," signed by the directors of the March, A. Philip Randolph and Bayard Rustin, appeared. In a separate statement in *New America,* Randolph commended the "Socialist Party's program for creating full employment and ending economic discrimination to the attention of all supporters of the civil rights movement." The "revolution for Freedom Now," he added,

. . . has moved into a new stage in its development. Its demands have necessarily become not only the end of all discrimination against black Americans, but for the creation of a new society—a society without economic exploitation and deprivation.

On the eve of the March, Michael Harrington, in a lengthy article in *New America,* praised A. Philip Randolph as "the most important Negro socialist of modern times," denied that socialists were " 'outsiders' trying to manipulate the [civil rights] movement for some secret pur-

[63] *Editorial, "A Step Toward Peace," New America (August 10, 1963), p. 2.*

pose," and insisted that "there must be a political realignment in America" since

> . . . *there cannot be full-scale civil rights without ranging social progress; and neither will come about unless there is a new movement, a political movement for realignment and a second party, in the United States.*[64]

The editor of *New America* saw the forthcoming "demonstration" as marking "a new stage in the revolution"; declared that "every step that this host of marchers takes will be toward a new kind of action on the part of outraged and oppressed citizens in the field of national politics"; rejoiced in the "towering fact that a coalition has been begun, and is strong enough that under its aegis masses of people will command the streets of the capital on the 28th, to voice a number of radical economic and social demands"; called on "every Socialist, every liberal, every trade unionist" to be "among those giving his wholehearted support to the March," and after the March to

> . . . *continue to back the movement in the fight it has outlined so well in its statement of principles—"our unalterable opposition to the forces ('Reactionary Republicans and Southern Democrats') and their century long robbery of the American people."*[65]

As for August 28, *Time* magazine judged it "a day that would never be forgotten." The March on Washington, it declared, "was a triumph. But after everybody agreed on that, the question was: Why?"[66] No doubt that question will be asked for some time to come. From the standpoint of rhetorical function, however, one might suggest that the March provided the "New Left" movement with a highly appropriate symbol: a symbol of solidarity—a massive symbol of people in *movement*—of people *identifying* in the name of *freedom, justice,* and *equality*—of people *committed,* and *acting* in *coöperation, hope,* and above all, *peace,* for "a better world."

4.

In September of 1963, then, as this analysis is completed, it seems reasonable to suggest that a "New Left" movement is now in its period of inception—and developing, indeed, toward maturer stages of that

[64] *Michael Harrington, "Socialists and Civil Rights,"* New America (*August 31, 1963*), *p. 3.*
[65] *Penn Kemble and Paul Feldman, "March Marks New Stage in Revolution,"* New America (*August 31, 1963*), *pp. 1, 12.*
[66] Time (*September 6, 1963*), *pp. 15, 13.*

period. One stage in the inception period of a movement (if it is to achieve its period of rhetorical crisis), is the decision of aggressor orators ("prophets") to forsake trite and ineffective appeals, to undertake new modes of argument.[67] If even a slight "reduction of international tensions" results from the Moscow Test Ban treaty, the "New Left" may be expected to continue its appeals for further *détente* with the Communist opponent, as well as for such broader "steps" toward "a better world" as those included in the TTP program—disarmament, development of non-violent forces for defense, aid for revolutions by the oppressed, economic planning, world community, world law. But the present interest of the "New Left" in the content and method of peace "communication" indicates, at least, that current modes of appeal are being scrutinized, and new ones considered. It may be that certain "lessons" of the civil rights movement (*urgency,* "Freedom *Now*"; the "use of the 'black body' against injustice . . . as a means of creating social disruption and dislocation")[68] will lead to alterations in the manner or mode of appeals for "peace"—e.g., to the widespread adoption of "direct action tactics" (i.e., a "physical rhetoric of resistance"). If so, an ethical confusion ("act" not in keeping with "essence") would seem to arise—at least for those who make a "god term" (term of "essence") of *sanity* (*the rational*) but whose rhetorical action is by choice *absurd* (i.e., essentially non-rational; coercive rather than persuasive; dependent on "seat of the pants" rather than "seat of the intellect"). If debate ("forensic drama," "reasoned discourse") is the creating myth of American democracy,[69] Rustin's justification of the necessity of "body" rhetoric on the ground that "the accepted democratic channels have been denied the Negro"[70] might be entertained in light of the Burkeian "scene-act ratio" (non-rational, non-democratic "acts" in a non-rational, non-democratic "scene"); but it would seem difficult for advocates of "peace" to claim lack of access to "accepted democratic channels" of persuasion.

Other stages in the inception period of maturing movements include the decision to address broader publics, and (in "Saving Remnant" movements)[71] the decision to speak openly ("overtly," unambiguously). It may be that Muste's advice to "dissenters"—that to improve "com-

---

[67] *Griffin, "The Rhetoric of Historical Movements," op. cit. (above, note 12), p. 186.*

[68] *See Muste, "Let's Radicalize the Peace Movement," op. cit. (above, note 24), and Bayard Rustin, "Birmingham Leads to New Stage in Struggle,"* New America *(June 18, 1963), p. 7.*

[69] *Hugh Duncan,* Communication and Social Order *(New York, 1962), p. 259.*

[70] *Rustin, "Birmingham Leads to New Stage in Struggle," op. cit., p. 7.*

[71] *Griffin, "The Rhetoric of Historical Movements," op. cit. (above, note 12), p. 186.*

munication" they must identify themselves openly to their publics—will be increasingly heeded. Harvey Swados has done so in his *A Radical's America;*[72] and it is interesting to note that the Council for Correspondence has decided to "go public" by making its newsletter available for "general circulation." Appropriately, the July-August issue of the newsletter bears a new name ("our old title was a study in calculated ambiguity"); and the editors indicate their awareness that, in openly addressing a broader public, they

. . . must assume a bit less—introduce our writers more carefully, explain the relevance of our topics, and generally design for the uncertain and perhaps only half-interested eye.[73]

Further stages in the development of an inception period—in addition to the abandonment of ineffective appeals, the adoption of new modes of argument, and the decisions to speak "overtly" and to address broader publics—include the intensified use of previously employed channels of propagation, as well as the employment and consolidation of new channels. With the effective utilization ("flooding") of all channels, the movement begins to "flower into public notice"—and the way is prepared for the final stages of the inception period: the emergence of "hosts of aggressor rhetoricians" and the consequent generation of the "moving tide of discourse" that precipitates the period of rhetorical crisis—the period of the collective, public (i.e., "overt") rendering of judgment.[74] Or to restate the rhetorical process of inception periods in Burkeian terminology: as problems of "communication" are solved, increasing numbers of individuals "identify" with the movement (that is, "reject" the prevailing "symbols of authority" and "accept" the symbolic ends of the movement); as they undergo "change of identity," become "committed" to the movement, they are freed from their "alienation," "repossess their world," "shift their co-ordinates"; in this shift they acquire new "perspective," gain a "sense of direction," "see around the corner"—and hence, they "prophesy."[75] Eventually, as the ranks of the "prophets" (aggressor orators) multiply, the period of rhetorical crisis arrives: the public renders its collective judgment, "accepts" the new "symbols of authority"—and "transcendence" ("transformation," "social change," "revolution") is achieved.

[72] *Harvey Swados,* A Radical's America *(New York, 1962), p. xiii.*
[73] The Correspondent: The Monthly Newsletter of the Council for Correspondence (*July–August 1963*), p. 38.
[74] *Griffin, "The Rhetoric of Historical Movements," op. cit. (above, note 12),* p. 186.
[75] *Burke,* Attitudes Toward History (*Boston, 1961*), pp. 268–270.

At the present writing, the "New Left" movement cannot be said to have "flowered into public notice" (as compared, for example, with the "neo-conservative" and "radical right" movements). This stage may begin to develop, however, as the "New Left" continues to improve and extend the range of its rhetoric. On May 31, just as the significant summer of 1963 was about to begin, David McReynolds expressed his encouragement at the many "communities of resistance" that he had found in his tours throughout the country; but he warned that

. . . the task to be faced is enormous. To translate the many local points of resistance into a powerful new American Left requires some nondogmatic rallying point, some forum through which we can communicate with each other as we build together. If we would build a new America, then we must build New America.[76]

And so he was "forced to the conclusion that one of the most vital functions of the socialist movement—perhaps its single most important function—is that of expanding its press, specifically *New America.*"

From the standpoint of rhetorical structure, the "New Left" movement seems indeed to have reached a stage which requires the expansion of its press, the broadening of its publics, the augmentation and consolidation of its channels of propagation. These requisites might be served, in part, through the coaching of party realignment, the rallying of the various "communities of resistance," the general achievement of "solidarity" between relevant ongoing movements. The broad problem of solidarity has for some time been of concern to Riesman.[77] Paul Goodman, disturbed by the "Caliban" theme ("Let's along and do the murder first") of Baldwin's *The Fire Next Time* and David Lytton's *The Goddam White Man,* has recently insisted that the "only grounds of solidarity" lie in "working at common worthwhile tasks"; that "in such effort men lose themselves and find themselves changed"; that "new identity" is found "in the achievement of great tasks"; that

. . . the general effort to live better, at home and world-wide, will be— if we survive at all—the solution of race problems. In the effort for peace, rational economy, good schooling, world community, etc., race prejudice is trivial and must wither.[78]

[76] *David McReynolds, " 'Communities of Resistance' Work Toward a New America,"* New America *(May 31, 1963), p. 6.*

[77] *Birnbaum, "David Riesman's Image of Political Process,"* op. cit. (*above, note 31*), *p. 224.*

[78] *Paul Goodman, "The Only Grounds of Solidarity,"* Liberation, *VIII (June 1963), 22.*

On the eve of the Washington March, *New America* observed that the "new coalition built around the March . . . provides a potentially enormous power base for a common political program," but it warned that "the growing participation of white liberals, religious organizations, and the more politically conscious sections of the labor movement" could "tend to slow down the pace of action"; and therefore, to

. . . prevent any loss of momentum during the growth of the movement, it becomes the task of the more militant civil rights activists, trade unionists and liberals to educate and move the tens of thousands of new participants so that they can catch up with the revolution underway. The enormous political weight that they can add to the struggle is needed now.[79]

Michael Harrington, in the same issue of *New America,* declared that the time had come for "a political realignment in America" and asked that "the powerful forces for social change band together as effectively as the forces for social reaction have done."

The Washington March, as suggested earlier, both as symbol and deed was an achievement in solidarity; and the concern for solidarity was undoubtedly a factor in the Socialist party's announcement of a "National Conference on the Civil Rights Revolution," to begin in Washington on the day following the March. Discussion was promised on such topics as "The New Phase: A Prospectus for Civil Rights," "A Political Strategy for Civil Rights," "Fair Employment—Full Employment," and "Toward Full Equality in a Progressive America"; and speakers scheduled for appearance included Norman Thomas, Bayard Rustin, A. Philip Randolph, James Farmer (of CORE), Robert Moses (of SNCC), and other figures identified with peace, civil rights, trade union, and socialist organizations.[80]

In the months ahead, the search for solidarity will no doubt continue to preoccupy the "New Left"; and in addition, efforts will be made—or theoretically should be—to expand the "New Left" press, reach broader publics, intensify use of available channels of propagation, seek new channels, and (possibly) to speak more overtly. The prevailing mood, at the moment, seems to be one of guarded optimism. Representative, perhaps, of the present mood, and suggestive of efforts to come, is the following account of the summer, 1963, convention of the Students for a Democratic Society:

SDS will attempt to draw the peace and civil rights movements closer together, where appropriate, with a common rejection of token solu-

[79] *Kemble and Feldman, "March Marks New Stage in Revolution,"* op. cit. (*above, note 65*), *p. 12.*
[80] New America (*August 31, 1963*), *p. 12.*

tions; aid the budding full-employment "movement"; and at the same time maintain lines of communication with less radical students, this last less as an organizational ploy than to help SDS itself avoid the hubris of the "New Left."

A fifth of SDS's membership attended the convention, a remarkably high proportion, but the most significant thing about them was that all were participants in local insurgency—university reform, peace politics and research, or civil rights activism. The developing SDS strategy therefore flowed as much from the gathering as from the analysis, and it was clear that in the coming year SDS members will be found where social change is to be found, working, learning and teaching at once.[81]

5. Postscript

I thought that as soon as I became my own master I would immediately enter public life. A sudden change, however, in the political situation diverted me from my plan.

—PLATO, *Seventh Letter*

Little more than a week after the preceding essay was completed the nation was shocked by news of the bombing of the Sixteenth Street Baptist Church in Birmingham. On September 22, a week after the bombing, a National Day of Mourning was held for the six children who had died in the tragic events of the previous Sunday. Tom Kahn, Bayard Rustin's assistant in the March on Washington, informed readers of *New America*:

It was obvious that the participants in this National Day of Mourning felt betrayed by the Federal government. In New York, 10,000 gathered in Foley Square, headquarters of the Justice Department, and heard Norman Thomas, Bayard Rustin, James Farmer, and James Baldwin indict the Kennedy Administration for its failure to protect beleaguered southern Negroes from racist terror. . . .[82]

In his speech at the Foley Square rally, Baldwin announced that "it is time that the government knew that if the government does not represent us, if it insists on representing a handful of nostalgic Southern colonels, the government will be replaced"; that "a government and a nation are not synonymous. We can change the government and

[81] *Todd Gitlin, "A Student Convention,"* The Correspondent (*July–August 1963), pp. 56–57.*
[82] *Tom Kahn, "March's Radical Demands Point Way for Struggle,"* New America (*September 24, 1963), p. 4.*

we will."[83] In a separate statement for *New America,* Baldwin declared that "the crimes committed in Birmingham Sunday must be considered as one of the American answers to the March on Washington." This "shameful day" was one of the

. . . direct and inevitable consequences of the power held in Washington by the Southern oligarchy. It is a day which utterly destroys any claim the Kennedy administration in general, or the Justice Department in particular, may make concerning its zeal or dedication in the field of civil rights. . . .

The "most reactionary forces" in the country were determined

. . . to smash the patience and break the will of the Negro people in order to create a situation which will justify the use of martial law. First, the Negroes, then all other dissenters and / or revolutionaries will find themselves intolerably coerced, and will be broken, in or out of prison or driven underground. . . .

It was not enough, therefore, "to mourn the dead children: what we must do is to oppose and immobilize the power that put them to death." Baldwin confessed that he had been one of those people "stampeded by the fear of Nixon into the Kennedy camp"; that he "would certainly never have dreamed of the coming [sic] of a 'Kennedy' man under any other compulsion." Certainly the time had come "to ask a sovereign people why they should continue so abjectly to choose between the interchangeable mediocrities with which Washington continually confronts us." He refused to believe that "we are unable to envision and achieve political alignments less unrealistic and less immoral." The great apathy which reigned in the country was symtomatic of "the bewilderment and despair of people who doubt that they have the power to change and save themselves." Such despair was "indescribably dangerous"; for when people

. . . allow themselves to feel that they can do nothing, they permit all manner of crimes to be committed in their names. Can anyone deny that this process is already under way in American life? And this means that the crimes committed Sunday in Birmingham will be as nothing compared to the crimes we will find ourselves committing, unless we take upon ourselves the responsibility of examining and revising our

[83] *James Baldwin, "We Can Change the Country,"* Liberation, VIII *(October 1963), 8. Foley Square rally speeches by James Farmer (p. 9) and Theodore Bikel (p. 5) also appear in this issue.*

institutions, and become more exigent than we are concerning the calibre of our representatives.[84]

In the September 24 issue of *New America,* speeches presented at the Socialist party's post-March "Conference on the Civil Rights Revolution" were reported (Rustin: "The civil rights revolution will succeed to the degree that we succeed in moving this country to the left. . . . We have an alliance now with trade union and religious leaders. Our problem is to keep that alliance alive for this period—with all the pressures that exist"). But under the heading "Political Murder," the editor of the paper devoted his entire analysis to the Birmingham tragedy. It was an analysis that largely agreed with Baldwin's. "The response of the Kennedy administration" had been "beyond belief, even for cynics." "The coalition of profits and racism" ("Southern Dixiecrats and right wing Republicans") had "demonstrated its enormous political and economic power." It had "gotten away with political murder." He warned that "the Federal government, by avoiding its constitutional duties, and those liberals in Congress whose hands still tremble, are forcing Southern Negroes to resort to violence to protect the lives of their families." There was only one alternative:

. . . tens of thousands of black and white bodies marching in the streets and "going to jail, and jail again," while at the same time carrying on an unremitting political struggle against the coalition of profits and racism.

"The lines are becoming more finely drawn," he concluded:

Either we march with the revolution for equality or we stand guilty with the Southern racists and their allies for the murders of the six Birmingham children and the terror yet to come.[85]

As the autumn advanced, tones of anger, despair, and foreboding colored "New Left" discourse in the North; in the South it grew dark with themes of death and blood sacrifice. Reporting late in September from Selma, Alabama, Ronnie Dugger noted:

Death has come up many times during the mass meetings of the Negroes. When he addressed them Monday night, Lewis [John Lewis, national chairman of SNCC] told them that if it was necessary, let blood

---

[84] *"James Baldwin Statement—Political Murder in Birmingham,"* New America (*September 24, 1963*), pp. 1, 4.

[85] *Paul Feldman, "Political Murder,"* New America (*September 24, 1963*), p. 2.

flow in the streets; but let it be Negroes' blood, he said, because it should be innocent blood. Again and again speakers said they are ready to die if they have to for this cause. Wednesday night, a Snick speaker asked the crowd of 500 if they were ready to die, and they broke into strong applause.[86]

In the issue of *The Correspondent* which printed Dugger's report, Howard Zinn proposed that the President create and send into the South a corps of special agents ("we might call them E-men, for Equality") with the power "to make arrests on the spot, the moment a move is made to violate federal law." Expressing doubt of Zinn's notion that "many demagogic Southerners do not have the courage of their apparent convictions," Riesman pointed out that

. . . for them shooting is a traditional way to create conviction. Are the Southern pieds noirs less capable than those of the French Empire of conspiracy and assassination? It may possibly be that the issue will come to this as our desperations combine and intertangle with each other. Fearing where that road leads, I wonder if other courses such as non-violence have shown conclusively their impracticality?[87]

Rustin, in the October issue of *Liberation,* called again for the use of "black bodies, backed by the bodies of as many white people as will stand with us." He insisted:

We need to go into the streets all over the country and to make a mountain of creative social confusion until the power structure is altered. We need in every community a group of loving troublemakers, who will disrupt the ability of the government to operate until it finally turns its back on the Dixiecrats and embraces progress.

He warned that

. . . unless those who organized and led the March on Washington hold together and give the people a program based on mass action, the whole situation will deteriorate and we will have violence, tragic self-defeating violence. . . .[88]

---

[86] Ronnie Dugger, "Dead End in the Deep South," The Correspondent (*November–December 1963*), p. 46.

[87] Howard Zinn, "A Question of Action"; David Riesman, "A Problem of Reaction," The Correspondent (*November–December 1963*), pp. 51, 54.

[88] Bayard Rustin, "The Meaning of the March on Washington," Liberation, VIII (*October 1963*), 13.

And yet, as the autumn advanced, events more heartening to "New Left" causes were occurring. In October the President approved the sale of wheat to Russia; the General Assembly of the U.N. condemned South Africa's policy of *apartheid;* the pacifist Linus Pauling was awarded the Nobel Peace Prize; Marshal Tito was welcomed at the White House—where the peripatetic ladies Nhu were officially ignored; and on November 1, with the assassinations of Diem and General Nhu, the "reactionary regime in Viet Nam" was abruptly brought down. Steps, however small, toward "peace," the "relaxation of tensions."

But in Dallas, where he had come to deliver a United Nations Day speech on "peace," Adlai Stevenson (*Time* reported) was "clunked" on the head with a picket's poster, and "a young man spat on him." Dallas, *Time* noted, "was shocked."[89]

The arrest of Professor Frederick Barghoorn by the Russians, on the day before the Viet Nam coup, was (in the light of post-test ban "euphoria") a retrograde act. Unnecessary. "Seemingly pointless," *Time* felt. Both abrupt and absurd. Understandable, perhaps, only as an existential political act—an act existential, in Norman Mailer's phrase, "precisely because its end is unknown."

On November 16, following the President's appeal, the Russians released the professor. The following week, *Publishers' Weekly* announced the appearance of Norman Mailer's book on existential politics, *The Presidential Papers.* A long-time "New Leftist," and long disappointed in President Kennedy's performance ("Tin soldier, you are depriving us of the Muse"), Mailer had written his book "to" and "for" the President. It was designed to give him an "existential grasp of the nature of reality." Its "unspoken thesis" was that "no President can save America from a descent into totalitarianism without shifting the mind of the American politician to existential styles of political thought."

If a public speaker in a small Midwestern town were to say, "J. Edgar Hoover has done more harm to the freedoms of America than Joseph Stalin," the act would be existential. Depending on the occasion and the town, he would be man-handled physically or secretly applauded. But he would create a new reality which would displace the old psychological reality that such a remark could not be made. . . .[90]

The President had every qualification for greatness, Mailer informed him, but one—he had no imagination. He was expert in translating political matters into arithmetic:

---

[89] Time (*November 1, 1963*), p. 26.
[90] *Norman Mailer,* The Presidential Papers (*New York, 1963*), p. 26.

Politics is arithmetic, but politics is also rhetoric, passion, and an occasional idea to fire the imagination of millions. For his arithmetic the President gets a mark of 98 per cent. For his imagination: zero. For his passion 40 per cent. For his rhetoric: 50 per cent.

"Existential politics," Mailer affirmed, "is rooted in the concept of the hero, it would argue that the hero is the one kind of man who *never* develops by accident, that a hero is a consecutive set of brave and witty self-creations." In John Kennedy the nation had a President with "the face of a potential hero," a President who was brave

. . . but politically neuter, adept at obtaining power and a miser at spending it, an intellectual with a mind like a newspaper's yearbook, and a blank somewhat stricken expression about the eyes, a numbed mind seems to speak behind them.[91]

And so Mailer offered his assorted papers to the President—papers on "Existential Legislation," "The Existential Hero" (*Superman Comes to the Supermarket*), "The Existential Heroine," "On Dread," on "Red Dread," on "Death." In his final paper, "On Waste," Mailer invited the President to go along with him "on an existential journey into the deeper meaning of scatology"; for it was necessary that a President

. . . be ready to contemplate everything human and inhuman in the psychic life of his Republic . . . including precisely those ideas which encounter the rude, the obscene, and the unsayable.[92]

It is unlikely that time remained for the President to profit by Mailer's scatological learning or to accompany him on his journey. Shortly after the book was published, John Kennedy was off on journeys of his own, political trips into Florida, into Texas. He went to San Antonio, Houston, Fort Worth—and came at last, on November 22, to Dallas.

He had come to deliver an address at the Merchandise Mart, an address which was to feature a warning against extremist "voices" on the Right, against those "who confuse rhetoric with reality and the plausible with the possible." He was struck down, all public evidence indicates, by a self-proclaimed "Marxist"; by an extremist of the Left, grown voiceless; by "a man of our century, for whom argument seemed a fraudulent smokescreen";[93] by a man, it is at least certain, for whom reality was not rhetoric but a rifle. From the standpoint of categorical

[91] Ibid., *pp. 5, 6, 7.*
[92] Ibid., *p. 270.*
[93] *Frederick D. Kershner, Jr., in "The Meaning of the Life and Death of John F. Kennedy,"* Current, *No. 45 (January 1964), p. 20.*

expectation, whether of the "New Left" or of the public at large, John Kennedy's death was as neatly and formally chiastic as any discourse in his life had been.

It was not, however, in the words of the philosopher Charles Frankel, a death that was "morally intelligible":

> . . . *what happened was an act of human will that was like an act of impersonal nature—unnecessary, purposeless, abrupt. . . . It is the kind of event that the existentialists have in mind, I suspect, when they speak of "absurdity."*[94]

Without question the Birmingham bombing, as well as the assassination of the President, both sickened and stunned the nation. These were acts of consummate violence; yet their impact, insofar as the developing structure of "New Left" rhetoric is concerned, is likely to be slight. Qualitatively, both acts might easily be characterized in words drawn from the "New Left" lexicon of "devil terms"—terms descriptive of scene in the Cold War world. Neither act, in brief, constituted a change in the "objective environment" of the "New Left"; both merely served to confirm its analysis of that environment. This being so, no significant change in rhetorical strategy is required; and thus the search for solidarity, for broader publics, for additional channels of propagation should proceed. Indeed, one week after the assassination, SNCC held its "Fourth Annual Conference on Food and Jobs"—a conference at which Baldwin and Rustin spoke; at which Jack Conway, Walter Reuther's representative to the March on Washington Committee, provided a "basis for joint struggle by the civil rights and labor movement around a common political and economic program which is concrete, radical and relevant."[95] And on December 13–15, in New York, Turn Toward Peace sponsored a conference attended by some 200 representative leaders of more than 100 organizations. In his speech at the conference, Rustin

> . . . *not only demanded the economics of the unusual in the struggle for peace and civil rights but specified that breakthroughs in both areas required fundamental changes in the structure of American society. He called for the most militant kind of pressure on President Johnson.*[96]

[94] *Charles Frankel, in "The Meaning of the Life and Death of John F. Kennedy,"* Current, *No. 45 (January 1964), p. 38.*

[95] *See "Conway of IUD Lays Basis for New Left,"* New America (*December 27, 1963), p. 5.*

[96] *Jerome Grossman, "The Peace 'Crowd,' "* The Nation (*January 20, 1964), p. 67.*

In his report on the conference, Norman Thomas has noted that if Turn Toward Peace "cannot push at this juncture such good specifics as SANE or the Socialist Party has advanced," it can nevertheless "provide mechanisms for bringing them under discussion and getting maximum possible cooperation at local, regional and the national levels."[97]

Even so, the prevailing current of the broad national rhetoric (a rhetoric of "non-extremism"), accelerating in the wake of the murders in Birmingham and Dallas, may serve to retard the "New Left" in the development of one stage in the inception phase of its movement—the decision to speak more overtly. While the rhetoric of continuity prevails (the "Eternal Flame" at Arlington; President Johnson: "Let us continue"); while "hate" remains the national scapegoat; while "rhetoric" itself stands charged with guilt (Burke: "So people went on bickering and carping, trying to catch him up . . . using the standard devices of rhetoric. . . . Go, please, and read Aristotle's *Rhetoric*. . . .";[98] Lippmann: "In the light of this monstrous crime, we can see that in a free country . . . unrestrained speech and thought are inherently subversive"[99]), public sanctions are likely to solidify against open appeals for radical change—whether from the Right or the Left. "Socialism," in consequence, is likely to remain "a word on the Devil's tongue," and the day deferred when the "New Left" can speak in its own name. Until it does, however, it cannot truly enter public life, cannot truly be its own master. In this sense, the bombing and the assassination may be viewed as diversions in the developing rhetoric of the "New Left" movement.

Archetypal Metaphor in Rhetoric:
The Light-Dark Family
by Michael Osborn

This study probes the possibilities of one form of "new criticism" occasionally mentioned by critics of rhetorical criticism—the idea that a fresh and sensitive look at the figurative language of a speech, focusing especially upon its metaphors, might yield a critical product rich

[97] *Norman Thomas, "Turn Toward Peace," New America (January 10, 1964), p. 2.*

[98] *Kenneth Burke, in "Reflections on the Fate of the Union: Kennedy and After," The New York Review of Books (December 26, 1963), p. 10. Other contributors to this symposium include Irving Howe, David Riesman, Paul Goodman, and Norman Mailer.*

[99] *Walter Lippmann, "Today and Tomorrow," The Washington Post (November 26, 1963), quoted in Current, No. 45 (January 1964), p. 23.*

From *The Quarterly Journal of Speech*, LIII, 2 (April 1967), 115–126. Used by permission of the author and the Speech Communication Association. Mr. Osborn is Associate Professor of Speech at Memphis State University.

and useful as some similar ventures in literary criticism.[1] For example, one could study the speeches of a man, or speeches of a certain type, or the public address of different ages, in order to determine preferred patterns of imagery or to trace the evolution of a particular image. One could even consider questions such as whether the quantity of imagery varies according to rhythms such as crisis and calm or development and deterioration within a culture.[2]

From this plenitude the present study selects for more extensive consideration what an earlier article has termed "archetypal metaphor."[3] Investigation indicates that the archetypal metaphor of rhetorical discourse has certain characterizing features.[4]

---

[1] *See for example: Martin Maloney, "Some New Directions in Rhetorical Criticism," Central States Speech Journal, IV (March 1953), 1–5, and Robert D. Clark, "Lessons from the Literary Critics," Western Speech, XXI (Spring 1957), 83–89. Various approaches in literary criticism are illustrated by: Richard Harter Fogle, Hawthorne's Fiction: The Light and the Dark (Norman, 1964); Caroline F. E. Spurgeon, Shakespeare's Imagery and What It Tells Us (Cambridge, 1935); and Stephen Ullmann, The Image in the Modern French Novel (Cambridge, 1960).*

[2] *Some work in these directions has already been accomplished, as occasional references to published research here will indicate. Among unpublished research, William Martin Reynolds provides a study of societal symbols and metaphors in his "Deliberative Speaking in AnteBellum South Carolina: The Idiom of a Culture," unpubl. Ph.D. diss. (University of Florida, 1960). Reynolds argues that when invention becomes exhausted during the course of a protracted argument, rhetorical energies may then be concentrated upon the development of stylistic devices in order to dramatize and reinforce entrenched argumentative positions.*

Examination of the annual listings in Speech Monographs *indicates that a movement towards image study developed at the masters thesis level in the early 1930's. This movement, which withered as quickly as it appeared, produced two works which deserve more than the usual oblivion reserved for masters theses. Junella Teeter's "A Study of the Homely Figures of Speech Used by Abraham Lincoln in his Speeches" (Northwestern, 1931) shows appreciation in the manner suggested by Clark of the functional, "communicative" aspects of imagery. Melba Hurd's "Edmund Burke's Imaginative Consistency in the Use of Comparative Figures of Speech" (University of Minnesota, 1931) is a highly competent study of the kind projected by Maloney.*

[3] *Michael M. Osborn and Douglas Ehninger, "The Metaphor in Public Address," Speech Monographs, XXIX (August 1962), 223–234.*

[4] *The usefulness of the term, "archetype," may be impaired somewhat by ambiguity, for writers in various fields have extended it to suit their purposes. The word may refer to myth and symbol, or to a certain "depth" responsiveness to great literature, or to ancient themes reverberated in literature, or even to structural phenomena of the brain that have developed as a kind of "race consciousness" to certain forms of recurrent experience. See for example: Philip Wheelwright, The Burning Fountain: A Study in the Language of Symbolism (Bloomington, 1954), pp. 86–93, 123–154, and Metaphor and Reality (Bloomington, 1962), pp. 111–128; Northrop Frye, "The Archetypes of Literature," in Myth and Method: Modern Theories of Fiction, ed. James E. Miller, Jr. (Lincoln, 1960), pp. 144–162; and Maud Bodkin, Archetypal Patterns in Poetry: Psychological Studies of Imagination (London, 1934). Despite such*

First, archetypal metaphors are especially popular in rhetorical discourse. Within the almost limitless range of possibility for figurative association, such metaphors will be selected more frequently than their non-archetypal approximations. For example, when speakers wish to place figurative value judgments upon subjects, they will more often prefer a light or darkness association over an association with Cadillac or Edsel, ivy or poison ivy, touchdown or fumble, etc.

Second, this popularity appears immune to changes wrought by time, so that the pattern of preferential selection recurs without remarkable change from one generation to another. A similar immunity belongs to archetypal metaphor considered cross-culturally, for such preferential behavior appears unaffected by cultural variation.[5] Thus, when Dante conceives of God as a light blindingly bright, and of Hades as a place of gloomy darkness, or when Demosthenes speaks of troubled Athens as launched upon a stormy sea, the meaning comes to us clearly across the barriers raised by time and cultural change.

Third, archetypal metaphors are grounded in prominent features of experience, in objects, actions, or conditions which are inescapably salient in human consciousness. For example, death and sex are promontories in the geography of experience.

Fourth, the appeal of the archetypal metaphor is contingent upon its embodiment of basic human motivations. Vertical scale images, which project desirable objects above the listener and undesirable objects below, often seem to express symbolically man's quest for power. Such basic motivations appear to cluster naturally about prominent features of experience and to find in them symbolic expression. Thus, when a rhetorical subject is related to an archetypal metaphor, a kind of double-association occurs. The subject is associated with a prominent feature of experience, which has already become associated with basic human motivations.

This peculiar double-association may well explain a fifth characteristic, the persuasive potency of archetypal metaphors. Because of a certain universality of appeal provided by their attachment to basic, commonly shared motives, the speaker can expect such metaphors to touch the greater part of his audience. Arising from fundamental interests of men, they in turn activate basic motivational energies within an audience, and if successful turn such energies into a powerful current running in favor of the speaker's recommendations. Certain archetypal

---

variation, the term carries the idea of basic, unchanging patterns of experience. The use here is consonant with that theme.

[5] *A general concept of cultural similarity in the use of metaphor gathers some empirical support from Solomon E. Asch, "The Metaphor: A Psychological Inquiry,"* Person Perception and Interpersonal Behavior, *ed. Renato Taguiri and Luigi Petrullo (Stanford, 1958), pp. 86–94.*

combinations such as the disease-remedy metaphors are quite obvious in this respect. They provide a figurative form of the threat-reassurance cycle discussed by Hovland *et al.*[6] Images of disease arouse strong feelings of fear; images of remedy focus that emotional energy towards the acceptance of some reassuring recommendation.

Finally, as the result of the foregoing considerations, archetypal metaphors are characterized by their prominence in rhetoric, their tendency to occupy important positions within speeches, and their especial significance within the most significant speeches of a society. One can expect to find such images developed at the most critical junctures in a speech: establishing a mood and a perspective in the introduction, reinforcing a critical argument in the body, and synthesizing the meaning and force of a speech at its conclusion.[7] And because of their persuasive power, their potential for cross-cultural communication, and their time-proofing, one can expect the perceptive rhetorician to choose them when he wishes to effect crucial changes in societal attitude, to speak to audiences beyond his own people, or to be remembered for a speech beyond his lifetime.

This paper focuses particularly on four sources of archetypal metaphor—light and darkness, the sun, heat and cold, and the cycle of the seasons—related by their affinity in nature and by their sharing of a basic motivational grounding. The paper's organizing metaphor is that of a solar system: it is most illuminating to think of these sources as a kind of spatial family in which light and darkness occupies the center, and the sun, heat and cold, and seasonal cycle sources range out from it in that order of proximity.

Light and darkness is the sun of its own archetypal system, in which the sun itself has only planetary significance. The reason for placing light and darkness at the center is that its motivational basis is shared in varying degrees by the other archetypes to be considered here. The nature of these motives and the rationale for their attachment to light and darkness are immediately apparent.

Light (and the day) relates to the fundamental struggle for survival and development. Light is a condition for sight, the most essential of man's sensory attachments to the world about him. With light and sight one is informed of his environment, can escape its dangers, can take advantage of its rewards, and can even exert some influence over its

---

[6] *Carl I. Hovland, Irving L. Janis, and Harold H. Kelley,* Communication and Persuasion: Psychological Studies of Opinion Change *(New Haven, 1953), pp. 59–96.*

[7] *Concluding sex and death metaphors are investigated in John Waite Bowers and Michael M. Osborn, "Attitudinal Effects of Selected Types of Concluding Metaphors in Persuasive Speeches,"* Speech Monographs, *XXXIII (June 1966), 147–155.*

nature.[8] Light also means the warmth and engendering power of the sun, which enable both directly and indirectly man's physical development.

In utter contrast is darkness (and the night), bringing fear of the unknown, discouraging sight, making one ignorant of his environment—vulnerable to its dangers and blind to its rewards. One is reduced to a helpless state, no longer able to control the world about him. Finally, darkness is cold, suggesting stagnation and thoughts of the grave.

What happens, therefore, when a speaker uses light and dark metaphors? Because of their strong positive and negative associations with survival and developmental motives, such metaphors express intense value judgments and may thus be expected to elicit significant value responses from an audience. When light and dark images are used together in a speech, they indicate and perpetuate the simplistic, two-valued, black-white attitudes which rhetoricians and their audiences seem so often to prefer. Thus, the present situation is darker than midnight, but the speaker's solutions will bring the dawn.

Light-dark metaphor combinations carry still another important implication which students of rhetoric appear to have neglected. There are occasions when speakers find it expedient to express an attitude of *inevitability* or *determinism* about the state of present affairs or the shape of the future. Change not simply *should have* occurred or *should* occur, but *had to* or *will* occur.

The deterministic attitude usually has more strategic value in speeches concerning the future. The speaker may wish to build a bandwagon effect: "you had better come join us: the future is going to happen just as we predict." In moments of public crisis and despondency, the speaker may wish to reassure his audience: "there's no reason to lose heart: good times are just ahead." Statements such as the latter will have not simply a public reassurance value, but also a personal rhetorical value: public declarations of confidence in a future desired by his audience will enhance the speaker's *ethos,* suggesting him as "a man of faith."

The combination of light-dark metaphors is ideally suited to symbolize such confidence and optimism, because light and dark are more than sharply contrasting environmental qualities. They are rooted in a fixed chronological process, the movement of day into night and night into day. Therefore, symbolic conceptions of the past as dark and the present as light or the present as dark and the future as light always

---

[8] *This conception of man in the presence or absence of light is influenced somewhat by the account of essential aspects of behavior offered by Charles Morris,* Signs, Language, and Behavior *(New York, 1946), p. 95.*

carry with them a latent element of determinism, which the speaker can bring forth according to his purpose.

Most often, it appears, this sense of historical determinism in rhetoric is tempered by conditions, and therefore can not often be equated with philosophical determinism. The latter eliminates the significance of all contingencies, and, in works such as Hegel's *Reason in History,* sees historical process as one ceaseless, remorseless flow toward a fixed end or "Absolute." Rhetorical determinism, while it also eliminates or ignores the myriad accidents and contingencies of life, nevertheless stops this reductive process one step short of philosophical determinism. It usually offers a conception of two patterned alternatives potential in historical process, depending upon a choice specified in the speech. One of those fundamental, possibly unconscious strategies of rhetoric, it therefore simplifies complex situations and facilitates choice, at the same time lending a certain dramatic significance to the rhetorical situation. If an auditor feels he is playing an important role in an elemental conflict, his gratitude for this feeling of personal significance may well predispose him in favor of the speaker's position.

The choice situation which a speaker thrusts upon his audience always concerns the acquisition of an attitude or the adoption of a solution; these forms of choice become conditions when a speech is imbued with rhetorical determinism. The speaker will say: "the present flowed from the past *because* you adopted (or did not adopt) my solutions or *because* you possessed (or did not possess) certain qualities. The future I envision will flow from the present *if* you adopt my solution or *if* you possess certain qualities." While both conditions may be present in a speech, the solutional condition is suited more to deliberative speeches, the qualitative condition more to ceremonial or inspirational speeches.

Whatever the conditions, patterns of light-dark metaphors can serve to suggest (where the determinism is left implicit) or to reinforce (where the determinism becomes explicit) the impression that some particular series of events had to or will occur. The metaphoric combination creates and strengthens this feeling by associating possibly controversial assertions concerning the inevitability of a particular process with a general, unquestionably determined cycle of nature. One could, therefore, simply classify this important work of light-dark metaphor combinations as argument by analogy. The classification, however, seems somewhat bald, especially when qualitative conditions are the hinge upon which rhetorical determinism turns. With such conditions, the symbolic combination emerges as an analogical form significant enough to be individuated as *argument by archetype.*

To discover the reason for this special significance, one must examine more carefully the effectiveness of qualitative conditions. This effectiveness depends upon audience acceptance of a basic ethical premise, which indeed animates a good part of the public discourse of Western nations and even provides much of the rationale for the significant occurrence of such discourse in the first place. This usually invisible axiom may be reconstructed in the following form: *material conditions follow from moral causes.* If a man or state qualifies by having certain specified virtues, the present condition of well-being is explained, or a radiant future is assured. Corresponding qualities of evil in a man or state have led or will lead to correspondingly opposite material conditions.[9] The Western quality of this submerged premise becomes apparent when one considers that the tracing of material conditions to moral causes tends to enhance the stature and responsibility of individual man within the historical process. The world is made to turn upon the struggle between good and evil within the human soul, giving a grand historical significance to intensely personal moral crises. An Eastern or Marxist point of view might well reverse the terms of the cause-effect relationship and, accordingly, diminish the stature of the individual.

An assertion that some series of events has been or will be determined, according to the presence of certain moral qualities, may depend therefore upon dual sources of support. First, the assertion rests upon a faith in moral causation and is the conclusion of a submerged enthymematic structure. Second, the assertion may call also upon an association with the fact of an unquestionably determined archetypal process. But the two forms of support do not operate independently. The faith itself is confirmed by an association with the fact of archetypal process, which constantly suggests to the impressionable mind of man that evil darkness contains the promise of light, good light the potential for darkness, in unending succession. Therefore, vivid symbolic representations of light and darkness may often perform a subtle but fundamental probative function in a speech, well deserving individuation in such cases as *argument by archetype.*

Among rhetoricians, ancient and modern, none has been more aware of the potential power of light and dark metaphors than Sir Winston Churchill. Indeed, Churchill in his war speeches shows a remarkably consistent preference for archetypal images in general. This favoritism

[9] *Kenneth Burke discloses an excellent example of the past-present relationship regarded as dependent upon moral qualities in his analysis of Hitler's rhetoric,* The Philosophy of Symbolic Form *(Baton Rouge, 1941), pp. 204–205. One infers from Burke's analysis that Hitler fused his views of the past and present, present and future into a panoramic interpretation and prediction of German history. To blame the present ills of Germany upon past moral degeneracy (sin) was to promise the future well-being of Germany when moral health should be restored (redemption).*

may be a symptom of a more general truth, that in moments of great crisis, when society is in upheaval and fashionable contemporary forms of symbolic cultural identity are swept away, the speaker must turn to the bedrock of symbolism, the archetype, which represents the unchanging essence of human identity. Audiences also are unusually susceptible in such moments to archetypal images, for it is comforting to return with a speaker to the ancient archetypal verities, to the cycle of light and darkness, to the cycle of life and death and birth again, to the mountains and rivers and seas, and find them all unchanged, all still appealing symbolically to the human heart and thus reassuring one that man himself, despite all the surface turbulence, remains after all man.

One example among Churchill's many finely wrought images illustrates clearly most of the characteristics discussed in the preceding section:

If we stand up to him [Hitler], all Europe may be free and the life of the world may move forward into broad, sunlit uplands. But if we fail, then the whole world, including the United States, including all that we have known and cared for, will sink into the abyss of a new Dark Age made more sinister, and perhaps more protracted, by the lights of perverted science.[10]

One first observes a fusion here between the archetypes of light and darkness and the vertical scale, a frequent combination because of the natural association of light with the above and darkness with the below. The opposing value judgments are intense, the presence of rhetorical determinism unmistakable. The situation has been simplified until there are two—and only two—alternatives, one of which must become the pattern for the future. The conditional factor is qualitative, whether the British people choose to remain steadfast in the face of danger. Their moral choice will determine the future material condition. Churchill utilizes symbolism to strengthen their commitment to this virtue, first by conceptualizing a reward, the "sunlit uplands," second by specifying even more vividly a punishment, "the abyss of a new Dark Age." By an intense initial contrast of light and dark images, Churchill reawakens the figurative tension of what could be—out of context—a threadbare metaphoric phrase, "the lights of perverted science." This reinvigorated metaphor provides a grotesque, unnatural association of light with evil, reinforcing the power of the threat. Thus the example is an impressive, apparently intuitive display of potentialities discussed previously.

[10] *"Their Finest Hour,"* Blood, Sweat, and Tears, *ed. Randolph S. Churchill (New York, 1941), p. 314.*

Churchill's purpose with this image was exhortation. When he intends comfort and reassurance, certain variations occur in the image patterns:

Good night, then: sleep to gather strength for the morning. For the morning will come. Brightly will it shine on the brave and true, kindly upon all who suffer for the cause, glorious upon the tombs of heroes. Thus will shine the dawn.[11]

This example forms much of the conclusion of his address "To the French People." He is speaking to a defeated people: because they are already in "the new Dark Age," he does not mention light and dark alternatives, and the sense of conflict and contrast has faded. There is only one pattern now for the future, the reassuring movement from darkness into light. The speaker sees this movement as so inexorable, so inevitable, that he does not even mention conditions. They are present only implicitly: the moral qualities of endurance, courage, and loyalty to the "cause" even to the point of suffering and death. To strengthen his assertion that the future is favorably determined, Churchill relies upon—and at the same time reinforces—his *ethos* as "a man of faith." But is such confidence actually more confidence than it is prayer, an effort to invoke the predicted future by a kind of public incantation? Whatever it is, the immediate effect of consolation and encouragement is compromised only if his auditors can sense uncertainty behind the brave words.

The nature of the figuration, as well as the patterns of figurative development, appear to have changed. The first example, consonant with its vigorous, exhortative temper, thrusts its changes of meaning directly upon the audience. "Sunlit uplands," "abyss," "Dark Age," are obviously metaphors from the first crack of the language. They force their auditors immediately into the experience of resolution.[12] But this second example illustrates a somewhat slower—perhaps more soothing—tempo of meaning change. Churchill's speech was delivered during the evening, and he has obviously taken advantage of the circumstance.[13]

---

[11] *"To the French People,"* Blood, Sweat, and Tears, *p. 403. See other prominent examples in "Be Ye Men of Valor" and "The War of the Unknown Soldiers."*

[12] *Osborn and Ehninger, pp. 226–231, offer a model which describes how the mind reacts when it encounters a metaphoric stimulus. Resolution is a critical phase within the reaction process.*

[13] *A similar exploitation for figurative purposes of a physical circumstance in the speech situation occurs in William Pitt's "On the Abolition of the Slave Trade," Select British Eloquence, ed. Chauncey A. Goodrich (New York, 1963), pp. 579–592. The conclusion of Pitt's speech, which develops a striking dawn image, happened just as dawn itself was lighting the windows of Parliament.*

"Good night . . . sleep to gather strength for the morning" could be taken quite literally. But from that moment the metaphoric intent begins to reveal itself, so that the movement into figurative meaning develops gradually throughout the example. One can not escape a certain physical similarity with the coming of dawn itself: a subtle onomatopoeic quality pervades the whole.

The sun is implicit in all light-dark images, and in the planetary system around light and darkness it is especially close to the center. But it does have special functions as an archetypal source. While light-dark images serve generally as value judgments upon the actions and conditions of men, the sun can symbolize more aptly human character. Most often it serves a eulogistic purpose, suggesting qualities of goodness which belong to a man. Thus sun images are at once less dynamic and more personal than metaphors of light and darkness.

An especially artful example occurs in Edmund Burke's "On American Taxation," in which the image first apotheosizes Lord Chatham, then comments less favorably by the subtlest form of ironic contrast upon the character of Charles Townsend:

For even then, sir, even before this splendid orb was entirely set, and while the western horizon was in a blaze with his descending glory, on the opposite quarter of the heavens arose another luminary, and for his hour, became lord of the ascendant.
This light, too, is passed and set forever.[14]

The example indicates still another implication of sun imagery. While light and darkness are grounded in a chronological sequence, there are also subordinate cycles in the various phases of the night and day. The night phases are not archetypally significant, but different moments of the day are charged with such significance. The dawn-twilight cycle emerges especially as a symbol for human life from birth to death, indicating that the birth-death cycle, itself an archetypal source, may require metaphoric illumination when it becomes the subject for discourse. MacArthur's sentimentalized self-portrait in his "Address to Congress" further exemplifies this usage. In both his introduction and conclusion, he sees himself "in the fading twilight of life." By positioning the images in these critical places, he reveals that his primary purpose in the speech is to focus sympathetically upon himself. To enhance further the symbolic appeal, MacArthur uses images contrast,

---

See *Philip Henry Stanhope,* Life of the Right Honourable William Pitt (*London, 1861*), *II, 145–146; Lord Roseberry,* Pitt (*London, 1898*), *p. 98; and J. Holland Rose,* William Pitt and National Revival (*London, 1911*), *p. 470.*
[14] *Goodrich, p. 259.*

referring in the body of the speech to "the dawn of new opportunity" in Asia.[15]

Sun metaphors may serve also to distinguish between qualities of light. Natural, sun-produced light is preferred over man-made light, permitting metaphoric value contrasts within the symbolic scope of light itself. Such contrasts occur infrequently, and are of a finer, more subtle sort than the obvious figurative oppositions of light and darkness. Edmund Burke provides an example in "Previous to the Bristol Election," which contrasts rather obscurely the light of open day with candlelight:

The part I have acted has been in open day; and to hold out to a conduct, which stands in that clear and steady light for all its good and all its evil, to hold out to that conduct the paltry winking tapers of excuses and promises, I never will do it. They may obscure it with their smoke, but they never can illumine sunshine by such a flame as theirs.[16]

Burke illustrates also a final potential of sun metaphors based upon the eclipse phenomenon. Eclipse has an obvious, trite connection with "bad luck," "misfortune," but in the hands of a master rhetorician it may acquire fresh, more interesting associations. Implicit in it is the suggestion that darkness may be momentary, that a period of misfortune in national life may be only transitory, and that the nation will emerge again quickly into its former brightness. Generally some modicum of sunlight remains to reassure and sustain the observer. Thus there may be an occasional rhetorical advantage in suggesting that a nation is in the darkness of eclipse, rather than in the darkness of night. Burke's example illustrates this potential only in a partial sense:

Tarnished as the glory of this nation is, and as far as it has waded into the shades of an eclipse, some beams of its former illumination still play upon its surface, and what is done in England is still looked to as argument, and as example.[17]

Somewhat farther distant from the center of the light-dark system is the contrast of heat and cold, represented most vividly and frequently in fire imagery. Fire partakes not only of the central light-dark motivational basis but also that of the sun to which it is contiguous. It

[15] The Speaker's Resource Book, *eds. Carroll C. Arnold, Douglas Ehninger, and John C. Gerber (Chicago, 1966), pp. 279–284.*
[16] *Goodrich, p. 293.*
[17] Ibid., *p. 305.*

has an extensive range of possible metabolic associations, as Philip Wheelwright's discussion indicates.[18]

Wheelwright notes that the warmth of fire associates it with bodily comfort, with the growth of the body and its food, and with the preparation of food. Its tendency to shoot upward relates it to the motivational basis of vertical-scale imagery: that which reaches above can symbolize the difficult effort by man to improve upon his condition, to aspire to "higher" ideals and attainments. Because fire is the most active, most rapidly changing of nature's elements, it can represent youth and regeneration. On the other hand, in its sun embodiment it can symbolize the permanence of nature, an association which gives meaning to the home's hearth-fire and to the church's altar-fire. Because fire burns and disintegrates substance, it can be viewed either as a destructive or as a purifying force: symbolically it can be either infernal or purgatorial. Because of its spontaneous generation and rapid reproduction, fire can represent also the birth of an idea and how it proliferates in the mind. Furthermore, just as a torch spreads flame from one place to another, an idea can leap from one mind to another.

With respect to the relationship between fire and light, Wheelwright claims an inseparable connection, such that fire suggests light, light fire to the mind of the recipient:

Modern household appliances have so successfully enabled us to separate light and heat, that we are prone to forget how naturally in ancient times the two phenomena went together. . . . Even on a cold winter's day the sun could be felt in one's marrow. Consequently, in those contexts where light served as a symbol of intellectual clarity it tended to carry certain metaphoric connotations of fire as well. . . . As fire, glowing with light, warms the body, so intellectual light not only instructs but also stimulates the mind and spirit.[19]

His suggestion, however, that the modern mind may no longer be as susceptible to the ancient association of fire and light is not supported by a prominent example from the rhetoric of John Kennedy:

Let the word go forth from this time and place . . . that the torch has been passed to a new generation of Americans. . . . The energy, the faith and the devotion which we bring to this endeavor will light our country and all who serve it—and the glow from that fire can truly light the world.[20]

[18] The Burning Fountain, *pp. 303–306; and* Metaphor & Reality, *pp. 118–120.*
[19] Metaphor & Reality, *p. 118.*
[20] *Arnold, Ehninger, and Gerber, pp. 226–227.*

The example confirms Wheelwright's notion that fire has a natural association with youth and regeneration.

While fire represents here dedication, a constructive impulse, Churchill provides an example which symbolizes destruction—and perhaps purification.

What he [Hitler] has done is to kindle a fire in British hearts, here and all over the world, which will glow long after all traces of the conflagration he has caused in London have been removed. He has lighted a fire which will burn with a steady and consuming flame until the last vestiges of Nazi tyranny have been burnt out of Europe, and until the Old World—and the New—can join hands to rebuild the temples of man's freedom and man's honor, upon foundations which will not soon or easily be overthrown.[21]

One notes again Churchill's tendency to build figurative, enlarged meanings out of literal conditions. The "conflagration" in London caused by Nazi bombings extends figuratively to the anger felt in "British hearts," and extends again to represent the nature of future retaliation. In such cases Churchill does not introduce *items for association* out of context, which is the usual practice in metaphor,[22] so much as he uses a previous subject as an *item for association* with subjects which follow. This practice provides a certain artistic cohesiveness in his image patterns.

One notes also the coupling of fire, symbolic destruction, with the activity of building, symbolic construction. This archetypal combination suggests that an especially arresting metaphor, because of the adventure of creating and resolving it, can establish an appetite for imagery in both speaker and audience which makes further vivid figuration appropriate and perhaps even mandatory.[23] The destruction-construction effects suggest also that, as with disease-recovery metaphors, some balancing function, partly aesthetic and partly reassuring, is served by the second member of the metaphoric combination.

The cycle of the seasons, most distant from the center in the light-dark system, impinges upon the motivational bases of all which precede it in proximity to that source. The variations in light and darkness from one season to another, the different qualities of sunlight, the extreme variations in heat and cold, all give seasonal contrasts a complex and

---

[21] *"Every Man to His Post,"* Blood, Sweat, and Tears, *p. 369.*
[22] *See Osborn and Ehninger, p. 227.*
[23] *The concept of form as "appetite" is developed in Kenneth Burke's* Counterstatement *(New York, 1931). See especially the discussion in Chapter VII. The appetitive aspect of metaphor-sequence mentioned here seems related to Burke's "qualitative" and "repetitive" forms.*

powerful potential for symbolizing value judgments rising from hope and despair, fruition and decay. Furthermore, the inescapable rhythm of seasonal succession provides another potential symbol for all stipulations of a determined present or an assured future. For these reasons the cycle of the seasons is immensely significant in poetry and fictional prose; Shakespeare, for example, made superb use of the source.[24] Therefore, it is surprising and somewhat perplexing that this basic environmental archetype is virtually ignored by rhetoricians.[25]

Understanding this strange neglect, which one must assume points to some special inadequacy or inappropriateness of the seasonal cycle for rhetorical purposes, requires a consideration of the nature of the source and a comparison with similar, more popular archetypes. Seasonal images are unpopular in rhetoric because of the subject matter with which the rhetorician typically deals and because of the usual nature of his audience. The succession of the seasons is a slow, deliberate process. It is suited more for long-range representations of the process of change and of the general condition of men within that process. It fits more the poet's or philosopher's elevated perspective upon time and the gradually evolving nature of man's destiny. But the subject matter of rhetoric is most often dynamic, immediate, and concrete. It has to do with specific problems and specific solutions. Some innate inappropriateness appears, therefore, between the subject matter of rhetoric and the symbolizing potential of seasonal contrasts.

A further reason for the unpopularity of the source lies in the psychology of audience and in the interaction between rhetorical subject matter and that audience. The succession of phases in light and darkness is immediate and vividly obvious: to promise light after darkness implies that a solution will come quickly, an attractive assurance for popular audiences who are impatient of long term effects or whose needs are felt concretely and acutely. The succession of the seasons, on the other hand, implies a slower and more deliberate process, not especially gratifying for such audiences. Moreover, while the succession of phases in light and darkness is rapid and spectacular, the prolonged process of seasonal change lacks dramatic impact for people who are not attuned aesthetically to long-range contrasts and subtle changes.

---

[24] *His use of seasonal imagery in drama is catalogued extensively by* Spurgeon, Shakespeare's Imagery.

[25] *The few examples encountered illustrate the concept discussed herein of an abstract subject matter and, significantly, occur in ceremonial speeches of a mixed rhetorical/poetic genre. See Franklin Roosevelt, "First Inaugural,"* American Speeches, *eds. Wayland Maxfield Parrish and Marie Hochmuth Nichols (New York, 1954), p. 502; and George Canning, "On the Fall of Bonaparte," Goodrich, p. 863.*

Thus the cycle of the seasons is an aristocratic source, which provides specialized symbols for subjects at higher levels of abstraction for the consideration of sophisticated audiences. One must conclude that the seasonal archetype provides a dimension of potential power and appeal from which the rhetorician, by the nature and circumstances of his art, is usually excluded.

The examination of one family of archetypal sources does not yield a complete, precise set of questions which the critic can use to exhaust the implications of any given rhetorical image. However, these explorations do suggest an initial pattern of inquiry.

Concerning metaphoric *invention,* what characterizes a speaker's selection of *items for association*? Does he have favorite metaphors for favorite subjects, and among these metaphors is there any kind of harmonizing relationship which would indicate an underlying unity of imaginative outlook on public questions? Does the speaker vary the tempo of meaning change in different situations, and if so for what purpose and to what effect?

With respect to *organization,* how significant is the position of an image within a speech? If its major appearance is in the introduction, does the metaphor echo and reverberate through the remainder of the speech in minor variations? Or if especially arresting, does it appear to create an eidetic disposition within speaker and audience, causing a chain-reaction of imagery to extend throughout the speech? If its major statement is in the conclusion, is the image prepared for by minor variations which condition the audience? If any of these phenomena occur, has one in effect an organization of images which runs parallel with the organization of topics? Does this image order dominate the substantive order, or is it subservient to that order? Do such patterns repeat themselves among the various speeches of a man, and if so, what can one infer that would individuate the speaker's rhetorical artistry?

Concerning *ethical proof* implications, does the intensive use of light-dark contrasts project the speaker as one who has little difficulty in making clear, decisive choices between good and evil? Does the speaker suggest himself as a man of faith or conviction by his symbolic representations of the past-present, present-future relationships? If he does communicate some sense of rhetorical determinism, does he attach conditions, and if so, what is their nature?

The *motive* basis of archetypal metaphor suggests other questions. Among the range of motivational attachments which surround an archetype, what particular motive does a specific image emphasize? Does this implicit motive stimulation reinforce, or run counter to, the system of motivational appeals made explicit within the speech? From the same subject comes a somewhat more general question with important implications for the rhetorical theorist. Might one construct inductively from the study of archetypes a system of motives particularly relevant to rhetorical discourse, rather than adopting by authoritative warrant some general list of "impelling motives"?

At least one important question may be asked relating to the *logical proof* function. Does an image embody some tacit enthymematic structure and function as a demonstration within itself, or does it serve more to dramatize, illustrate, and reinforce a logical structure made explicit elsewhere in the speech?

Two final possibilities and questions, directed as much to the theorist as to the critic, merit discussion. The first concerns the long-pursued relationships between rhetoric and poetic. Published research for some time now has been seeking general distinctions between the two arts, and while often suggestive seems, perhaps fortunately, not to have produced final answers. The discussion of seasonal images here supports the possibility that a more microscopic venture, concerned with tracing fine distinctions according to the imagery appropriate to each art form, might advance this inquiry.[26]

The second question concerns the relationships between archetypal and non-archetypal metaphor. At what moments might the non-archetype be preferable to its archetypal counterpart? That there are such moments is suggested by Laura Crowell's analysis of Franklin Roosevelt's 1936 presidential campaign address at Pittsburgh.[27] The critic finds a sustained baseball image and explains that the speech was given at Forbes Field. Thus the same kind of special circumstance which enhanced Churchill's images of dawn and fire made in this case a non-archetypal figure more appropriate.

A more significant possibility is raised by a different interpretation of the evidence presented in Wilcomb E. Washburn's excellent survey of early American political symbolism.[28] In the perspective here Washburn's evidence suggests that archetypal images may be especially crucial not only when a society is in upheaval, but also in its formative stages before it has achieved a certain national identity. Such images, which appeal to *all* men, must bear the burden of figurative persuasion before the emergence of images which appeal to *these* men. Thus, in the popular demonstrations of 1788 which urged the adoption of the federal constitution, structural and ship-of-state images were empha-

[26] *See also Osborn and Ehninger, pp. 233–234; and Michael Osborn, "The Function and Significance of Metaphor in Rhetorical Discourse," unpubl. Ph.D. diss. (University of Florida, 1963), pp. 274–299.*

[27] *"Franklin D. Roosevelt's Audience Persuasion in the 1936 Campaign,"* Speech Monographs, *XVII (March 1950), 48–64.*

[28] *"Great Autumnal Madness: Political Symbolism in Mid-Nineteenth-Century America,"* QJS, *XLIX (December 1963), 417–431.*

sized. But by 1840 a set of indigenous symbols—"log cabin," "hard cider," and the "plough"—had emerged to dominate the political imagery of the day. Such images are creatures of the moment, but they are more timely even as they are more evanescent. They may permit a more precise focusing upon whatever values and motives are salient in society at a given time.

The Future of Rhetorical Criticism:
Paradigmatic or Pluralistic?

T HE twentieth century has witnessed tremendous scientific advances. These advances have been accompanied by and perhaps even made possible by a strong sense of the reality of science and the efficacy of its method. On a strong scientific basis the world, or at least the economically advantaged portion of it, has become increasingly re-formed on a technological basis. So complete have these changes been that some social critics have been referring to the United States, Western Europe, and the Soviet Union as "technocracies."[1]

More recently, however, increasing portions of the citizens of these nations have become convinced that their technical proficiencies have so deeply affected their societies that not only economic means but social existences have been technologized. One concomitant of the technical advances has been a plundering of the natural environment to the degree that life itself is threatened. More and more voices have been raised against the seeming consequences of technical sufficiency and spiritual poverty. Part of the outcry, of course, has arisen because, in spite of the plenty produced by bureaucratized industry, education, and government, economic poverty still exists in pockets in the advanced nations and in large segments of the disadvantaged world. These pockets of poverty are often attributed more to a lack of will than to a lack of ability.

Although it seems foolhardy to us to assert that the blame for these conditions should be laid at the door of science, we are confident that one result has been and will continue to be a resurgence of humanistic scholarship. Humane traditions are even making themselves felt in the philosophy of science. Thomas S. Kuhn's work, on which we have depended heavily, places science in a much different light than that typical earlier in this century and is still the most prevalent viewpoint. Such thinkers as Michael Polanyi and J. Bronowski stress the humane values of science itself.[2]

We believe that there will be an increasing ability in academia and

---

[1] *For a review of technocratic forces and references to some literature, see* Theodore Roszak, The Making of a Counter Culture: Reflections on the Technocratic Society and Its Youthful Opposition, *Garden City, N.Y., Anchor Books, 1969, chap. 1.*

[2] *See Michael Polanyi,* Personal Knowledge: Toward a Post Critical Philosophy, *New York, Harper Torchbooks, 1964; and J. Bronowski,* The Identity of Man, *Garden City, N.Y., American Museum Science Books, 1965, and* Science and Human Values, *New York, Harper Torchbooks, 1965; Stephen Toulmin,* Foresight and Understanding, *New York, Harper Torchbooks, 1963 is also relevant, as is, of course, Thomas S. Kuhn,* The Structure of Scientific Revolutions, *Chicago, University of Chicago Press, 1962.*

in public interchange to tolerate the pluralistic tendencies that seem endemic in humane studies, and we believe that rhetorical criticism is and will remain consistent with this trend. Within a humane tradition rhetorical criticism will be fundamentally subjective, leaving the field open for numerous approaches.

Increasingly, rhetorical criticism is becoming much broader, as interest and research in communication become more complex. Within the broad scope of that criticism, individual critics are finding and will need to find particular focuses if their work is to be productive. Methods will develop from the variety of questions asked and the public communicative processes that are probed.

In his review of the theoretical writing on rhetorical criticism, Barnet Baskerville concluded that "alone among recent writings, Mouat's 'An Approach to Rhetorical Criticism'[3] rejects pluralism and seeks for a uniform approach."[4] We believe that this criticism is even more valid today than it was in 1967. The forces that brought about the general acceptance of pluralism have, if anything, become stronger since Baskerville surveyed the literature.

We conclude then that no paradigm will soon arise to gain the adherence that neo-Aristotelianism had in the 1930s and 1940s. If a pluralistic attitude becomes generally recognized and understood, we should see a lessening of interest in theorizing about criticism and a revitalized concern with criticizing public discourse.

At the very least we should expect a lessening of interest in traditional methods of theorizing. It seems fair to say of academic speech criticism during the first part of the twentieth century that a unified theory was rather well accepted before it was applied to the reality of discourse. The process was deductive. Even when faith in the paradigm began to break down, theorists persisted in the deductive mode. In the future rhetorical theory will probably be developed more inductively, as abstractions from the study of discourse. In a sense, this development will mean less distinction between theory and criticism.

A productive "closeness" of theory and criticism will result if the abstractions from critical practice take on the character of tentative principles, which are held tentatively, applied, confirmed (to some degree), and modified by further criticism of public discourse. If theory is to be descriptive of the process of public discourse in a rapidly changing society, then rhetoric must be a constantly growing and changing body of knowledge.

[3] *Lawrence H. Mouat, in* The Rhetorical Idiom, *Donald C. Bryant (ed.), Ithaca, N.Y., Cornell University Press, 1958, pp. 161–177.*
[4] *Barnet Baskerville, "Selected Writings on the Criticism of Public Address, Addendum, 1967," in Thomas R. Nilsen (ed.),* Essays on Rhetorical Criticism, *New York, Random House, 1968, p. 189.*

Accompanying the pluralism, tentativeness, and change that we predict, we see a shift from the traditional critical interest in speakers (or the sources of discourse) to the interactions that make communication a process. Thus, rhetoric as such will be closer to the center of critical interest. Critics are now assuming that rhetoric is not something added to the deliberation of a set of issues by spokesmen but rather something integrally associated with the reality of whatever those issues are.[5] Although critics will be interested in what speakers, writers, or demonstrators have to say, they will be more concerned with the forces that seem to permeate public discourse, issues, campaigns, or movements.

These generalizations about the future may not be completely accurate, of course, but they are based on what present practice appears to indicate. In concluding, we would like to stress one more potentiality. In the future critics are apt to find themselves dealing rhetorically with rhetorical materials, that is, they are likely to enter the arena of social influence, at least to the extent that the manner in which messages are received and made meaningful will be determined in some part by the general critical sensibilities of audiences. If the critic finds the persuasive implications of his own messages, then he should be willing to take responsibility for the evaluations that he will inevitably make.

[5] *On this point see Robert L. Scott, "On Viewing Rhetoric as Epistemic,"* Central States Speech Journal, *XVIII, 1 (February 1967), 9–17. Excellent examples of well-integrated criticism of the sort we suggest are Edwin Black, "The Second Persona,"* The Quarterly Journal of Speech, *LVI, 2 (April 1970), 109–119; and Parke G. Burgess, "The Rhetoric of Moral Conflict: Two Critical Dimensions,"* The Quarterly Journal of Speech, *LVI, 2 (April 1970), 120–130.*

Selected Bibliography

Books

Aly, Bower, *The Rhetoric of Alexander Hamilton,* New York, Columbia University Press, 1941.

Auer, J. Jeffery (ed.), *Antislavery and Disunion, 1858–1861: Studies in the Rhetoric of Compromise and Conflict,* New York and Evanston, Harper & Row, 1963.

Black, Edwin B., *Rhetorical Criticism: A Study in Method,* New York, Macmillan, 1965.

Bormann, Ernest G., *Theory and Research in the Communicative Arts,* New York, Holt, Rinehart & Winston, 1965.

Braden, Waldo W. (ed.), *Oratory in the Old South, 1828–1860,* Baton Rouge, Louisiana State University Press, 1970.

Brigance, William N., *A History of American Public Address,* 2 vols., New York, McGraw-Hill, 1943.

Brockriede, Wayne and Scott, Robert L., *Moments in the Rhetoric of the Cold War,* New York, Random House, 1970.

Bryant, Donald C. (ed.), *Papers in Rhetoric and Poetic,* Iowa City, University of Iowa Press, 1965.

Burke, Kenneth, *Counter-Statement,* New York, Harcourt, Brace, 1931.
————, *Permanence and Change,* New York, New Republic, 1935.
————, *The Philosophy of Literary Form,* Baton Rouge, Louisiana State University Press, 1941.
————, *A Grammar of Motives,* Englewood Cliffs, N.J., Prentice-Hall, 1946.
————, *A Rhetoric of Motives,* Englewood Cliffs, N.J., Prentice-Hall, 1950.
————, *The Rhetoric of Religion,* Boston, Beacon Press, 1961.
————, *Language as Symbolic Action,* Berkeley, University of California Press, 1966.

Cathcart, Robert, *Post Communication: Critical Analysis and Evaluation,* Indianapolis, Bobbs-Merrill, 1966.

Fogarty, Daniel, *Roots for a New Rhetoric,* New York, Teachers College Press, 1959.

Graham, John (ed.), *Great American Speeches of the Twentieth Century, Texts and Studies,* New York, Appleton-Century-Crofts, 1970.

Grover, David H., *Debaters and Dynamiters,* Corvallis, Oregon State University Press, 1964.
———— (ed.), *Landmarks in Western Oratory,* Laramie, University of Wyoming Press, 1968.

Golden, James, and Rieke, Richard, *The Rhetoric of Black Americans,* Columbus, Ohio, Charles E. Merrill, 1971.

Goodrich, Chauncey A., *Select British Eloquence* (1859), Indianapolis, Bobbs-Merrill, 1963.

Hillbruner, Anthony, *Critical Dimensions: The Art of Public Address Criticism,* New York, Random House, 1966.

Holland, De Witte (ed.), *Preaching in American History,* Nashville, Tenn., Abingdon Press, 1969.

Howes, Raymond F. (ed.), *Historical Studies of Rhetoric and Rhetoricians,* Ithaca, N.Y., Cornell University Press, 1961.

Linsley, William A. (ed.), *Speech Criticism: Methods and Materials,* Dubuque, Iowa, William C. Brown, 1968.

Lomas, Charles W., *The Agitator in American Society,* Englewood Cliffs, N.J., Prentice-Hall, 1968.

Nichols, Marie Hochmuth (ed.), *A History and Criticism of American Public Address,* Vol. III, London, Longmans, Green, 1955.

————, *Rhetoric and Criticism,* Baton Rouge, Louisiana State University Press, 1963.

Reid, Loren (ed.), *American Public Address, Essays in Honor of Albert Craig Baird,* Columbia, University of Missouri Press, 1961.

————, *Charles James Fox: A Man for the People,* Columbia, University of Missouri Press, 1969.

Richards, I. A., *The Philosophy of Rhetoric,* New York, Oxford University Press, 1936.

Rueckert, William H., *Kenneth Burke and the Drama of Human Relations,* Minneapolis, University of Minnesota Press, 1963.

———— (ed.), *Critical Responses to Kenneth Burke,* Minneapolis, University of Minnesota Press, 1969.

Scott, Robert L., and Brockriede, Wayne, *The Rhetoric of Black Power,* New York, Harper & Row, 1969.

Smith, Arthur L., *The Rhetoric of Black Revolution,* Boston, Allyn & Bacon, 1969.

Thonssen, Lester, and Baird, A. Craig, *Speech Criticism: The Development of Standards for Rhetorical Appraisal,* New York, Ronald Press, 1948. Second edition, 1970, with Waldo W. Braden.

Wallace, Karl R. (ed.), *A History of Speech Education in America,* New York, Appleton-Century-Crofts, 1954.

Weaver, Richard M., *The Ethics of Rhetoric,* Chicago, Henry Regnery, 1953.

Wrage, Ernest J., and Baskerville, Barnet (eds.), *American Forum: Speeches on Historic Issues, 1788–1900,* New York, Harper & Row, 1960.

———— (eds.), *Contemporary Forum: American Speeches on Twentieth-Century Issues,* New York, Harper & Row, 1962.

Articles on Theory

Backes, James G., "Rhetorical Criticism: Yet Another Emphasis," *Western Speech,* XXVI (Summer 1962), 164–167.

Baird, A. Craig, "The Study of Speeches," *American Public Addresses, 1740–1952,* New York, McGraw-Hill, 1956.

Baskerville, Barnet, "Principal Themes of Nineteenth-Century Critics of Oratory," *Speech Monographs,* XIX (March 1952), 11–26.

———, "The Critical Method in Speech," *Central States Speech Journal,* IV (July 1953), 1–5.

———, "The Dramatic Criticism of Oratory," *The Quarterly Journal of Speech,* XLV (February 1959), 39–45.

Black, Edwin, "The Second Persona," *The Quarterly Journal of Speech,* LVI (April 1970), 109–119.

Brockriede, Wayne, "Toward a Contemporary Aristotelian Theory of Rhetoric," *The Quarterly Journal of Speech,* LII (February 1966), 33–40.

———, "Dimensions of the Concept of Rhetoric," *The Quarterly Journal of Speech,* LIV (February 1968), 1–12.

Bryant, Donald C., "Some Problems of Scope and Method in Rhetorical Scholarship," *The Quarterly Journal of Speech,* XXIII (April 1937), 182–189.

———, "Aspects of the Rhetorical Tradition," *The Quarterly Journal of Speech,* XXXVI (April 1950), 169–176, XXXVI (October 1950), 326–332.

———, "Rhetoric: Its Function and Scope," *The Quarterly Journal of Speech,* XXXIX (December 1953), 401–424.

———, "Rhetorical Criticism in *The Middlesex Journal,* 1774," *The Quarterly Journal of Speech,* L (February 1964), 45–52.

Burgess, Parke, G., "The Rhetoric of Moral Conflict: Two Critical Dimensions," *The Quarterly Journal of Speech,* LVI (April 1970), 120–130.

Burke, Kenneth, "Rhetoric—Old and New," *The Journal of General Education,* V (April 1951), 202–209.

———, "A Dramatistic View of the Origins of Language," *The Quarterly Journal of Speech,* Part I, XXXVIII (October 1952), 251–264; Part II, XXXVIII (December 1952), 446–460; Part III, XXXIX (February 1953), 79–92.

Byrne, Richard B., "Stylistic Analysis of the Film: Notes on a Methodology," *Speech Monographs,* XXXII (March 1965), 74–78.

Cain, Earl R., "A Method for Rhetorical Analysis of Congressional Debate," *Western Speech,* XVIII (March 1954), 91–95.

Clark, Robert D., "Lesson from the Literary Critics," *Western Speech,* XXI (Spring 1957), 83–89.

———, "Biography and Rhetorical Criticism" (review essay), *The Quarterly Journal of Speech,* XLIV (April 1958), 182–186.

Croft, Albert J., "The Functions of Rhetorical Criticism," *The Quarterly Journal of Speech,* XLII (October 1956), 283–291.

Dell, George W., "Philosophic Judgments in Contemporary Rhetorical Criticism," *Western Speech,* XXX (Spring 1966), 81–89.

De Vito, Joseph A., "Style and Stylistics: An Attempt at Definition," *The Quarterly Journal of Speech,* LIII (October 1967), 248–255.

Duhammel, P. Albert, "The Concept of Rhetoric as Effective Presentation," *Journal of the History of Ideas,* X (June 1949), 344–356.

Ehninger, Douglas, "On Rhetoric and Rhetorics," *Western Speech,* XXXI (Fall 1967), 242–249.

Ellingsworth, Huber W., "Anthropology and Rhetoric: Toward a Culture-Related Methodology of Speech Criticism," *Southern Speech Journal,* XXVIII (Summer 1963), 307–312.

Ericson, Jon M., "A Critique of Rhetorical Criticism," *The Quarterly Journal of Speech,* L (October 1964), 313–315.

Gregg, Richard B., "A Phenomenologically Oriented Approach to Rhetorical Criticism," *Central States Speech Journal,* XVII (May 1966), 83–90.

Griffin, Lelend M., "The Rhetoric of Historical Movements," *The Quarterly Journal of Speech,* XXXVIII (April 1952), 184–188.

———, "The Edifice Metaphor in Rhetorical Theory," *Speech Monographs,* XXVII (November 1960), 279–292.

Haiman, Franklyn S., "Rhetoric of the Streets: Some Legal and Ethical Considerations," *The Quarterly Journal of Speech,* LIII (April 1967), 99–115.

Hance, Kenneth G., "The Historical-Critical Type of Research: A Reexamination," *Central States Speech Journal,* XIII (Spring 1962), 165–170.

Hendrix, J. A., "In Defense of Neo-Aristotelian Rhetorical Criticism," *Western Speech,* XXXII (Fall 1968), 246–251.

Hillbruner, Anthony, "The Rhetorical Critic's Role in Society," *The Quarterly Journal of Speech,* XLIV (February 1958), 100–102.

———, "Creativity and Contemporary Criticism," *Western Speech,* XXIV (Winter 1960), 5–11.

———, "Criticism as Persuasion," *Southern Speech Journal,* XXVIII (Summer 1963), 260–267.

———, "Speech Criticism and American Culture," *Western Speech,* XXXII (Summer 1968), 162–167.

Holland, L. Virginia, "Rhetorical Criticism: A Burkeian Method," *The Quarterly Journal of Speech,* XXXIX (December 1953), 444–450.

———, "Kenneth Burke's Dramatistic Approach to Speech Criticism," *The Quarterly Journal of Speech,* XLI (December 1955), 352–358.

Hunt, Everett, "Rhetoric and Literary Criticism," *The Quarterly Journal of Speech,* XXI (November 1935), 564–568.

———, "Rhetoric as a Humane Study," *The Quarterly Journal of Speech,* XLI (April 1955), 114–117.

————, "Thoughts on a History and Criticism of American Public Address," *The Quarterly Journal of Speech,* XLII (April 1956), 187–190.

Johannesen, Richard J., "Richard Weaver's View of Rhetoric and Criticism," *Southern Speech Journal,* XXXII (Winter 1966), 133–153.

Karstetter, Allan B., "Toward a Theory of Rhetorical Irony," *Speech Monographs* XXXI (June 1964), 162–178.

Lee, Irving J., "Four Ways of Looking at a Speech," *The Quarterly Journal of Speech,* XXVIII (April 1942), 148–155.

Lomas, Charles W., "Rhetorical Criticism and Historical Perspective," *Western Speech,* XXXII (Summer 1968), 191–203.

Macksoud, John S., "Kenneth Burke on Perspective and Rhetoric," *Western Speech,* XXXIII (Summer 1969), 167–176.

Maloney, Martin, "Some New Directions in Rhetorical Criticism," *Central States Speech Journal,* IV (March 1953), 1–5.

Mouat, L. H., "An Approach to Rhetorical Criticism," in Donald C. Bryant (ed.), *The Rhetorical Idiom,* Ithaca, N.Y., Cornell University Press, 1958.

Murphy, Richard, "The Speech as Literary Genre," *The Quarterly Journal of Speech,* XLIV (April 1958), 117–127.

Nichols, Marie Hochmuth, "Lincoln's First Inaugural," in Wayland Maxwell Parrish and Marie Hochmuth Nichols (ed.), *American Speeches,* London, Longmans, Green, 1954.

Nilsen, Thomas, "Criticism and Social Consequences," *The Quarterly Journal of Speech,* XLII (April 1956), 173–178.

North, Helen F., "Rhetoric and Historiography," *The Quarterly Journal of Speech,* XLII (October 1956), 234–242.

Olian, J. Robert, "The Intended Use of Aristotle's *Rhetoric,*" *Speech Monographs,* XXXV (June 1968), 137–148.

Osborn, Michael M., "Archetypal Metaphor in Rhetoric: The Light-Dark Family," *The Quarterly Journal of Speech,* LIII (April 1967), 115–126.

————, "The Evolution of the Theory of Metaphor in Rhetoric," *Western Speech,* XXXI (Spring 1967), 121–130.

————, and Ehninger, Douglas, "The Metaphor in Public Address," *Speech Monographs,* XXIX (August 1962), 223–234.

Parrish, Wayland M., "The Study of Speeches," in Wayland M. Parrish and Marie Hochmuth Nichols (eds.), *American Speeches,* New York, Langmans, 1954.

Redding, Charles, "Extrinsic and Intrinsic Criticism," *Western Speech,* XXI (Spring 1957), 96–102.

Reid, Loren D., "The Perils of Rhetorical Criticism," *The Quarterly Journal of Speech,* XXX (December 1944), 416–422.

Rosenfield, Lawrence B., "Set Theory: Key to the Understanding of Kenneth Burke's Use of the Term 'Identification,' " *Western Speech,* XXXII (Summer 1969), 178–183.

Rosenfield, Lawrence W., "Rhetorical Criticism and an Aristotelian Notion of Process," *Speech Monographs,* XXXIII (March 1966), 1–16.

———, "The Anatomy of Critical Discourse," *Speech Monographs,* XXV (March 1968), 50–69.

Scott, Robert L., and Smith, Donald K., "The Rhetoric of Confrontation," *The Quarterly Journal of Speech,* LV (February 1969), 1–8.

Simons, Herbert W., "Confrontation as a Pattern of Persuasion in University Settings," *Central States Speech Journal,* XX (Fall 1969), 163–169.

———, "Requirements, Problems, and Strategies: A Theory of Persuasion of Social Movements," *The Quarterly Journal of Speech,* LVI (February 1970), 1–11.

Steele, Edward D., "Social Values, the Enthymeme, and Speech Criticism," *Western Speech,* XXVI (Spring 1962), 70–75.

Thompson, Wayne, "Contemporary Public Address: A Problem in Criticism," *The Quarterly Journal of Speech,* XL (February 1954), 24–30.

Tompkins, Phillip K., "Rhetorical Criticism: Wrong Medium?" *Central States Speech Journal,* XIII (Winter 1962), 90–95.

———, "The Rhetorical Criticism of Non-Oratorical Works," *The Quarterly Journal of Speech,* LV (December 1969), 431–439.

Wallace, Karl R., "The Substance of Rhetoric: Good Reasons," *The Quarterly Journal of Speech,* XLIX (October 1963), 239–249.

Wichelns, Herbert, "The Literary Criticism of Oratory," in A. M. Drummond (ed.), *Studies in Rhetoric and Public Speaking in Honor of James A. Winans,* New York, Century, 1925.

Wrage, Ernest J., "Public Address: A Study in Social and Intellectual History," *The Quarterly Journal of Speech,* XXXIII (December 1947).

———, "The Ideal Critic," *Central States Speech Journal,* VIII (Spring 1957), 20–23.

Wright, Warren E., "Judicial Rhetoric: A Field for Research," *Speech Monographs,* XXXI (March 1964), 64–72.

Critical Articles

Andrews, James R., "Confrontation at Columbia," *The Quarterly Journal of Speech,* LV (February 1969), 9–16.

Auer, J. Jeffery, "Tom Corwin: 'King of the Stump,' " *The Quarterly Journal of Speech,* XXX (February 1944), 47–55.

Baird, John E., "The Rhetoric of Youth in Controversy Against the Religious Establishment," *Western Speech,* XXXIV (Winter 1970), 53–61.

Baskerville, Barnet, "Joe McCarthy, Brief Case Demagogue," *Today's Speech,* II (September 1954), 8–15.

Bosmajian, Haig A., "Nazi Persuasion and the Crowd Mentality," *Western Speech,* XXIV (Spring 1965), 68–78.

Bostrom, Robert N., "I Give You a Man—Kennedy's Speech for Adlai Stevenson," *Speech Monographs,* XXXV (June 1968), 129–136.

Braden, Waldo W., and Brandenburg, Earnest, "Roosevelt's Fireside Chats," *Speech Monographs,* XXII (November 1955), 290–302.

Brandenburg, Earnest, "The Preparation of Franklin D. Roosevelt's Speeches," *The Quarterly Journal of Speech,* XXXV (April 1949), 214–221.

——, "Franklin D. Roosevelt's International Speeches: 1939–1941," *Speech Monographs,* XVI (August 1949), 21–40.

Brock, Bernard L., "1968 Democratic Campaign: A Political Upheaval," *The Quarterly Journal of Speech,* LV (February 1969), 26–35.

Brockriede, Wayne E., and Scott, Robert L., "Stokely Carmichael: Two Speeches on Black Power," *Central States Speech Journal,* XIX (Spring 1968), 3–13.

Brooks, Paul D., "A Field Study of the Johnson and Goldwater Campaign Speeches in Pittsburgh," *Southern Speech Journal,* XXXII (Summer 1967), 273–281.

Burgess, Parke G., "The Rhetoric of Black Power: A Moral Demand?" *The Quarterly Journal of Speech,* LIV (April 1968), 122–133.

Campbell, Finley C., "Voices of Thunder, Voices of Rage: A Symbolic Analysis of a Selection from Malcolm X's Speech, 'Message to the Grass Roots,' " *The Speech Teacher,* XIX (March 1970), 101–110.

Casmir, Fred L., "An Analysis of Hitler's January 30, 1941, Speech," *Western Speech,* XXX (Spring 1966), 96–105.

Crowell, Laura, "Franklin D. Roosevelt's Audience Persuasion in the 1936 Campaign," *Speech Monographs,* XVII (March 1950), 48–64.

Devin, Lee, "Lincoln's Ethos: Viewed and Practiced," *Central States Speech Journal,* XVI (May 1965), 99–105.

Faries, Clyde J., "Private Allen's Strategy of Reconciliation," *The Quarterly Journal of Speech,* LII (December 1966), 358–363.

Fletcher, Winona L., "Knight-Errant or Screaming Eagle? E. L. Godkin's Criticism of Wendell Phillips," *Southern Speech Journal,* XXIX (Spring 1964), 214–223.

Golden, James A., "John F. Kennedy and the 'Ghost,' " *The Quarterly Journal of Speech,* LII (December 1966), 348–357.

Gravlee, G. Jack, "Franklin D. Roosevelt's Speech Preparation During His First National Campaign," *Speech Monographs,* XXI (November 1964), 437–460.

Griffin, Leland M., "The Rhetorical Structure of the 'New Left' Movement: Part I," *The Quarterly Journal of Speech,* L (April 1964), 113–135.

Haberman, Frederick W., "General MacArthur's Speech: A Symposium of Critical Comment," *The Quarterly Journal of Speech,* XXXVII (October 1951), 321–331.

Hayes, Merwyn A., "William L. Yancey Presents the Southern Case to the North; 1860," *Southern Speech Journal,* XXIX (Spring 1964), 194–208.

Heisey, D. Ray., "The Rhetoric of the Arab-Israeli Conflict," *The Quarterly Journal of Speech,* XVI (February 1970), 12–21.

Henderlider, Clair R., "Woodrow Wilson's Speeches on the League of Nations, September 4–25, 1919," *Speech Monographs,* XIII (March 1946), 23–34.

Hillbruner, Anthony, "Rhetoric and Politics: The Making of the President, 1960," *Western Speech,* XXIX (Spring 1965), 91–101.

Hunter, Charles F., "Thomas Hart Benton: An Evaluation," *The Quarterly Journal of Speech,* XXX (October 1944), 279–285.

Jensen, J. Vernon, "The Rhetorical Strategy of Thomas H. Huxley and Robert G. Ingersoll: Agnostics and Roadblock Removers," *Speech Monographs,* XXXII (March 1965), 59–68.

Kane, Peter E., "Evaluating the 'Great Debates,' " *Western Speech,* XXX (Spring 1966), 89–95.

Kennedy, George, "Anthony's Speech at Caesar's Funeral," *The Quarterly Journal of Speech,* LIV (April 1968), 99–106.

Kennicott, Patrick C., "Black Persuaders in the Antislavery Movement," *Speech Monographs,* XXXVII (March 1970), 15–24.

Kerr, Henry R., "The Election Sermon: Primer for Revolutionaries," *Speech Monographs,* XXIX (March 1962), 13–22.

Lanigan, Richard L., "Urban Crisis: Polarization and Communication," *Central States Speech Journal,* XXI (Summer 1970), 108–116.

Leathers, Dale G., "Fundamentalism of the Radical Right," *Southern Speech Journal,* XXXIII (Summer 1968), 245–258.

Ling, David A., "A Pentadic Analysis of Senator Edward Kennedy's Address to the People of Massachusetts, July 25, 1969," *Central States Speech Journal,* XXI (Summer 1970), 81–86.

Martin, Howard H., "The Rhetoric of Academic Protest," *Central States Speech Journal,* XVII (November 1966), 244–250.

McBath, James H., and Fisher, Walter R., "Persuasion in Presidential Campaign Communication," *The Quarterly Journal of Speech,* LV (February 1969), 17–25.

McGuckin, Henry E., Jr., "A Value Analysis of Richard Nixon's 1952 Campaign-Fund Speech," *Southern Speech Journal,* XXXIII (Summer 1968), 259–269.

Newman, Robert P., "Under the Veneer: Nixon's Vietnam Speech of November 3, 1969," *The Quarterly Journal of Speech,* LVI (April 1970), 168–178.

Oliver, Robert T., "Wilson's Rapport with His Audience," *The Quarterly Journal of Speech,* XXVII (February 1941), 79–90.

Ritter, Kurt R., "Ronald Reagan and 'The Speech': The Rhetoric of Public Relations Politics," *Western Speech,* XXXII (Winter 1968), 50–58.

Rosenfield, Lawrence W., "A Case Study in Speech Criticism: The Nixon-Truman Analog," *Speech Monographs,* XXXV (November 1968), 435–450.

Scott, Robert L., "A Rhetoric of Facts: Arthur Larson's Stance as a Persuader," *Speech Monographs,* XXXV (June 1968), 109–121.

———, "Justifying Violence—The Rhetoric of Black Power," *Central States Speech Journal,* XIX (Summer 1968), 96–104.

———, "Rhetoric That Postures: An Intrinsic Reading of Richard M. Nixon's Inaugural Address," *Western Speech,* XXXIV (Winter 1970), 46–52.

Sloan, Thomas O., "A Rhetorical Analysis of John Donne's 'The Prohibition,'" *The Quarterly Journal of Speech,* XLVIII (February 1962), 38–45.

———, "Persona as Rhetor: An Interpretation of Donne's *Satyre III,*" *The Quarterly Journal of Speech,* LI (February 1965), 14–27.

Smith, Robert W., "Rhetoric in Crisis: The Abdication Address of Edward VIII," *Speech Monographs,* XXX (November 1963), 335–339.

Stelzner, Herman G., "The British Orators, VII; John Morley's Speech-Making," *The Quarterly Journal of Speech,* XLV (April 1959), 171–181.

———, "Speech Criticism by Journalists," *Southern Speech Journal,* XXVIII (Fall 1962), 17–26.

———, "'War Message' December 8, 1941, An Approach to Language," *Speech Monographs,* XXXIII (November 1966), 419–437.

Tompkins, Phillip K., "The Rhetoric of James Joyce," *The Quarterly Journal of Speech,* LIV (April 1968), 107–114.

Vasilew, Eugene, "Norman Thomas at the Townsend Convention of 1936," *Speech Monographs,* XXIV (November 1957), 233–243.

Wallace, Karl, "On the Criticism of the MacArthur Speech," *The Quarterly Journal of Speech,* XXXIX (February 1953), 69–74.

Williams, Donald E., "Andrew D. White: Spokesman for the Free University," *The Quarterly Journal of Speech,* XLVII (April 1961), 133–142.

Windes, Russel, Jr., "A Study in Effective and Ineffective Presidential Campaign Speaking," *Speech Monographs,* XXVIII (March 1961), 39–49.

———, and James A. Robinson, "Public Address in the Career of Adlai E. Stevenson," *The Quarterly Journal of Speech,* XLII (October 1956), 225–233.

Wrage, Earnest J., "E. L. Godkin and the *Nation:* Critics of Public Address," *Southern Speech Journal,* XV (December 1949), 100–111.

———, "The Little World of Barry Goldwater," *Western Speech,* XXVII (Fall 1963), 207–215.

Wylie, Phillip, "Medievalism and the MacArthurian Legend," *The Quarterly Journal of Speech,* XXXVII (December 1951), 473–478.

Index

71 72 73 74 7 6 5 4 3 2 1